THE EGO AND THE FLESH

Cultural Memory
in
the
Present

Mieke Bal and Hent de Vries, Editors

THE EGO AND THE FLESH

An Introduction to Egoanalysis

Jacob Rogozinski
Translated by Robert Vallier

STANFORD UNIVERSITY PRESS

STANFORD, CALIFORNIA

Stanford University Press
Stanford, California

The Ego and the Flesh was originally published in French under the title *Le Moi et la chair* © Les Éditions du Cerf, 2006.

This book has been published with the assistance of the French Ministry of Culture, National Center for the Book, and the University of Strasbourg.

Cet ouvrage a bénéficié du soutien des Programmes d'aide à la publication de Cultures france/Ministère français des affaires étrangères et européennes. This work, published as part of a program of aid for publication, received support from Cultures France and the French Ministry of Foreign Affairs.

Printed in the United States of America on acid-free, archival-quality paper

Library of Congress Cataloging-in-Publication Data

Rogozinski, Jacob.
  [Moi et la chair. English]
  The ego and the flesh : an introduction to egoanalysis / Jacob Rogozinski ; translated by Robert Vallier.
    p. cm. — (Cultural memory in the present)
  "Originally published in French under the title Le moi et la chair, Les Éditions du Cerf, 2006."
  Includes bibliographical references and index.
  ISBN 978-0-8047-5988-5 (cloth : alk. paper) —
  ISBN 978-0-8047-5989-2 (pbk. : alk. paper)
  1. Self (Philosophy) 2. Ego (Psychology) I. Vallier, Robert.
  II. Title. III. Series: Cultural memory in the present.
  BD450.R557413 2010
  126—dc22

                                                        2009053225

Typeset by Westchester Book Services in Adobe Garamond 11/13.5

Contents

Acknowledgments

I would like to express my gratitude to Michel Henry, my teacher and friend, who advised me to "follow my idea."

I would also like thank Richard Figuier, who encouraged me to write this book.

And finally, thanks to Heinz Wismann, who welcomed it into his collection "Passages" at the Editions du Cerf.

JACOB ROGOZINSKI

Translator's Note

Translating any work is difficult, and every work has its own unique set of challenges. Such challenges are augmented when the work is by a synthetic thinker like Jacob Rogozinski. The many threads woven through texture of *The Ego and the Flesh* are drawn from ontology, phenomenology, psychoanalysis, modern philosophy, and contemporary thought, and Rogozinski's partners in dialogue range from Descartes to Deleuze, Lucretius to Lacan, al-Hallaj to Heidegger, to name just a few. But neither a list of interlocutors nor the very title *The Ego and the Flesh* do justice to the content of the book, and may even obscure it. Through this critical dialogue, Rogozinski elaborates an "introduction to egoanalysis," which frequently demands that he reinvent old concepts and sometimes invent new ones. His own introduction, in the form of a conversation between at least two voices, announces the themes of the work and points out the roads he will travel, allowing me to limit myself to just a few comments about translation here at the outset.

The first word of the title—Ego—is already both the first theme of the work and the first problem for the translator. In French, the ego is translated as *le moi*, which, when stripped of its definite article, is, of course, the accusative subject, *moi*, me. Rogozinski often plays with this ambivalence, such that one cannot tell whether he is talking about *ego* or *me*. Such confusion is part of his philosophical argument, of course, but it is sometimes difficult to render in English. *Eclats de moi*, for example, using the partitive "de," could be "pieces of me" or "fragments of ego." Sometimes the ambivalence is so great that I have used an appositive, such that *c'est moi* and similar phrases are occasionally rendered as "it's me, the ego." The situation is compounded by existing English translations of, for example, Lacan, where a phrase like *qu'est-ce que ça veut dire d'être un moi* are rendered as "what does it mean to be an I?"—that is, a nominal subject, a *Je*, rather than an accusative subject, *un moi.* For Rogozinski, both the nominal and the accusative refer to, and are derived from, the more originary phenomenon of the *ego.*

So the book is indeed about the ego, and in a word, Rogozinski wants to save the ego from egocide. In French, *égicide* is coined by the author to mean, in effect, the killing of the ego. The word names both the act itself and the agents of the act but also has the homonymical virtue of sounding like *régicide.* Recall the start of Foucault's *Discipline and Punish,* which details the long list of tortures inflicted on Damiens, the unsuccessful regicide, the one who has attacked the king's body or person. The egocidal thinker, the ego killer, wants to dethrone His Majesty the Ego through an act of egocide. Parts I and II of this book examine and try to defend against egocide.

The ego thus has the lived experience of itself as other, especially when it sees itself in and is captivated by its specular image in the mirror. This other that it sees is perceived as other—*autre*—than it, but the ego is equally captivated by the Other—*Autre*—whose many figures include the They in Heidegger and the Symbolic in Lacan. Other people, who are egos like me, are *autrui,* others. There is a difference, a divergence, *un écart* between myself and myself-as-another, or between myself and an other person. This divergence is sometimes a gap, an interval, or a hiatus, even a gaping hole, preventing the other and the ego from completely coinciding or fusing. Indeed, this function of opening a divergence (*fonction d'écart*) is a function of *the remainder, le restant,* one of Rogozinski's key notions here, referring to the noncoincidence of the touching and the touched. An attempt at articulating an egoanalysis, he tells us, necessarily involves (perhaps even is) *a phenomenology of the remainder,* which may be a better description of what one will find in this book. The mode of the remainder's appearance is a nonappearance, or a haunting, *une hantise,* which provokes *fantasies, phantoms,* and *phantasms* of different kinds, whose styles of being are elucidated by Rogozinski's careful analyses.

Rogozinski throws a lot of words around—including thrownness, being-thrown, throwing-out, ejecting, dejecting, abjecting, and rejecting. None are terribly difficult to translate, but it is worth noting that whatever the ego expels from itself, its waste, is never thrown very far away from it. It remains nearby, in the ego's orbit, or in its *mouvance,* another key concept here, and a fine old English word associated not only with some very important person's retinue or entourage (the way flocks of birds or bees seem to fly as a coordinated unit can also be described as its *mouvance*) but with a territory of influence. It sees itself as other, as the first *foreigner* or *stranger* (*étranger*) within itself, devaluing and denigrating it, humiliating and hating it. This devaluation is a figuring, which may well scar the face, *la figure*, of the other. Sometimes it disfigures, transfigures, refigures, or configures it, before possibly recognizing it as its own self.

The second word in the title—*la chair*—is also both a philosophical theme and a problem for translation, if only because of its history and its meanings. In English it becomes *flesh*, but that then doubly obscures its provenance. Derived from the Latin *carne*, which can be both living flesh and dead meat, *la chair* in French, at least among many phenomenologists, is used to translate Husserl's *Leib* (itself derived from the verbal *Leben*, to live), that is, the living body, as distinguished from a dead one, a *Körper*. Most English translations of Husserl render *Leib* as Body, but one of the major elements of Rogozinski's analysis is precisely the difference between the body (*le corps*) and the flesh (*la chair*), corporeality and carnality, incorporation and incarnation. One therefore ought not hear in this term some metaphysical or mystical notion.

So the book is indeed about *The Ego and the Flesh*, but as I have just tried to indicate, it is also about much more than what these two terms name—or maybe it is the case, inversely, that these two terms contain much more than we ever thought, in which case we owe Jacob Rogozinski a great debt of gratitude for offering us this introduction to egoanalysis. In many ways, translation itself always risks disfiguring the text it translates. Rogozinski's sentences are often long and complex, his syntax demanding, his wordplay clever, and his manner of critically blending ideas drawn from diverse discourses challenging. I have sometimes had to break up and rearrange sentences to suit the demands of English or to accommodate differences in the translation of primary texts. I have tried to keep editorial insertions to a minimum, generally indicating them with square brackets; and I have tried to keep to Rogozinski's sometimes idiosyncratic use of capitalization and italicization, though sometimes such formatting has had to be altered for the sake of clarity. All of this raises the risk of disfigurement, and there is no doubt that I have lost a play on words or two along the way, but I have above all tried to remain faithful to his thinking and to his argument. I hope I have left no scars.

Translation is also a solitary and lonely undertaking but not one that can ever be completed alone. So, if they can bear it, allow me to acknowledge the kind help, generous support, and warm friendship of a number of others from whom this translation has benefitted in ways great and small: François Raffoul, Michael Naas, Pascale-Anne Brault, Bernie Flynn, Judith Walz, David Krell, Elizabeth Rottenberg, Philippe van Haute, Dan Selcer, Chelsea Harry, Heather Radke, and Peter Murphy. I would also like to acknowledge both the dean of Liberal Arts and Sciences, Chuck Suchar, and the director of the Honors Program, Helen Marlborough, at DePaul University, who very kindly arranged for me to have an academic quarter away from my administrative duties so that I could finish this project. Emily-Jane Cohen at Stanford University Press has been the very model of patience, and both she and her assistant Sarah Crane Newman provided both moral support and gentle prodding at key times. And finally, let me warmly thank Jacob Rogozinski himself, not only for this work of philosophy but also for his enthusiastic involvement in the project.

BOB VALLIER

THE EGO AND THE FLESH

Introduction

"What's new, friend? Is there anything new to think about?"

"If I answered 'me,' what would you say?"

"That you're joking."

"And yet, that's my answer. What remains to be thought today is me [*moi*]."

"Surely you mean 'the ego' [*le moi*]. Is it your view that the concept of 'ego' should become, once again, a major stake for thought?"

"Even more, that 'the' ego, the concept of ego in general, means nothing. A universal ego, a 'me' that would not be *me* is only an empty form, one that we could easily replace with an It or an X. The meaning of the concept of ego is entirely given by the experience I have of it at every moment, the experience of being a living and singular ego. And so the matter to think now is indeed *me*!"

"I asked you what was new to think about, and you give me one of these old yarns of humanism and of the philosophy of the subject?!"

"I didn't say anything about the human or the subject; I said ego. A singular ego, which is not easily assimilated into the general notion of humanity, nor the idea of the subject. It is a question of thinking the mystery *that I am*."

"Oh now, come on! How could I not know that I am? Why be interested in trivial things as blindingly obvious as that I am myself?"

"Exactly because it blinds me and dissimulates what I am. Everybody notices, every once in a while in a brief flash, that this question has not been answered, that each of us still remains a mystery for others and for ourselves. Suddenly the question 'who am I?' comes over me. It arises in anxiety, in the extreme intensity of passion, joy, or suffering, or even in that 'sickness unto death,' the despair of being only despair, the despair of not truly being myself. The questions always arises anew, because it remains unanswered. Nothing is more foreign to me, nothing is more distant from me, than myself—because I never stop forgetting myself, letting myself be captivated by others and the world, to the point that I persuade myself that I am not me, that I am nothing.

"Surely your egocentrism spares you. Look around you! The disaster of modern times gets worse day by day. The task of thinking is to make our world intelligible, to decipher the events of world history—if we want to help humans resist violence and injustice. But you prefer to devote yourself to narcissistic introspection."

"And yet each of these humans you speak of lives and experiences life first of all as a singular ego. All resistance finds its source in the experience that each has of this threatened singularity. Were there no ego, if each of us did not live as an ego, *who* then would stand up to resist?"

"All right, I'll give you that: resistance to oppression presupposes a subject capable of resisting. But I doubt that it can be a matter of one ego, of one isolated individual. Resisting is not the affair of one *me*, but of an *us*—of a people, a class, or let's say instead a multitude."

"Of a multitude composed of individuals, each of whom lives its life immediately as *ego*, engaged in a singular relation to its body, the world, and others. This ego feels its pain or joy, its desire or hatred, its anxiety or despair—if it were not affected in this way, then how could it have the experience of the intolerable suffering brought on by oppression and injustice? It is because it feels these affects in its flesh, in its life, that it can decide to resist, to join with others in a community—and this decision remains always *its* decision, which no other ego can take in its place."

"And there it is: what you're proposing is a return to Descartes, to a solitary individuality closed in on itself, which one day just decides to leave its sphere and go looking for others. But this solipsistic ego doesn't exist: we gave up that old metaphysical fiction a long time ago. Or rather, if it ever 'existed' anywhere, it was in the dominant ideology that represents our society as an aggregation of selfish, rival individuals. The ego that you're praising and which puts its narcissism on parade is not the subject of possible resistance but rather the effect and the agent of submission to power. The philosophy you preach is indeed in the air these days."

"You're right on that point: the exaltation of the sovereign individual is one of the major traits of the epoch. But is the ego that thus shows itself really me? Allow me to cite one of Nietzsche's aphorisms: 'In ordinary egoism, it is exactly the non-ego that dominates, that profoundly banal being.' This narcissistic ego whose hegemony you criticize is an ego that totally identifies itself with others, or rather, with *images* of the Other, glorious figures that shine on the screens of the Spectacle. It's a strange and deadly paradox: whenever it believes that it is 'authentically' affirming itself or expressing itself in its own name, it is exactly then that the Other is speaking in its place, *breathing* its words to it—dictating to it, yet at the same time eluding it. To designate this situation, I would like to go back to the almost forgotten notion of *alienation*. In truth, the 'autonomous' ego that our era celebrates is an ego under-the-influence, an alienated ego. But this does not mean that our ego is entirely reducible to the subjugated ego, captive to its alienating identifications. Let's avoid confusing *the alienated ego* and *the true ego*—otherwise we would not even be able to imagine the possibility of a deliverance or a healing. How could I resist my alienation if there were not a point of truth in me capable of escaping the influence of the Other?"

"So now we're fully into metaphysics. This 'true' ego that you're invoking is an inconsistent fiction, and Descartes' error was long ago refuted. This substantial permanence and personal identity that he attributed to the ego are nothing but illusions of our reason: nothing proves that I remain *myself* from one moment to the next. Instead of a permanent subject, we are dealing merely with a series of impressions succeeding one another in a discontinuous manner. Instead of an ego sure of being itself, there is only a blind flux from which anonymous events arise. By making the 'I think' into originary evidence, Descartes naively imagines that thought necessarily has a subject and that this subject is always defined as an ego. Nothing is less certain. We must allow the possibility of a thought that would no longer be *my* thought but rather an impersonal event, a *cogitatur* and not a *cogito*: it is not me who thinks, desires, or speaks but rather *it*."

"So you would then define the ego, my certainty of being myself, as a pure and simple illusion?"

"Absolutely."

"Well then it would have to be a universal illusion, because all humans consider themselves in this way, live their lives as ego, in every epoch and in all known human cultures. Language attests to it: certain languages do not know our distinction between present, past, and future, and others do not have the verb 'to be'—but all of them include a first person singular. Perhaps 'Being' or 'time' (or 'God') is not said in every language, but there is no human language that ignores the *I*. Not even the language of the psychotic, when he declares that '*I* am no longer *myself*,' that '*I* feel that *I* become an other,' or when he, like Nietzsche when slipping into madness, claims that '*I* am all the names of history.'"

"But it is not enough to say 'I' in order to be aware of being 'me,' in the sense we understand it, we Occidentals of modern times. As historians and anthropologists have shown, the Cartesian cogito had no meaning for Hindus or the Ancient Greeks. Since they did not practice reflective introspection, their self-consciousness was that of an impersonal *It* or of an *Us*, of a member of a community and not as an individual I."

"If we allow that these analyses are correct, and I admit that I have difficulty believing them, this does not in any way mean that Buddha or Socrates did not have an ego or did not live their lives as singular egos, but only that they had not brought this concrete experience that was the ground of their lives to the level of the concept. It is this 'still mute experience that must be led to the pure expression of its proper meaning,' as Husserl said, and I have the weakness of thinking that such meaning cuts across every historical epoch, that the certainty and the mystery of being ego are encountered, albeit under different forms, in all times and in all human cultures."

"You're opposing me with a de facto argument there. Even if we allow, with reserve, that all humans from all times take themselves as egos, this only shows that they are all fooling themselves."

"If that were the case, we would still have to take account of such a radical illusion. And for this, we would have to postulate the existence of a Great Deceiver—call it the Unconscious if you prefer, or Metaphysics, or the Imaginary, or Ideology . . . in any case, the existence of some Other = X that would engender the illusion of being ego in 'me.'"

"That's right."

"But it is me that it tries to deceive: by making me its target, it reveals to me that I exist, and the more it tries to deny me, the more it confirms me in my existence."

"So, 'if it deceives me, then I am.' This is the old argument of the Evil Genius that you're trotting out for us. You are decidedly Cartesian."

"This focus of a radical illusion, which Descartes called the Evil Genius, has been given other names by the moderns, without them noticing that they were repeating the Cartesian argument—or that Descartes had already answered them. *I am, I exist*: this statement resists every attempt to refute it."

"You're not going to claim that Descartes would have responded in advance to the criticisms addressed to him by Hume, Kant, Nietzsche, Heidegger, analytic philosophy, and psychoanalysis, are you?"

"Why not? None of these thinkers, none of these theories, have succeeded in explaining in a convincing way how, on the basis of an Other = X, of an entity that is not me (and we could call it the Imagination, the will to power, Being, language, the unconscious Id, it doesn't matter), the certainty of being ego, of being me, is necessarily constituted. None of them have been able to show how the ego could be derived from a more originary non-ego. The moment has come to recognize the failure of all of these *ego killers,* these *egocides.*"

"Don't you mean regicides?"

"No, I mean egocide, this tendency—massively dominant in contemporary thought—that denounces the ego as an illusion which should be conveniently dissolved. I'll tell you, for a long time I let myself be charmed by the egocidal thinkers, before understanding that my teachers had been led astray. Most often it was a matter of radical thinkers, very critical with respect to power and society, who had not fully measured the consequences of their orientation. By considering the ego as a simple mirage, they annihilated every possibility of resistance. By refusing to recognize in it a personal identity, that is, the power to persist in its duration, they favored its decomposition into innumerable ephemeral 'personalities,' a *liquidation* of every identity that characterizes the 'liquid,' exploded, moving universe that is our own. In traditional societies where the hierarchy of the body politic assigns a preestablished place to each person, such a critique can have a subversive importance. In a 'disembodied' society, which requires of its subjects a flexibility and a limitless mobility, it is important, on the contrary, to defend our personal identity, threatened by incessant dispersion. Resistance to alienation subsequently passes through a combat for the unity of existence. Were there only discontinuous impressions or impersonal events succeeding one another in an anonymous flux (or if I resembled the amnesiac who forgets from one moment to the next who he is and what he does), then how could I make a radical decision, for example, to resist or to take a *coherent stand* [*m'y tenir*], remain constantly faithful to myself throughout my life?"

"You are relying here on the most radical egocidal thinkers, those who make the ego into a simple and inconsistent appearance, thus facilitating your own task. But it is a matter not of denying the existence of the ego but rather of limiting its claims, removing it from its sovereign place, while avoiding constructing it as ultimate foundation. What we call our ego is in fact only a derived entity, produced by another more originary agency."

"It's possible, but the difficulties begin as soon as it becomes a matter of explaining how the ego could be derived from an originary non-ego, and *without taking account* that it derives from it. It then cannot avoid appearing as a mask, a sort of screen dissimulating the non-ego that engenders it, like the source of an illusion that must be brushed aside. After all, if it thinks in me without me knowing it, I could indeed be merely the dream of this Other who thinks the thought 'me' . . . Inevitably egocide is radicalized, and it seems impossible to destitute the ego, to derive it from an Other, without sooner or later destroying it. As soon as egocide is initiated, it is already too late to save the ego."

"The ego is nonetheless posited as an ego by opposing itself to an Other, by ejecting it outside of its sphere—and this Other does not necessarily have the traits of an Evil Genius: it is the weak, the humiliated, the one I have wronged, whose supplicating face accuses and obliges me. As Pascal has already said, 'the ego is detestable' and 'unjust' because it claims 'to become the center of everything.'"

"This ethics of the Face that you are reclaiming is sublime, but I cannot adhere to it. I fear recognizing in it a subtle variation of egocide, which does not negate the existence of the ego but tries to lessen and humiliate it, in order to submit it without reserve to the Other. By what right do you claim that to be ego is always to be guilty, or that the Other would always be my innocent victim, or that I more than any other would be responsible for everything before all? Why do you refuse to *share in this wrong*, to admit that there is also *a violence of the Other*, an injustice, a cruelty, a treason that it can commit against me? And moreover, whenever this Other that you religiously invoke speaks, it always expresses itself by saying 'I,' exactly like me. I conclude from this that it is not wholly Other, an infinitely other Other, but another myself, *an alter ego*. if I want to understand *who* the Other is, then I must start from myself and try to show how I constitute *in me* the meaning of being an other-than-me. Such a method in no way implies any 'narcissism' or any violence to others: it is the only path that could lead me to them."

"Perhaps you are right about that. But you cannot deny that the ego most often refuses to welcome the Stranger or Foreigner, to be vulnerable and exposed to it, to be devoted to it. This indifference to the Other is not only a fault that the ego would be free not to commit: it is also a question of an ontological egoism that reveals the very truth of the ego to us. 'This is mine,' 'that's my place in the sun': this is the origin of all violence and injustice."

"You're giving the ego a hard time for its indifference to the Other. It seems to me on the contrary that we are *not indifferent enough*, that we are constantly under the influence of the Other, captive to it, subjugated by it. This is how our ego is constituted in the world—by identifying itself with different figures of the Other. But the more I identify myself with it, the more it appears to me as a threatening rival that seems more 'me' than myself. The alienated ego then turns back against the Other and tries to negate it in its turn. Identification thus turns into hatred, and this culminates in a murderous desire. Despite whatever Levinas may say about it, it is not the claimed 'egoism' of the ego that would be the major source of violence—it is the mastery of the Other over me. In order to stop considering the Other as my rival or my persecutor, I must first find myself. You were wrong to believe that the affirmation of the ego impeded it from opening itself to the other. On the contrary: the ego that rejects and accuses the Other is envious of and hates the Other, is an ego that has *not sufficiently* affirmed itself. What then is lacking in 'the humanism of the other human,' in all the psychological or moralistic discourses about the 'desire for the Other,' and in the respect or the love for others? Each time, we believe we know what the ego is, what the Other is, and how they relate to one another. But in truth, I still do not know *who* I am—and as much as my true ego escapes me, I also no longer know who the Other is, or how I am able to encounter it, to recognize it as an other, or to identify myself with it."

"I am having difficulty following you. You seem to admit that the ego is constituted by identifying itself with figures of the Other, but you immediately designate this identification as an intolerable alienation, and then you call on the ego to 'un-alienate' itself by affirming itself, to 'come back to itself'—as if it were a lost paradise before the Fall, a primordial Self preceding every alienation."

"Let's say this instead: an originary ego, a singular I (and not some anonymous 'self'), which is given to itself before giving itself to an Other or identifying with it. This is why our alienation is not originary and why it must be possible to be dislodged from it, up to a certain point."

"But I was nothing before identifying myself with the Other! You know what psychoanalysis teaches us: it is only when it manages to recognize itself in the mirror that the infant becomes aware of being an ego. This derivation of the ego on the basis of a non-ego, which seems so mysterious to you, is easily explained: the ego is formed by unconsciously identifying itself with an image presented to it as the image of an other. My relation to myself is marked by an original alienation at the outset: how would it be possible to dissipate this illusion, which is the same as me?"

"I know this thesis, and it is not at all satisfying to me. I recognize, however, that psychoanalysis is one of the very rare theories to try to describe the genesis of the ego on the basis of a non-ego. It thus presents us with one of the most convincing versions of egocide. But to respond to you, I will have to analyze this theory of the 'mirror stage' in a more precise manner, along with the conception of identification subtending it. I hope to be able to show you that Freud's and Lacan's hypotheses about the genesis of the ego or the subject are not grounded, and that they disfigure our experience and dissimulate the truth of the ego."

"Are you going to succumb to this detestable fashion that condemns psychoanalysis as a scientific imposter?"

"Let me reassure you that, like you, I distrust these doctrines that believe that 'thought is a bone,' or rather a network of neuro-connections, and which imagine being able to cure us by enclosing us in chemical camisoles, or by reconditioning our behaviors, as if we were just lab rats. What motivates them is their horror at the truth. They loathe this singular, enigmatic truth that traverses the history of each ego, that is dissimulated for my unhappiness or is discovered for my liberation. It is this truth that psychoanalysis is seeking, and for this, it merits support against the thought police. But this must not inhibit us from criticizing the limitations of Freudian theory."

"I have another objection for you. You claim this Cartesian gesture for yourself that posits the ego as first truth. But Descartes did not question the Being of this ego, the *sum* of the *ego sum*. He thus ratified this forgetting of Being, which since the Greeks has condemned the Occident to errancy. By erecting the human ego as supreme principle, the French philosopher has worsened this errancy: he grounded modern metaphysics in the Subject, and this culminates in an absolute will to power seeking to conquer the Earth. Are you going to renew this blindness?"

"Do you really believe that Descartes is at the origin of this metaphysics of the Absolute Subject or this conquering Will that unfurls itself on the world? Heidegger's charge against the Cartesian cogito has a very specific meaning: it radicalizes the egocide that he had already initiated in *Being and Time*. For him, Dasein, that is, the existing being that I am, is not *me*—it is the *Da-* of the *Sein*, the 'there' of Being, and everything that it is, is granted to it by the enabling-favoring of Being. By thus submitting us to the call of Being, Heidegger strips us of our freedom, and this egocidal gesture is not foreign to the political positions that he'll take in 1933."

"You are going to have to demonstrate that!"

"I am ready to do so, to submit the ontological 'destruction' of the *ego cogito* to a rigorous critique. It is high time that this were done with the pretended priority of the question of Being over the question of the ego. From Heidegger, at least, I retain this: a philosophical question is recognized by a fundamental trait, according to him—whoever questions is included in the question. We must then allow that more than any other question, "who am I?" is a *radical* philosophical question, because whoever questions is entirely included in this question, is *one with it*. It is in effect a matter of *a question that I myself am*. Whenever I question Being or time, I understand myself in my questioning (since I am and since I exist temporally), and it could be that the analysis of my existence is a privileged access to the meaning of Being—but *I am not* Being or time *as such*. If the proximity, or even the identity, of whoever questions and the stakes of the question characterize philosophical questioning, then the question that concerns the ego is the most radical of philosophy."

"It is not only Heideggerian ontology that you will have to criticize but also psychoanalysis and even the whole of contemporary thought."

"To be able to return to the truth of the ego, to find the path that leads me back to myself, I must begin by brushing aside what obstructs it, namely, those doctrines issuing from the *self-forgetfulness* of the ego. Be assured that I will limit myself here to those two major thinkers of the twentieth century whom you have invoked, those grand masters of egocide, Heidegger and Lacan, while leaving others the task of extending this critique to Hume, Nietzsche, Sartre, Merleau-Ponty, and Deleuze, without forgetting Wittgenstein and his various epigones. This critical detour seems necessary to me—it is in being confronted with what is most powerful in adverse thoughts that a new thought of the ego will be able to be unfolded. But this critique of ontology and psychoanalysis would be but a sterile polemic if it did not allow for positing the question of the ego on new bases. For this, we will have to confront Descartes: will he who had discovered the originary truth of the ego be able to keep it up all the way to the end? Does he not then submit the cogito to an Other Subject that would be its ground and its truth? And if it turns out that he too gave in to the temptation of egocide, what would remain of the Cartesian gesture? We are going to have to go one step further toward a more radical thought of the ego. It is only in the last part of this book that we will approach this unknown, which is me, ego. New questions will arise there, with new concepts that will allow for an elucidation of them. We will be able to question the relation of the ego and the flesh, wonder who is the first foreigner I discover in myself, delimit the enigma of the encounter with others, understand the passage from hatred to love, death, and the resurrection of the ego. We will perhaps then begin to understand what the origin of our alienation is and to glimpse the path of our deliverance."

PART I

AGAINST EGOCIDE

Ego Sum Moribundus, or
Heidegger's Call

In the text "European Nihilism," Heidegger evokes the "sovereignty of the Subject in modern times," a subject that manifests itself as an "unconditional will to power" and tries to become the "absolute lord of the Earth." For Heidegger, the origins of this conquering subject are found in the Cartesian cogito: "it is Descartes, with his proposition *ego sum*, who forces open the door into the essential domain of this sovereignty understood metaphysically." Heidegger adds: "We today are witnesses to a mysterious law of history which states that one day a people no longer measures up to the metaphysics that arose from its own history; that day arrives precisely when such metaphysics has been transformed into the absolute."[1] The meaning of this enigmatic sentence becomes clearer if we remember that this text dates from 1940: it was the French people who no longer "measure up to" the Cartesian philosophy that they had produced, at the moment when this philosophy, blossoming into the absolute metaphysics of the will to power, turned back on and crushed itself, as carried out by the *Wehrmacht*. The most legitimate heir to Descartes, therefore, is Hitler: from the *Discourse on Method* to *Mein Kampf*, the same project is unfolded and achieved. But let us be cautious: in making this claim, Heidegger is seeking not to justify Nazism (he had already renounced it some time previous) but rather to deconstruct it by revealing its metaphysical foundations. Hitler's vision of the world and his political project would therefore be rooted in the "modern metaphysics of subjectivity," that is, in the most extreme forgetfulness of Being. By installing the human subject at the center of beings, modern metaphysics has left us defenseless against its sovereign nihilistic will, which wants nothing other than itself, and whose blind power is unleashed as the devastation of the world and the earth. Descartes' cogito is really just one among many modes of this metaphysical subjectivity, a still indigent prefiguration of it. Because the French philosopher remained prisoner to an "egoist" interpretation of subjectivity, reducing the subject to an isolated ego, he is principally responsible for the "aberration" that is modern individualism. Once this new principle is fully unfolded, it is no longer an individual ego with which we deal but rather a collective subject, a historical community that "wills [itself] to be a people, nurtures [itself] as a race, and finally, empowers [itself] as lord of the earth."[2] But it does not matter if it is an isolated "individual," or the "man" of the rights of man, or the German "people" united behind their *Führer*—the same project governs all of the fundamental principles of modern times.

I do not here intend to discuss Heidegger's analysis of Descartes, his polemical engagement with the author of the *Meditations,* to which Heidegger would constantly return over a half century.[3] For the moment, let us note only that through Descartes, Heidegger attacks both the "metaphysics of the ego" that characterizes our epoch, and its concrete consequences—namely, the fall into "the nonbeing of subjectivism," the submission to "an 'I' reduced to its random desires and abandoned to an arbitrary free-will."[4] As a simple and deficient variation of the modern Subject, the Ego would be—like Spirit, Man, People, or "Race"—an illusion that quickly leads us astray and therefore must be deconstructed. Heidegger thus accomplished one of the most powerful and radical egocides ever conceived, and this destruction of the ego still weighs heavily on French philosophy today. The focus of my inquiry here is to question the reasons for this egocide. How can Heidegger claim that the ego is only an illusion? How does he come to consider the ego cogito as a metaphysical Subject bent on the conquest of the earth? Is this claim legitimate, or does it instead rest on a profound misinterpretation of both Descartes' thought and *the ego as such*, our ego? To respond to these questions, we have to go back to Heidegger's master work, to the revocation of the ego that began some years earlier in *Being and Time.*

"I am the others"

"The question [of Being] has today been forgotten": so begins *Being and Time*. Western philosophy is grounded in this *forgetfulness of Being*, and it is not only philosophers but all humans who, in their everyday existence, allow themselves to be absorbed by things, by *beings*. We endlessly rush about from one being to another, never pausing to wonder what makes each being be what it is, never questioning the Being of these beings.[5] Opening a new path to the question of Being is the task of a thinking that first defines itself as *a fundamental ontology*. But Being is given each time as the Being of *a being*, as the singular *manner of being* proper to this being. Amidst all the beings surrounding us and that we are, we need only locate that "exemplary being," the analysis of which will allow us to pose the question of Being anew. This privileged being is the only being able to ask the question of Being—that is, "the being which in each case we who question ourselves are." Heidegger calls this *Dasein*, and as it is the only being that *exists* in the strict sense, the only being whose "essence resides in its own existence," I propose that this be translated as "existing being" [*l'existant*].[6]

Who, then, is this existing being? Who is Heidegger's Dasein? It is the being "which in each case I myself am."[7] This is why existing being exists only in the singular and why this term is therefore not suitable for man or any other collective entity (people, race, nation, state, etc.). It is not a matter of *the* ego or even of the general and anonymous notion of an "I," because "it pertains to egohood that the ego is always mine. A nameless ego is an absurdity."[8] In other words, this existing being is *me*, which is why it is "always mine"—because at every moment, *I am it*. And yet existing being is also *not me*, no more than it is a subject or a man (nor is it consciousness, the unconscious, soul, spirit, person, or individual). We must be sure that "violence is not practiced on Dasein by preconceived notions of *ego* and subject drawn from the theory of knowledge,"[9] because characterizing it that way would lead us to misconstrue the singular mode of being that is its own—the enigmatic, still fleeting, and indeterminate singularity of the existing being that I am. But it is for yet another reason that Heidegger renounced all those old names such as "ego," "subject," and "man" and substituted "Dasein" for them: he says that he was trying "to characterize with a single term both the relation of Being to the essence of man and the essential relation of man to the openness ('there' [*Da*]) of Be-ing [*Sein*]."[10] To change the name of the ego to Da-sein is therefore to de-cide (1) to think the "I am" on the basis of the "am," that is, from *Being* rather than from the *I*; and (2) to understand the Being of Dasein on the basis of its *Da*, its "there," that is, an *over there*, "a being-outside-of," an Outside—and thus to think of it as *transcendence*. By privileging the *ego* and not the *sum*, by representing it as a subject turned back in on itself and deprived of all transcendence, the traditional conception of the hu-man ego becomes an obstacle to the disclosure of Being. In order to have access to this existing being, all the traditional definitions of the human ego (and especially its modern determination as Subject) must be revoked, and we even have to get rid of the name "ego" altogether: the existing be-ing that "I" am is no longer an *I*. In *Being and Time*, an egocide—a desti-tution, a destruction of the ego—is thus achieved.

And yet, existing being is defined as *this being that I myself am*, and it can be determined only as such, that is, as an ego. If being-mine or being-ego [*être-(à)-moi*][11] belongs to existing being as one of its essential characteristics, it becomes very difficult to reject every reference to the ego. But even if Dasein is not an ego, it is nonetheless *nothing other than me*.[12] But now let us examine more closely the motives that led Heidegger to reject all references to the ego. Something obvious imposes itself in re-sponse to the question of knowing *who* the existing being is: "it is in each case *an 'I'*—not others—that is this entity"; "when Dasein addresses itself in a way which is closest to itself, it always says 'I am this being'" (*BT,* 150–51). Taking this indication literally would lead us to complete error: "What if the aforementioned approach, starting with the givenness of the I to Dasein itself, and with a rather patent self-interpretation of Dasein, should lead the existential analytic, as it were, into a pitfall?" (*BT,* 151). By passing itself off as an ego, existing being fools itself for at least three rea-sons. By determining existing being as ego, (1) we enclose it in an absolute solitude, without world or others, and thus misconstrue its transcendence; (2) we make it into a substance, a subject, that is, a "subsisting being," and thus mistake its mode of being; and (3) we think that it is always properly itself when it says "I" and thus erase the difference between its inauthentic existence and its possible authenticity. Heidegger attributes all three of these mistakes to Descartes, who would then be the origin of all the prin-cipal errors ruining modern philosophy. If we want to discover what existing being really is, it must be thoroughly differentiated from the ego, which would require the destruction of Cartesian philosophy. By determining the ego as a "thinking thing" or "substance," the French philosopher attributed to it an unsuitable and inappropriate way of being—namely, that of "subsisting" [*vorhanden*] beings as they present themselves to a purely theoretical and abstract investigation. Assimilating the ego to a substance amounts to conferring a permanence or the stable identity of a thing on it. Now, we all do indeed have the spontaneous tendency to consider ourselves in this way, to imagine our ego as an always present support or as the "subject" that sustains all our thought and invariably persists throughout our life. Always similar to itself, this ego-subject seems to enjoy an immutable and faultless certitude, without ever questioning itself about the meaning of its existence. The whole effort of *Being and Time* consists in liberating existing being from this false understanding of itself and in distinguishing the permanent presence of things from the temporality proper to Dasein, the temporality of a being always in projection, whose existence is always "ahead of itself," and which is temporalized in the horizon of the future rather than in the present—a being who must yet find itself and always risks losing itself. If it is true that since Descartes, the term "ego" has designated an "ego-substance" or an "ego-thing" always present to and certain of itself, then that name is no longer suitable for such a being.

Heidegger does not even imagine another possibility, such as an ego that would be neither "substance" (in the sense of a subsisting being) nor a "subject," that is, an ego whose name could define the existing being that I am without betraying it, and that would perhaps be better suited for it than the name *Dasein*. And moreover, this is exactly how existing being designates itself: each time it calls out to itself by asking "who are you?" it always responds "Me." Does not such a self-assured response reveal it in its truth? That is not how Heidegger understands it: when existing being says "I," then "Dasein *is not itself*" (*BT*, 151) and thus most grievously mistakes itself as to what it is. In what context does existing being so noisily present itself by saying "me, me, me"? In the context where we encounter it most often—in its everyday life, as it addresses itself to others around it. However, Dasein in its everydayness is never truly itself, and this mode of existence throws it into fallenness [*Verfallenheit*]. Everyday existence is characterized by a particular relation to Others: existing being finds itself under the influence of Others and in their grip, from which it is unable to twist free or distinguish itself. In this indistinct mix, "one's own Dasein is completely dissolved into the kind of Being of 'the Others'" (*BT,* 164) such that "everyone is the other, and no one is himself" (*BT,* 165), and thus *I am the Others.* How can Dasein exist in this mode, not simply *like* an Other (by imitating it, taking it as a model, etc.), but by identifying itself completely with the Other? Heidegger sometimes names the initial relation of existing being to the world and to Others as an "identification," which is presented as a captivation, a dispossession of self, an "alienation" [*Entfremdung*] whereby existing being becomes alien, *fremde,* foreign to itself, letting itself be trapped by its own inauthenticity (*BT,* 222ff.). What must Dasein, the singular existing being that I am, be in order to abdicate its singularity by always identifying itself with others? Are there only these alienating identifications such as fallenness, or is another form of identification possible? Heidegger gives no answers to these questions and thus leaves the origins and fundamental structures of our fallenness in profound obscurity.

In *Being and Time,* his analysis is centered on another question that tries to determine who everyday existing being is, dispersed and lost among others. Within this mass where everything is confused with everything else, "the 'who' is not this one, not that one, not oneself, not some people, and not the sum of all of them. The who is the neuter, the 'they' [*das Man*]" (*BT,* 164). Each acts, each thinks as *das Man* thinks, and it is with this generic Other = X that the everyday I is identified: at first, I am the others "in the mode of being the They." This word here designates "the 'leveling down' of all possibilities of Being," an anonymous, multiform, and proliferating power from which no sphere of existence seems able to escape (*BT,* 165). From where does the They get this unrestrained power? How does it happen that the existence that is always mine also forgets itself to the point of being constantly lost among others? If it is always already alienated to this extent, will it ever be able to overcome its fallenness and have enduring access to its authentic existence? To know if this deliverance is possible, we must look for *who* is most capable of resisting the power of the They. The leveling that it effects consists in rendering all individuals and all situations interchangeable, crushing the singularity of the existing being that I am and erasing all differences between me and others. Heidegger emphasized the "ontological difference" that demarcates Being and beings, without ever taking into account the dividing line that differentiates me from everything that is not me. This other difference—which I will henceforth call "the egological difference"—seems to me more decisive when it comes to dissociating oneself from the They. How does one resist the domination of the Collective, this "recruitment" that submits individuals to the "leveling down of organized uniformity"—without relying on an irreducible singularity, impossible to level or to substitute for another? Where is this rebel singularity discovered? Is it still that of an ego, of a certain way of being me? Or is the ego never singular enough to resist its neutralization in the They? When I say "I," when I think that I am speaking in my name, it is instead the They who speaks through my mouth, and the more narcissistically I claim my originality, the more I am subjected to this Other. Does this mean that I have not yet found my proper voice, my own ego, and that I have to find myself by myself while freeing myself of the Other? Or does it mean that I will never be authentically myself as long as I am ego?

Heidegger chooses the second hypothesis, which is that of egocide. For him, the "who" of everyday inauthentic existence is not an ego—it is nothing other than the They. But authentic existing being is likewise not "ego." Why not? Because the true name of Dasein in its authenticity is not me or ego but rather Self [*Selbst*]. In the resoluteness that frees it, "authentic Being-one's-self . . . does not keep on saying 'I' " (*BT*, 370), nor does it have to say it because it is no longer an ego and has successfully "surrender[ed] its I-ness so as to attain itself as an authentic self."[13] This is a particularly habile strategy: Heidegger had at first pretended to take up the defense of the being-ego or being-mine, which was threatened by the alienation and leveling of the They, but he did so only to prepare us better for the elimination of the ego to the benefit of the Self. Most of his successors have endorsed this forceful gesture, which is how and why the Self has massively invaded French philosophy, each time implying a depreciation or a destitution of the ego.[14] What is Heidegger's Self, which pretends to evict the ego? This term designates an anonymous entity, which is neutral with respect to the Me, the You, the He, or She, and is even more primordial than the They: "only because Dasein as such is determined by selfhood can an I-self comport itself towards a you-self . . . selfhood is neutral with respect to being an 'I' and being a 'you.' "[15] The being-one's-self [*Selbstsein*] of Dasein is then presented as an essence common to all existing beings, and this Self that I share with so many others no longer has anything to do with my singular existence. Heidegger ends by recognizing this: "The manner and the way in which man is man, that is, himself . . . by no means coincides with I-ness."[16]

In truth, this Self, which is no longer mine or another individual's but which governs all my relations with others, this anonymous Self that neutralizes any difference between me and others, has all the characteristics of the They. What was supposed to define authentic existence strangely turns out to resemble the principle of fallenness and inauthenticity. Both are grounded on the same erasure of singularity, the same denial of egological difference, and I do not see what could distinguish them except for the peremptory claim that the They alienates me, while being-one's-self frees me and opens to me the path toward an authentic existence. I have always wondered what magic would allow a universal and neutral Self to grant me access to myself, even though the ego was unable to do it. Rather, the contrary is true: only what most strongly resists the influence of the They can free me from my alienation, and this could not be enacted by a Self, but only by an ego, the me that I myself am, the ego that is always mine. By defining the *Selbst* as the "primordial ground" of the ego, Heidegger entirely reverses the order of grounding. But no one truly first has the experience of being a "self": each existing being initially experiences itself as being *me, ego*. It is the ego that, from out of itself, constitutes the meaning of being an other or an alter ego, of being "yourself" or "him or herself"—and it is only then, on the basis of myself and my relation to others, that I form the notion of a Self common to all. For an existing being that is each time its own, the deliverance from alienation and the access to an authentic existence will necessarily occur only through a return to myself, to the ego that I am. And since there is no longer any reason to renounce designating this existing being as an ego, I propose henceforth that wherever Dasein is concerned, we must hear and understand "ego."

The reader will perhaps judge that I am wasting time with vain subtleties and finally contenting myself simply by replacing one word with another. But words are important, for what is at stake here is the truth of our existence. By substituting the name "Dasein" for "ego," Heidegger hoped to distinguish himself from Descartes (and from his own teacher, Husserl), but also from the everyday illusion and the "pitfall" into which existing being constantly falls by representing itself as an ego. He wanted to commit an egocide. In order to safeguard the singularity of existing being, he had decided to eliminate the ego, but he substituted for it the more general and neutral notion of the Self, which crushes its singularity more violently still. He is thus exposed to an insurmountable contradiction: he persists in characterizing existing being as always mine, pretending all the while to avoid any reference to the ego. To get out of this impasse, he would have had to renounce either egocide or mineness. Heidegger would take the second option, first by reinterpreting mineness on the basis of Being rather than the ego[17]—which robs it of all concrete meaning—and then by abandoning every reference to this notion. In the text in which he had first introduced it, he declared that the fact that "it is in each case mine . . . is a thoroughgoing, constitutive [determination] for this Being. Whoever crosses it out has lost whatever part of his theme he is talking about."[18] But Heidegger would himself cross Being out just a short time later, by giving existing being over to the moral violence of the Neuter.

"I am (not quite) dead"

Everywhere resonates the voice of those who preach death . . . They say "Life is refuted!" But only they are refuted, and their regard which sees only a single facet of existence.
    —Friedrich Nietzsche, "The Preachers of Death," in *Thus Spoke Zarathustra*

Who am I, such that I am always identified with others? How is it possible to resist the omnipresent domination of the They, the Neuter, the Collective? Do I have the power to escape their grasp and finally become myself? These questions would have no meaning if existing being were not in every case my own, each time me: this is why I can decide whether to be myself, to be truly the existing being that I am, to be "authentically" myself. The possibility of an authentic existence supposes a decision of truth, a decision *for* truth, and it is each time me who decides, me who chooses myself—or who chooses not to choose. By opening itself to the world and to itself, Dasein exists; and this openness, this "there" of the existing being, is the truth itself, "the most originary phenomenon of truth" (*BT*, 271). And so, as the existing being that we are, *"Dasein is 'in the truth'"* (*BT*, 263), which does not mean that it is always right about everything but rather that it is the ultimate condition of the truth: there is truth only if I, the existing being, am there. This does not mean that *I am* the truth or that existing being would be identified with the truth as such: it is simply the condition and addressee of it—that *to whom* and *by whom* the truth is revealed. This difference between truth and its condition, never questioned by Heidegger, prohibits us from thinking of the revelation of truth as an *auto-revelation*, wherein truth would be given without being distanced from itself. A fault line is found here, which risks opening into an abyss: as we will see, Heidegger will soon dissociate existing being from the truth in order to entrust truth to the guardianship of Being, and finite existence will fall still further away from the truth, in the shadows of errancy and forgetfulness.

In the perspective of *Being and Time,* existing being thus has the possibility of being opened to itself in truth, of being truly itself, of existing in an authentic manner. But it also has the inverse possibility of closing itself off from itself and from Being. It is most often found in this dissimulative position: "because Dasein is essentially falling, its state of Being is . . . *in non-truth*" (*BT,* 264), and by this fact, it is "equiprimordially both in the truth and in untruth" (*BT,* 265). From this follows a paradoxical thesis, which is also one of Heidegger's most beautiful discoveries. Since they both belong to existing being as two paths that it could take, truth and non-truth are not mutually exclusive in the same way that simple logical contraries are (such as True and False in the traditional conception): by confronting one another with the greatest violence, each calls to and is intertwined with the other in the stranglehold of their combat. Said more soberly, non-truth is not opposed in an exterior manner to truth but is rather the countertruth *of* this truth, initially belonging to its essence; and in each case, truth must tear itself away from the veiling of non-truth. Of all the names that have been given to truth, the Greek word *alétheia* is most suitable, if we recognize that the prefix (*a-*) is here a privative attesting to a *dis*-covering or *dis*-closure or *un*-veiling of a truth that pulls itself away from a more ancient and more powerful non-truth (*BT,* 265).[19] Truth is first of all the truth of Dasein, of an existing being deeply marked by the battle between truth and non-truth and which, in the tearing away and distress, must in every instance make a decision for one or the other. Such a decision is free, is freedom itself: without it, no truth could be given.

But we may wonder how such a decision is possible, how an existing being that finds itself "always already and most often" in illusion could open itself to the truth—a truth that has always escaped it. Having lost itself in the anonymity of the They, existing being must be called back to itself in order to take hold of itself again. An "attestation" must be presented to it, testifying that its deliverance is possible, and it seems to come to it from the outside, carried by an "alien" or "foreign voice," by a "call of conscience" (*BT,* 314, 317ff.). What does this silent voice say to suddenly quiet the incessant gossip of the They and to summon existing being to itself? On the one hand, "Taken strictly, nothing. The call asserts nothing, gives no information about world events, has nothing to tell" (*BT,* 318); it possesses no ontic content (relative to beings), provides us with no moral, religious, or political message. On the other hand, its ontological meaning is entirely determined: if it says nothing about worldly affairs, it is because it cries out for the Nothing—and the Nothing is presented as the recall of a *Schuld,* a guilt or a debt (*BT,* 326–27). To whom am I in debt, and how do I discharge myself of it? The concern here could not be for an ethical obligation or for a universal moral imperative indifferently addressed to everyone: "Conscience, in its basis and in its essence, is *in each case mine*" (*BT,* 323). As with the door of the Law in Kafka, conscience is destined only to me. From whence does this conscience of indebtedness that transfixes my existence come? At first blush, the origin of the call remains entirely indeterminate: "It calls [*Es ruft*], against our expectations and even against our will" (*BT,* 320), like an injunction that resounds "from afar unto afar" (*BT,* 316), and surprises me every time, giving me the impression that it is not me, but another, who calls me. We must, however, reject any interpretation of the call that would attribute it to an "alien power" (*BT,* 323). In truth, this voice from the outside is not the voice of an other: "Dasein, as conscience, calls [itself]" (*BT,* 322). It is surely presented at first as an alien or foreign voice, but nothing is more foreign to me than myself. Ensconced in the banality of my everyday life, I feel secure in my world, and the calling of the call—which is only myself—does not belong to this familiar world: "it is Dasein in its uncanniness, thrown Being-in-the-world as the 'not-at-home'—the bare 'that-it-is' in the 'nothing' of the world" (*BT,* 321). The voice that clamors in the desert of the world is never anything other than my own voice, which calls me back to myself in order to help me to find myself.

For this reason, the sender and the addressee of the call are one and the same, which reveals an essential trait of Dasein to us: it always addresses itself to itself, exists only *in view of itself.* Such is its singular disposition, an attestation for which is given by the analysis of conscience, but which is transparent in each of its ontological determinations (its "existentials"): whether it is a matter of the understanding, in which existing being "in a primordial manner gives itself both its Being and its potentiality-for-Being as something which it is to understand" (*BT,* 120), or of affection, in which "Dasein is always brought before itself, and has always found itself" (*BT,* 174)—each time existing being is affected by itself. And even when it loses itself in its everyday destitution, it is always away *from itself* that it has turned and *toward itself,* toward its inauthentic existence, that it flees. We can designate this irreducible relation or openness to self as an *auto-affection* or rather as an *auto-donation* or self-givenness.[20] Existing being is not limited to receiving the call or to being passively affected by it; existing being is also what calls itself, and in calling itself is carried toward itself, thus becoming the gift of a possibility for existence. In the call, in the understanding or decision, existing being gives itself to itself—and it is for this reason, in offering itself in this way, that it is always possible for it to find itself or to lose itself. By giving itself to itself, it reveals itself as the singular existing being that it is. And yet, most often, existing being does not see itself as this power that is its own. It is its strange fate that its own call first reaches it as if it were the call of an Other: it is at odds with an *intimate stranger,* which at the end of the account will be revealed as another part of itself.

Curiously, Heidegger does not question this enigmatic internal alterity traversing existence. He is interested above all in the ontological meaning of debt and in what such a phenomenon reveals. When I discover that I am in debt, I feel that *I am not* what I am to be, that I am *not truly* myself. By recalling the existing being to its debt, the call reveals that existing being "constantly lags behind its possibilities" (*BT,* 330), that its initial choice of its existence forever escapes it. Dasein cannot ground itself, it can never be master of its grounding, because it is passively *thrown* into its *there,* thrown into existence without having decided to come into the world. The date and place of my birth, my filiation, my body, my sexual identity, my first childhood—all these ontic determinations that I have not chosen—are the traces of this primordial dejection that I will never be able to overcome (*BT,* 329–32). The feeling that I have of being in debt is thus the index of a conflict between my primordial possibility of *giving myself to myself* and my condition of thrownness, my abandonment, which Heidegger calls "facticity." Which of these two dimensions of existence takes precedence over the other? In the perspective of *Being and Time,* it seems that self-givenness prevails over facticity: were this not the case, the fallenness of Dasein would be insurmountable. Yet is it possible to respond authentically to the call, "to project oneself upon one's *ownmost* authentic potentiality for becoming guilty" or to be in debt (*BT,* 333–34)? By deciding to be itself, existing being returns to itself, it "stands together with itself primordially" (*BT,* 333), and only an existing being that is self-given is also able to return to itself from its most extreme alienation. The possibility of this decision proves that its self-givenness is more primordial than its thrownness, as the analysis of the call decisively confirms: it shows us that the alterity, the uncanniness of the Voice seemingly assaulting existing being from the outside, is purely appearance, and that this Voice instead belongs to or is a part of the existing being's call to itself. The same is true for every dimension of facticity or thrownness, which seemed to unburden me of myself and condemn me to an insurmountable passivity. All of this is included in the decision, as my initial *situation* from which I cannot be separated, but which I myself must freely take up—because it all belongs to my existence, and because my thrownness, my filiation, my birth, my body, are all *mine,* belong to me, are me.

In what does such a decision consist? Heidegger characterizes it as "resoluteness" (a deliverance, a "declosion," *Entschlossenheit*), but he has often been reproached for the indeterminacy of this notion, an indeterminacy that could then justify any engagement or respond to any call whatsoever. We know that in a 1933 course, one of his students described himself as very "resolute" to act but wondered why he should "resolutely" reread Heraclitus rather than join the Sturmabteilung (SA). Are all concrete choices, all possibilities of existence, absolutely equivalent? Or do some of them correspond better than others to the resolute decision? To this question, Heidegger gives an answer that shifts the problem in an unexpected direction. For him, resoluteness becomes authentic only "when it no longer projects itself toward" any possibilities whatsoever and toward instead its "ownmost" and "most extreme" or "uttermost possibility," which is the ability *to die* (*BT,* 353–54). It is my capacity to "run ahead of" or "outstrip" my death, to anticipate it in anxiety, that gives resoluteness its meaning: death allows us to decide between the different possibilities of existence and to privilege as the most authentic the one that most assuredly runs the risk of death. All ontological determinations of existence will from then on be seen in this somber perspective. Fallenness will thus be redefined as fleeing before death, as "diversion" [*divertissement*] in Pascal's sense; truth will now be identified with the certitude of having to die; and the call will be authentically understood as the "memento mori" reminding me of the always possible imminence of my death. Death's shadow extends over all of *Being and Time,* and Heidegger's thought consequently reveals its true face: this ontology is *a thanatology.*

In what sense is existing being called upon to run ahead of or outstrip its death? This notion comes from an "existential" concept of death, which must be distinguished from the ordinary meaning. At first glance, what we know about death does not come from our own death, of which we have no direct experience, but solely from the death of others. But this is only a false knowledge—we only ever witness the death of others from the outside, without having the experience of death as such. Death is the most singular and most personal experience, it is my ownmost possibility—no one can die in my place—and no one else's death could teach me anything about death as such. This is why the possibility of its own death "summons Dasein as singular," "isolates it from itself," and manages to free it from its alienation in the They. This absolute singularity sees itself erased in the common notion of death, which understands death as an anonymous, indeterminate event (*one dies, they die*) that indifferently strikes everyone in general yet concerns no one in particular. By understanding it as an indifferent and distant terminus ("we all end up dead"), existing being flees from the anxiety of its death, forgetting that death is an always imminent possibility and is possible at any moment, always accompanying its existence. These different characteristics define what Heidegger calls "Being-towards-death," which means both being endlessly turned *toward* death and being *at the point of* or *on the brink of* death, that is, attached to it, always dying, always exposed to the imminence of its death. It is not a matter of abstractly meditating on this possibility but rather of being identified with it, of "coinciding with one's death." In my being-toward-death, I do not think of my death as a future event, but rather, *I am* my death; only in this way do I exist authentically: "only in dying [*im*

Sterben] can I to some extent say absolutely *I am*."[21] This paradoxical position becomes more comprehensible if we distinguish death [*Tod*] considered as the terminus yet-to-come of a life, from death considered as the always already present possibility of dying [*Sterben*]. This dying-without-death is what is at stake in "running-ahead" or "outstripping," in the strange experience of a being-toward-death that must not quite go *all the way to* death, a being that is carried toward the extreme limit of its death while constantly holding itself back on this side of the limit. It is right to say that Heidegger never takes into account death as such;[22] as long as it is *toward* death, existing being remains *living*—and so, in fact, the entire analysis concerns nothing but life, this very singular mode of living that dying is.

How does one die without really dying, without being dead? How can we describe the terrifying experience in which someone dying but still barely alive manages to utter the paradoxical phrase, "I am dead"? In "The Facts in the Case of M. Valdemar," Edgar Allan Poe tells us the story of a dying man who, just before dying, is successfully hypnotized.[23] The hypnosis prolongs his agony by maintaining him for months in a state of living death. The only trace of life in his inert body is his voice, which occasionally resonates like a voice from beyond the grave, proffering this impossible claim: "I tell you I am dead." This goes on until the hypnotist who, in trying to awaken him, actually hastens his death, and Valdemar immediately decomposes into "abominable putrefaction." Why are we so fascinated by this story? By revealing the essential link of the saying-I to death, by letting it be understood that as soon as I say "I," I am already dead, Poe articulates the intolerable truth of our existence. And if the truth of the "I" is that "I am dead," we must conclude from this that the "I" is dead, that my sense of being a living ego is only an illusion, that the ego does not exist. In Valdemar's phrase, egocide is linked to thanatology.[24] From Kafka to Artaud, from Genet to Blanchot, this dark message continues to haunt the literature of our time. With Heidegger, Poe's Valdemar enters into philosophy. The destitution of the ego to the benefit of Dasein finds its ultimate meaning in the linking of the death of the ego to the paradox of the "I am dead." It is in this respect that Heidegger criticizes Descartes. The French philosopher would dodge the possibility of the ego's death by defining the ego as an always self-identical and permanent substance. Descartes would not have understood that the truth of the ego is not to be found in the illusory permanence of the *cogito sum* or that the ego had to be understood instead as *sum moribundus*—which does not mean that I would be moribund, gravely ill, or dying: "insofar as I am, I am *moribundus*."[25] Such would be the "fundamental certitude of existing being": *ego sum moribundus*, I am my dying, I am toward death.

What are we to think of this? Is the ego essentially defined as being-toward-death? Does my relation to death ground the radical singularity of my existence and give its truth to it? We have seen that Heidegger dismisses the false knowledge that we think we have learned from the death of others and that he tries to maintain a strictly solipsistic approach to death. From this point of view, we would even have to say that *others do not die*: they may be deceased, or they may absent themselves from the world or fall into nothingness, but only I alone am able to die. Only Dasein dies, because it is mine, because it is me. But from where does existing being gain this absolute certitude of having to die? How does this strange knowledge come to me if not from my experience of the death of others, on the basis of which I anticipate my own? I dread my death as the possibility that I *no longer exist*, that I *am no more*: in this case, the nothing, annihilation, would be the ultimate meaning of death. But from where does this determination come? Is it not once again from this absence, this hole of nothingness that the other's death furrows into the world? And from where does this certitude that my death is imminent or possible at any moment come if not from the astonishment and shock that I am plunged into when the other's death is announced? This impossibility "to give myself my death [*me donner la mort*: to kill myself]" or to experience it in advance obliges me to approach it indirectly, to anticipate it by analogy with the death of others, even though this has nothing in common with my death and, strictly speaking, cannot teach me anything about it. Heidegger's whole analysis is grounded on this analogy, without recognizing it: he transgresses its own rule, starts from the other rather than from Dasein, steals the determinations of another's death and passes them off as those of my own death. This was no doubt inevitable as soon as I claimed to articulate a knowledge about my death. If my death arises from "the nothing," if it can let itself be thought of as a mode of the nothing, then the other's death is no longer a question of a relative nothingness or of determinate negation or of the other's absence from the world, but rather of a more radical Nothing that annihilates the world itself. This is what obliges me to make recourse to analogy, to fiction, or to faith when I desire to give a meaning to this non-meaning, a face to my faceless death.

If Heidegger is wrong here, it is not so much for having appealed to the other's death (how could one not?) but rather for having dissimulated the appeal by presenting a simple analogy as a rigorous analysis of my being-toward-death. What favors this double fault, and prevents Heidegger from seeing it, is Dasein's equivocal character as mine without really being me, defining itself at once both as the singular existing being that I am and as a universal and neutral Self. Under the cover of this neutrality, in which all difference between me and the other disappears, certain determinations of the other can be secretly transposed to Dasein. The principal error in his approach is thus not its solipsism, as has often been claimed, but rather that it is *not solipsistic enough* and does not sufficiently preserve the egological difference. At the end of the account, my "ownmost" and "most singular" possibility reveals itself to be absolutely improper, not my own, already contaminated by the death of the other: the being-able-to-die is what is most common and most impersonal, effacing all individuality in the cold anonymity of death. In truth, it is never me who dies, but *They die* through me. This impersonal neutrality of death seduces so many egocidal thinkers, who see in it the most radical way to eliminate the ego's singularity. Blanchot thus marvels that in the experience of my death, "*I* do not die, I am deprived of the power to die, in my death *one* dies," and Deleuze celebrates the "splendor" of this anonymous One, "in which *it* dies like *it* rains."[26] It thus cannot be "my" death that grants the character of always-being-mine to my existence. If it is true that "no one can take my dying away from me," then it is also true that no one can love, hate, feel, think, or live in my place. No other ego can substitute itself for me, and not because I would be an *ego moribundus* but rather because I am *ego*—and because the life of the ego is each time singular, each time mine.

In *Being and Time*, Heidegger's introduction of being-toward-death responded to an essential exigency: he had to give a more concrete signification to the concepts of resoluteness and authenticity and to allow choosing the most authentic possibility of existence from among many—but this attempt fails, and Heidegger ultimately recognizes it: the running-ahead or outstripping of death remains a formal and empty structure, incapable of concretely determining a possibility of existence (as the astonishing section 74 establishes). In order to overcome its indetermination and to give it concrete meaning, he will designate it as a "sacrifice." We learn that outstripping "enables Dasein to understand that giving itself up [*Selb-staufgabe*: self-sacrifice] impends for it as the uttermost possibility of its existence" (*BT*, 308) and that the "resoluteness is the freedom . . . to give itself up" (*BT*, 443). Consequently, the only authentic existence will be one that freely carries itself toward death. What distinguishes true sacrifice from suicide is that it requires dying for something other than the self, for another human, a people, a country, or an idea: it calls on me to die for an Other. By reinterpreting being-toward-death in terms of sacrifice, Heidegger thus renounces solipsism and recognizes that the authentic existing being never dies alone, that it gives itself death by giving itself to the Other. This dimension of his thought has escaped most of his readers. Consider Levinas, who thought it possible to oppose the solitary heroism of Dasein to an ethic of sacrifice, which would lead beyond Heideggerian ontology:[27] he did not notice that the sacrificial dying-for-another was already at the heart of this ontology. But where does this apology for sacrifice come from? From Hegel and his "freedom for death"? Or from Nietzsche, who also sang the praises of "free death" that stops one from becoming "too old for his truths and his victories"? Or from his reminiscences of Christian theology? Ultimately, it does not matter, because all sacrificial philosophies are always grounded on an egocide. Because these philosophies take the ego for nothing, for an inessential moment of the life of the spirit, for a fiction forged by the will to power, they can call it to a heroic death, a death in which its empty existence will finally find its meaning and its dignity. There had once been a philosopher at Syracuse named Hegesias, to whom has been given the surname Pisithanates, the Counselor of Death, because his doctrine consisted in defending suicide. He preached it with such eloquence that after hearing him, his disciples threw themselves off of the high cliffs into the waves. Chroniclers do not tell us whether he ultimately applied to himself the same remedy that he had prescribed. But we should not rush to make Heidegger into a new Pisithanates. On the contrary, Heidegger teaches us that an authentic relation to dying prescribes staying alive, remaining an always living *moribundus* in order to be able to stay ahead of death—this is true at least as long as he maintains the demarcation between *Sterben* and *Tod*. It suffices to imagine this running-ahead as a sacrifice, so that dying may then be identified with an effective death, and so that the thought of existence may then be changed into a preaching of death. In the service of which or what Other, what community, can Dasein (which acquires authenticity only by separating itself from others in the solitude of its resoluteness) sacrifice itself? By accepting dying for the Other, does one not also accept at the same time killing in the service of this Other? Let us now examine these questions as they were posed and all too briefly considered by Heidegger in the period from 1927 to 1933.

"The individual is worth nothing": On Heidegger's Nazism

In the "Call to German Students," written in November 1933, Heidegger declares that "the Führer and he alone is the present and future German reality, and its law . . . Heil Hitler!"[28] How could he have signed that? There is both indignation and anger in such a question. But a great injustice has also been committed—and first of all toward the name "Martin Heidegger," who is above all the author of *Being and Time*. The fate of thought is always assigned to the name of a singular existing being, with all its errors and its baseness. The name is an implacable constraint whereby the work is left compromised by Heidegger's signature, held hostage by it, and returning to him afterward as a figure of his destiny. Hostages: indeed, such is the status of Heidegger's "words," essential motifs of his thought, when we find them linked to the proclamations of the Nazi rector. What could Dasein, resolute decision, and authenticity subsequently mean once they have been charged with a political meaning and have reappeared in a discourse arguing for the raising of the Führer to the status of Law? By placing it in Hitler's service, does Heidegger betray his own thought, or is this disaster already secretly announced in the theses of *Being and Time*? Every possible response has been given to these questions, ranging from the disciples' obstinate refusal to recognize the least relation between Heidegger's thought and his support for Hitler, to those who, like Adorno, consider Heidegger's philosophy "fascist through and through." What is problematic in Heidegger's case is not that the only political decision he ever made was to support Hitler but rather that he tried to justify this decision philosophically and to engage all of his philosophy in this justification. For some months (or for some years; it does not matter), he tried to elaborate on the foundations of his own ontology a more authentic philosophy of Nazism, which would conform better than its official expressions to what seemed to him to be "the truth and the greatness of this movement." By wanting to build on it a sort of metaphysical Nazism, he compromised his philosophy in his political drift, and it is legitimate to look for what in this thought could have authorized such a drift. For this, it is important to read and reread Heidegger patiently—and not to purge him from our libraries, as we are sometimes invited to do today.

This research, which I have elsewhere undertaken,[29] can take as its starting point the theme of the "call." Most often, Heidegger's rectorial proclamations are presented as calls (to students, to workers, to Germans, etc.), and even when this is not the case, the proclamations are marked by the rhetoric of injunction: they summon those to whom they are addressed to submit themselves to a call for the "German revolution," that is, for the Führer. What do this injunction and the "call of conscience" described in *Being and Time*, a call that is supposed to tear existing being away from its captivity in the They, have in common? We know that such a call "asserts nothing, gives no information about world events" (*BT*, 318), and certainly, since it says nothing, it is always possible to make it say what it does not say, just as one makes a dead man speak, by identifying this call with the Führer's call to the German people. But this would be to do violence to it: such a call would be addressed to no people, no class, no community—because it is this singular call by which an existing being is called to itself "in the solitude of its abandonment" (*BT*, 320). This existing being is neuter (neither male nor female, neither Jew nor Greek nor German, etc.); it is the Exiled; it is always "Dasein in its uncanniness, thrown Being-in-the-world as the 'not-at-home'—the bare 'that-it-is' in the 'nothing' of the world" (*BT*, 321). As it addresses the call to itself, its call can come from no one other than it, which it would have to obey. Nor is the call destined to an other whom it would try to subjugate: every position of mastery, every claim to exert a spiritual or political *Führung*, or to pass itself off as Hero or Guide, thus sees itself revoked in advance by the call. Considered from the perspective of *Being and Time*, Heidegger's adhesion to Nazism appears to be the height of inauthenticity. By engaging it, he repudiates himself, but this repudiation had been favored by an initial ambiguity in his thought. He would probably not have ceded so easily to the Führer's call had he remained faithful *to his own call* or if he had held on to his initial thesis of the absolutely singular character of Dasein as being always mine. Because the concept of Dasein is profoundly equivocal (both mine and other than me), Heidegger tends more and more to play its neutrality against its being-mine, in order finally to identify it with an anonymous Self. Dasein thus loses its ownmost singularity, which had prevented it from being totally alienated in an Other. We begin to glimpse one of the motives that could have allowed him to cede to Hitler's call: what made his adhesion to Nazism possible is the renunciation of the singularity of Dasein as always mine— and that is an egocide.

Of course, the revocation of the ego is insufficient to explain this political drift, for two reasons: first, because such an extreme engagement is never based simply on "ideas" or philosophical theses: it puts into play what is most opaque in existence, the share of non-truth—blindness, phantasm, madness—that haunts our freedom; and second, because the destitution of the ego can, on the contrary, be connected to a politics of resistance to tyranny. Another condition must be required for a deconstruction of the ego or the subject to drive a philosopher to kowtow to the tyrant. Whether we reread the various "calls" that the rector issues or the funerary homage he gives for the Nazi "hero" Schlageter, we find Heidegger's texts impregnated with the same pathos and subtended by the same injunction to sacrifice oneself in the service of the German people and its Guide.[30] We have already seen this slippage in *Being and Time*, when being-toward-death, which was supposed to isolate me from others so that I could be revealed to myself, ended up being confused with the demand to sacrifice myself for another. Heidegger certainly did not in 1927 imagine basing a politics on being-toward-death. But his reserve dropped some years later, when the communitarian dimension of heroic sacrifice led him away from the solitary character of dying as always mine. From this, he came to ground "the primordial community" on the ordeal of the war, on the "camaraderie of the soldiers at the front," because "the proximity of death in the form of sacrifice has first lead each of them to the same nothingness, which has become the source of an absolutely belonging-ness to each of the others. It is precisely death . . . and the acceptance of sacrifice that death requires, that create above all the space of the community."[31] With this sharing in dying, we will discover the grounding experience of the community: "the people" is revealed as a community of combat against death. This is where that strange figure of a "historical Dasein of the German people" emerges, a collective Dasein (which was unthinkable in the framework of *Being and Time*) that recuperates all determinations of individual existence and transposes them onto the plane of the community.[32] What then becomes of the freedom-for-death and the call to sacrifice in this chilling prose? They are addressed to the people, in the form of a defense of military service, celebrated as the "obligation to be the utmost engaged," to give one's life for the Chief. In the "Rectoral Address," military service is connected with the service of Work and of Knowledge, guaranteed at the highest levels by philosophy. The Knowledge in question here is defined as "the most trenchant imperiling of Dasein," as the unveiling of its being-toward-death. And so the Führer of Knowledge, the thinker who thinks death, agrees with the Führer of the War, who wages war in the name of the People, and their voices are united in the same call to death.

The Heideggerian politics of 1933 can thus be defined as a politics of being-toward-death. This does not necessarily mean that it justifies murder, mass terror, or extermination: with Heidegger, the call to death remains above all an injunction to sacrifice oneself, probably because the limits of his thought forbid him from imagining the other's death, of taking into account the always present possibility of murder.[33] However, what characterizes the Dasein of the people is precisely the ability to inflict death on others and, first of all, on other individual existing beings who risk their lives in its service. Does not demanding that another sacrifice himself amount to killing him? And just how far does this sovereign power of the People of the Heroes extend? As far as the ordered annihilation of another people? Our philosopher never asked these questions. Of the "hero" who risks death, he wanted to retain only the willingness for self-sacrifice. He did not see that a man, for whom his own life and ego are nothing, is equally able both to sacrifice himself and to massacre others, as today's suicide bombers demonstrate. We understand that certain leaders of the Third Reich were able to speak ironically about the "private Nazism" of the rector of Freiburg and his pretension to impose his own vision of national socialism in the place of the official ideology. What he lacked was precisely this call to murder, which is at the heart of the Hitlerian program. Despite his efforts, Heidegger never succeeded in being "authentically" Nazi.

I do not here intend to go deeper into the question of Heidegger's political engagement. I merely would like to look at what allowed him to transpose his philosophy politically and thus place it in the service of Hitler. What authorizes this drift is egocide—more exactly, it is the conjunction of egocide and thanatology, of a sacrificial interpretation of being "toward death." This was probably not a fatal alliance but was favored by the paradox of the *ego sum moribundus*, in which the revocation of the ego is linked to the certitude of being "toward death." Let us learn a lesson from this: one must never give up on the egological difference. It is sufficient to posit at the outset that the existing being that I am is not "me," not "ego," and everything else follows from there: this existing being will gradually be dispossessed first of its being-mine, then of its finite singularity and its freedom, and it will finally and completely blend in with the Dasein of the people, which will confiscate all of its essential traits. The very notion of a "Dasein of the German people" supposes a primordial identity of the mode of existence of a collectivity with that of the individual. Heidegger inherits his postulate from a long tradition of political philosophy: it led Plato to identify justice in the soul with justice in the city, as if the same letters had been writ "here in small and there in large letters," and the consequence of this postulate is always the subordination of the individual to the more eminent reality of the city, the state, or the people. But such a prejudice does violence to the phenomena. When we erase every demarcation between the mode of being of the ego and the mode of being the community, then not just individuals are subjected to the dictatorship of the Collective, but the essence of the community itself is also disfigured by applying to it determinations foreign to it. For this transposition misconstrues the mode of existence of the community, its originary plurality, in order to subject it to the figure of the One [*Un*]. Heidegger's politics are inscribed in this tradition, leading him to submit singular Dasein completely to the domination of a community, which takes on the form of the One People or the total State. The philosophical egocide begun in *Being and Time* thus finds its practical application in the directives of the Nazi rector. For instance, when Heidegger summons the professors to participate in the reform of the University "on the basis of the forces and requirements of the national-socialist State," he concludes with these words, heavy with meaning: "The individual, wherever it crops up, is worth nothing. The destiny of our people

in its State is worth everything."[34] The political transposition of Heideggerian philosophy ends up here with the enslavement of singular Dasein.
What the totalitarian state wants to break is a fundamental trait of existing, namely, its ability to call itself by itself: henceforth, it is an Other that
calls it and gives it its Being.[35] For an existing being, this is equivalent to
an alienation much more radical than it was subjected to by the influence
of the They. Just as existing being was identified with the They, so too
does this new alienation lead it to be identified with the Chief, giving it
the illusion of thinking and acting by itself, even though it is its Guide
who decides and acts in its place. Prisoner to such an identification, it is
even ready to give its life for the Führer, to battle for servitude as if it were
freedom.

A conclusion imposes itself: by transposing his philosophy onto a
political plane, Heidegger disfigures it. His engagement coincides with a
decisive turn in his thought. We have seen that *Being and Time* was marked
by an antinomy, since Dasein is defined there both by its self-givenness—
its ability to give itself freely to itself—and by its facticity, its thrownness,
its impotence to ground itself. When Heidegger redefines it as submission
to the Führer, this tension is resolved in favor of facticity. His maintenance of the previous vocabulary dissimulates this sharp turn, as does the
pathos of anticipatory resoluteness and self-affirmation, which masks Dasein's extreme alienation and its passive submission to the call of an
Other. Yet even after having distanced himself from Nazism, Heidegger
will not reconsider this turn and its principal consequence, the renunciation of self-givenness. Certainly he will situate himself once again on a
purely ontological plane, so that it will no longer be the Führer but Being
itself who calls existing being. The call's origin will have changed, but its
meaning will remain the same: it orders us to make ourselves available for
the "most noble gift," that of sacrifice, and this sacrificial offering alone is
"the path to preserving the favor of Being."[36] The rupture with the theme
of *Being and Time* is consummated, since existing being is no longer
called by itself but now responds to a call that comes to it from elsewhere.
This inversion of the relation between man and Being is what we custom-
arily call the *Kehre*, the turn of Heidegger's thought—without noticing that
it merely prolongs the true and only turn already effected in 1933. It is in
this context that the thinker subsequently attacks the "metaphysics of the
Subject" issuing from Descartes, accusing it of being at the origin of the

disaster of our epoch and, notably, the unleashing of the Nazi "will to power." If the individual Ego, the Man of the rights of man, and the People or the "Race" of totalitarian ideologies are in truth only variations of the same principle, then the specific character of Nazism is diluted in the darkness of modern times, and it becomes absurd to try to resist it, for example, in the name of democracy. What allows Heidegger to settle his accounts at little cost is to burden the unfortunate Descartes with the responsibility for Heidegger's own engagement with Hitler. His turn can be interpreted as an attempt to deconstruct the "metaphysical" foundations of his adhesion to Nazism and to justify his decision to leave *Being and Time* incomplete by claiming that this work was "in danger of becoming merely another entrenchment of subjectivity."[37] The work was too "Cartesian" and thus too close to Hitler. In making this claim, Heidegger completely dissimulates the political meaning of this turn by which he had renounced the self-givenness of existing being and its singularity of being always mine. And his other writings will only bury the political meaning deeper still by radicalizing the egocide, by imposing the dogma of an originary passivity of man and of an absolute necessity for the history of Being. It is not me who has access to thought, speech, or truth—it is Being that grants me thinking; it is the "Being of language that plays" with me, the truth of Being that is revealed and destined to me. The later Heidegger will no longer celebrate the saga of Being, which "claims" man and sovereignly disposes of him, lavishing its favor on him or abandoning him to errancy—all while insisting on the passivity of man, his total submission to the "hidden decree of Being." One of Heidegger's major legacies to French thought is a defense of passivity. Though the reference to Being will have been set aside in favor of Structure, the Other, or Life, we will nevertheless continue to affirm the absolute passivity of the subject or of the ego, and this heavy heritage has long impeded us from accepting the possibility of acting, this reversal of passivity into resistance whereby the ego tries to free itself from its alienation. We often oppose the "serenity" of the later Heidegger to the "voluntarism" of his Nazi period, without noticing that the rhetoric of decision and sacrifice in fact covered over a *destruction* of acting. By substituting Hitler's call for Being, Heidegger maintained the arrangement that justified the submission to the Guide's inflexible will, this alienating identification in which existing being grants the full powers of his life to an Other. The later Heidegger's thought is grounded entirely on this *ontological alienation*. But it is an illusory projection: in truth, it is never Being that calls, that gives or refuses itself, reveals or dissimulates itself—it is Dasein that calls; it is *me*. When the ego abdicates its freedom, when it becomes a passive spectator of its own existence, the times are ripe for the philosophies of History—and it is true that the "thought of the history of Being" strongly resembles Hegel's and looks like an inverted Hegelianism in which errancy is substituted for the victorious march of Spirit's progress in an always growing forgetfulness of Being. What these two doctrines have in common is their acceptance of what happens, the tendency to justify everything in the name of the superior necessity of History.[38] We are sometimes astonished that Heidegger, who is so sensitive to the devastation of the earth and to the destruction of forests and rivers, lacks the words to deplore the extermination of millions of people, words that Paul Célan expected of him. By his silence, his refusal to answer, Heidegger remained faithful to the lines of force of his thought, to his inability to think murder, to his passive submission to destiny. For him, everything that happens—including the worst disaster—proceeds from a decree of Being and must be welcomed with serenity. Here again there is a lesson to be retained: as soon as one renounces the ego's freedom, as soon as one denies it the power to be called by itself, the temptation to bow before a figure of Fate, God, Hero, Führer, or Being is great.

The Cross of Being

If there is something like catastrophe in the creative work of great thinkers, then it consists not in being stymied and in failing to go farther, but precisely in advancing farther—that is to say, in their letting themselves be determined by the initial impact of their thought, an impact that always deflects them. Such going "farther" is always fatal, for it prevents one from abiding by the source of one's own commencement.[39]

When Heidegger declared this at the end of the 1930s, he was hardly thinking of himself—although his march forward had already led him to disaster. He had forsaken his thought of Dasein because it seemed to him too close to the metaphysical subjectivity in which he had seen the grounds for Nazism. And nothing more assuredly resists the call of the Guide (or any other collective entity) than does the singularity of existing being, its being-mine or being-ego, its self-givenness—all of which makes it akin to an ego. This is what the philosopher would have had to maintain had he remained faithful to the source of his thought. But this was impossible for him, since existing being is not "me": the catastrophe was in progress from the beginning, from the initial decision to call this existing being that I am Dasein rather than ego. What is problematic in this term is not just the *Sein*, but also the *Da-*: its ontological dimension grounds existence on its relation to Being and above all its transcendence. Because this "there" means "over there," or "on-the-outside-of," Da-sein must be understood as a *being-outside-of.* The term "transcendent" does not designate some distant afterworld or objects situated beyond my consciousness but rather the ability to transcend *oneself,* which belongs to a finite existing being. With Heidegger, this thesis has a polemical weight: it attacks Husserl, his teacher in philosophy, who, as he said, had "given him eyes to see." The founder of phenomenology opposed the immanence of consciousness to the transcendence of the world, which, Heidegger notes ironically, amounts to "thinking the subject as a kind of box with an interior, volume, and exterior,"[40] whereas Dasein is not a subject closed in on itself and seeking to "exit" itself to an outside. It is always already outside itself, which is what allows it to be itself: "the possibility and the necessity of the most radical *individuation*" reside in its transcendence (*BT,* 62).

It is time to question the primacy of transcendence. I am not certain that it truly manages to ground individuation or to confer onto Dasein the singularity that is each time its own. Existing being becomes authentically itself by choosing itself by itself, by returning to itself in order to overcome its everyday alienation. Its transcendence is what makes this return to self possible by allowing it to pass beyond the beings in which it was caught. But this possibility of always projecting itself beyond is also what had already thrown it into the world, alienated it to this world and to others. How can the same power be both the condition of its failure and its authenticity? How can it throw outside of itself while also leading it back to itself? This ambiguity is at the heart of the concept of transcendence. Toward what or where does it direct itself? Toward the world, toward the Being of beings "in general"? Or toward the Being of that being that I myself am? Heidegger refuses to choose between these two possibilities: opening itself to the world, existing being is opened to itself in the same gesture. We can, however, wonder whether the two perspectives are not incompatible. Let us suppose that the destination of transcendence is the world: as always already thrown outside of me, forever deprived of "myself," of a proximity to or intimacy with self, I am forever lost, and my alienation risks being insurmountable. Let us posit on the contrary that the destination is existing being itself, so that the provenance and the destination are now one and the same: I call myself to myself; I give myself to myself. The essence of transcendence is then revealed as self-givenness, and it can ground the project of an authentic existence. But in what sense can we still speak of a "transcendence" or "being-outside-of-self," since this movement coincides with the self-givenness of the ego, and since I leave myself only then to return to myself—and therefore never truly exit myself? The most suitable term to designate what resides in itself, what gives itself to itself without ever leaving itself, is "immanence." The truth of transcendence is therefore immanence[41]—and we must then recognize that the thought of Dasein and of existence is grounded on a primordial dissimulation, a forgetfulness of immanence.

What masks the opposition of these two perspectives, of these two senses of "transcendence," is the paradox of being-toward-death, in which being-outside-itself and the return-to-self are linked. Nothing throws me outside of myself in a more extreme manner than does my death, but my death is also my ownmost possibility whereby I reappropriate my Self in my most profound dispossession. At least, this is what Heidegger claims. In fact, we have discovered that *Being and Time* fails to ground being-toward-death on the basis of Dasein and that the meaning of my death comes from my experience of the other's death. Thus "my" death is never really my death, and the transcendence of my being-toward-death is not what allows me to be myself: it is because I am a living ego that I can transcend myself toward others, identify myself with them, and live as mortal. I must be alive in order to anticipate the possibility of my death, as Heidegger knew well, since he recognized that "death, in the widest sense, is a phenomenon of life" (*BT*, 290). He also knew that "life lives in that it bodies forth," by being incorporated in a flesh through which "flows the stream of life."[42] Taken strictly, this would have had to lead him to consider death as a *phenomenon of the flesh*, to imagine the carnal immanence of life as the condition of all existence and all transcendence. He would have had to admit that the question of the flesh is at least as radical as the question of temporality and that the relation between the ego and the flesh is perhaps more decisive than the relation of Being and time. Heidegger was never able to accept this, because his thought of Being is built on a forgetfulness of life and of the living ego. It is in this way that he rejoined those preachers of death whose gaze "sees only one sole facet of existence."

This misconstrual is all the more astonishing in that he had first tried, in the beginning of the 1920s, to elaborate a philosophy of "factical life" before renouncing it and turning toward the question of Being. This refusal to determine Dasein on the basis of life prevented him from rallying to a "zoology of peoples," that is, to the biological racism of the Nazis. By a strange paradox, this ideology of hatred and death is grounded on a metaphysics of life, but the "life" that it exalts is not that of the singular individual; it is a universal and blind principle whose implacable "laws of selection" condemn those "inferior races [*Untermenschen*]" who are "inept at living" to death. As soon as life ceases to be my life, as soon as it is torn away from the immanence of the ego and transferred to a collective entity, fascism is not far behind. In truth, the primordial phenomenon of life is an always singular life, always mine: life is given in each living ego and each time in a different manner. Heidegger did not want to understand this, and though he may have taken his distance from the metaphysics of universal Life, he did so only in order to submit existence to the grip of death. He thus styles himself as the crooner of the "Viva la muerte!"—this call to death which is at the heart of fascism. If we desire to resist this mortifying captivation, this ontological fascism that menaces thought, we will have to try *to liberate thought from death*. We will have to think of our existence, our life, without them being governed and ordered by being-toward-death—and we will also have to think of death otherwise, by delivering it from thanatology and from the metaphysics of sacrifice. To believe Heidegger, existing being "is never to be defined ontologically by regarding it as life" (*BT,* 75). In effect, "living beings . . . are separated from our eksisting essence by an abyss."[43] As existence is defined on the basis of being-toward-death, this schism between existence and life leads to an equally radical schism between life and death, and this in turn prohibits us from understanding how life comes to be linked to death, how it is able to resist it or, on the contrary, let itself be captivated by it. Not only is Heidegger unable to think death, but he likewise also fails to think life, to determine it on the basis of an existence dedicated to death. I wonder if we ought not choose the inverse route and try to understand death *on the basis of life*, as an immanent possibility that life gives itself, as a *mortification*, a necrosis of its living flesh. This amounts to establishing the priority of living over dying, of the flesh over temporality, of immanence over transcendence— and this is the path that I will be exploring in this book.

Heidegger's ontology is grounded on a double refusal: revoking the ego in the name of Dasein (the egocidal thesis) and turning away from life in the name of being-toward-death (the thanatological thesis). These two gestures attest to the same rejection of immanence, which he considers a prison without doors or windows. Unlike Dasein, whose existence is grounded on its transcendence, the immanent ego of Descartes and Husserl would be a subject crumpled up on itself, without any opening to the world, others, Being. This is a fatal mistake: far from grounding my individuality, transcendence makes the threat of a *disindividuation*, whereby I risk losing myself, weigh heavily on my existence. There are at least three reasons for this: (1) existing being transcends itself *toward the world*: it is originarily being-in-the-world, but the world is a system of references, a universal economy wherein anything can be substituted for anything else, and each human is worth the same as any other; there is no place in this world for the radical singularity that I am; (2) by transcending itself toward the world and others, existing being identifies itself with them: since I am always already outside of myself, I exist *only in the other*, under the other's influence, and so there is no place for me to return to myself; my transcendence condemns me to an alienation without return; and (3) existing being is most radically torn away from itself *by dying*: the ultimate meaning of transcendence is being-toward-death, and I am truly myself, *ego moribundus*, only by projecting myself toward my death, by sacrificing myself, by sinking into nothingness. It is on this terrain of transcendence that Heidegger and his epigones thought it possible to ground the authenticity of existence, the freedom of the subject, the truth of desire—and we know that their attempts were destined to failure.

The moment has come to change tack and to look elsewhere for the path of our deliverance. Heidegger himself has taught us that what allows existing being to come back to itself is the call that it addresses to itself. But he was mistaken about the meaning of this call, which has nothing in common with the transcendence of Dasein: the call is destined to myself;

it belongs to my self-givenness. Only an ego that has already come to itself is capable of coming back to itself: the ego's immanence is what saves it from being lost in the world. I can accede to myself only by putting out of play the reality of the world and all the transcendental entities that captivate me and separate me from myself. Only a return to the immanence of my life will be able to free me from this captivation. Understood in this way, immanence is no longer anything like a closed box or a prison. Husserl had responded in advance to his disciple's objection: "things given immanently are not, as it first appeared, in consciousness as things are in a box, but rather that they present themselves in something like 'phenomena' . . . that in a certain sense create objects for the ego."[44] He means that immanent phenomena make possible our experience of things in the world, that the sensations of smoothness, cold, or white "create" a thing like the table for me. The border between these two planes is not impervious: all transcendent reality is constituted on the basis of and in these immanent data. We must go further and try to describe these phenomena in their primordial givenness, on this side of all openness to the world and all constitution of an object. And we must show how, by giving itself to itself, the ego unfolds its field of immanence. This is how I understand the *im-* of immanence: it designates less a residence "in" me than a path toward me, a *passage*. By carrying me toward myself, my self-givenness is in movement; it is the same as the mobility of my life, and the "mouvance" wherein I unfold myself without ever being distanced from myself is the source of my freedom and the condition of all transcendence.[45] Only an ego that is already given to itself is able to receive what is given to it and is also able to give itself to the world and to others and to be open to them, or to "transcend itself" in Heidegger's sense. This is why my self-givenness is *more primordial* than the transcendence that carries me toward the world. The rhythm and style of my existence, my loves and hatreds, my alienation and the possibility of my deliverance, the morning blossoming of my birth and the unfigurable horizon of my death, and everything that happens to me in the world must first be announced or prefigured in the elementary phenomena of my immanent life. Describing such phenomena is the task of a radical thinking of the ego, and I will try to elaborate this egoanalysis in the second half of this book.

The most rigorous thinkers of immanence are most often content to oppose the two planes, without considering the passage from one plane to the other, or the genesis of transcendence in immanence.[46] But this is precisely what we must try to understand, this equation of element $=$ X, which is at the origin of all transcendence—and we must imagine it as an event *internal* to immanence, the trait of a limit that immanence gives to itself. Heidegger had discovered that because it is projected toward beings, transcendence bumps up against some X that will be "opposed to it [*dawider*]" and "offer it as a cessation."[47] This internal objection or Opposing of transcendence is rooted in Being itself: *Dawider* is one of the names of Being, which is why the philosophy of transcendence calls for an ontology. However, Heidegger never wonders how transcendence itself is possible or how it can be constituted on a plane of immanence. This supposes that another Dawider had already arisen on this plane, that the ego has addressed to itself this gift of a cessation. Transcendence would thus run the risk of a more radical objection than that of the "object $=$ X," namely, the objection of an adverse pole that would be opposed to me in immanence, even within my flesh and my life. What is this Opposing that my life carries in it? Must we call it "my death"? Does it still belong to Being? Unless it has nothing to do with Being, the world, or death, unless it is possible to subtract it from every ontological interpretation, only then will we have taken a step beyond Heidegger.

Being is eminently transcendence: this is one of the cardinal theses of *Being and Time* (e.g., *BT*, 62).[48] This does not mean that it will sit enthroned far away from us in some Beyond; the transcendence in question here is that of existing being, from which it comes; but it is to Being that it is oriented. Being is that toward which transcendence transcends, its destination, its Dawider. Carried by its transcendence, existing being passes beyond all beings, including the being that it itself is. Why must it constantly surpass itself, tear itself away from itself, in order to go beyond itself toward Being? Is this not a way of *fleeing* from itself? Of being alienated from Being, of forgetting itself in it? Certainly it is a matter of a Being that is always mine, of *my manner of being*: by transcending me toward it, I only ever go beyond to myself. But this is precisely the "mineness" of Being that Heidegger calls into question at the end of *Being and Time*, when he left aside the analysis of the being of Dasein in order to inquire into the question of Being in general (*BT*, section 83). He was going to try over the next few years to think of Being in its difference from beings. By transcending all that it is, Being becomes a Neuter (not my

Being nor the Being of any other being), and its neutrality is transmitted, as we have seen, to existing being, which then becomes an anonymous Self, which is not me, not you, not anybody. The clearing of the *ontological difference* between Being and beings is thus paid for by an abandonment of the *egological difference* between the ego and the non-ego—that is, an always more decisive egocide, which would become even stronger in the 1930s after Heidegger's Turn. There again, his trajectory has an exemplary value: the more I devote myself to Being "in general" (or to the Other, to "God," or any other Transcendent) and the more I am distanced from myself, the more I forget myself. Heidegger's ontology is one of the ways of this forgetfulness. His principal innovation consisted in linking transcendence to the question of Being: all that which in transcendence threatens to subjugate or destroy the ego, to mislead it in the world, to alienate it without return, to dedicate it to death—all of this finds its source in its initial orientation to Being. Ontological neutrality, being-in-the-world, being-with-others, and being-toward-death are the four vectors of transcendence, the four branches of the cross of Being to which the ego is nailed. This is what we must free it from, by ceasing to determine it on the basis of Being and of transcendence and even by renouncing designating it as "existing being." Neither *ek-* nor *Da-* nor *Sein*—only the name *ego* suits it, and it no longer belongs to Being: at the limit, we no longer even have to designate it as an *I am* (or we can keep the "am" but only *under erasure*, between parentheses, or in quotation marks).

It is time to return to the starting point, to the criticism that Heidegger addresses to Descartes (and ipso facto to Husserl), when he accused Descartes of being centered on the *ego* while forgetting the *sum*, forgetting to question the Being of the *I am*. How would the French philosopher have responded to this? Perhaps in this way: that he did not deny that, prior to enunciating the cogito, he had failed "to know previously what thought, existence, and certainty are; and similarly to know that it is impossible that that which thinks does not exist." But Descartes would have immediately added that these notions "do not give us knowledge of anything that exists" and thus do not merit being taken into account.[49] In other words, he would have said that a thought of "being" or "existence" necessarily lacks the singular reality of the ego. By centering himself on the *sum*, by wanting to think of the ego on the basis of its being and not of itself, Heidegger was completely mistaken about the meaning of the ego.

He did not understand that the immanent nucleus of the ego escapes from the influence of Being, that it "is" not, does not "exist" in any manner. The ontological indifference, the disinterest in the question of Being for which he reproaches Descartes, is not the sign of a failure but of an unprecedented audacity, of a breakthrough to the mystery of an ego foreign to Being. Husserl came close to it when he claimed that the immanent ego escapes from the world and from Being by putting them out of play, or that this ego "precedes" Being, or that it is a question of a "primordial fore-Being [*Vorsein*]" of an originary life but also of an "absolutely concrete ego."[50] This was a thought that was too new to be understood: the majority of his successors would follow Heidegger's path and keep the ego or the subject within the horizon of Being. Such is the case with Sartre, for whom the for-itself and the in-itself, the transcendence of the human subject and the compactness of things, "both belong to Being in general." And such is also the case with Merleau-Ponty, who discovers the phenomenon of the flesh but sees in it an "element of Being" and immediately reabsorbs it in the universal "flesh of the world." So too is it the case with Levinas, who certainly tries to think "otherwise than Being" but reserves it to the Other by confining the ego to the selfish enjoyment of the "landlord of Being." And we must not forget our latest great ontology, Deleuze's, in which all identity is dissolved in one sole "clamor of Being."

Whenever philosophers fail, it falls to a poet to endure this "unswayable cruelty of living and of not having to be." For Artaud, Being is a mortal threat, "a sort of death sentence," and the cross of Being comes to bar or block the flux of life. He calls on us to think of life on this side of Being and, within this life, of a primordial ego-body that "does not tolerate being," that does not accept becoming the tool of Being. He would have had to traverse madness in order to be able to attain this plane, in order to complete the "disengagement of [his] true ego," which would allow him to sign anew in his name, to "remake a body," to retranscribe his experience in writing.[51] But how is it possible to engage on this path that has provided access to the truth of the ego, given that our philosophical concepts have, since the Greeks, been riveted to Being and have turned away from the ego? Must we not make recourse to another discipline, the only one to have flirted with the boundaries of madness and tried to understand "this madness whereby a human thinks he is human?" I would now like to turn to psychoanalysis: perhaps it, better than philosophy, will allow us to approach the enigma of the ego and to understand from where this invincible certitude of being "me, ego" comes. But I first add the caveat that psychoanalysis too may have succumbed to the prejudices of an ego-cidal epoch, to the temptation to reduce the ego to a simple reflection, a sparkling decoy on the surface of an empty mirror.

2

I Am the Dead Person I See in the Mirror, or Lacan's Subject

A painting from the sixteenth century attributed to Furtenagel shows the married Burgkmair couple; the wife has in her hand a mirror bearing the inscription "know thyself."[1] We perceive in the mirror not their reflection, however, but rather their fleshless skulls. This is a classic allegory of the "vanities," and we would have hardly noticed it but for this detail: the couple looks directly at us rather than being fascinated by the symbol of their death, as we might expect. By means of a very subtle visual snare, our gaze is captivated by the gaze of the living dead and then, as if by ricochet, is irresistibly turned toward the mirror so effectively that we now contemplate our own death in their place—all by means of a strange reshuffling whereby the spectators and the painted figures, the living and the dead, fleshy and skeletal faces, the painting and the mirror, vertiginously change positions. What the painter makes us see here is something that one of the riskiest writings of our times also recognized: "And so I am dead," wrote Jean Génet, "I am a dead man who sees his skeleton in the mirror." We find an only slightly altered version of this same vision in the prehistory of the Freudian discovery. Josef Breuer's patient Anna O. would faint as soon as she entered a certain room. Hypnosis finally provided the key to this mystery: when she entered the room for the first time, "she had seen her pale face reflected in a mirror hanging opposite the door; but it was not herself that she saw but her father with a death's head."[2] Whereas the painter tried to figure the impossible experience of seeing oneself dead, the hysteric does not (or refuses to) recognize her death mask, and she denies her anxiety about death by projecting it onto another, substituting her father's image for her own. The Burgkmairs, however, no less than Anna, cannot tolerate the ordeal since, by turning their gazes away from the mirror and to the spectator, they try in some way to discard their death to the viewer. The painter will at least have brought the ruse to light by placing it in the scene of a visual montage, thus disarming it.

How can one see oneself dead—or say that one is dead? How can one utter the unsayable statement "I am dead" without immediately dissolving into a decaying carcass? What intrepid Oedipus would be able to confront the mystery of the mirror and recognize his mortal truth in it without being blinded by it? In one of his first seminars, Jacques Lacan tries to show that the ego is grounded on an "imaginary" illusion, and he insists on the fundamental relation linking the ego to death. It is in this context that he refers to Edgar Allan Poe's story of Valdemar, which reveals the truth of life, the submission to death of a life that "wishes only to die."[3] We thus once again find in Lacan the same paradoxical gesture already seen in Heidegger and in most contemporary thinkers: Lacan also associates the statement "I am dead" with the announcement of *the death of the I*, its destitution. This egocide's singularity, and what distinguishes his from other egocides, is that Lacan looks for the origin of the illusion of being *me*, an ego, and thinks he finds it right there in the sinister reflection where the Burgkmairs' gaze deflects our own—in the mirror. This is where each of us, in the earliest years of life, will gain access to the deceptive consciousness of being an ego. Lacan defined the analyst as a mirror held up before the analysand, not a "living mirror" but rather an "empty mirror," a mirror "without brightness showing a surface where nothing is reflected" (E, 151). Because he also maintains that the psychoanalytic cure consists in a "subjectification of his death" (E, 289), the identification of the emptiness of the mirror-without-reflection and of the emptiness of death is not prohibited. Furtenagel's painting is therefore valuable as an allegory of psychoanalysis. "Wo Es war, soll Ich werden" is Freud's phrase,[4] which Lacan endlessly translated and commented on. It can also be understood in this way: "Yes, that's how I get there, where it was (to be): who knew, thus, that *I* was dead?" (E, 679). Psychoanalysis is thus submitted to Valdemar's law. Is this the only authentic understanding of the "soll Ich werden," the Freudian imperative to *become ego*? From where does this omnipresence of death in Lacan's thought come? For what reason does he reduce the ego to a mere illusion? Is this egocide not also doomed to failure, just as with Heidegger? Does not the ego return in Lacan's thought as a leftover that is impossible to eliminate, a specter haunting Lacanian psychoanalysis?

The Mirror Stage as Mortuary

We have to go back to the beginning of Lacan's work, to his famous theory of the mirror stage.[5] This is what led him to claim that the ego is a "mirage," a lure of the imaginary, and so is at the heart of the Lacanian egocide. Moreover, the mirror stage is not Lacan's personal discovery; instead, he had borrowed it, without acknowledgment, from Henri Wallon. Wallon had noted that unlike monkeys of the same age or other animals more generally, the human child is able to recognize itself in the mirror beginning at about six months of age, which helps the child to construct the image of its body. Seizing upon this empirical observation, Lacan raises it to the rank of an "ontological structure of the human world" and concludes that the child *identifies itself* with its specular image. Lacan sees in this identification the very origin of the ego, "the symbolic matrix in which the *I* is precipitated in a primordial form" (E, 76). It is a matter of an originary identification: prior to the crucial experience of the mirror, there had been no ego and no unitary image of the body, and the child had understood itself only as a fragmented body. I am able to overcome this primitive fragmentation only by identifying myself with an image—which is why the ego is *imaginary*—and I will never be me, will never be an ego, except by the intermediary of this exterior image. The reflection that I discover in the mirror is certainly *my* image, but it also appears to me as outside of me, like the image *of an other*. In this sense, "the ego is always an alter ego" (S, II:321): in being identified with this image, I am identified with the other, so much so that I will never be myself—forever separated from myself by this double, this foreign yet familiar "other" who is me without really being me. And "so the ego is constituted in its nucleus by a series of alienating identifications" (E, 347), in the experience of an intimate submission to the other, to a Master. This alienation supposes a radical misrecognition, since I think I recognize *myself* in the image of the other.

We know that in the myth of Narcissus, his blind fascination with his own reflection leads him to death; on the basis of this, Lacan points out the simultaneously murderous and suicidal character of our narcissistic relation to the mirror: here we see that "the primordial ego, as essentially alienated, is linked to the first sacrifice as essentially suicidal . . . In other words, we see here the fundamental structure of madness . . . the madness by which man thinks he is a man" (E, 187–88). The ego is mad, and to believe in the ego, to believe that I am me, is a madness. Every relation to an other is grounded on this mortifying relation of the ego to its own image—for this double that looks back at me in the mirror is more me than I myself am; I fear it as a rival constantly trying to kill or annihilate me, and my relations with others will forever carry the mark of this insane death struggle. Lacan thus engages psychoanalysis on the path of a radical egocide.

I would like to show that the theory of the mirror stage is at least partially true but that it had been falsified by Lacan's interpretation of it to serve certain polemical ends. For it plays a capital role in his return to Freud initiated in the 1950s. Against those who claimed to reform Freudian theory by recentering it on the ego and those who proposed to "reinforce" the "feeble ego of the neurotic" so that it becomes adapted to social reality, Lacan insisted on the demarcation between the ego and the "true subject" of the unconscious. The concern is not to readapt this "eccentric" subject to reality but rather to lead it to "recognize and name its desire" and thus "to enter into relation with true others" beyond mirages of the imaginary. Let us say it very bluntly: the proclaimed return to Freud instead leads us very far from him. Not only does the founder of psychoanalysis not really know of the distinction of the ego and the subject that Lacan so generously attributed to him, but moreover, Freud conceived the ego in an entirely different manner. For Freud, far from being reduced to a single narcissistic dimension, the ego is the agency of the psychical apparatus, giving us access to the exterior world and allowing us to act on it. The imperative of the "soll Ich werden" is inscribed in this perspective: the mission of psychoanalysis is to "strengthen the ego, to make it more independent of the super-ego, to widen its field of perception and enlarge its organization, so that it can appropriate fresh portions of the id."[6] And yet, despite this divergence, the Viennese master and his French disciple agree in their shared rejection of the Cartesian heritage. For them, the existence of the ego would not be an originary truth that "depends on nothing else" but merely the result of a series of identifications and, as such, will necessarily remain subordinate to those more originary agencies (the id, the Other) from which it derives. Lacan observed this lucidly when he exposited the mirror stage: the conception that psychoanalysis has of the ego "sets us at odds with any philosophy directly stemming from the *cogito*" (E, 94). Either Descartes and the ego's originary affirmation or Freud and the ego's derivation from another agency—such are the alternatives.

Descartes had already responded to this type of objection. When Lacan claims that belief in the ego is a madness, he is in his own way restating the argument of the Evil Deceiver, who tries to persuade me that I do not exist. The mirror takes the place of the Cartesian deceiver from now on; as a new variation of the Evil Genius, the mirror is exposed to the same refutations: "If I err, I am." That is, I must indeed already be for this Other to be able to deceive me into believing that I am myself. This is the blind spot of the theory of the mirror stage, the question that Lacan never wanted to pose: *who* must this anonymous seer be such that it can recognize itself in its image and recognize itself as *me, ego*? Who is identified with this reflection if not me, an ego more originary than the identification supposedly constituting it? An ego that would, for all that, not be reduced to a psychological ego, to an ego-in-the-world more or less adapted to society—hence, an I without qualities, without repressed psychical representations, without any preliminary relation to an Other or to objects. The theory of the mirror stage thus leaves open the possibility of an originary ego that would not issue from an alienating identification. For there are many ways of being "I," and Lacan certainly knew it. In his early seminars, he presents the subject of the unconscious as an I, but as an I that "is not me" (S, II:44). At the end of the analysis, this initially anonymous and mute subject will take up speech by saying "I": where there once had been a silent subject is where the I must now arise to name itself. If this subject finally manages to say "I," then does not this possibility belong to it from the beginning? Is it not always already necessarily ego? Has not the I in some way necessarily *preceded* it in order to be able to reemerge and to be named at the end of the cure? Like the "always my own" character of Heidegger's Dasein, the I-subject is likewise *not me*, but it is *nothing other than me*. This affirmation of an originary ego is precisely what Lacan refused to allow. In order to avoid all confusion between the

subject and the ego, there was only one solution available to him: eliminate every reference to the ego, and stop characterizing the subject of the
unconscious as an I. He would consequently define it as "an a-cephalic
subject, a subject who no longer has an ego,"[7] a "barred" subject that is no
longer anyone, an X, an empty place, a "subjectification without subject"
(S, XI:184–85). Here, then, we see what, thirty years later, would lead him
down the same path as Heidegger: in order to escape the difficulties provoked by egocide, he radicalizes it and thus digs himself ever deeper into
an impasse.

So many difficulties are rooted in the conception of the mirror
stage. Lacan gives the power to generate the ego to sight: the possibility of
seeing oneself determines the fundamental characteristic of the ego, its
transcendence—because I am ego only by identifying myself with an image that always stands outside of and beyond me. He qualifies the fascinated contemplation by which the child is absorbed in the vision of its
reflection as "an interminable ecstasis." Of all of our senses, sight is what
most separates us from ourselves, projects us beyond ourselves in the distant horizons of the world. This is why the "ecstatic" conception of knowledge dominating Western philosophy since Plato has privileged vision,
and Lacan is included in this age-old tradition in which the paradigm of
the mirror plays a major role. There are at least two ways of representing
vision: in the classical way, as an eye receiving light from the outside, allowing it to see; or in the case of the modern optic, as a look that throws
itself toward the world, scrutinizing and inspecting it in order to grasp all
aspects of the visible. Whether it is given to me without coming from me
or whether it arises in me without returning to me, vision is characterized
by a cleavage between its origin and its destination, that is, by its transcendence. We know that, far from grounding the possibility of individuation,
the logic of transcendence subsequently tends to dissolve the singularity
of the ego in the general economy of the world, alienating it, even annihilating it by hastening it toward the nothingness of its death. Lacanian theory is no exception to this. Certainly, unlike Heideggerian theory, it no
longer supposes a preexisting subject, a Dasein that would *itself* transcend
itself by projecting itself toward the world. On the contrary, a transcendent image, coming from the Other, is carried toward the seer in order to
imprint on him the form of a body and the appearance of an ego. The
emphasis will therefore no longer be placed on the freedom of existing

being ("freedom?" Lacan would exclaim, "I have never used this word!") but rather on the extreme passivity of the subject or the ego, their submission to the different figures of the Other, their originary and insurmountable alienation. The ego receives everything from its image—and, foremost, the illusory possibility of being an ego: how could it free itself from this?

The image is invested with such power and is able to create the ego ex nihilo and forever captivate it, only because there is neither ego nor unified body in front of the mirror—only, rather, the chaos of a fragmentary body. Lacan's entire effort rests on a double postulate: (a) the fragmentary body cannot be unified *by itself,* cannot give itself the form of a one-body, a total body, without passing through the transcendent exteriority of the Image; and (b) it cannot form the nucleus of an ego *from itself.* If that were possible, if the originary body could be constituted by itself as *my* body, then we would have to recognize that the ego exists prior to the mirror, and it could no longer be considered as a mirage of the imaginary. This hypothesis will not even be evoked. Lacan could not imagine that the ego is given to itself in an immanent manner without depending on any Other. By postulating that the ego is constituted by identification, on the plane of transcendence and in the horizon of sight, Lacan condemned it to an alienation without return. The experience of the mirror will thus be that of an intimate servitude, and "the ego is this master the subject finds in an other, whose function of mastery he establishes in his own heart" (S, III:93). Who is this Master that implants my image in me? What have I seen in the mirror that fills me with terror and imposes on me a submission without reserve? Similar to the witch's mirror from which the necromancer calls forth spirits, the Lacanian speculum suddenly unveils to us the grimace hidden beneath its glistening reflections: "This image of the master, which is what he sees in the form of the specular image, becomes confused in him with the image of death. Man can be in the presence of the absolute master. He is in his presence from the beginning, whether he has been taught this or not, in so far as he is subjected to this image."[8] This mirror is a mortuary [*ce miroir est un mouroir*]: by seeing myself in it, I see myself as a phantom contemplating its own death. The Burgkmairs' skulls reflected in the mirror, or the pale death's head suddenly appearing in the mirror in front of Anna O's eyes, would not manifest a pathological deviation of the human experience but rather reveal its unspeakable truth. This image of my death is indeed *my* image; it is *me.* The ego is therefore presented as the "nearest and most intimate apparition of death," as this "gap . . . whereby death makes itself felt" (S, II:210). It is no longer sufficient to say that "I am dead"—because in truth *I am death.*

It is difficult to descend much further into egocide. But by what right does Lacan identify my image with the faceless approach of my death? By what magic could we see ourselves dead? How does the transcendence of vision rejoin the invisible frontier where it is abolished in its night? A more specific analysis of the seeing-oneself [*se-voir-soi-meme*] and of its relation to the being-outside-of-self of the look is necessary here. When Lacan criticizes the Cartesian cogito, he assimilates it to an "I see myself seeing myself" [*je me vois me voir*], to the *illusion* of seeing-oneself-seeing [*se voir voyant*], the narcissistic illusion in which the *look* disappears: even if I could see my eyes in the mirror, I could never perceive my gaze. Ungraspable, fading, the look always escapes beyond the field of vision, and this scission, this "schize," between the visible eye and the seeing gaze prohibits me from seeing myself seeing myself. It is the mirror itself that is broken, and Lacan seems tempted for a brief moment to come back on this side of sight, toward a self-perception nearer to the self, more "immanent" to the body, which can only be tactile:

For, I *warm myself by warming myself* is a reference to the body as body—I feel that sensation of warmth which, from some point inside me, is diffused and locates me as body. Whereas in the *I see myself seeing myself,* there is no such sensation of being absorbed by vision. Furthermore, the phenomenologists have succeeded in articulating with precision, and in the most disconcerting way, that it is quite clear that I see *outside*, that perception is not in me . . . And yet I apprehend the world in a perception that seems to concern the immanence of the *I see myself seeing myself.* (S, XI:80–81)

This reference to phenomenology (favorable, for once) could have led Lacan to root the cogito in the experience of the touching-touched, or what Merleau-Ponty called the "tactile chiasm." But this is not the path Lacan chose: he does not oppose a more originary immanence to the illusory "immanence" of the seeing-itself-seeing but instead opposes the transcendence of the look of the Other, which surrounds me from all sides and precedes my own vision (S, XI:72). The Lacanian optic is displaced toward the field of the Other, toward a more radical and foreign transcendence. We will have the chance to observe it again: this decentering toward the

Other, toward always more transcendence, is the answer Lacan gives every time to the difficulties affecting his conception of the ego or the subject.

By thus slipping from my vision to the look of the Other, Lacan avoids drawing the consequences of his critique of the seeing-oneself-seeing. Taken literally, the hypothesis of a "schize" or split of the eye and the gaze tends to ruin the theory of the mirror stage. I will never take hold of those lifeless eyes, those cold orbs that I see in the mirror, the furtive sparkle of my gaze; and so we will have to apply to the mirror what Lacan had said of the picture, namely, that the central focus of vision "cannot but be absent, and replaced by a hole," the black hole of the pupil "behind which is situated the gaze" (S, XI:108). If I do not see myself seeing myself, then we must conclude from this that I never see *myself*, that I perceive only my visible figure in my reflection—that is, only a thing among other things in the world—and not my capacity of seeing from which the living ego that I am radiates. The specular identification is revealed to be impossible: breached in its center by the effacement of the gaze, it could only constitute a partial and divided ego, an *ego-hole*. Deprived of the gaze, the eye that I see (whether it be mine or an other's in the mirror) will always remain a blind eye, a dead eye, the eye of a dead person. If the specular image refers me to the absolute Master, it is because the scission of the eye and the gaze, petrifying my reflection, made the image of my death arise in its place—but it is only an image, and I can see myself only *as if* I were dead. No one is really able to see oneself truly dead: a cadaver no longer sees anything at all and surely no longer sees itself; and it is not their own death that Anna and the Burgkmairs are contemplating, but only a pale stain of color on the painting, a pale reflection shining on the mirror's surface. The theory of specular identification ends up at a double impasse: it is impossible to see oneself seeing—that is, living—and equally impossible to see oneself dead. And nevertheless, I see *myself*, I recognize myself in the blind face, as if I had captured my gaze in it. So that I may identify myself with my reflection and transfer to it the character of being mine, of being me or ego, I have to be *already* identified with myself. In order to recognize the image of my body in the reflection, I must *have a place of residence* in this body, live it already *as mine*. Clinical experience teaches us, in contrast, what happens when this initial self-identification, this carnal residence, *does not take place*: incapable of experiencing its body of flesh as its own, the psychotic or the autistic individual does not recognize himself in the reflection and becomes anxious about the unknown Thing staring back at him from the mirror. Because his own gaze escapes him, he is also unable to recognize in the other's eye the living gaze that inhabits it: "instead of seeing the other," a schizophrenic declares, "I see only the surface of his eyes"; and other patients avoid meeting the other's gaze "because of the black hole in the middle" or because they think "death is looking them directly in the eyes."[9] Lacan's thesis is perfectly suited for this limit-experience of madness. But does it also agree with our common experience? Is it true that this Medusa's face that he thought he had discovered at the heart of the mirror secretly haunts our reflection?

Let us dare to say that these brilliant analyses that show Lacan's genius on every page . . . are false! "Fascination," "impotence," "paralysis," "terror": such are the terms he uses to describe the ego's hypnotic captivation by its image. The fragmentary body can hope to leave its chaotic dispersion behind only by letting itself be astonished by the frightening gaze that fixates on it from the mirror. Let us confront this theory with the real experience of the child or of psychotics in therapy trying to restructure their decomposed image: they approach the mirror not in terrified submission (even if anxiety sometimes surfaces) but, on the contrary, in an intense activity of motor exploration and a joyous experimentation with postures, gestures, rhythms, and spatial perspectives. "Normal" children as described by Wallon thus make an effort to repeat these gestures in front of the mirror, play with their image, touch it, embrace it, and so forth. Likewise, a young psychotic girl of four years of age who first avoids the mirror will progressively take up her body image during her analysis, sketching out gestures while facing the mirror, moving around in front of it, trying to compare her image to the analyst's.[10] What is wrong with Lacan's conception is above all this dimension of bodily *movement* that subtends the process of recognition of and identification with the image. Whether it be partial or total, still fragmentary or already unified, narcissistically contemplated in the mirror or symbolically structured by the signifier, the Lacanian body is always immobile, frozen, and petrified as if under *a death sentence.* Freud's position was wholly different, emphasizing the body's motility, its "motor discharges," and the importance of tactile impressions for the ego's genesis. By concentrating on the single horizon of sight and by reducing it to a hypnotic fascination, Lacan will have missed the truth of the body, this body movement that touches and palpates and takes hold of itself and that, well prior to the mirror stage, begins to overcome its initial fragmentation.

Is this mouvance of the living body unfurled *without me*? Does the ego's genesis begin only with imaginary identification, or do we have to imagine pre-specular cores or nuclei of the ego? Since Lacan constantly appeals to experience, let us stay on that plane for a moment. The example of the blind gives us an element of an answer: if the Lacanian thesis were true, those blind from birth would be fated to psychosis, would never have consciousness of being an ego nor of having a body. Yet we know that even if they take longer to differentiate their body from exterior objects and from the bodies of others, blind children are nonetheless able to access the psychical functioning of the ego without difficulty. This must therefore be rooted on this side of the mirror, in the sensorial and affective experiences to which those blind from birth have access—the experiences of a tactile ego, an ego-body in movement that touches and is touched, as well as an ego that hears the voices of others and its own voice. Each affect, each stratum of the perceptual field, each fragment of the fragmentary body, would already be inhabited by an equally fragmentary ego, which tries to rejoin and be united with other shards of the ego, constituting an increasingly fuller field of experience and increasingly longer and more continuous temporal phases. The mirror stage is only a phase within this process. By identifying my flesh "here" with my reflection "over there," my immanent motor impressions with a transcendent visual image, the process intertwines the tactile and the visible, offering me new access to my own body and the other's body. A living, and not an empty, mirror, *a mirror of life* reflecting the movement of a living ego, permits the ego to unfold itself in the world. Wallon had understood this better than Lacan: according to Wallon, this process above all allows the child to distinguish itself from its image and thus to "unify its ego in space," and "to take hold of itself as a body among bodies."[11] This means that the mirror is not a lure and that, on the contrary, it frees me of the illusion of reality initially attached to my image, leading me to differentiate the real and the imaginary better, and to stop imagining my reflection as a double or a rival, but rather as a *simple image* that is also *my* image.

In what way, then, is it an alienation or a submission to the Master that Lacan says characterizes the mirror stage? How do they accord with the dis-illusion by which the child frees itself of the prestige of the image? Some psychoanalysts propose an altogether different interpretation of the mirror phase: it would mark not the beginning of an alienating identification but rather the "culminating point of a long process of projection the point of which is to constitute in its difference the face of the other with which the subject is first identified."[12] During the first months of life, the child would first identify itself with its mother's breast and face, an originary identification wherein the maternal face covers over or fills the entire field of the visible and is merged with the subject itself. The child would not be able to get beyond this original alienation except by finally recognizing its own face in the mirror, differentiating it from its mother's: this specular recognition "comes to interrupt the originary identification in the face of the other," accomplishing a "disindividuation of the mother's face, followed by an identification with another face that is its own."[13] This then explains both the child's triumphant jubilation when it is freed of its captivation in the other's image and its depressive anxiety provoked by this disidentification through which it learns of and fears the possibility of its disappearance or death and the definitive separation from the mother. There would therefore be a third person, more originary than the paternal signifier or the Oedipal law, and it would be the mirror itself, the projection of an image of the living body interposed between the body of the mother and the body of the child. The imaginary would no longer be merely the focus of illusion and alienation but would also be the condition of truth, of the coming-to-self of a true ego. This disalienation is surely accompanied by a new identification with an exterior image. This should not surprise us: in the transcendence of the world, the ego always passes from one alienating identification to another—and yet these identifications do not have the same weight, do not affect the ego's singularity in the same manner. By identifying itself from now on with the image of its own body, the child no longer lets itself be captivated by the image of the mother and begins to disengage from its influence, from the illusion of a fusional unity with the other: the child begins to affirm itself in the horizon of the visible. Traversed and worked over by truth, the "mirror stage" is the site of this unveiling and this deliverance.

It is thus difficult to follow Lacan when he determines that the mirror stage is the imaginary matrix of the ego and the prototype of all identification. On this point, he diverges from Freud, who admitted the possibility of an original identification "preliminary to any object-choice." Neither specular nor symbolic, it is a question of an *affective* identification that constitutes a "very important form of attachment to someone else, probably the very first."[14] Lacan could not allow this, because he refuses to recognize an affectivity more originary than any relation to the signifier. And yet, just like his French disciple, the founder of psychoanalysis considered the ego to be the residue of a series of elementary identifications. By leading us ever further toward the origin, toward the enigma of a primitive incorporation or an initial (purely affective, fusional, and blind) identification with the maternal breast, Freud merely displaces the difficulty. He will return to it again in a note written just before his death: "the child likes to express the relation to the object by identification: I am the object . . . the breast is a portion of me, I am the breast. It is only later that I have it, that is, that I am not it."[15] This raises the same question once again: if I am to be the breast, is it not necessary that first of all *I am*? For me to identify myself with the breast or the face of my mother, with the image of my body, or with the name of my father, or with the heroes I have chosen, an I must precede these identifications, and my ego must have come to itself prior to any relation to the Other. What can this preexistence mean? Do we not risk falling back into obscure speculation about an intra-uterine "subjectivity" and the "primary narcissism" of the fetus? Let us brush aside that mistake: the ego's *originary* character must not be understood as an *original* state that can be situated in the time of the world. The ego's coming-to-self "precedes" its coming into the world and its first contacts with others, just as a *condition* precedes what it makes possible, like the source-point of an immanent genesis or of a "continuous creation" that begins and recommences at every moment in the ego's field of immanence. Because he had not reached this plane, Freud was condemned to confuse the original and the originary, to seek the ego's source always further back in my infancy, to alienate me to an Other more ancient than me. He does so without ever imagining the possibility of an originary identification of the ego with itself, an originary *self-identification* that would be the condition of every relation to the Other. Are we still dealing here with an alienating identification, and if so, in what sense? What relation is there between this self-identification and the successive identifications with a foreign Other described by psychoanalysis? Neither Freud nor Lacan has given any answers to these questions. We must, however, confront them if we want to describe the immanent genesis of the ego and, within this genesis, disengage the truth of the mirror stage. For we must also wonder why we do not stop identifying ourselves with these scintillating figures that are projected on the screen of the phantasm or the scene of the Spectacle, as if they were projected on the wall at the bottom of the cave where we are held prisoner.

"So who knew I was dead?"

The Lacanian conception of the imaginary suffers from two defects: not only is it impossible to have access to the mirror stage, but it is also equally impossible to leave it behind. It is impossible to be identified with an image that is not mine, since I do not see my seeing gaze in it; and, supposing that identification could be produced, it is impossible to overcome it and be differentiated from this double *that I am.* Lacan took account of this by recognizing the irreducible character of the illusions of the ego and of consciousness: to those who asked him whether it is possible to "force someone out of their consciousness," he replied with his characteristic biting irony that "I am not Alphonse Allais, who would respond to you: skin him."[16] Unless it lets itself be skinned alive, we do not really see how the subject could disengage itself from its narcissistic enclosure and, at the end of an analysis, finally address itself to the Other *in truth.* By conceiving the cure on the basis of the mirror stage, as a projection of unconscious images on the "empty mirror" that is the analyst, Lacan risked making the cure interminable. To get out of this impasse, he, like Alice, had to go *through the looking-glass* and look for a "beyond" of the imaginary. For the imaginary relation is a dead end, the closed field of a mortal joust between the ego and its other. Whereas Wallon foregrounded the integrating function of specular recognition, the dis-illusion it provokes in the child in reconciling it with the child's image, Lacan on the contrary insists on the rivalry opposing me to my double. Because he approaches it through a philosophical framework, he applies a Hegelian scenario to the mirror stage, interpreting it as a death struggle for recognition. From the impossible vision of my death sketched in the mirror, he slips into the possibility of murder: though I may never be able to see myself dead, I can no doubt anticipate the encounter with the absolute Master in the gaze of the other who is ready to kill me. This can only reinforce the egocidal tendencies of Lacanian psychoanalysis: because the ego is nothing for Hegel, it must pass through the death struggle and murder in order to become self-consciousness. For there to be a true recognition, the struggle must go to term, to the death of one of the combatants. But this then suppresses the very possibility of recognition: just as I cannot see myself dead, I likewise cannot be recognized by a dead person or admire myself in the blind mirror of a dead person's eye. By killing its double, the ego bars itself from being identified with it and consequently from identifying itself as "ego": as in Poe's story "William Wilson," the murder of the narrator's rival annihilates them both, and the imaginary relationship is completed in a suicidal impasse.[17]

Where the madness of the ego was, I must arise as subject and detach myself from the mortal prestige of the image, overcoming the mirror stage. For Lacan it would not be a matter of coming back to this side of the mirror, to the immanent experience of an invisible life supporting and secretly animating the transcendence of the gaze. Lacan wanted to know nothing of this experience. The sole issue he could imagine consisted in passing beyond the imaginary *along the lines of the imaginary itself* by radicalizing its ecstatic transcendence. For vision is unfaithful to its own transcendence, and the indigent alterity it generates is never other enough, does not sufficiently tear me away from myself and my narcissistic madness. He will thus go in search of a more radical alterity, an "absolute Other," "beyond all imaginary others," and it is in this way that the famous character, the symbolic Big Other, will make its appearance in his work, as an emergency solution destined to overcome the absence of an exit from the imaginary relation. This new version of the Other depends narrowly on the terms of the aporia it is supposed to relieve but will instead reproduce, with all its determinations, as the *third*, interposing itself in the specular relation as the guarantor of the *peace treaty* of the death struggle and as the stakes of *true speech*. And so it is from the mirror that we must begin again, from this fascination in which the child, captivated by its own reflection, risks drowning in it. Lacan had first sought *in* the specular relation itself a "function of exclusion" capable of countering this captivation and helping the ego to differentiate itself from its other and *to fixate on* its image.[18] The ego could thus free itself *by itself* from its captivity in the image. This probably grants too much to the ego, and the thesis will quickly be abandoned. From then on, Lacan will have recourse to an exterior third, to this other that is the parent, the adult accompanying the child at the mirror, to whom our cherub will turn to ask for a word, a gesture, a look, or the least little sign capable of distinguishing him from his double.[19] Lacan will assimilate this libratory gesture whereby the Other demarcates me from my imaginary double to the Freudian *einziger Zug*, the single trait of identification constituting the subject. As mythical as it may seem, this new conception of the mirror stage nevertheless indicates the path beyond narcissism, a possible alternative to the death struggle. Reconstructing the Hegelian dialectic of master and slave in his own way, Lacan supposes that a preliminary pact had been agreed to, at least tacitly, by the combatants in order to save the life of the vanquished: "In the final analysis, the loser must not perish if he is to become a slave. In other words, a pact always precedes violence before perpetuating it, and what I call the symbolic dominates the imaginary, allowing us to wonder whether or not murder really is the absolute Master" (E, 686). Such an accord demands being guaranteed via the mediation of a Third, by the word of an Other who takes no part in the struggle and prevails over the Hegelian Master.

Who is the "symbolic Other" invoked by Lacan, this veridical Other who guarantees truth? No one other than Descartes' God. In his seminar on the psychoses, Lacan introduces this reference to the Cartesian God, to a true Other who protects us from the Evil Genius of madness. The experience of the psychotic shows us what happens when this anchoring fails: "in delusional speech, the Other is truly excluded, there is no truth" (S, III:53), and only the persecuted figure of the Lying God, a mad god who reigns over delirium, persists. We can be saved from disaster only by the assignation of *a point of truth*, by the affirmation that "there is something that is absolutely nondeceptive" (S, III:65). For Lacan, this radical truth is not that of the ego but of the Other, that is, of God. Despite all of this, he discovers the ego's affirmation in the name of "God," a god who says "I am." This allows him to link the question of truth to the affirmation of a subject capable of saying "I," the subject whose voice is addressed to Moses through the burning bush. According to Lacan, the message on Sinai designates the I as the "ultimate ground" of all speech and all truth: it means that "speech clearly profiles the being of the I as its ultimate ground."[20] We will therefore no longer say that the "I is an other"—but rather that the Other is that which says "I" and can say "I" in truth. The originary I in question here is certainly not the narcissistic ego of the mirror stage, and yet it is nothing other than *me, ego*. It is the *Ich* of the Freudian imperative, the I-subject that finally, at the end of analysis, leaves its silence; and this saying-I is *true*; it is the ultimate condition of all truth. I, the ego, *I am the truth*—and the truth itself, when it is articulated, always says "I." This would be a convenient way to understand the famous Lacanian sentence, "I, the truth, am speaking."

We should thus wonder how the truth of the ego can, between breath and cry, blossom into speech. We should question what Merleau-Ponty called "the frightful birth of vociferation," the mystery of the voice.[21] But Lacan is not engaged in this direction: he sets up language [*langage*] as the "radical condition" for all creative speech (S, II:313), and his references to "true speech" will become ever rarer and more mocking. This primacy of language defines the Lacanian conception of *the symbolic order*. Borrowed from Levi-Strauss, this term designates the very structure of language, the total system of *signifiers*—phonic or graphic marks whose linkage generates the signified, that is, meaning. And he will identify (a little too rapidly) this "signifying chain" with the unconscious of psychoanalysis. By celebrating this baroque wedding of Freud and Saussure, he thinks he has finally found an exit from the impasse of the imaginary— because the symbolic dominates and is opposed to the imaginary, just as "the place of truth" is opposed to the reign of illusion and just as the pact grounding coexistence is opposed to the death struggle. If imaginary space is the space of the ego and its rivalry with the "object-a" [*l'objet petit-a*], which is its specular double, the symbolic is defined as the field of the *subject*, determined by its relation to the Big Other, that is, to the unconscious itself, which is "structured like a language." This demarcation of the narcissistic ego from the "true subject of the unconscious" will give the Lacanian egocide its definitive status. We would be wrong to reduce this theory to its structuralist trappings: with those then-fashionable linguistic terms, Lacan was in search of a more radical transcendence. The "true speech" was still too close to the living voice of a singular subject, and its truth might seem to depend on a saying-I, an ego capable of *taking up speech*. Conversely, the "ek-sistence" (the radically exterior position) that he attributes to the signifying chain, and the "exstatic relation to the Other" it implies, will allow him to give an absolute priority to the signifier over the subject, to alienate the subject from the signifier, and to eliminate from the subject the least trace of living subjectivity in order to reduce it to a "subject without ego."

What, then, is the subject for Lacan? It is "what the signifier represents for another signifier." Always absent from discourse, the subject is the element missing from the signifying chain, and it is never able *to be said*, to be articulated in spoken language without letting itself be represented by the signifier substituted for it. This certainly does not mean that I existed as a subject *before* being displaced by the signifier: the "priority of the signifier over the subject" implies that I am *nothing* before the signifier "I" (or any other signifier supposedly representing me) calls me to exist as subject. This is why the subject is entirely submitted to this Other that is the cause of it: it exists only as "subject" of the signifier (in the feudal sense of the term), subjected to it in an alienation without return. If the signifier represents the subject, it is always "for another signifier," because there are signifiers *only* in a network or chain, taken up in a structure that puts them in relation to others. There must be *at least two* signifiers to engender a subject: the first signifier convokes it, makes it arise from out of its nothingness—for example, in the mode of a question, an appeal, a shout-out ("hey you over there!"). But as soon as the subject rises up to speech, the second signifier takes hold of and fixates it ("yeah you, buddy!") and "the ready-to-speak that *was to be* there . . . disappears, no longer being anything but a signifier" (E, 713). By calling the subject to present itself, the first signifier alienates it immediately to the second signifier, which represents it. Torn between these two signifiers enclosing it, invoked by the first and then immediately revoked by the second, the subject is torn apart, eclipsed, withered. The Lacanian subject thus resembles the tightrope walker in *Zarathustra*: he has at most taken one step before the demon of the signifier, which was behind him, jumps in front of him and pushes him into the abyss.

I admit that I long admired this theory for its apparent rigor and radicality. But now I find it profoundly equivocal. Let us consider anew its fundamental thesis: the subject is what the signifier represents to another signifier. We can understand either that it sustains the relation of the signifier to the signifier *in general*, that is, the signifying chain as such; or that it is the effect of a *singular* relation between two signifiers, which are themselves singular. In the first case, the subject is only the *subiectum*, the impersonal support of the signifying system. To "subject itself," to become a subject, would then consist in being inserted in the chain, identifying with the total network of signifiers, that is, with the Other—and such a subjectification amounts to disappearing as a singular and living subject. But it is possible to interpret the canonical formula in a completely opposed perspective: it would define a singular subject constituted in its relation to the Other by a unique and incomparable "trait," by a relation, different each time, to the singular object of its desire. In this sense, each subject differs from other subjects and from the Other, and it becomes impossible to consider it merely as the anonymous support of an unconscious structure. "The subject is what is named," what is identified on the basis of the "first signifying nucleus" that is its name.[22] Where the unnamable Thing was, it must now arise as an I and take up speech in the first person and in its own name. How could it do so if it were only the empty support of a universal function? Lacan did not ever really choose between these two perspectives: he oscillates as the texts dictate, designating it sometimes as the anonymous *subiectum* that is the Other and sometimes as a living subjectivity capable of saying "I"—with a marked preference for the first option. Even in the 1960s, when he tries to effect a return to Descartes, he reduces the Cartesian cogito to an impersonal quasi-subject, an "I think which is not I," and his rereading of Descartes is completed with a radical egocide: "*Cogito ergo Es*, I think, therefore, there is the Id."[23]

He did indeed know, however, that this dissociated and fading quasi-subject, a mere inert toy for the signifier, has nothing to do with the living subject that I am, a subject capable of being named, inscribing its name in language, and extricating itself from the influence of the Other. He had understood that his conception of the symbolic as structure without subject had nothing to say about this singular life unfurled between the event of my birth and the possibility of my death: "There is, in effect, something radically inassimilable to the signifier. It's quite simply the subject's singular existence. Why is he there? Where has he come from? What is he doing here? Why is he going to disappear? The signifier is incapable of providing him with the answer, for the good reason that it places him beyond death. The signifier already considers him dead" (S, III:179–80). One fine day, while reading the newspaper, President Schreber had the unpleasant surprise of learning the news of his own death. It had already been some time since God, in his "powerfully deep voice," had begun treating him as a decaying carcass and since divine rays had transformed him into a "leprous cadaver," thus attesting that the subject of psychosis is lived as always-already-dead. Schreber's hallucinated experience here rejoins Poe's tale: what Poe's hero Valdemar announces is not only that "I am dead" but also an "I tell you that I am dead"—as if it were the very fact of saying it, of giving his "I" access to the signifier that immediately delivered him to death. Valdemar is indeed a Lacanian hero. He is one of the possible names of the subject who was nothing before being called by the signifier and who fell back into nothingness as soon as the signifier convoked him. The more I "subjectify" myself in the Lacanian mode, the more I annihilate myself as a living subject. If the imaginary ego found its truth in the impossible test of seeing itself dead, the symbolic subject discovers its truth in this utterance from beyond the grave that crosses Valdemar's bloodless lips: in the equally impossible experience of *saying one is dead* [*se dire mort*]. It is once more death that leads the dance: "*Wo Es war, soll Ich sterben*: there where it was, I must die."

In the "battle of giants" between the life drives and the death drives, Freud chose the side of life, of "the Eros of poets and philosophers that brings all living things together," of the desire that interrupts and defers our inexorable "slide towards death." He would thus be surprised to hear his French disciple attributing to him the thesis of submitting life to death and proclaiming that the psychoanalyst "must acknowledge the prestige of but one master—death" (E, 289). Why does Lacan thus reverse Freud's approach? One answer to this question imposes itself: his emphatic insistence on death comes from Heidegger. In his project of regrounding Freudian theory, Lacan had made massive recourse to Heidegger, going as far as identifying the Other with Being, the return of the repressed with *alétheia*, and the death drive with Dasein's being-toward-death.[24] The analytic cure thus becomes the equivalent of the conversion to authenticity whereby existing being assumes itself as *ego moribundus*—and this therapy that should free us from the mortifying effects of the compulsion for repetition, our unconscious guilt issuing from the death drive, is transformed in its turn into the preaching of death. We can wonder whether these hazardous rapprochements do violence both to Heidegger's thought and to psychoanalysis. But his fascination with the Heideggerian onto-thanatology is not alone responsible for this drift. Lacan can assimilate the subject of the symbolic to being-toward-death because death already reigned over his thought and because he had interpreted (by denaturalizing it) the mirror stage in terms of the death struggle. Because the mirror exposes us to the encounter with the absolute Master, the "human animal is capable of imagining itself mortal," and "without this gap that alienates him from his own image, this symbiosis with the symbolic in which he constitutes himself as subject to death, could not have occurred" (E, 461). Lacan thus renounces his fundamental thesis: what he advances instead is the idea that the imaginary precedes and radically grounds the symbolic. It is remarkable that these same terms that had formerly qualified the imaginary double are found again here characterizing the subject's relation to the signifier, which "petrifies" or "freezes" it, destines it to death,[25] as if the submission of the subject to the symbolic order merely repeated on another plane the ego's mortal subjection to its reflection. In passing from the imaginary to the symbolic, we again find the same motifs—exstatic identification, originary alienation, exposure to death—that already governed the mirror stage. The charms of the speculum have not been exorcised, and the symbolic "true subject," which was supposedly opposed in every way to the ego's narcissism, appears at the end of the account as its twin or double, its reflection in the mirror. It could not be otherwise: Lacan tried to respond to the aporia of imaginary transcendence with an overdose of transcendence, substituting another more radical ecstasy for the specular ecstasis, without perceiving that this orientation towards ecstatic transcendence had precipitated his thought into an impasse. The passage from the imaginary to the symbolic is thus limited to replacing one alienating identification with another, and so we do not really clearly see how the subject could dissociate itself from the Other, since its alienation is what makes it be a subject. But such a deliverance must be possible; otherwise psychoanalysis would be only a vain imposter. The subject must, at the end of the cure, "break through the plane of identification," must manage to *be dis-identified from* the Other. But how could it, if it exists only by being forever identified with it?

Wo Es war, soll Ich werden: where there had been only a subject alienated from the Other, now I, me, the ego, must arise as subject of my desire. This supposes that alienation is not the ultimate term of my relation to the Other; and many Lacanians forget that Lacan knew this very well. The proof is this passage from the seminar on the *Four Fundamental Concepts of Psychoanalysis*, wherein, after having described the structure of alienation, he introduces a "second operation" that he names *separation* (S, XI:213–15). And he specifies that it has the meaning of a *self-separating* that allows the subject to defend itself [*se parer*] against the strikes of the Other and thus "to engender" itself (which in Latin is *se parere*). Separation begins when "in order to attribute to himself [*se parer*] the signifier to which he succumbs, the subject attacks the chain . . . at its interval" (E, 715), which is the point of weakness for the Other, the failure of its discourse. There is a gap between the signifier that calls it and the signifier that fixes it—a brief moment of silence when the subject can turn itself back to the Other, address itself to it, question it about its desire ("what do you want with me?")—but its question goes without response. In the space opened by the silence of the Other, the subject is able to ask itself the question of its own desire and stops desiring only what the Other desires—and it is here that it "finds the path of return from alienation." We do not see very clearly, however, how it will succeed in overcoming its alienation or come back to itself by separating itself from the Other, since it was nothing before being subjected by it. By what miracle would a subject engendered by the signifier and totally alienated from itself be able to loosen the vise of the signifying chain? For separation to be possible, alienation must not be originary, and instead an originary nucleus of the subject must precede its identification with the Other and be capable of resisting its influence, just as the Cartesian ego is able to resist the evil genius. Lacan could never allow this, no more than he could imagine an ego more originary than the mirror stage. His egocidal prejudice hastens his fall into an impasse: he claims that separation is a decisive moment of the subject's constitution, even though the situation of the subject prohibits it from unsticking itself from the Other. Separation is absolutely necessary, yet also perfectly impossible, and as it is what should finally lead the patient to give his analyst a break, we understand why the cure tends to become interminable. Consequently, the high priest of psychoanalysis can rule without sharing power, because he has eliminated in advance whatever could resist his power and because he has reduced all living subjectivity to a bloodless X, a fading specter similar to those "shadows of thrashing men" in Schreber's visions.

Wo Ich war, soll Ich werden (a Return to Freud?)

With Lacan's return to Freud completed, egocide triumphs in psychoanalysis. Instead of liberating the I-subject from its alienating identifications, one radically submits it to the Other: where I, me, the ego, was, the Other now comes forth to subject me [*m'assujettir*]. Yet the ego's destitution fails to totally eliminate it. As with Heidegger, it reappears in the thought that had sought to exclude it, condemning it to incessant oscillations. After having first defined the ego as an imaginary illusion, and the subject of the symbolic as an "I" distinct from the ego, Lacan then denies that the subject is an "I." But the same ambiguity is found in his conception of the subject, which he sometimes presents as a universal and neutral function and sometimes as a singular subjectivity capable of naming itself, of saying "I." The strange "return to Descartes" undertaken in the 1960s will hardly allow Lacan to be done with these equivocations, since he henceforth identifies the subject of psychoanalysis with the Cartesian cogito, all the while refusing to consider it as an ego. What barely varies in this problematic is the subject's or ego's originary, total, and insurmountable alienation, the alienating identification that subjects it to its specular double or to the signifying chain. Whether "I" am defined as an imaginary ego, an I-subject or a subject without an I, I always exchange one alienation for another. All these attempts simply come down to displacing the initial aporia, in a game of hot potato that passes from the imaginary to the symbolic, then from the symbolic to the "real," without ever succeeding in overcoming it. Why chase after an unfindable exit when we can find it behind us, where Lacan never looked: on this side of the mirror and its "interminable ecstasy"? His privileging of the exstatic transcendence of sight leads him to situate the ego's origin outside of the ego itself; the passage to the symbolic retains what is essential in this arrangement, substituting the exterior of the signifier in place of the exteriority of the image. The ego or the subject is determined as the passive effect of an originary identification with a transcendent Other, which prohibits it from being disidentified with, or being separated from, this foreign otherness, since it was nothing before prior to having alienated itself from it. No matter how we read this conception of identification, we are inevitably lead to a dead end. Does not all identification necessarily consist in being identified with an other than self? Must the subject or the ego not be first identified *with itself* in order then to be able to identify with this other? How can I identify myself with an other if it is not me who recognizes myself in the other, or if I did not already exist prior to any identification? Lacan's thought does not allow for a response to these questions, because he never wanted to admit either that the ego can exist prior to the mirror stage, prior to any relation to the signifier, nor that ego was even the originary condition for imaginary or symbolic identifications. To get out of this impasse, another return to Freud is necessary, but it is a return to another Freud, the Freud who made the "soll Ich werden"—the exigency to become me, to become ego—the major imperative of psychoanalysis.

Freud, who was not Lacanian, did not think that the ego could be totally reduced to a residue of alienating identifications. He maintained that the ego "is formed to a great extent out of identifications"—but not completely, that is, *only in part.*[26] Where does the other part of the ego come from? It comes not from an image, from a gaze or from a voice, and even less from a signifier—but rather from the body. For Freud, the ego is "above all corporal" and is an "ego-body [*ein Körper-Ich*]." It is "ultimately derived from bodily sensations, chiefly from those springing from the surface of the body."[27] Before being able to be identified with an image or with a trait of the Other, the ego-body must first be unfolded on the surface of, and differentiated from, the id. If not, if this surface is not constituted, then no reflection, no symbolic mark, no partial object, could ever be inscribed there, and no identification would be produced. In fact, when this surface is torn or becomes porous or brittle, as happens in certain psychoses, then we are dealing no longer with an identification in the strict sense but rather with an "incorporation," an injection in the body of fragments of the other's body. The ego is thus formed right on [*à meme*] the body, as an *ego-skin*:[28] it derives by projection from the *tactile* sensations diffused across the corporal surface, which allows us to understand why those blind from birth have no difficulty accessing the feeling of having a body and being an ego. The privileged role that Lacan was going to attribute to sight is granted by Freud to the touch, to the "internal perception" of the body that it makes possible: he remarks that "a person's own body, and above all its surface, is a place from which both external and internal perceptions may spring. It is *seen* like any other object, but to the *touch* it yields two kinds of sensations, one of which may be equivalent to an internal perception."[29] These tactile sensations constitute the nucleus of the ego, its most originary layer on which are deposited other layers issuing from different perceptual experiences. Freud sometimes evokes an "acoustic cap" or "cap of hearing" set on the surface of the body, or auditory traces that are "by differentiation within the ego" at the origin of the superego; nothing then prevents us from imagining visual experiences completing this genesis: the mirror stage could find its place in this process but only as a derivative, later phase wherein the ego would finally have access to a perception of the body's total form. It is not only identifications with others that constitute the ego but above all its perceptual experiences, along with the accompanying affects of pleasure, displeasure, or anxiety: the ego is rooted in these "signs of perception," which Freud considered as more originary than either conscious or unconscious mental representations.[30]

The originary tactile surface could be neither unfolded nor crossed with other perceptual layers without a series of movements. No perception is truly possible without movement, without a hand advancing to grasp or lightly touch, without a gaze glancing or fixating. Whereas the Lacanian mirror petrifies the body, freezes it in the inert stature of a cadaver, Freud insists on the contrary on the role of motility and "motor discharges." He is thus able to define the hysterical symptom as "phantasies translated into the motor sphere, projected onto motility, and portrayed in pantomime,"[31] or to evoke the sublimation of the death drive, its transformation into an instinct to master by derivation from motility.[32] Yet such notations remain rare and allusive: he will never seek to specify which conceptions of the body are at stake in his theory; and his remarks on the corporeal origin of the ego, on the primacy of touching or the originary "signs of perception," will remain inconsequential for the development of psychoanalysis. There is an astonishing paradox here: for the Freudian discovery had dealt with just that—the body, the suffering and rejoicing of the body. It was by listening to, and by trying to understand and heal the somatic symptoms of hysterics—such as Emmy von N.'s spasms, or Elisabeth von R.'s painful legs, or Dora's cough—that Freud had laid down the bases of psychoanalysis. He had discovered that their symptoms arise not from the objective body as studied by science but from a "phantasmatic anatomy" that escapes the traditional opposition of body and soul. And yet, like all great explorers, he was unable to recognize or even to name the unknown earth that he had just come upon: he immediately falls back into dualism by considering the psychical and the physical as two entirely distinct planes and hysterical symptoms as "conversions" or "translations" that in no way affect the separation of the two planes.

It would have been difficult to avoid: at a time when this dualism reigned completely over the sciences, and in order to ground *psycho*-analysis,

Freud had to restrict his field to the unconscious psychical reality by demarcating it from every investigation concerning the body or the "obscure biological substrate" of the drives. Psychoanalysis is thus grounded on *a denial of the body*, which will never be called into question—and the price of such a denial is heavy. By excluding the somatic from the field of analysis, Freud barred himself from thinking what he calls the "ego-body." Instead of anchoring the ego in this originary unity—that of an ego that would be body, of a body that would be ego—he dissociates it. He makes it into a "mental projection" of the corporeal surface, its transposition on the psychic plane, as if it were a matter of two different surfaces, one of which would be derived (who knows how) from the other. Since it arises from corporeal sensations that are not yet "me," the ego would not be an originary phenomenon: Freud and Lacan share here a common rejection of Descartes, even if the master attributes a double origin to the ego (by projection of corporeal sensations and by identification with others), while his disciple limits himself to just one, identification. As with Heidegger and all egocides, Freud never wonders how an originary non-ego could manage to engender the ego. He did not see that if my ego is able to "derive" from tactile sensations, then these sensations must already be mine: they must already belong to an ego-body capable of projecting itself on other planes.

This derivation of the ego from a non-ego or a body that would not yet be *my* body was not the only possible route for psychoanalysis. In the *Interpretation of Dreams*, Freud always claims that "dreams are absolutely egoistic," that all the people figuring in them are only "disguises" for the ego: "In cases where not my ego but only a strange person occurs in the dream-content, I may safely assume that by means of identification my ego is concealed behind that person."[33] Given that the dream is the "royal road to the unconscious," we must conclude that the unconscious itself is "egoistic," that the representations it contains are only different disguises for the ego. This confirms the analysis of the *phantasm*, that is, the apparently anonymous scenario ("a child is being beaten") whose true subject is no one other than the ego ("I am the child being beaten"). By introducing the concept of narcissism in 1915, Freud extends this "absolutely egoistic" character to sexual desire and to the libido itself. He advances the hypothesis of an "originary libidinal investment of the ego," which will subsequently be turned toward exterior objects without ceasing to be fundamentally narcissistic. It is no longer even possible to oppose a "libido of objects" to a "libido of the ego" (or, if one prefers, a purely narcissistic desire to the desire for the Other): in effect, "in the state of narcissism," these two kinds of libido "are found first reunited and indiscernible," and this originary narcissistic investment persists in all object-choice.[34] In brief, by desiring the Other, it is always me that I desire. Whether it is a matter of a dream, of a phantasm, or of a desire, the Other would only ever be a substitute for the ego. The same goes for the different instances of the psychical apparatus and notably for the superego and the ego-ideal, which Freud distinguishes clearly from the ego—but while claiming that they still belong to the "system of the ego," that is, that it is a matter of self-differentiations internal to the ego.

To remain faithful to this orientation, Freud would have had to recenter psychoanalysis on the ego, converting it into an *egoanalysis*. And yet, after the 1920s, he would go in the completely opposite direction, hypothesizing that the ego is a derived moment of the id. By making it a mirage of the imaginary, Lacan will only radicalize this Freudian gesture. We here reach the limit of psychoanalysis, a theory that seeks to ground itself as an objective science of the "psychical reality" *within the world*. By this fact, it is never *me* it attains, never my immanent ego in my absolutely singular life: it is an ego-in-the-world and in relation to innumerable other subjects, whose existence precedes its own and determines it in all its aspects: an "ego" that is always already identified with the Other, alienated from it, and therefore never able to become itself. The *soll Ich werden* will thus remain a pious wish, an inaccessible ideal, promised to the patients yet endlessly deferred throughout the interminable cure. How could I ever become myself if I had not *already* come to myself? As archaic as they are, rooted in the most original experiences of childhood, alienating identifications are not originary: they suppose a *self-identification* of the ego. It is *me* who built this stature that fascinates me, this structure that crushes me; it is my own flesh that I project in the mirror or on the Other and that animates them with a semblance of life. The specular image would be nothing if I had not already recognized it as my reflection, and the signifier would remain a dead letter if I had not already invoked it in my speech. The ego's priority over the Other will allow it to be dis-identified and separated from the Other. If we want to remain faithful to the Freudian imperative, then we must take a step beyond Freud—or rather a step backward from him and toward this thought that recognizes in the ego a first truth, an originary affirmation that "does not need any Other to exist." We have to return to Descartes.

No science can edify itself if it is not rooted in a founding truth that gives it its *index sui*, the criteria for all other truths that it could discover. This ultimate ground of experience is what is lacking in psychoanalysis and what a radical theory of the ego could offer. I will designate this theory, which is yet to be constituted, as an *egoanalysis*: it claims not to substitute itself for psychoanalysis but rather to enter into dialogue with it, in order to allow it to reground itself, to recenter itself on the truth of the ego. It is not a question of once again ceding to the original sin of philosophers, to the old temptation to rectify psychoanalysis—but rather of listening to it. But it does so without returning to this normalizing therapy already combated by Lacan, a therapy that sought to readapt the "weak ego of the neurotic" to social reality. What egoanalysis tries to discover is the originary nucleus of the ego, *the true ego* of which Proust spoke, and which is not reducible to the *mundane ego* alienated from others. It thus once again calls into question the alienating identifications that constitute the "well-adapted" personality and should help in being freed from them. How can we approach this originary ego? Does it still lead back to an effect of language, or is it rather a matter of a *tacit ego*, an inhabitant of the silent country where the very possibilities of being in the world and of speaking arise? And if it takes hold on this side of the signifier, how will we be able to name or describe this still unexplored domain? Must we say, with Freud, that it is a matter of *an ego-body*? There is a great risk of reducing it to its biological substrate, or of ceding to the triumphant imperialism of the neurosciences whose most dogmatic adherents claim today to be done with that "imposter" psychoanalysis, a risk we may avoid only if the originary corporeity of the body-ego is rigorously distinguished from what the sciences study, perhaps by giving it another name. Some weeks before his death, Merleau-Ponty wrote this sibylline note: "Freud's philosophy is not a philosophy of the body but of the flesh—the unconscious—the ego (correlatives) to be understood on the basis of the flesh . . . as differentiations of one sole and massive adhesion to Being that is the flesh."[35] It must be possible, following Merleau-Ponty's clue, to reground the Freudian theory by understanding it "on the basis of the flesh," a flesh that would no longer be considered a universal element of Being—of a flesh that is *always mine*. If we situate ourselves in this perspective of an originary linkage between the *ego* and the *flesh*, the brilliant intuitions that run throughout Freud's work are clarified in a new way: the "absolutely egoist" nature of the dream, phantasm, desire, the "originary narcissism" of the libido, the importance of corporeal movement and of the rhythm of "motor discharges"—this "ego-body" issuing from tactile perception of the corporeal surface, these acoustic traces, these fragments of voice inscribed on the surface of the ego in order to form the superego—all this will find a new meaning in the perspective of an egoanalysis.

Perhaps we will then be able to understand the drama that was played out in the first beginnings of psychoanalysis, before Freud ever turned toward the suffering body of hysterics, and that would then decide its future orientation and blindness:

Anna was sitting at the bedside with her right arm over the back of her chair. She fell into a waking dream and saw a black snake coming towards the sick man from the wall to bite him . . . She tried to keep the snake off, but it was as though she was paralyzed. Her right arm, over the back of the chair, had gone to sleep and had become anesthetic and paretic; and when she looked at it the fingers turned into little snakes with death's heads.[36]

From the beginning of the scene, the young woman's arm is immobile, as if her hand has to avoid advancing on her father's body. What cannot take place on the plane of touching suddenly surges forth in vision, in the form of the tempting serpent, a figure in which are condensed both the hand that touches and the organ touched, Anna's arm and the object of her desire, her father's erection. It is the hallucinatory figuration of a forbidden jouissance. At this limit-point, where the incest-prohibition could horribly fail, it is no longer just the object of fantasy but also the Law itself that comes to be inscribed in Anna's body by paralyzing the guilty arm. But is it not here that the Thing surges forth again, demultiplied, in the fingers metamorphosed into little snakes of death? Me, Anna O, I am she who will make my agonizing father have an orgasm, I carry in my flesh the emblem of his jouissance, and I am also my father who is dying, I am the black serpent who announces his death, and I already anticipate in my own flesh this death that is also mine.

Is psychoanalysis sufficient to take account of all this? We must have recourse to another approach if we want to understand this intrigue in which the interdiction on touching, the rupture of an originary unity, is inscribed right on the flesh. What must the flesh be for it to be fragmented and *mortified*, to the point that Anna no longer recognizes her hand of flesh in this hand-thing-become-numb, discovering the image of her death at the end of each paralyzed finger? If the Law prohibiting incest can be translated corporeally, it is only by reviving a more ancient wound, a rip in which the flesh is torn away from itself. This is already what is played out in the mirror stage: the possibility of recognizing myself in my image and thus of conjuring up the foreign Thing, the face of Medusa who fixates me in the mirror. But how is the flesh able to recognize and be intertwined with itself, to identify with itself? Is not this identification always partial, precarious, and doomed to failure? Is it not this weakness of identification that paralyzes Anna's arm and makes the "pale face" of her death appear in the mirror? How can I avoid becoming this dead person who sees his skeleton in a mirror? We know how she tries to escape from this horrible vision: by projecting on the Other the funereal reflection, by recognizing in it "not her own face, but the face of her father with a head of death." Projecting the abjection that haunts us onto the Other: how do we avoid ceding to this, which nourishes our phantasms and sometimes our mass graves? It is a miserable expedient, since the Other is issued from my flesh, since it is a part of myself that has become foreign to me. The ego-flesh would have to confront its torment, take it up in itself, instead of projecting it outside of itself: from that hole of jouissance in which the Thing pulses, from where that ancient wound was, I must come forth to myself and to my body—but I will be able to do so only if I had already been there, only if I recognized this wound as mine, and this unnamable Thing as the flesh of my flesh. By ceasing to reject the flesh, to project itself on and to lose itself in the Other, the ego will finally be able to find itself. *Wo Ich war, soll Ich werden*: there where I have always and forever been is from where I must arise.

3

Return to Descartes

Psychoanalysis will have succeeded no better than ontology in eliminating the ego. It too presents itself as an alternative to Descartes, as an implacable critique of the illusion of being "me," an ego, but just as with Heidegger's Dasein, Lacan's subject also finally had to pass itself off using the old name "ego." The effort was wasted: this existing being that I have yet to be is always mine, always ego, and the subject of psychoanalysis, the I that I must become, is nothing other than ego. The ego's obstinate persistence in existing being or the subject had led Heidegger to abandon the privilege of Dasein and turn toward Being and led Lacan to reclaim a "subjectivation without a subject." They thus both ended up submitting the singular ego entirely to the supremacy of a Neuter, a Being, an Other, which for a while in Heidegger takes on the characteristics of the Führer and annihilates both the freedom and the truth of the ego. From the earlier to the later Heidegger, or from Freud to Lacan, egocide is inexorably worsened, and no one is ever able to explain where in each of us the absolute certainty of being ego comes from or how this illusory ego could derive from a more originary non-ego. And if we look to other thinkers, we will once again find the same aporias, the same radicalization of egocide, and the same return to the ego in a thought that was supposed to go beyond it. Thus, Nietzsche, after denouncing the charms of the cogito, finally invokes an *ego fatum* that would be the enigmatic "subject" of the Eternal Return.[1] And Sartre, who first described the ego as a transcendent object or as a mere "mirage," will reintroduce an "ego-subject" in *Being and Nothingness*.

And we will find an analogous oscillation and the same antinomy in Derrida.[2] Egocide is thus condemned to oscillate between a revocation and a restoration of the ego, as if never finished with the ego.

One of the principal difficulties of *Being and Time* concerns the possibility of resolute decision, that conversion whereby Dasein is freed of its original fallenness in order to have access to an authentic existence. This conversion has to be able to be accomplished, and the truth of existence has to be able to be revealed and give us new access to the question of Being, for if not, the project of a fundamental ontology would be stripped of meaning. The same problem is found in Lacan, for whom the subject has to overcome its original alienation by separating itself from the Other: if this separation were impossible, psychoanalysis would be a pure and simple imposture. Under what conditions is such a deliverance possible? How can Dasein—thrown passively into existence, into a facticity that it cannot master, as existing being always outside of itself and always fallen—decide to be itself and to return to itself? To do so, it must call itself by itself, it must have the power to be recalled to self, to give itself to itself—and this self-givenness must be more originary than its thrownness and its fallenness. The same is true for the psychoanalytic subject, which is able to dis-identify itself from the Other only on the condition that its alienation had not been absolutely originary, that is, that it had already been identified with itself prior to being identified with the Other. In each case, the possibility of deliverance supposes that some element X predates fallenness and alienation and is always *already self-given* prior to being identified with the world or with the Other. For Dasein to be able to open itself to the truth of existence, and for the subject to be able to undo the charms of the imaginary, this X must already be *in truth*: it must possess the power *to be revealed to itself* in truth. Finally, in order to be able to resist alienation or neutralization in the anonymity of the They or of Structure, this X must be radically *singular*. Self-givenness, self-revelation, singularity: what would be capable of satisfying these three conditions? Neither existing being nor the subject has been able to do it: not only are they not singular enough nor are they sufficiently demarcated from an anonymous neutrality, but they are also determined on the basis of a transcendent alterity (as the There of Being or a function of the Other) without ever having access to self-givenness. Neither ontology nor psychoanalysis will be able to determine this element X—and yet, by some strange lapsus, Heidegger,

Freud, and Lacan each time designate it by its name: this X that is the truth of Dasein or the psychoanalytic subject *is the ego, it is me.* The failed wish of the egocidal thinkers leads us back to their old adversary, that philosopher whom they try to refute without ever really doing so. If I want to understand *who* this ego that I am is, then it is time to return to Descartes.

"If I err, I am"

Descartes' solitude. Everything from the most trivial opinion to the loftiest thought always arises in opposition to Descartes. Whenever common sense wants to attack a rationalism judged to be too restrictive, it denounces the "Cartesian spirit." Whenever an adept of the cognitive sciences, perhaps a bit less uncultured than some of his colleagues, wants to show that our reason cannot arise from the affects, he calls his book *Descartes' Error.*[3] On an entirely different level, when Heidegger wants to determine the origin of errancy, of the devastation of the world that characterizes modern times, he attacks the cogito, to the point, as we have seen, of making Hitler the heir of Descartes. And when Foucault describes that forceful turn in the classical age that reduces the voices of madness to silence, it is again Descartes who is invoked and incriminated for this rejection of madness effected in the first *Meditation.* The Cartesian philosopher would be contemporary, and in some way complicit, with the Great Imprisonment that sends the mad, naked and in chains, to be devoured by rats in the dungeons of Bicêtre. But what an epoch excludes allows us to see its hidden unity better. This rule is also valid for that great excluded cogito of Descartes, this pariah of our philosophy. Where does this unanimity constantly formed against it come from? What is it about the affirmation of the ego—its singularity, its truth, its freedom—that horrifies so many of our contemporaries?

There is no thinker after Descartes who did not try to refute the *cogito ergo sum,* even if they differed on how to understand it. Some, after Kant, focus on the "therefore," on the logical connection of the "I think" and the "I am." They then posit an insurmountable duality between being and thought, between the I that thinks and the I that is. "I think where I am not, thus I am where I do not think," Lacan writes ironically. Others question the very unity of the ego cogito, the identity of the ego with "its" thought, which leads them to substitute an anonymous thought for it—an "it thinks," a *cogitatur*.[4] The first objection can be easily refuted. These philosophers are simply wrong; they have concentrated their attacks on a minor statement that does not fundamentally express Descartes' discovery. If we take the second *Meditation* literally, we note that the famous formula "I think therefore I am" is not found there (though it is certainly found in the *Discourse on Method* and in the second *Response*).[5] The Cartesian discovery is more soberly stated: *ego sum, ego existo*, "I am, I exist." This bare affirmation of the ego's existence, which is immediately given here without the least trace of a logical deduction, thus showing the passage of the ego to thought or of thought to being, greatly embarrasses the commentators. By foregoing the "I think" and the "therefore," Descartes avoids in advance the various traps the commentators will use to try to catch him.

It is more difficult to respond to the second objection, which refuses to admit that it is the *ego* who is or that the "subject" whose existence is affirmed is necessarily an *I*. In fact, this affirmation of the *ego sum* only takes up another, previous, statement, giving it the form of a thesis. At the beginning of the second *Meditation*, Descartes evoked the hypothesis of the Evil Deceiver and the possibility "that there is absolutely nothing in the world, no sky, no earth, no minds, no bodies." But this very hypothesis of a universal deceiver prohibits me from doubting my own existence; and it is in this context that, for the first time, the indubitable affirmation of the "I am" is stated: "there is a deceiver of supreme power and cunning who is deliberately and constantly deceiving me. In that case I too undoubtedly exist, if he is deceiving me; and let him deceive me as much as he can, he will never bring it about that I am nothing so long as I think that I am something."[6] The revelation of my existence thus comes not from a theoretical reasoning or a reflection on my acts of thought but rather from a more disturbing proof, from the initial experience of the threat of a deceiving power that wants to make me be nothing and tries to annihilate me. This power is presented as an Evil Deceiver capable of tearing me away from my certainties, and this universal deception is imposed on me as a nontruth, a countertruth more powerful than all sensible or rational evidence, including the naive certainty that I exist and am myself. We too often weaken Descartes' thought by considering this countertruth as an inconsistent and immediately rejected hypothesis. The deceiver is much more than a mere fiction destined to reinforce my reasons to doubt: we must instead see in it a real threat or menace, an unknown power that assails and seeks to destroy me.

There are many ways of denying that I am, and they correspond to very different perspectives. It could be (a) that I mistake myself when I claim that I am an "ego." The ego would be only an illusion that has to be dispelled: this is the gesture that I call egocide. Or it could be (b) that I am not who I think I am, that I mistake myself for another when I imagine myself to be me—and this would be madness. The threat of madness, apparently spared at the outset of the first *Meditation*, reappears here.[7] Another threat is also sketched out: (c) the Deceiver (who takes on the traits of the Great Persecutor) unfurls his power *ut nihil sim*—so that I am nothing. Can we qualify this promised annihilation as something other than a death threat, an endlessly reiterated attempted murder? A *reductio ad nihilum*: that is what the synopsis of the *Meditations* calls the disappearance of finite substances, their destruction by the withdrawal of divine support, which has sustained them in existence— and it is to this "reduction to nothingness" that my persecutor destines me. Certainly, by not knowing who I am or even *if* I am, I do not yet know if I can die or what meaning my death will have for me. But let us be content for the moment with observing this strange link whereby the initial countertruth is linked to the still meaningless possibility of my death. The Cartesian claim of the *I am* has meaning only by resisting this triple threat of illusion, madness, and death, all of which Descartes condenses in the figure of the Deceiver. *Si me fallit, ego sum*, "if I err, I am." This statement can be understood in several senses: (a) if an Other seeks to deceive me when I think I am an ego, then that is indeed the proof that I am, that I exist in the form of an ego since this X deceives *me*; (b) even if I am mad or delirious for believing that I am myself, this madness is mine, confirms for me that I am, and that I am still *me*; and (c) if one tries to annihilate me, it must be that I am, that a part of myself resists what persecutes and tries to kill *me*; and even if one could persuade me that I am already dead, this proves again that I am, because only a living being I can utter that "I am dead." For this reason, the proposition "I am, I exist" is "necessarily true"; and it is also why it is a matter of a truth that is impossible to call into doubt—thus, an absolute truth. For this truth attests to an affirmation more powerful than anything that pretends to deny it; it is able to resist its most extreme negation, to turn negating powers back against themselves in order to put them in the service of its own self-revelation. There is thus *at least a truth*, the stopping point of a truth that escapes from illusion and resists this universal negation and triumphant nihilism of modern times, the advent of which was prefigured by the Cartesian deceiver. This truth is irreducible and is *my* truth, the strange singular truth *that I am*—because such a truth is always given "in the first person," as an I. The very validity of the Cartesian argument depends on this truth: unlike the statement "I exist," which is absolutely impossible for me to deny, the proposition "X exists" can be completely and easily contradicted by the equally valid proposition that "X does not exist," which means there is no assurance that X necessarily exists. Refusing to consider the "subject" of this truth as an I, reducing it to an anonymous *subiectum* which has nothing in common with ego, amounts to annihilating this truth, submitting it without reserve to the Evil Genius.[8]

"But I do not yet have a sufficient understanding of what this 'I' is, that now necessarily exists." (M II, 5:17). *Who,* then, am I? This might seem an absurd question since I am so certain of being "me," of defining myself by my personal identity, by my name, my history, the place I occupy in the world. All of these certainties vacillate when tested by doubt, because it affects me *myself,* in my singular existence. I thought I was René Descartes, born in the Touraine, former student at La Flèche, later an officer in the king of France's armies. I remember German navy men who tried to assassinate me. I remember this wood-burning stove near which I meditated throughout the winter on the banks of the Danube, and I remember the three dreams I had there, when I discovered the foundations of an admirable science. I decided today to free myself from all beliefs, in order to go in search of a firm and stable ground. This is how my certainty of being this man fell into the night of doubt: no longer the gentleman mathematician or the French cavalry officer, I am now constrained to revoke all the memories constituting the framework of my life, because they, too, can be fictions of the Evil Genius. I am, I exist, this is absolutely certain, but who am I? Nothing other than a pure, anonymous ego. And yet this ego is not an abstract concept or some common notion of an Ego true for all men. As neutral and impersonal as it may appear, it nevertheless attests to a singular existence, with the style that is its own, its inimitable manner of sensing, of being incarnated in its flesh, of being affected by its life. In truth, this ego *is mine*, it is *me.*

Nothing is more difficult to conceive than this ego without qualities, this ego = X, because I have the habit of identifying my ego with a human individual existing in the world among others, taken by the intrigues of history, and inserted in a complex network of symbolic and social relations. I will come to consider this individual, this subject, this human person with its particular manner of being in the world, as myself. And I have come to love it, to rejoice narcissistically in being it and in persevering in my being. Like Nessus's tunic sticking to my skin, I cannot free myself of it without tearing away the flesh to which it adheres. This evidence must be called into question. By doubting the existence of the world and of all that exists in it—figures and places, minds and bodies, other people I meet around me—I *also* call into doubt this mundane ego, the subject that I am within the world: from then on, I discover that the core of my ego does not coincide with this human individual to which I had reduced it. Certainly I can no longer doubt that I am, and my certainty of existing is necessarily true—but the truth of my existence does not stop slipping away: I will never be certain of truly being what I am, and I will never be able to be assured that it is indeed me who speaks when I say "I." This lag or hiatus will thus be maintained between my consciousness of existing and my knowledge of myself, which remains very obscure and indeterminate. Existing without knowing who one is means existing in the mode of an enigma. I thus remain an enigma for myself, and every attempt to determine the essence of the ego will fail to dissipate the enigma *that I am*. An uncertainty persists, which prohibits me from totally identifying myself with the mundane and narcissistic ego, the character in the social comedy that I do not stop showing in the place of my true ego. This uncertainty sometimes lets us have a glimpse of the persona behind the theatrical mask dissimulating it, glimpse the strangeness of an ego without a face and without a name. This ego would not be entirely *subjected*, alienated by a subjective identity; it could be desubjectivated or *dis-identified*, and so could change life, could change its manner of living its life, or could even be reborn with another identity, reappearing as a *more true* figure, less forgetful of its primary truth.

I know while writing this that I am doing violence to Descartes: this demarcation between the ego-in-the-world and an originary core of a still enigmatic and indeterminate ego revealed through the experience of doubt barely even appears in his work. I am trying, however, to remain faithful to the radicality of a step that calls into question the obviousness of being in the world, being with others, being a human individual among others, in order to see the dawn when I discover *that* I am without yet knowing *who* I am. Descartes will have thus preserved the fortunes of a question that philosophers no longer ask: Who am I? *Who is ego?* This question sometimes erupts in my life when the ground of all my certainties vacillates: "It feels as if I have fallen unexpectedly into a deep whirlpool which tumbles me around so that I can neither stand on the bottom nor swim up to the top" (M II, 1:16). We encounter this loss of all ground or solid foundation in the experience of madness, which Descartes marginalizes; we also encounter it in the experience of deception or persecution, in the threat of an Other who deceives and tries to negate the ego. We will find it again in other limit-experiences of existence—the extreme violence of love, when I wonder *who I am* to be able to love so much; in the intensity of despair, when I wonder *who I am* such that every future slips away from me; and in all of those ordeals that make the ego foreign to itself and to its familiar world, when its *uncanniness* is revealed to it. I will not examine these other modes of access to the question here; for the moment, I will rely only on Descartes' thought experiment, that is, this threat that a very powerful Deceiver makes weigh on me. We must start there if we want to try to understand what this ego that I am is.

I do not yet know anything of this ego at the outset of the second *Meditation*, except that it suddenly arises as an act of resistance, a sort of jolt able to undo the illusion that blinds it. It is a jolt that nothing announced, that nothing preceded, except this anonymous power, this Other = X, which is perhaps only *my own* power turned back against me. And moreover, the deceiver would not threaten *me* if I did not already exist: should we conclude from this that my resistance comes first, that the ego precedes this Other that had initially seemed to precede it? These formulations can lead us astray if we represent threat and resistance as actions succeeding one another in the world. Let us put this mundane representation aside and try to take hold of the moment when the *ego sum* comes forth, the unique moment of my birth. I arise as a persecuted ego, the prey of this threat that reveals me to myself; but the threat can take aim at me only insofar as I exist and thus resist it. The persecutor and the paradoxical point that escapes its grasp arise at the same time in a unique co-birth. I thus do not successively pass from a state of passivity to a revolt and self-affirmation, but rather, my passivity and my act of resistance are two versions of one and the same event. We can speak of the ego's "originary passivity," but only on the condition of recognizing that its passivity is the inverse of a primordial act, a decision to resist. Such a decision is not identified with an empirical choice, as if my resistance were merely one possibility or one attitude among others that I may or may not choose to adopt: for the ego, *existing is resisting.* In other words, the ego is not "substance"; rather, it subsists only to the extent that it resists and only as long as its resistance endures. As soon as the resistance is interrupted, as soon as it lets itself be trapped or deceived and alienated by the deceiver, it ceases to exist as an ego. The affirmation that *ego sum* finds here is its ethical meaning and is rather unexpected in a philosopher who is so respectful of the established authorities and who teaches us to "change our desires rather than the order of the world." It grounds an *ethics of resistance* wherein the ego finds access to its truth and its freedom, tearing itself away from the grip of the Other. It must be possible to remain faithful to this originary affirmation of itself throughout a life, to perform it again in each new decision, or to deny it in a passive submission to the Evil Deceiver.[9]

If my primordial experience of the Other is one of persecution, if I can affirm myself as ego only by resisting this threat, then between the ego and the other a deep gap is opened up, an abyss that will perhaps be impossible to fill. I attain myself only by revoking all alterity—"in so far as I consider myself alone, and as if there were only myself in the world" (M IV, 15:39)—and my existence seems radically *solipsistic.* Even after the third *Meditation* had overcome absolute solipsism by showing the existence of an infinite Other called "God," and even after the sixth had reestablished the certainty of the existence of the world, Descartes would still obstinately evade considering the existence of the other, of other men who would be my similars—as if the initial defiance toward the deceiving Other, the necessity of being affirmed against it and *without it*, persisted after the conversion of this Other into a bountiful God; as if this rejection or revocation of the Other were from then on deferred *from the Other to others.* This never-surmounted temptation of solipsism, this porous border traced between the ego and others, is thus indissociable from Descartes' method. One often concludes from this that solipsism is a fundamental vice of his method, arguing that a thought that takes the affirmation of a solitary ego as a starting point would be incapable of attaining the alterity of the other. By making the ego "the center of everything," the method will reveal its "injustice," its narcissism, its allergy to the Other (Fichte and later Husserl will be the target of the same criticisms). This argument can be easily turned back against those who make it: how can those who start with the Other and who are initially installed in being-with-others find access to the ego? When they think they have determined what the ego is, is it not an *already alienated* ego that they have encountered, an ego-in-the-world that is not my true ego? They are wrong to imagine that the originary affirmation of the ego prohibited it from being opened to others: in order to meet the Other *in truth* and to stop fearing it as my persecutor or my double, I must have first found myself. It is *my* truth that will give me authentic access to others; if I want to find the path that will lead me to them, I must first return to myself.

Is this self-affirmation of a solitary ego indeed Descartes' lesson? *Si me fallit, Ego sum*. If an Other deceives me, if I exist only by resisting it, then is not this proof that I am not alone? From the origin, this Other would be addressed to me—in order to deceive me—and its call is what convokes me to existence. By discovering that the ego necessarily exists, Descartes would have discovered at the same time the originary alterity that its existence presupposes, and with the same gesture, he will have overcome the impasse of solipsism.[10] But where must this alterity be situated? *Who* is the Other that deceives me? One could make rapid progress by determining this unknown power as an Other distinct from me, but Descartes made room for the possibility that I have deceived myself. "Is there not a God, or whatever I may call him, who puts into me the thoughts I am now having? But why do I think this, since I myself may perhaps be the author of these thoughts?" (M II, 4:16). The focus of illusion is manifested here as an anonymous pole of alterity, as yet unable to determine whether it is a matter of an internal or external threat or whether I have within me this power that traps me. It could be that I am my own deceiver. At this point, it is still too early to decide; but the fourth *Meditation* will give a clue to this mystery by showing that the origin of my errors is in me. We can recognize from now on in the figure of the Evil Genius the double of the ego, blinded to or by itself, at once both the deceiver and the deceived, both subject and object of the illusion. While I deceived myself about all things and about myself, I added a supplemental illusion to this blindness: without being aware of it, I created a fiction of a malicious

Other and transposed the cause of my error on to it. The ego would possess the strange capacity to project a part of itself outside of itself, to transfer an *internal* alterity that it does not yet recognize in itself onto the plane of the Other. By dividing myself, without even taking account of it, into a deceiving ego and a deceived ego, I have the illusion of being affected, threatened, and aggressed against by an Other, even though I am affected only by myself. A new imperative is subsequently added to the originary decision to resist the Other, which calls on me to stop blaming the Other for my errors, to stop considering it as an absolute threat, and instead to recognize that the source of the illusion is in me. What then must be understood is the status of this intimate alterity, this focus on illusion that I reject outside of me and that comes back to me from the outside in the disguise of a foreign Other. Descartes will no longer be of any help in thinking this. We will have to discover a method, a path that leads to this unknown part of myself, to this other-in-me that I will call the *remainder:* this will be what is at stake in the last part of this book.

And so I deceive *myself* whenever I think that an Other different from me is trying to deceive me—which confirms *post facto* the radical solipsism of the second *Meditation.* Faced with all those powers that alienate and crush us, that press us to deny ourselves, solipsism at least has this virtue: it teaches us to respect our ego, to not forget its singularity or the irreducible demarcation that distinguishes it from every other, which I have characterized as the *egological difference.* To affirm this difference is first of all to recognize that my ego is unique, incomparable, and that it does not let itself be substituted for or identified with anything else; it belongs originarily to no community. This solitude has nothing in common with the solitude of a mundane individual who chose to be isolated from others, because it precedes all relation to the world and to others. This is why every attempt to insert the ego into a common genre or to define it on the basis of a universal concept (such as Man or Subject) does violence to it and can therefore only fail. As soon as I am considered an element of an ensemble, a member among others within a human community, I am already no longer myself, and the egocide has already prevailed. Descartes knew this well: "by 'thought' I do not mean some universal which includes all modes of thinking, but a particular nature, which takes on those modes, just as extension is a nature which takes on all shapes."[11] This is why he refused to consider the statement "I think therefore I am" as a logical deduction (a syllogism), because that would amount to deriving my existence from a preexisting universal rule ("everything which thinks, is; . . .")—whereas no other thought, no other thinking being different from me, preexists the evidence that I am.[12] It is better to have recourse to the formulation of the *Meditations*, which immediately affirms the existence of the ego without deducing it from a preliminary *cogitatio*. If we decide to call *singular* that which, unlike the *particular*, is *not* derived or deduced from the universal, one will say that my ego is an absolute singularity. This affirmation of the singular is what those who attack Descartes' (or Husserl's) solipsism cannot tolerate. In fact, one would have to reproach him for *not being solipsistic enough* and for too quickly renouncing (in the third *Meditation*) the singular position of the ego; he also cedes to this self-forgetfulness whereby the ego is alienated from the different figures of the Other. A third imperative consequently is imposed: do not forget the egological difference; do not cede ground on my singularity. We will then have to look for how the ego can affirm itself without denying the Other and be opened to the other without being alienated by it.

In this "provisory ethics" that I have tried to dislodge from the *Meditations*, this third imperative is linked to the first imperative of resistance. Even if it consequently seems that the power threatening me is not a power of an Other, the exigency to resist it retains all its value: inseparable from my existence, it reemerges throughout my life, when I am confronted by these mundane powers that try *to subject me*, to make me a passive "subject" similar to others. They always exert their domination in the name of a universal, a common norm: in trying to submit the ego to the order of the world, they attack both its capacity for resistance—its freedom—and its singularity. When I decide to resist them, I at the same time affirm my radical difference, and I exempt myself from the Universal. The ego thus gives birth to itself in this way, as an exception to the universal illusion imposed by the Evil Genius—and an ego that remains faithful to itself chooses to remain constantly in this state of exception. According to an ancient tradition, the Law is lifted and exception is imposed in place of the rule at the time of the coming of the Messiah. In the imperative to become myself (*soll Ich werden*), I want to hear an echo of this messianic promise of a time when every ego would be its own messiah. It is this truth that we are going to have to think, the absolutely singular truth that I am—because this truth is, for each of us, "the narrow door through which the Messiah passes."

Neither Human nor Subject

If we ask ourselves what we are, each of us will immediately respond "a human." Belonging to the human species characterizes what is most essential about us: such is the postulate, the fundamental belief that defines humanism. In an epoch that, more than any other, will have had the experience of the inhuman, humanism ended up imposing itself as an imperious exigency for grounding all ethics, politics, and thought on the humanity of human beings and human rights. To the point of throwing the worst opprobrium on those philosophers who had formerly tried to question its presuppositions: outside of humanism, only barbarity reigns! Such a unanimity merits being questioned. Combat against those who claimed to exclude millions from humanity and the affirmation of our belonging to a universal human community once sustained the resistance to the unnamable—the resistance of Antelme, Primo Levi, Chalamov. But this petition of humanity no longer has meaning today. In a society where we no longer encounter the most extreme forms of exclusion and terror, where the respect for human rights is the object of universal agreement, their incantatory invocation amounts to legitimating the established order, celebrating our Western democracy as the best of all possible worlds: the exaltation of Man has become its supplemental soul, the spiritual aroma of this world without spirit. In truth, the current hegemony of humanism is a disaster for thought because it prohibits questioning this enigma that we are. Is it indeed all that certain that I am "a human," that such massive obviousness suffices to define me? Descartes had already encountered this question, and it seems indecent to raise it again in our day; I admire the serene audacity with which he dismissed the naive certainty of humanism: "What then did I formerly think I was? A man. But what is a man? Shall I say 'a rational animal'? No; for then I should have to inquire what an animal is, what rationality is, and in this way one question would lead me down the slope to other harder ones, and I do not now have the time to waste on subtleties of this kind" (M II, 6:17).

The recourse to the concept of the human rests on a double mistake: (a) it tries to determine a simple essence—that of my ego—on the basis of a composite and complex notion; and moreover, (b) it claims to define a singular existence on the basis of the universal concept of humankind. Yet as soon as it tries to derive the singular from the universal, it does a violence to its singularity. For the certainty of belonging to the human species is mundane: it supposes existence with others in a common world into which the ego is thrown, and where its singularity is already lost. "To be radical," the young Marx said, "is to take a thing by its roots, and the root for Man is Man itself." But Man is only an abstraction, a universal genre composed of a multitude of living individuals, innumerable singular egos, for each one of which its "root"—its origin and its truth—is the ego itself. By submitting the ego to the authority of Man, humanism disfigures it, not only because it crushes its singularity under a common notion uniformly abstractly valid for everyone but also because it betrays its indetermination by imposing on it a particular conception of Man and of what is properly "human." Today, the most wide-ranging understanding of the human being identifies it with the *victim*, the suffering, oppressed, humiliated individual whose rights must be defended.[13] Such is, for example, Levinas's thesis: the face of the other is the face of my victim whom I have wronged by the mere fact that I exist; the other "is the weak, even though I am the strong; it is the widow and the orphan." The humanity of the human will be defined by its situation as persecuted or hostage, that is, by its passivity, its insurmountable impotence, its nonfreedom. It is indeed in this way that the Cartesian ego first appeared to us: threatened with death, persecuted by an Other that seeks to destroy it. But the situation is immediately reversed, and we have discovered that this threat is what calls it to existence, and that its existence is inseparable from its resistance to the Great Persecutor. But what the victimism of this humanism refuses to admit is this paradoxical experience in which the passivity of the persecuted is reversed in an act of resistance, where the ego undergoes the ordeal of its freedom, a freedom more sovereign that any power in the world.

If am not human, what then am I? Would I be a subject? We remember from the Heideggerian indictment that Descartes inaugurates the epoch in which the human Subject is posited as the supreme principal of beings, which aggravates to the extreme our forgetfulness of Being. For Heidegger, the "I think" has the sense of a "I represent (to) myself." It means that the ego is represented with absolute certainty as the "unshakeable ground" of itself and of beings. For the ego cogito revisited by Heidegger has all the characteristics of a conquering despot: its *cogitatio* is a *co-agitatio*, a violent "agitation" that goes on the assault against beings in order to take hold of and master them in the unity of its representation. In this nihilistic will to power unleashed on the world in 1940, Heidegger recognized the characteristic traits of the Cartesian cogito. It is difficult to be so profoundly wrong about an author. Let us return to the letter of Descartes' text, instead of abstractly reconstituting his thought; let us go back to the first beginning in which the ego is revealed to itself. We will immediately discover that the "I think" is not an "I represent": at the moment of its birth, the ego does not yet represent anything at all, cannot arrange anything in front of itself to take hold of. In this obscure night of doubt where the entire world is out of play, there is nothing outside of it at its disposal to do with as it pleases; it is so stuck to itself that it is simply unable to represent itself, to be separated from itself in order to reflect on itself, to *re-present* itself in its reflection. Heidegger confused the transcendence of the ego-in-the-world and the immanence of the originary ego. Such an ego—the result of radical doubt, surrounded and threatened by a deceiving power—has nothing in common with a self-certain Subject assured of its domination over beings. It does not assault the world in order to submit it to its influence but is instead the target of a mortal threat. Heidegger confuses here the persecuted and the persecutor, the freedom of the ego—its impoverished and fragile resistance—and the omnipotence of a Master or Guide. His position appears to be symmetrical with Levinas's: whereas the German thinker sees in the Cartesian ego only a conquering will to power, the author of *Otherwise Than Being* celebrates the absolute passivity of a "self-cornered" ego, incapable of turning itself back against its persecutor. Both of them are mistaken about the ego, about the paradox of its birth: they misconstrued the indissociable unity of its passivity and its resistance, wherein the distress of the persecuted is inverted into affirmation.

Heidegger commits another mistake when he identifies the ego with a "subject," understood in its initial metaphysical sense as *sub-iectum*, the subjacent Ground or permanent and stable support. Insofar as the ego is itself this always-present Ground, it would be capable of grounding itself and of durably grounding all things, and this power is what allows it to claim influence over the world. This thesis decides the final meaning of the Cartesian ego: if it proves correct that the ego does not benefit from permanent presence, that I am unable to persist by myself in time, then I will never be able to ground myself by myself. I will never be Subject. Our habit of considering ourselves as human "subjects" confronting a world of "objects" is so strong that we do not perceive that this conception is recent: it has been at most two centuries—starting with Kant—since the subject-object binary has been massively imposed, allowing us to think about our relation to the world. Those who condemn Descartes for having "grounded the modern metaphysics of the Subject" forget just one thing: our philosopher never assimilated the ego to a "subject" and never characterized it as such. However, even if the word "subject" is not there, it could be that another notion allows Descartes to conceive of the ego as a metaphysical subject. That term is "substance," for it also names what "stands below" (*sub-stans*), a stable and persistent support. By defining the ego as a "thinking substance," Descartes would have erected it as Subject, and the disaster of modern times would have already begun. But is this so certain? "By *substance* we can understand nothing other than a thing which exists in such a way as to depend on no other thing for its existence,"[14] hence a thing that exists by itself in an absolute manner. This is not the case with any thing in the world, above all not with corporeal reality (which he also wrongly considered a substance). Through the proof of doubt, I discover an absolute existence: mine. I am thus the sole and unique substance: it is a matter of notions that "I do not see why they cannot originate from myself" (M III, 20:30), and if understood in this way, only the ego duly merits this title. But if it is true that *I exist* by myself, it does not mean that I also have the power *to subsist*, to persist in time: I could be substance (in the precise sense that Descartes gives to this term) without being subject. We must wonder (a) what this strange "substantiality" that Descartes attributes to the ego signifies and how it is possible to accede to existence without the need for any Other and (b) whether I have the power to endure by myself, to maintain my identity across time without any foreign help. If I were substance in this second sense, I would also be subject, and the Cartesian ego would indeed be the prefiguration of the Absolute Subject that was going to go on the assault against the Earth. And if not, if I were not capable of subjectifying myself, what would follow? How would I be able to tie up the unity of my life—and simply to remain the same from one moment to the next? If I am neither Subject nor Human, what then am I? And how can I tear away these masks that dissimulate my true face?

I Am the Path, the Truth, the Life

So many questions lead me back to the enigmatic truth that I am. How am I able to determine an absolutely singular truth that would be true only for me? Let us return once again to Descartes' experience, to that initial moment when universal illusion is reversed into affirmation. "If I err, I am": the truth of the ego cogito is revealed in its relation to an originary nontruth, which is not exterior to it, not opposed to it as the true is normally opposed to the false. The countertruth of the deceiver and the truth of the ego seem to be indissociable from one another—if the Other did not deceive me, I would not be—and I know now that this countertruth is not foreign to me and that the deceiving Other will finally be revealed as a hidden face of myself. Thus, the ego attains its truth in an endless combat against an illusion rooted in the deepest depths of itself. Descartes will try to ground the criteria of truth on a "general rule" of clarity and distinction—"whatever I perceive very clearly and distinctly is true" (M III, 2:24)—but nothing proves that this rule suits the truth of the ego: first, because it is a matter of *a truth of exception*, that cannot submit to any general norm; but also because this Cartesian rule skips over the *clair-obscur*, the originary link of the truth to the countertruth, and thus does not take account of the conflict that puts them at odds *in* the very revelation of the truth. This truth is not exteriorly opposed to the countertruth but is linked to it in an essential unity and arises only by tearing itself away from the veiling of an initial countertruth—and as such a truth, it can no longer be defined as the evidence of a clear and distinct idea. We must instead understand it in the way Heidegger does: as unveiling, a disclosure, *a-lèthéia*. It does not let itself be enclosed in a theoretical statement: it *gives itself* in a different manner each time, as an always singular event; and in giving itself, it reveals each time the *Lèthè*, the obscure Ground of veiling and forgetfulness from which it has torn itself away. One would completely betray the Cartesian method were one to assimilate this truth to a representational certainty, to this representation that I create of myself by reflecting on myself. This misunderstanding is what impedes Heidegger from perceiving the proximity between his own conception of the truth as *alèthéia* and the truth of the Cartesian ego. It is a still enigmatic truth that can no longer be imagined as the adequation of a subject and an object or of a subject with itself. It is a precarious truth, deprived of the assurance that representational adequation provides and that paradoxically coincides with the uncertainty of a nonknowledge: it could be that I am never able to know truly who I am. And yet this truth is capable of resisting the highest power of nontruth, the universal doubt into which all the evidence of the world sinks.

What is revealed in the discovery that *I am*? Nothing other than myself, the singular truth of my existence. The term "unveiling" must not lead us to error: there is nothing hidden behind the veil of illusion awaiting unveiling. Nothing precedes my revelation—no Other, *nor any other ego*, no preexisting entity with which I may or may not coincide. It is myself that is revealed to me, and I exist only in the moment of this revelation. I am thus not the *condition* of revelation of a truth different from me, as Heideggerian Dasein is the condition of the disclosure of the truth of Being. When I am revealed to myself, nothing yet exists outside of me: there is no other truth than me; *I am the truth*.[15] According to Spinoza's famous formulation, "verum est index sui": the truth is its own criterion. I assert that this is true, and indeed even more so for the truth of the ego, "verum index mei": the truth that I am is the "index" of my existence, its source and its law. By thus indicating my truth to myself, by revealing it to me, I reveal *myself* to myself: I am both the agent and the outcome of revelation, what reveals and what is revealed, the condition of truth and the truth itself. It is in this sense that the ego can be called "substance," because it is at the origin of itself, because it has no need for anything else to be revealed and thus to exist. Where does such a revelation lead me? Neither toward Being nor toward the Other nor toward God—only toward myself. It is the path that leads me back to me, and it is me who is this path: I am the truth, *and I am the path*.

This first of all means that no exterior criteria, no preexisting condition, can decide the truth of my ego (or its nontruth). For this truth is *index sui*: it is revealed by itself and has no need for anything else in order to be true. In being self-revealed, I do not discover an ego that would already exist, as a subject "unaware" of its own existence: I did not exist before revealing myself, and this means that my revelation *makes me exist*, that it creates me *ex nihilo*. By tearing myself away from nothingness, I engender myself, I give life to myself, I give birth to myself in a mad genesis in which I am both "my son, my father, my mother, and me."[16] The self-revelation of the ego thus coincides with its self-givenness, with the strange power to be given to itself. Heidegger conferred this power on Dasein, but he immediately reduced it to the sole power of calling oneself, without perceiving that, by calling itself, the always-mine existing being *gives itself* originarily to itself, freely accords itself its own existence. How are we to understand this self-revelation that is also a self-givenness? The theoreticians of language acts define such statements as *performatives* ("the session is over," "I take you as my spouse," etc.) that do not describe a preexisting exterior reality but rather produce it in the very act of stating it. One could well characterize the Cartesian *ego sum* as a performative[17]— *if* this did not risk assimilating it to a linguistic operation or reducing it to the utterance it states by arbitrarily excluding the possibility of an ego that would not limit itself to the act of saying "I." By affirming that the statement "I am" is true "whenever it is put forward by me or conceived in my mind" (M II, 4:17), Descartes let the possibility that the truth of the ego is not identified with a linguistic utterance be glimpsed. Some years later, in his incomplete manuscript, "The Search for Truth," he would even go as far as to call all speech and all interlocution into doubt.[18] If we want to remain faithful to the radicality of his method, we will not take the royal road of contemporary thought, which reduces the *ego sum* to a statement, a signifier, or a language act. The linguistic turn of the twentieth century distracts us from what is essential: because the linguistic approach is centered on the "subject of the statement," on the "receiver" of phrases or of the act of saying "I" in ordinary language, it always tends to make the *I* into a *universal* agency that is indifferently valid for all speaking subjects. By being placed on this terrain, in the anonymous generality of the signifier or of language games, then what is unique about the *I am* is necessarily missing. Thus the pronoun *I* is only ever a *pro-noun*, a borrowed name, a sort of pseudonym that dissimulates the truth of the ego.[19] "*I tell you* that I am dead," said Valdemar, perhaps suggesting that in the moment when the ego passes to the plane of language, its living singularity is lost: as soon as I say "I," I am no longer what I say I am; I am already dead. It is by placing out of play all relation to language that we will be able to approach the singular ego, the *tacit ego* whose silent self-givenness subtends all expression and enunciation.

It is best to call this pure irruption starting from nothing—that is, that which arises without anything announcing it—an *event*. This term lets the coming of what happens be heard, the sudden and forced entry of the absolutely new. It qualifies what comes forth as singular, as an exception, each time different (an event is never repeated), passing (no event perdures), without cause and without goal (like the rose, the event is *without a why*; it "blooms because it blooms"). It underscores its unforeseeable and in a sense *impossible* character—because a true event always transgresses the limits of the possibility, comes forth as *the possibility of the impossible*: nothing seems able to escape the influence of the deceiver—no truth, no existence—and yet, here I am. Since Deleuze, French philosophy has placed the theme of the event at the fore, almost always presenting an impersonal "it happens," an anonymous coming that precedes all subjectivity. It is because one is centered on the events *of the world*, those affecting the ego from the outside, fashioning it, exalting it, or breaking it. But none of these events could happen without a recipient capable of welcoming it, recognizing it as an event, keeping it in memory—and yet also being turned away from and forgetting it. No event could take place without a witness, and it could not affect the witness if the witness were not already given to itself as an ego capable of welcoming the event: there would be no event without the archi-event that I am.

What is the meaning, the "content," of such a revelation? It teaches us nothing about exterior phenomena and does not allow us to ground any objective science or justify any action in the world: it reveals nothing other than myself to me. At the end of the second *Meditation*, I exist alone, without a world, without a body, without any truth other than myself. Does this mean that I am closed in on myself, blind, deaf, and dumb to all that exceeds my pure certitude of existing? Certainly not. "For example, I am now seeing light, hearing a noise, feeling heat. But I am asleep, so all this is false. Yet I certainly *seem* to see [*videor videre*], to hear, and to be warmed. This cannot be false; what is called 'having a sensory perception' is strictly just this, and in this restricted sense of the term it is simply thinking" (M II, 9:19). This is a capital passage in which is discovered the ultimate meaning of the Cartesian truth, the essence of revelation, that is, *sensing*. What is revoked by doubt is never a perceptual or intellectual content but instead is the way that this content has of giving itself to me: in a *videre*, in the vision of a thing presented as a reality existing outside of me. What resists doubt is given in another way: in a *videor*, in the experience of sensing oneself seeing, hearing, or touching.[20] It is this originary sensing that Descartes here identifies with thought, and we finally understand what *cogito* means: the Cartesian "I think" is not an "I reason" or an "I represent" but an "I sense." And this sensing is *always true*: even if an Other deceives me, even if all things outside of me are merely illusory appearances, I cannot doubt that I think of these things, that I sense them; and whatever they appear to me to be is what they are in truth. On this plane, there is no longer any separation between "appearing" and "being": in pure sensing, *what gives itself coincides with what is given.*

One is mistaken when one characterizes the Cartesian ego as an isolated monad or an autistic consciousness folded in on itself. For the truth of its existence is extended to all that it can think—and its thinking opens unto the light of the world, listens to its rumor, caresses and savors the flesh of things, but by experiencing these mundane realities as so many of the immanent experiences in which it senses itself seeing, hearing, touching. "Cartesian doubt" is thus not really doubt, that is, a *negation* of the world, but rather a suspension or putting out of play of its real existence: far from denying or negating the world, this suspension allows it on the contrary to be manifested, to be unfolded in appearance. An unforeseen difficulty arises here: I experience this primordial Sensing even though my body is out of play. I am here confronted with the mystery of touching without hands, of a vision that senses itself seeing without light and without eyes. What can we name this sensing prior to the world and prior to the body? What is the domain of this primordial experience, the site of the "je suis"? Let us come back once again to the first emergence of my ego: I was experiencing an adverse power that tried to annihilate me and made the threat of death weigh on me. If there is an indissociable link between the countertruth and death, we must also recognize inversely that the truth of the ego is linked with life, that it carries the promise of a life more powerful than the forces of illusion and death. The statement "I am, I exist," means "I sense," that is, *I live, I am living*—because only a living being can sense and be sensed. By coming to itself, the ego comes to life, in the marvel of a birth that nothing could have preceded. One can certainly designate it as a cogito but only on the condition of no longer reducing its "thought" to a purely intellectual activity or abstract reflection: "cogito" is one of the names for life, for the feeling that I experience when I sense myself living or when I am affected by my life. This is indeed how Descartes understood it: when he defined the ego as a "thing that thinks," it was to distinguish it from the "the whole mechanical structure of limbs *which can be seen in a corpse,* and which I call a body" (M II, 6:17; my emphasis). A thing that thinks means for Descartes a living thing, entirely distinct from the dead mechanics of a body (and of course, as such, it is no longer a "thing" in the ordinary sense of the word). This dualism of soul and body, for which he has so often been reproached, consists above all in affirming the irreducible duality of the living and the dead. I am, I exist, I think, I sense, I live—these terms are all perfectly synonymous, and they all proclaim the same truth, a truth valid only for a living ego, which is the truth *of* its life—the life itself as site of truth. The self-revelation of the *ego sum* is therefore manifested in an experience that is in every case singular, the originary unity of truth and life, and each of us—we who say "I"—would have the right to state in his or her own name this phrase: "I am the path, the truth, life."

We can call this ego that raises itself into life without anything else intervening—no cause or no anterior event—and determines it to exist "free"; and we know that Descartes made freedom an essential trait of the ego. I do not intend to confront the Cartesian doctrine of freedom: to understand what my freedom is, it is better once again to question the event of my arrival, to find the trace of my birth. The freedom of the ego is rooted in this archi-event, this originary resistance whereby I manage to outwit the ruse of the deceiver: "But whoever turns out to have created us, and however powerful and however deceitful he may be, in the meantime we nonetheless experience within us the kind of freedom which enables us always to refrain from believing things that are not completely certain and thoroughly examined."[21] The affirmation of my freedom is presented here as an act of resistance, an act of defiance marking the stopping point of the evil jouissance of the other. It is identified with the action of doubting, with the capacity that delivers me from my alienation to the idols of the world. Understood in this way, the ego's freedom is indissociable from its truth, from the event of truth—so singular, as fleeting as any event—in which I am revealed and am given to myself. And yet, the ego's freedom is so radical that it could *also* decide *against* the truth and deliberately choose falsity and evil. After having hesitated for a long time, Descartes finally recognized the possibility of a *freedom for evil*, "this positive power which we have of following the worst although we see the better."[22] The fact that the ego possesses this power or that I have the capacity to decide for truth and for nontruth is not at all astonishing, since I am my own deceiver: I am the truth and the path, and I am also the focus of this illusion that blinds me. But how can I get so lost, even when I have put out of play these fictions that mislead me and even when I am revealed to myself in a primordial sensing whereby everything given to me is true? We touch here on one of the most difficult questions, the possibility of a self-illusion of the ego in the very movement of its self-revelation. Such an illusion can no longer concern the phenomena I perceive in the world—even if this fire burning me exists only in my dream, I truly sense the burning—but rather only the ego itself. How can I deceive myself? In at least two ways: (a) by mistaking myself for another, mistaking a part of myself as a foreign phenomenon; and (b) by mistaking another for me. The first case refers to the projection constituting the fiction of an Evil Genius, even though this deceiving Other is *in me*, originating in an unknown part of my ego. Descartes briefly evokes the second case by alerting us to the danger of "taking something else to be this 'I,'" literally placing it "in place of my ego" [*in locum mei*] (M II, 5:16)—without questioning the status of this alterity, capable (but by what magic?) of being introduced in me in order to dislodge me from myself while passing itself off as me. This is indeed what happens to me when I discover that I am identified with a "one," an anonymous Other that speaks through me when I think I am speaking in my own name. In the two cases, the border between the ego and the Other has been transgressed, and these two apparently opposed illusions presuppose an effacement of the egological difference. There is a third mode of illusion, a confusion between the immanent ego and the mundane ego alimenting narcissistic individualism, the naive certainty that the ego exhibited in the world is my sole and true ego. But this third case leads back to the second, since it is in fact an "other," a pseudo-ego alienated from others, that I mistake for me. In each case, the difference between the ego and the other has been forgotten. This forgetting dissimulates me to myself, leading me to represent myself as a human individual among others, a member of a great Whole, figuring me on the basis of the world and of mundane realities, like a "thing" that persists by itself—a subject.

The Moment of My Failure

Each of us is certain of being a subject endowed with an individual indivisible identity throughout life; each of us always naively believes this. Nothing is more common and "obvious" than such certainty—and yet Descartes will call it into question. We too often forget that at the moment of stating the "I am," he puts a restriction on it: this statement is "necessarily true" but only "each time that I say or conceive it." Does this mean that if I were to stop saying or thinking that I exist, the affirmation of my existence would cease to be true? This is a strange and worrisome eventuality that can no longer be avoided: "I am, I exist—that is certain. But for how long? For as long as I am thinking. For it could be that were I totally to cease from thinking, I should totally cease to exist" (M II, 7:18). I do not precede the event of my revelation and I would not survive it, *for I am this event* and nothing else: I am as passing and ephemeral as it is, I arise when it happens and I fade away with it. But if my ego disappears, how is it able to reappear each time? How can the event that I am be repeated once again and innumerable times? What poses a problem here is the *quoties*, the "each time" of the ego, its distributive, plural, and discontinuous character that seems to make it splinter into a multitude of successive acts of thought, each distinct from one another. Does this mean that my ego would endlessly disappear and be reborn? If that were the case, how could I be certain that it is indeed me, the same and unique me, that reappears each time? This question is found again in Hume, Kant, and all those who would try to contest the subjective unity and continuity of the ego. The question would not arise if the continuity of my existence were given to me at the outset as a necessary property of my ego, that is, if I were endowed with a substantial permanence, if I were a subject. In the sole and same movement, all the phases of my life, all the appearances of my ego, would be fused together in one unique melody without pauses or rests. This certainty of possessing a subjective identity, of being able to endure by itself in time, is an overwhelming obviousness that Descartes rejects. He claims that "a lifetime can be divided into countless parts, each completely independent of the others."[23] This is a highly paradoxical thesis, and no other thinker has supported it in this form. For Descartes, it is convenient to distinguish "time considered abstractly," where moments continuously follow upon one another, "from the time or the duration of the thing itself."[24] If "abstract" time (that is, the time of the world, the objective time of science) is characterized by its seamless continuity, "my lifetime," in contrast, is presented as a staccato, discontinuous succession of moments disjoined from one another, as if the past had no connection to the present. This unlinking or disjunction of the moments of my life therefore implies that I "may cease to be at any moment of my duration" and thus seems to condemn me to radical *precariousness*.

What are we to call this possibility of no longer being, this immi-nence of my disappearance or death [*disparition*]? For a living being, to stop existing amounts to dying. There would thus be a death immanent to life, a syncope, an eclipse of the ego similar to the "self-death" invoked by Proust, a death that "is perpetrated unbeknownst to us, against our will, every day." Like a blinking quasi-subject, the ego continuously dies in or-der to be reborn in a constant series of appearances and disappearances, whose scansion gives rhythm to the ego's life. This is not the first time we encounter the imminent possibility of my death: it was already present in this threat of annihilation that the deceiver made weigh on my existence, and there is an essential link between this death threat and the temporal precarity of the ego. The always present risk of my disappearance or death testifies that the threat has not been overcome—except for always too brief a time when I affirm myself as ego by resisting the powers of the coun-tertruth. For my certainty of existing only *quamdiu cogito*, "as long as I think," finds its meaning in another *quamdiu*, in the grace period that I have won through my resistance to the Great Deceiver: "In that case I too un-doubtedly exist, if he is deceiving me; and let him deceive me as much as he can, he will never bring it about that I am nothing so long as I think that I am something" (M II, 4:17). With this revelation *that I am*, a decisive vic-tory has been won—but it is also limited and provisory, since the focus of the menace has not been destroyed. The deceiver continues to reign outside of me and, in a sense, in me. I am, I exist: that is absolutely certain but only as a pure solitary thought, without body, world, or others—and without any duration. I exist only *in the moment*, carried by the dazzling intuition of the *ego sum*. I will have to reconquer myself at every moment, always af-firm myself anew in an incessant battle against the adverse power that tries to negate me, but without being able to link this new affirmation of myself to any of those affirmations preceding or following me—that is, without being able to be unfolded in or across time. Incapable of annihilating me, the deceiver nevertheless succeeds in dissociating me from myself, frag-menting me, dispersing me to infinity, each enclosing me in a point of time separated from all others.[25] But we know already that the Evil Genius is nothing other than myself: this temporal disjunction must therefore find its source in the very life of the ego. It is not the discontinuity of time that makes the ego vacillate; instead it is the ego's own deficiency that must be at the origin of the discontinuity of time.

Descartes characterizes this deficiency as a weakness, a lack of force or power: if the moments of our life are not linked together in a continuous and necessary manner, it is because "we easily understand that there is *no power in us* enabling us to keep ourselves in existence."[26] This will lead Descartes to appeal to an all-powerful and perfect Other, who alone can supplement this deficiency. As long as this Other's existence has not been demonstrated, the ego's life will remain a prisoner of the moment, fugitive and incapable of grounding any knowledge or *itself.* Begun as a search for a "fixed and assured point," an absolute foundation, the second *Meditation* ends with a vertiginous collapse. Neither the possibility that the ego is only an illusion nor the indistinction between dream and reality (which is to say also the threat of madness) has been conjured away. What is lacking from these phantasms, these vain simulacra haunting our dreams, is the necessary and continuous linkage of our perceptions: "If, while I am awake, anyone were suddenly to appear to me and then disappear immediately, as happens in sleep, so that I could not see where he had come from or where he had gone to, it would not be unreasonable for me to judge that he was a ghost [*phantasma*], or a vision created in my brain, rather than a real man" (M VI, 42:61–62). We now discover that this temporal continuity and necessary linkage are missing *from the ego itself.* How are we to distinguish this ego, so sure of its own evidence, from a phantasm or a specter? I, René Descartes, believed myself to be awakened from my dream in discovering the absolute truth of the ego. I now perceive that I have perhaps not stopped dreaming, that I am similar to those prisoners who dread waking up and conspire with their dreams in order to continue sleeping. How can I escape from this spectral existence? By triumphing over the deceiver, who at every moment dissociates me from myself: either I find a force in myself sufficient to prevail over this deceiving power, or another force comes to my rescue. The first hypothesis seems absurd, because the ego is defined precisely by its deficiency, its impotence to endure by itself. We will have to go in search of an Other more powerful than me who could overcome the discontinuity of time; the third *Meditation* is oriented in this direction. After having claimed that my lifetime is divided into innumerable moments separated from one another, and after concluding from this that "it does not follow from the fact that I existed a little while ago that I must exist now," Descartes adds this: "unless there is some cause which as it were creates me afresh at this moment—that is, which preserves me. For it is quite clear to anyone who attentively considers the nature of time that the same power and action are needed to preserve anything at each individual moment of its duration as would be required to create that thing anew if it were not yet in existence" (M III, 33–34).

One of most admirable Cartesian inventions is announced, the theory of *continuous creation*, that is, the paradox of a perpetual creation, that would for us coincide with a simple preservation. It is therefore not really a matter of a "creation" in the usual sense of the term, since it is not preceded by any destruction and seems only to repeat or preserve what already exists. But neither is it a pure preservation: it is not limited to repeating the identical, precisely because *it creates*; it is completed in every instance as if it were the first time. By always beginning anew, it *re*-commences, reproduces the preceding creation without coinciding with it: it performs it, is identical *and* different, just as a returning musical motif is both same and wholly different each time it returns throughout the melody. Always different, each time new, creation remains the same—it follows on itself and continuously endures, maintaining itself through the rupturing of moments and maintaining what it (re)creates, the motif of its creation. In creating the motif, it endlessly continues it, that is, preserves it as what it was, so well that creation and conservation fuse in the unity of the moment. The key to the paradox is found in the distinction between the two modes of temporality, between the time of the ego and the time of the world. In the "my lifetime," in the immanent temporality of creation, of the event, of freedom, each new creation takes everything up again *ex nihilo*, and temporality is indeed presented as a discontinuous succession of free creative moments.[27] It is only in the time of the world that the series of successive creation appears as a continuous preservation. The continuity of my existence is grounded on this plane; I am maintained and I endure in time, I exist as subject, whereas on the other plane the scansion of my originary temporality remains absolutely discontinuous. For the persistence of my subjective identity does not efface the always new event from which the *I am* arises, and as its radical condition, the time of my mundane existence refers to the instant of my birth, to the time of my freedom.

It is indeed a matter of birth here, or rather an incessant rebirth, *an eternal return*. As long as I only considered the disjunction of moments and my impotence to overcome it, the threat of an imminent death seemed to weigh on me at every moment. Now that I discover that this discontinuity harmonizes with a continual re-creation, the possibility of dying passes to a second plane, and the emphasis is placed on the inverse possibility of a new birth. As Descartes strongly underscores, no preliminary destruction precedes each new creation.[28] This is because there can be no dead time from one instant to another, no interval of nothingness: the always renewed flux of creation does not leave room for any reflux, for total disappearance, and so the possibility of my death becomes only the inverse of my birth, the menacing horizon from which it is each time detached, the *nihil* of creation *ex nihilo*. When the ego transgresses the cloture of the moment, when it is unfolded in the whole duration of its life by always being reborn, the being-in-birth becomes the ultimate horizon of existence. Descartes here rejoins the heroic line of thinkers who, from Plato's *Parmenides* to Nietzsche's *Zarathustra*, are confronted with the enigma of the Moment.[29] Since each present moment is linked continuously to all other moments, the theory of continuous creation finally gives me what I had been lacking, the force to endure, to fill up the breach of time, without necessarily making recourse to an Other. For this, it would be sufficient to allow that the moments of my life are intertwined in a purely immanent manner, without any foreign cause, and to admit that it is the ego's life itself that is created and continually recreated. It would be sufficient to identify what Descartes calls "creation" with the self-revelation that gives the *ego sum* to itself, this marvel of a birth without progenitors, of a creation without a transcendent Creator. But Descartes could not resolve himself to this: instead of considering continuous creation as an irruption of the ego *from nothing*, he assigned it to this foreign Cause that he calls "God." From then on the meaning of this theory is entirely inverted. Reduced to total impotence, the ego now need only submit itself without reserve; my life depends entirely on this Other-Cause, since it is what preserves me in existence by constantly recreating me, and only its good will allow me to continue to exist at every moment. The nightmare will not have ended: the threat of death and the precariousness of the ego are not always conjured away, and they even impose themselves more strongly despite the new perspective of continual creation, *or perhaps because of it*. For it is the continuity of my (re) creation by God that grounds the continual possibility of my annihilation, and this God who gives me life could indeed also destroy me—which is exactly what is declared in the "Synopsis" of the *Meditations*: "all substances,

or things which must be created by God in order to exist, are by their nature incorruptible and cannot ever cease to exist unless they are reduced to
nothingness by God's denying his concurrence to them."[30] Who then is
Descartes' God, such that he lets the shadow of nothingness and death be
glimpsed anew, beyond the reassuring attributes of his perfection and infinite goodness? Such a question concerns not only theologians and historians of philosophy. If the ego is not first of all subject but instead must
become one, can this happen *by itself*, by continuously recreating itself? Or
must it appeal to the support of an Other to break through the cloture of
the Moment? How is it able to make itself a subject [*se subjectiver*] without
immediately being subjected [*s'assujettir*] by the Other? These are the questions that Descartes legates to us who, in the solitude of our lives, groping
our way in the dark, try ourselves to open up for a path toward ourselves
and toward the Other.

Larvatus pro Deo: Descartes' Legacy

> Like an actor wearing a mask, I come forward, masked [*larvatus prodeo*], on the
> stage of the world.
>
> —Descartes, *Pensées privées*

We too often represent the trajectory of the *Meditations* as a victorious march forward, where, after having firmly grounded the certainty of
the ego, Descartes turns his attention to other "objects"—God, then material things—in order to demonstrate their existence and complete his
system. [31] There is nothing to this. Far from establishing the ego as an
unshakeable foundation, even further from erecting it as Subject, the second *Meditation* confronts us on the contrary with the ego's collapse, and
the failure of this foundation obliges Descartes to look elsewhere for another, more powerful, and more stable foundation than the ego, in an
Other which may finally be Subject. What can the name of this Other be?
When, in the third *Meditation*, we place all of our ideas under review, we
discover that one of them possesses such a high degree of objective reality
that the ego could not have caused it by itself. Descartes concludes from
this that "I am not alone in the world, but that some other thing which
is the cause of this idea also exists" (M III, 18:29). This *something else*, this

Other-Cause is presented first as an anonymous alterity, but this reserve will quickly be abandoned: since the idea in question is the idea of the infinite and since the name "God" designates an "infinite substance," the anonymity will be lifted, and we will have "to conclude necessarily from all that I have said before that God exists." We witness here a *forcing of the name,* wherein the initial indetermination is covered over by an overwhelming designation. "God" becomes the *surname* of the Other, and by this term I understand both the most eminent Name—the overarching Name, *sur-Nom*—and a sort of pseudonym or sobriquet imposed on him. What makes this sur-nomination possible is the powerful entry of a theology that attributes infinitude, perfection, omnipotence, absolute goodness to this God and that is engaged in proving that He exists (but then again, what is so divine about a "God" whose existence could be demonstrated by human reason?). With this theological turn, all the discoveries of the second *Meditation* will be negated, and above all the primacy of the ego, its privilege of being the first and the only absolute truth. The idea of God will be presented as the truest of all my ideas, the unique source of all certainty and all truth, and we will understand then that "my perception of the infinite, that is God, is in some way prior to my perception of the finite, that is myself" (M III, 23:31)—more ancient in me and more true than me. Destitute, relegated to a subaltern rank, the ego will now only be submitted to the Other's omnipotence, and the third *Meditation* finishes with a fascinated contemplation of the divine majesty, inviting us to welcome, admire, and adore it. It is indeed a matter of a turn here, a total reversal of perspective. Some readers (and not bad ones: Levinas, Lacan, and Guéroult, among others) believed to see in this turn a decisive progress, the moment when Descartes overcomes the "ontological narcissism" of the solipsistic cogito. For my part, I see a disaster that ruins his adventure, a disaster to which his most fecund advances will be abandoned.[32] It is probably always like this every time we try to figure the Other or give it a name, because we simply project our own characteristics and our own impoverished words on that which remains without a face; only a fabulous reflection of ourselves enchants us, which we never stop admiring and adoring.

In what way could Descartes' turnaround still interest us, given that he abandons the primacy of the ego to the benefit of the God of the theologians? We have given up trying to prove the existence of such a "God" a

long time ago, and yet the question of the relation of the ego to the
Other—the question of knowing whether the ego is or is not an originary
phenomenon, whether it needs any Other in order to be ego, or whether it
depends on the Other, letting itself be entirely determined by it—is still
and always will be our question. After having announced the death of
God, our epoch has worked desperately to give new names to the Other,
but these modern surnames have been ever more quickly exhausted. These
nominations also imply a forcing of the Other, and every time these figures have won their supremacy by subordinating individuals and their
singular ego, by successfully captivating their desire and enslaving their
freedom. This subjection of the ego to the transcendence of an Other posited as its Master, its Cause, its Law, is what defines our servitude; the
critique of this alienation must once again become one of the major tasks
of philosophy. By discovering that the ego is an originary phenomenon,
that I am myself before any Other is, Descartes makes a radical critique of
the ego's alienation possible. The disaster of the third *Meditation* shows,
however, that it is very difficult for this critique to stand and that a perhaps irresistible tendency—all the power of an Evil Genius—presses each
individual to abdicate his singularity and to submit to the dominating
figures of the Other. His "divided" philosophy at least has the merit of
indicating two possibilities to us, the path of resistance and the path of
submission, as well as the exact point at which these two paths bifurcate.
What our French cavalier was undoubtedly missing was the audacity to
sustain the privilege of the ego up to the end, this mad audacity that,
three centuries earlier, had led an old master to claim: "In my birth all
things were born and I was the cause of myself and of all things; and if
I would have wished it, I would not be nor would all other things be. And
if I did not exist, 'God' would also not exist. That God is 'God,' of that I
am a cause; if I did not exist, God too would not be 'God.' "[33] It is obviously not a question of playing Eckhart against Descartes, but only of
indicating this point of excess from which Descartes had in the end di-
verged, this *Durchbruch* or breakthrough whereby "I am above all the
creatures, and I am neither God nor creature, but I am what I was."

Is there any sense in playing Descartes against Descartes? Is it possible to save his thought from this theological drift? In truth, was he not
satisfied with sur-naming the Other by imposing on it the name "God":
Descartes also claims to determine the attributes of this God, and above

all, it is God's truthfulness, his infinite goodness, that prohibits us from believing that he may deceive us. At the moment when the first *Meditation* encountered the figure of a Deceptive God, it immediately rejected it: it would be better to deny the existence of God totally than to admit this, and the fiction of the Evil Genius specifically allowed Descartes to uphold the possibility of a radical countertruth without God being implicated. But as it happens, Descartes lets the disquieting grimace of a *Deus deceptor* be glimpsed beneath the reassuring mask of the Evil Genius, and he does not hesitate to imagine the possibility that universal illusion finds its source in God's *pleasure*, in the horrible joy he would take in misleading us.[34] The name of "God" is charged with a strange ambiguity here, since it designates both a master of deception and the "sovereign source of truth," both a persecutor who plays with and seeks to destroy me and He who brings me to life and sustains me in existence. Let us risk a hypothesis: this equivocation affecting the concept of "God" would be rooted in the thing itself, in the phenomenon that this name designates. It would be the clue to *a cleavage of the Other* in its relation to the truth, of an originary division of the Other that Descartes would have recognized, while immediately denying and dissimulating it. By calling both the great Deceiver and the guarantor of life by the same name, "God," Descartes came close to the enigmatic point where the truth is linked to the nontruth and where they become nearly indiscernible. What will have allowed him to take such a risk is his very audacious conception of a God as "the creator of the eternal truths." This God who has freely decreed that $2 + 3 = 5$ could have decided it otherwise. Since he is not subject to a truth that he himself has established, God could have made this truth be not true, so that I would be wrong every time I did this addition. This amounts to affirming the possibility of *a nontruth of truth* as the consequence of the freedom and omnipotence of God. A focus of illusion thus persists in the Other, and nothing can guarantee that such a God does not deceive me. This God is, however, also characterized by his absolute perfection: he would be unable to lie, since "all fraud and deception depend on some defect" (M III, 40:35). This lets a sort of conflict subsist in God, a tension between his freedom and his goodness, his omnipotence and his perfection. This Other with two faces, who exposes me to a radical illusion but is revealed to be *more true* than myself, this Other who creates and recreates me in every moment but also threatens to reduce me to nothingness—why must we obstinately call it "God"? What other unheard-of name might still suit it?

This conflict will be overcome when the third *Meditation* once and for all conjures away the menacing shadow of the deceiving God. The theological turn that identifies the Other with God is immediately succeeded by a second turn that identifies it with the *Good God*. If Descartes finally refuses to allow the coexistence of the truth and the nontruth in God, it is because he does not think the essence of the truth radically enough: he assimilates it here to *veracity*, to the moral attitude of a subject disposed to tell the truth. From then on, truth will no longer be opposed to the highest powers of nontruth—to the reserve of the secret, to illusion, to madness—but only to voluntary deception, to the lie. The question of the truth of the Other is displaced on the ethical plane, where it becomes a matter of sincerity, rectitude, and goodness. Now, the die was cast on this a long time ago. Everything was already decided at the dawn of our history, when this speech was addressed to the souls of the dead gathered before the daughters of Necessity: *theos anaitios*, "God is blameless."[35] Plato grounded a major current of occidental thought, the theodicy that seeks to prove that God is not the cause of evil. When Descartes defines deception "as nonbeing towards which the supreme being could never tend,"[36] he yields in his turn to this ancient tradition. We will have to wait a century, until Kant, to call this old identity of Being and God into question; to be able to conceive an evil, a radical evil, that would not be reduced to a simple negation, in order to stop identifying the infinite with supreme perfection; and to be able to imagine the infinite without "God." Only then will the path be open for new divine figures, freed of the blandness of the Good God. Such figures include the "Supreme Being of Evil" invoked by the Sadian libertine and the devouring and mortifying jouissance of Schreber's or Artaud's God, as well as the God-whore offering itself naked and insane in a spasm of agony to the shadow of the door Saint-Denis—for "God is nothing if not the overcoming of God in every way, so that she now becomes a vulgar being, full of horror and impurity; in the end, she becomes nothing."[37]

It is not just the metamorphoses of the divine that give us pause here but the consequences of Descartes' turn, his decision to erect God as the foundation of all truth. By eliminating the hypothesis of a deceitful God, he makes the threat that weighed on the ego disappear. An *other relation to the Other* is then opened, which will no longer proceed by lie, persecution, or conflict. It would be finally possible to affirm the ego without denying the Other, without making it a rival, and this new relation relieves the ego of its insufficiency, sustains it in its existence, gives it the time to unfold itself and endure. But this opening to the Other—to an Other that would no longer be my persecutor—is paid for with a heavy price: a profound dissymmetry, an infinite separation of the ego and the truthful and perfect Other, which amounts to making the ego entirely responsible for nontruth. Thus, the revelation of the truth of the Other dispossesses me of my own truth, leading me to submit completely to the Other. In this sense, the Good God of the third *Meditation* is a more ferocious and more dangerous rival than the deceitful God. A complex intrigue takes shape between the ego and the Other, the stakes of which we have barely begun to glimpse. The threads of this intrigue have to be unraveled if I want to know who the *ego* is. The third *Meditation* initially designates that the name "God" "proceeded from some substance which really was infinite" and not from myself (M III, 22:21), the only reality whose idea I was not able to create in myself: a transcendent alterity absolutely foreign to me. Yet this infinitely other Other will progressively appear to me as what is nearest and most intimate. It will be revealed as the Cause that re-engenders me in every moment, taking on the face of the Father who created me "in his image," whose mark I carry within me—that is, the idea of the infinite that is like the signature of the artist on his work. Descartes contributes a capital precision here: he underlines that "the mark of the craftsman stamped on his work . . . need be anything distinct from the work itself" (M III, 39:35), that it would be futile and absurd to look for the artist's tag in the margin of the tableau or to try to discern something in me that would refer back to the Other. I do not possess the idea of the infinite as one notion among others: *I am this idea*, I am the trace of the Other in me, and this trace is the same as me. Just as I immediately perceive that a certain phrase or quote is one *of* Celine's or one *of* Proust's, so too do I discover that *I am of the Other*. What had seemed absolutely foreign to me now reappears in the heart of myself; that which is most *my own* in me is what brings me closest to and most identifies me with the Other. In other words, the *in-* of the *in-*finite signifies not merely the negation of the finite but also its immanence, its belonging to the finite, its residence *in* me. The *in-*finite is the Other in the Same, the revelation of the Other in the deepest depths of the ego.[38] Does this Other already exist outside of me before being manifest to me? Absolutely not. By radical doubt, I have placed all transcendent reality out of play, including the Other named God. If there is an Other, if it is revealed to me, it could only be revealed *in me*. The idea of God or of the Infinite is not a representation referring to a reality exterior to it: the infinite *is nothing other than* its idea, its trace in me. So much so that my "resemblance" to the Other takes on a new meaning: it names my intimate relation to an alterity that I carry in myself, which is in me, which is me. We are no longer really dealing with a *resemblance* in the strict sense here, with a similitude between two exterior terms, but rather with an *identity*, which was not initially given to me. I "experienced it in me"; I gradually discovered it by overcoming an initial distance: it is less a question of an identity than of an *identification*.

Who must this Other be so that I can identify myself with it? It can no longer be a matter of a wholly-Other, an infinitely other Other, which would never let itself be led into an identity with the ego. Upholding this notion of the "infinite" leads Levinas astray, impeding him from envisaging the Other as an *internal alteration* of the ego. It leads him to think of the Other as absolutely separated from the ego, and it then becomes very difficult to understand how this infinite can be revealed to me and *in* me. We must be careful not to imagine it as a Subject always already there, preexisting the ego's discovery of it: there is an Other only in an internal excess, a self-alteration of the ego; there is an Other only in the event of my revelation, in this trace that it has engraved in me and *that I am*. Strictly speaking, we should no longer even be talking about an Other in the sense of an exterior entity foreign to me; though first presented in this way to a certain moment of experience, it is now revealed as an intimate alterity, a separation between me and myself. No longer just the deceiving Other but also now the truthful Other must be considered as an illegitimate projection, a part of myself that I transfer outside of myself without knowing it. Nobody—neither the Evil Genius nor the Good God—precedes the event that I am; no Other is revealed to me from the outside as this Infinite that would accuse my finitude; no Other shows itself to me for my salvation or my loss, to lead me astray and to kill me, or to engender and sustain me in my duration. And if all support is lacking for me, if I cannot count on the goodness of God or the call of Being, on the desire of the Other or the face of an other, then it is in me alone where I will have to find the resource that will allow me to stand firm, to maintain myself from one moment to the next, and to endure throughout my life. It falls to the ego and to it alone to sustain itself and to become its own subject.

Is it possible that Descartes was not aware of this secret identity of the ego and its "other"? *Larvatus prodeo*, I go forward masked: such was our philosopher's motto. What unknown facet of his thought will we discover were we to tear away this mask in which he has prudently dressed himself? Like the stolen letter on the minister's desk, the secret cipher of the *ego cogito* was indeed visible, right in the middle of the most well-known text of his entire oeuvre, where the evidence of the *ego sum* is stated. This statement is followed immediately thereafter by a tortured and almost untranslatable phrase, that we will now try to render: "But I do not yet have a sufficient understanding of what this 'I' is [*quisnam sim ego ille*], that now necessarily exists [*qui jam necessario sum*]."[39] In the "sim ego . . . qui . . . sum," an attentive reader will spot, like a watermark, a cryptic variation of the formula "ego sum qui sum"—I am what I am (or I am who I am)—in which we recognize the words of Sinai, the revelation of the Name of the Elohim through the burning bush. My hidden name, the clandestine truth of my ego is the name of the Other. This is a strange avowal, already announced in the *Discourse on Method* when Descartes evoked "this 'I'— that is, the soul by which *I am what I am*."[40] There was thus no need to wait for the following *Meditation* for the Other to be revealed or for me to discover the immanent identity of the Other and myself, because its name is intertwined with mine from the moment of my birth. The mark of the artist has forever been one with his work, and our two signatures, that of the Father and my own, are merged together in a unique monogram. We begin to understand why Descartes had to prove that God really exists outside of the ego. It was imperatively necessary for Descartes to mark an infinite distance between Him and the ego, because their demarcation did not go without saying; the secret formula of the second *Meditation* tends on the contrary to bring them closer together and even to identify them. What then lies in wait, more worrisome than the evil genius, is the possible merging together of the ego and the Other in that vertiginous moment when the ego discovers that it is one with God. The existence of a transcendent God must therefore be demonstrated in order to protect the ego from this vertigo so that it does not fall into madness. We can wonder whether Descartes succeeded in guarding against this threat and in grounding the transcendence of the Other in truth. Since I carry his signature in me, the trace of his Name, since *I am* this Name, how can I be certain that I am not God? And what does this unheard-of affirmation of the identity of the ego and God (or of his name) mean? Is this the hidden truth of the *Meditations*? *Larvatus prodeo*: perhaps this motto is also cryptic; perhaps we should hear *larvatus pro Deo*—not "I go forward masked" but "masked before God." Is it the reverent sign of our philosopher humbly "hiding his face before the face of the Infinite"?[41] Or is it instead an audacious ruse whereby he tried to escape from the gaze of the Other, to advance toward it in disguise in order to try, madly, to evict it and take its place ("masked in place of God" is another possible meaning of *larvatus pro Deo*)? We would be dealing no longer with a deceiving God but rather with a *deceived* God—abused by the feint of the ego. The masked philosopher would secretly initiate the great turn of modern times, the triumphal advent of this Subject who claims to supplant God.

This reading is not the only possible one, and there are several ways to understand this strange message in which the *ego cogito* seems to express itself as the voice of Sinai. Instead of seeing in it a metaphysical coup d'état by which the human Subject tries to dethrone God, we could instead recognize an attempt of the ego to reappropriate its power to say "I," which had been alienated in the Other, confiscated by God—but without trying to evict it and identify with it. It seems to me that the first interpretation does not correspond to Descartes' intention, nor does it take any account of the numerous passages in the *Meditations* that reaffirm the imperfection and the finitude of the ego, the infinite distance that separates it from God (or from the Absolute Subject of modern metaphysics). I will thus risk another interpretation: the proximity between the ego and God would be grounded not on an identity of essence but rather on the common form of their statement. In his commentary on *Exodus*, Meister Eckhart argues that the pronoun "I" "belongs to God and to him alone."[42] Let us size up this fundamental thesis. Certainly the ego also expresses itself in the first person by saying "I"—but this statement would be illegitimate, reserved uniquely for God. The possibility of saying "I," which seems to belong to each speaking subject, would in fact be the privilege of one sole subject, the only one capable of affirming *I am* without restriction.

This is what sanctions the expropriation of the ego, dispossessed of the power to call itself or to give itself to itself by calling itself "I." This usurpation of the saying-I is not the fact only of "God" (or rather of the idol that we so designate) but of all the dominant figures of the Other—the Father, the Master, the political Sovereign—that have always forever arrogated the power to say "I," to speak in my place and in my name. They are, however, able to do so only to the extent that I myself have granted them the privilege. The moment to be free of this alienation would have come, and this is what Descartes will call upon us to do by revealing to us that the statement of the ego is the same as God's, that we—as much as the Other, perhaps even more than it—have the power and the right to say "I." It would be a matter not of gaining possession of the Other's sovereign power, of proclaiming oneself God (as the metaphysical interpretation presses us to do), but rather of restituting my power *to call me to myself.*

We will probably never know what Descartes meant. But it is as if the metaphysical interpretation were imposed as the only one possible. Instead of holding on to a nominal identity between the ego's saying-I and God's saying-I, philosophers have taken it as an essential identity and have ended up claiming that the human Subject must become god in the place of God. Of course, the new God will no longer be called such; it will be baptized as the general Will or the absolute State, Man, the People, the Proletariat, and the Will to Power; but Subject is still the name that best suits these sovereign powers—and these subjects are imposed on me by speaking in my name and acting in my place. The deceiver worked desperately, but in vain, to reduce me to nothingness; the more he tried to negate me, the more I affirmed my existence. In Descartes' successors, we witness the reverse movement: the more the ego seeks to affirm itself, the more it is negated. The more the ego tries to free itself of its subjection to God by becoming its own foundation, the more it is submitted to an Other-Subject. All the prerogatives of the Cartesian God have been conferred on it—but is the absolute Subject that claims to be installed in the place of God still *me*, still *ego*? Tyrannical figures that subjugate living individuals are substituted for a solitary and fragile ego, persecuted by the Other. And yet these idols of our modernity, these new gods that live off of the ego's death, are also the heirs of the Cartesian ego, as if its destiny was to overcome itself by becoming God. Descartes would certainly not have subscribed to this posthumous destiny of his work.[43] In his search for a first foundation, he never stopped oscillating between the ego and God, between the affirmation of the ego's infinite freedom and the affirmation of its total submission to the Other. His successors inherit *a failed god*, a quasi-Subject who aspires to absolute autonomy yet is unable to give this autonomy to itself, because it *does not have time* to be itself. By relieving it of its deficiencies, by allowing it to be maintained in time, Descartes' successors complete his project.

With his lantern lit at full noon, the madman looks for God in the places and streets of the town. When he reveals to the crowd that God has not simply faded away, that his death is in fact a murder ("*we have killed him*—you and I"), he concludes his discourse by wondering: "do we not ourselves have to become gods merely to appear worthy of it?"[44] This God that we have killed was our sun and our horizon, the ground on which our world rested, and if we as God's murderers are unable to elevate ourselves into gods, we risk sinking into a bottomless night. There is a great naiveté in thinking that the glorious reign of dis-alienated Man would begin with the decline of religious faith. For the murder of God takes all the sovereign figures pretending to take its place with it into nothingness, thus announcing a major crisis of the Subject, of Man, of the Ego. This is why Nietzsche's madman is Descartes' heir. At the same time that the second *Meditation* affirmed the ego's absolute truth, it also discovered its extreme precariousness, namely, the deficiency of an ego unable to persist by itself in time. It was thus necessary to look for a more stable foundation, and Descartes thought that he had found it in God. It is then sufficient to radicalize doubt, to call into question the possibility of demonstrating the existence of God for the ego, deprived of all support, to be dislocated and to collapse. This *ego without subject*, this fragmented ego without a fixed identity that so many contemporary thinkers will present to us, is the ego of Descartes, as soon as it lacks the support of God—an ego whose fugitive, spectral existence resembles that of a phantasm, a nightmare, or delirium. The Cartesian foundation of the ego thus allows the possibility of a *desubjectification of the ego* to be glimpsed: this is the perspective that egocide will adopt, along with its most extreme consequences, including the ego's annihilation, its total dissolution in the dream of a dream. Even Fichte will present this as the ultimate consequence of the theoretical foundation of the cogito: "I know absolutely nothing and am nothing. Images alone are . . . fleeting images that pass . . . images without significance or aim. I myself am one of these images; nay I am not even this, but merely a confused image of other images."[45]

I have no taste for great historical frescoes, and the concern here is neither to look for "the sources of the ego" nor to retrace the history of its critiques. I observe only that the ego's truth, far from being imposed as an absolute evidence, has been contested by all of Descartes' successors and that this contestation continually becomes more radical. When Spinoza in book 2 of his *Ethics* posits as an axiom that "man thinks," *homo cogitat,* this proposition designates for him no longer a first and absolutely necessary truth but the de facto existence of a "man" who can just as well not exist. The evidence of the cogito is not annihilated; it is only maintained in a subaltern place, subordinated to the divine infinite Substance of which our soul is but a finite mode. One will notice, moreover, that this proposition is no longer stated in the first person, as an "I think," a cogito in the strict sense. It designates no longer my singular thought but rather the universal and neuter thought of Man in general. The Cartesian position of the ego is thus succeeded by its disposition, a destitution that dislodges it from its sovereign place. And this first egocide will soon be followed by a second, more radical one, a destruction that denounces the ego's identity as a simple illusion. For Hume, permanent substance, real identity, or continuous existence does not exist; there are only fleeting impressions that succeed one another in our perception, and it is only a fiction of the imagination that creates the appearance of a personal identity for our ego. It is difficult to be any more egocidal, and very often our contemporaries, from Nietzsche to Deleuze, will simply take up the Scottish philosopher's arguments. From then on, the unity of our life is dissolved in a multiplicity of impressions, events, or dissociated states of consciousness. Like amnesiacs who always forget what they have just experienced a moment ago, we are here condemned to a punctual existence, closed in on an immediate present, unable to assume our past or to project our future.

And yet, it is as if philosophers did not give up on the *I think*: every phase of destruction is succeeded by a return of the cogito. Kant, first of all, ensures this new foundation by erecting the *I think* as a supreme principle, the condition for the possibility of all experience. In fact, this refoundation leads us very far from Descartes, because the Kantian transcendental Subject or the Fichtean absolute Ego does not truly coincide with the singular ego that I am, and because this universal principle is indifferently valid for all thinking beings, an abstract principle defined by the logical identity I = I ("I am I"). But this universal I, which is not me, is no longer truly an *I*. And Kant even gives up calling it as such in order to designate it instead as an *It*, an X, a "thing that thinks in me."[46] The refoundation of the ego is equivalent here to a destitution, which is then aggravated in his successors, such as when individual consciousness becomes a simple moment of the absolute Subject who infinitely overcomes it. Schelling will soon propose abandoning the cogito, designating it instead as a *cogitatur* ("one thinks," "something is thought"). One step further and the destitution is completed by Nietzsche in a radical destruction of the ego's illusions, of the subject or of consciousness that would be merely some useful errors for life, fictions created by the will to power. One could easily show that the same cycle, the same three-step waltz, is repeated once again in the twentieth century, when Husserl's regrounding of the ego will result in a new destitution in favor of Being or the Other, then a new destruction. It seems that philosophy can neither get past the ego nor hold on to it, that it oscillates between a return to the ego and an egocide. This reveals the profound *instability* of the ego, incapable of positing itself as a principle without being immediately deposed—but it also attests to its irreducible *persistence*, since it is always reborn from its ashes in a new foundation. Egocide seems necessarily destined to failure, and the egocidal philosopher is always constrained to reintroduce the ego he had sought to eliminate, as we have already seen with Heidegger and Lacan. But philosophies of the ego also fail to establish it definitively, and every attempt at foundation hastens them into new crises. Such an instability must find its origin in the ego itself, in a weakness of the ego, which a very powerful force exploits to renounce the ego—to the point of imagining that "I is an Other," that the ego does not exist, or that I am already dead.

Our return to Descartes thus ends up at an unexpected result. We were hoping to find this absolute truth that *I am*, but its field is so limited that the ego is able to persist in its identity only by passively submitting itself to the Other or by seeking to be identified with it, "to make itself in some way the same as God." In both cases, the ego is alienated from itself to an Other-Subject, allowing its truth, its power to call itself, to give itself to itself, to slip away. Descartes would therefore be the first egocidal thinker. The rot has already set in: the very conditions of his discovery result in the destitution of the ego and hastens it into an always more profound crisis.

The return to Descartes is not sufficient for us. We will have to be more "Cartesian" than he. To do this, we will have to radicalize doubt and put out of play all the traditional determinations of the Other, all the proofs of its existence, of its truth or falsity, of its evilness or goodness, of its infinity, its divinity, its humanity. We would have to consider these figures of the Other as the ego's projections, transcendent figurations of an intimate alterity. We would have to try to demarcate the true ego from the mundane ego alienated to the Other and to stop conceiving the ego on the basis of the Other, in its submission to or rivalry with it, its respect, hatred, or desire for it, in order to imagine it as an originary phenomenon that has no need for any Other in order to be ego. Only thus can we approach the decisive questions of the life of the ego, of our life, and wonder whether it is possible to become oneself and to persist in life without identifying oneself with transcendent figures, and whether every identification with the Other amounts to an alienation; only then can we ask what this internal alterity, whose trace precedes in me all relation to others, might be. All these questions—this question *who am I?*, which in our time we are no longer able to pose—are made possible by Descartes. On this plane of thought, we owe him everything. We owe him this vigilance, guarding against anything that might harm, diminish, or deface the ego, against the innumerable feints of the great Deceiver (which today we call will to power, language, unconscious, or Being), which tries to persuade us that "I" means nothing and that there is no ego. Our French cavalier taught us how to undo these ruses before finally succumbing to them himself. A return to Descartes means going against Descartes himself, against what led him to deny the privilege of the ego sum. A return to Descartes requires defending the ego against the egocides, to reconstruct a radical thinking of the ego—because I do not always know what this ego that I am is.

PART II

INTRODUCTION TO EGOANALYSIS

4

The Equivocations of Phenomenology

So who, then, am I? Am I so certain of living and of being me? How will I finally manage to be myself, to become this "I" that I already "am"? How will I persevere in my identity? How can I be subjectified without alienating myself, without identifying myself with a foreign Other? None of the different deconstructions of the subject or of the ego has given us a response to these questions, and our "return to Descartes" also ended up in an aporia, since we discovered that the foundation of the *ego cogito* leads to its own collapse. It is time to go one step further and to take up again these questions in a different perspective. What I wish to sketch here is a new thought of the ego: an *egoanalysis*. In what way is this required today? Why should we make the ego into an object of an analysis when the certainty of being "me" is irresistibly imposed on each of us? Because I am not certain of *truly* being myself, of knowing who I am in truth. Apparently, nothing is closer to me than is my ego, since *I myself am it*—and yet at the same time, nothing is more foreign to me. The most distant galaxies and the tiniest microparticles are closer to and easier for me to understand. Even questions of God and Being are less opaque for me than am I for myself. Our everyday experiences show that our ego constantly tends to flee from itself, to dissimulate itself to itself, to identify itself with an anonymous Neuter or with a They or with others, and to be alienated from itself and lost in them. Our rereading of Heidegger, Lacan, and Descartes has confirmed it for us: scarcely glimpsed, the truth of the ego is immediately brushed aside to the benefit of a foreign entity that our egocidal thinkers present as the origin of the ego and the site of all truth. Nothing is more tenacious than this forgetting of myself, this *deceptor* that pushes the ego to deny itself, to let its truth be stolen by an Other. We know, however, that egocide always ends up at an impasse, that the gesture that was supposed to brush aside the ego each time ends up reintroducing it: *si me fallit ego sum.* The more one seeks to prove to me that my ego is only an illusion, the more I am confirmed in my own existence. The ego is thus *irreducible* and is in no way a derivative of a non-ego, which means that it is an *originary* event and that I am self-given, with no need for any Other for me to be given to myself. This same ego that endlessly forgets itself and abdicates its singularity is also able to resist the great Deceiver, to call itself back to itself in the project of an authentic existence, and to be separated from the Other in order to accede to its subjective truth. We have to take account of both its alienation and its resistance—that is, we will try to understand how I can identify myself with the world or with others, with my mother's breast or with my reflection in the mirror (that is, with all these transcendent realities *that I am not* and that remain forever foreign to me), as well as how I could ever free myself from this identification once it has taken place. We have to look at how an ego that would have surmounted its alienating identifications is able to unfold itself temporally, to exist without the help or reinforcement of a transcendent Other. The question we must reexamine is that of the subjectification of the ego, of its continuous re-creation, without ceding to this solution of distress that is the call of a bountiful God—and without engaging ourselves in the same impasse as Heidegger, when he claimed to ground the unity of my existence on the anticipation of my death.

We now understand better why it is necessary to establish an egoanalysis as a radical rethinking of the ego that can enter into dialogue with what is most fecund in ontology and in psychoanalysis. This thought will have to blaze its own trail and come to its question, without presupposing anything about what it will discover. For this, it will need a method capable of orienting it toward its "object," toward the still unexplored continent of the life of the ego. Such a method must above all be engaged in freeing the ego of the illusions that dissimulate it—to reveal me to myself in truth. Where will I find access to this path that would lead me back to myself? In a more precise determination of the obstacle that it is supposed to remove, this Stranger that dispossesses me of myself, prohibiting me from acceding to my truth. Whether we are dealing with God or Being or the big symbolic Other or the Face of the other person, this entity appears each time as a *transcendence*. We noted earlier that egocide seems indissociable from an "ecstatic" orientation toward a foreign transcendence that tears the ego away from itself, disfiguring it and giving it over defenseless to the power of the Other, the Neutral, death. If I want to discover who I am prior to any alienation or disfiguration, I will have to try to eliminate all transcendence. What will we call this primordial dimension of the ego, more originary than any that covers it over and affects it from the outside? We can call the "opposite" of transcendence an "immanence," which remains in-itself without ever leaving itself. In Latin, *immanere* means "residing on the inside," which is indeed the condition of the ego when it is revealed to itself by putting out of play all that exists outside of or beyond it. This is a suitable term to designate the site of the ego, its place of life—a place that is nothing other than its life itself—and its singular manner of existing and of living its life. I adopt this term for yet another reason: the prefix *im-* evokes a movement, invites thinking of the opening up of a path, an advancing that unfolds the ego as *a field of immanence* without going outside of it. What I designate with this term therefore possesses the same characteristics as the "plane of immanence" theorized by Deleuze—although for him it is a matter of an impersonal immanence, and the events traversing it remain "pre-individual singularities." Deleuze's conception remains prisoner to the contemporary prejudice that assigns the ego to transcendence: he refuses to imagine the possibility of an *immanent ego* coinciding with its plane of immanence. The question is posed, then, of knowing how an immanent ego is nevertheless able *to transcend itself* toward the world and toward others. How could it "leave" its field of immanence without immediately becoming altered or disfigured as a thing of the world, alienating itself to the Other without return. And how can this purely immanent (or purely "narcissistic") ego avoid disfiguring the other or misconstruing its transcendence by reducing it to an imaginary projection, a reflection, or a double of myself? These are some of the many questions that an egoanalysis will have to confront. But we will first have to clarify what we understand by "immanence" and "transcendence." The opposition between what resides "in the ego" and what is found "outside the ego" is marked by the mundane distinction between inside and outside. It leads to representing immanence falsely as a "closed box," a prison in which the ego would remain riveted to itself. What, then, is its authentic meaning?

Most often, the field of immanence is concealed. In order to disclose it, we must brush aside the transcendent entities that dissimulate it. This is precisely what Descartes had tried to do: even though he never used this term, Cartesian doubt had the purpose of revealing the immanence of the ego cogito. Was Descartes really able to achieve this? As doubt is a *negation* of the world ("I have already denied that I have any sense or any body . . . I am persuaded that there was absolutely nothing in the world"), then it is a matter of a *privative* operation that cuts the ego off from all transcendence and lets it merely subsist as the residue. Concentrated in one point, closed in on the moment, this ego is incapable of grounding any truth other than its own. In order to provide more certain bases for the science of the world, Descartes had to renounce the privilege of the ego and appeal to an Other-Subject called God, because Cartesian doubt is purely *provisory*: I doubt only in order to overcome doubt, and each newly discovered truth distances me further from my initial doubt, rooting me more firmly in the reality of the world. But this going outside of immanence is paid for with a heavy price: by abandoning doubt, Descartes immediately falls back into the "old opinion" that he had revoked—the belief in the infinite goodness of God—and the ego, dispossessed of its truth, is submitted without reserve to the transcendence of the Other. If we want to avoid this disaster, we have to change methods. Without renouncing the radicality of doubt, it is convenient to modify the process in one essential point: to brush aside transcendence without denying it—to *leave it aside*. Such is the path followed by Descartes' last heir, the only heir to remain faithful to him in the epoch of egocide. Husserl called this method the *epokhè* (a "suspension") or *the phenomenological reduction:* it consists in putting transcendence out of play (especially the transcendence of the world) and in suspending the "natural attitude," the naive belief in the existence of the world. Everything given in my everyday experience is placed "in parentheses," suspended. This does not mean that I *deny* that there is a world or that I call into doubt the real existence of things and others in the world. I still hear and see the noises, voices, and silhouettes marking the horizon. Nothing disappears, but the meaning of all these things is modified: instead of imagining them as realities existing in themselves,

I now consider them as they appear to me when I direct my attention to them, that is, as simple phenomena. The table that I perceive in front of me, the melody that I listen to, this strange flesh that I touch—none of this is given to me as an exterior object that I would merely record or passively receive: I have to constitute them by myself and *in me*, in my own field of experience. Nothing in the immense region of the world is lost, but rather things are no longer given as self-evident or with natural evidence. The *epokhè* restitutes the strangeness and mystery to the world, giving everything the air of an enigma. It breaks me out of my passive submission to existing reality and grants me the power to give meaning and a face to phenomena, to bring them to birth in some way by welcoming them— and thus to regenerate the world: because "anything not yet born can still be born provided that we do not allow ourselves to remain simple organs of recording."[1]

Understood in this way, the phenomenological reduction no longer has anything "reductive" about it, nothing restrictive or negative: it consists in a leading back [*re-ducere*] of our naive way of experiencing the world to the elementary phenomena that make this experience possible. Far from limiting our experience, the reduction frees it from its limitations, liberates it from its subjugation to existing reality in order to allow it access to a new domain that knows no limits. As not negative, the *epokhè* is not provisory, and so the concern is not to overcome doubt by appealing to divine veracity but rather to be installed in the reduction, to radicalize it by constantly putting every trace of transcendence out of play. The concern is no longer to escape from immanence in order to return to the world but rather to go always more deeply into the infinite field of my immanent life, where no God and no Other could sustain me in existence and where I encounter nothing other than myself. One would be wrong, however, to oppose Husserl and Descartes, for the founder of phenomenology is closer to his French forebear than he believes. We have already noted that Cartesian doubt is not a "doubt" in the strict sense and does not truly deny or negate everyday realities but instead lets them appear as they appear *to me*, as I seem to see them [*videor videre*], touch them, or hear them. Even though he believed he had denied the reality of the world, Descartes was, in fact, content to hold it in suspense—and thus he already practiced a sort of phenomenological *epokhè*. He did not know how to recognize, describe, or name the path he followed or the continent he discovered.

After the great explorers come the cartographers, and thus a Husserl was necessary in order to think Descartes' thoughts and to give a name to this unknown country that Descartes had begun to explore.

Whether it is a question of the ego's status, of immanence, or of the flesh, most of the Husserlian "inventions" are inscribed in Descartes' wake and merely cast light on what he had already found. Moreover, Husserl quite clearly recognized this: he underlines that Descartes "stands on the threshold of the greatest of all discoveries," that of the immanent ego, "and in a certain manner, has already made it—yet he does not grasp its proper sense" and had confused it with a human ego within the world.[2] The French philosopher did not realize that the originary ego did not belong to the transcendence of the world or that it "carries within it" the phenomenon of the world because it constitutes and gives meaning to it. But by considering the ego as a parcel or a region of the world, a "thinking substance" distinct from extended substance, Descartes fell back into the ancient dualism of soul and body. He barred himself from understanding what this *videor* is in truth, namely, the primordial Sensing that is the very stuff of the ego, and which Husserl calls "flesh" [*Leib*].[3] The immanent ego is not lodged in its flesh in the same way that a captain is in his ship or that the Cartesian soul resides in the pineal gland: it is its flesh; it is *Ichleib*, an "ego-body" or "flesh of the ego," an originarily incarnated ego;[4] it is the marvel of marvels, an originary source of always new phenomena, a "sphere of absolute position" such that "no real 'thing' . . . is necessary for the Being of consciousness."[5] Even in the terms he uses, Husserl recognizes the Cartesian determination of substance, its most authentic determination that suits only an ego that is freely self-given and has no need for anything else in order to be ego. As purely immanent, it must be able to endure, to be unfolded temporally without the support of any transcendent reality. We find the ultimate foundation of this free temporal unfolding in time itself. Husserl had discovered an essential character of immanent temporality, its capacity to be linked to itself, to unify itself by continually intertwining present impressions and primary memories ("retentions"), in which these impressions are intended as already-past. From then on, the present and the past—in other words, the originary impression and its retention—are no longer joined together as if they were two exterior terms, but rather their difference is furrowed within the living present itself. This present is no longer reduced to a mere point in time or fading moment but is instead unfolded as *a field of presence*, a phase of the flux, embracing its past and its future. The ego does not overhang this temporal flux from the outside like an intemporal Kantian subject: it temporalizes itself, it is one with its immanent temporality, and what Husserl calls the "living present" is nothing other than this living presence of the ego to itself.

Thus, all the aporias that trip up philosophers seem to be alleviated. For the first time, the self-givenness of the ego seems established. The *epokhè* invented by Husserl has proven its fecundity and truth as the only method that lets the ego's field of immanence be discovered and thus as the only method suitable for an egoanalysis. But egoanalysis will not be a "phenomenology" in the strict sense. It may well be that every phenomenology has failed to disclose the truth of the ego and that Husserl's successors have all taken part in egocide by destituting the ego in the name of Being or the Other, the Flesh of the world or absolute Life. Husserl himself was looking for other paths to the reduction that would no longer be centered on an originary ego. In his 1924 *Erste Philosophie*, he tried to open up a "non-Cartesian psychological path," whereas his incomplete philosophical testament, *The Crisis*, privileged the way of the lifeworld. Is this an avowal of the failure of the Cartesian way? Will we once again find this strange failure that, since Descartes, has affected every attempt to ground or reground the ego? We are not concerned here with a doctrinal problem that would interest only historians of philosophy; I see here the clue to a major difficulty that is impossible to escape. Why does the field of immanence belong only to *an* ego, a me, and not to an *us*, without taking account of my relation to others surrounding me and who join me in giving the world a figure? And why attribute the field of immanence only to an ego and not to an impersonal consciousness or a life that would no longer have the status of an ego? Must the reduction I undertake necessarily lead me back to myself? And if so, what "me," what ego, is in question here? In what way is it distinguished from the everyday ego suspended by the reduction? These questions are posed very early on in Husserl's lifetime, and here they are posed again— because phenomenology is not a doctrine but rather a path toward the things themselves, a possibility of thought.

We would be wrong to believe that Husserl always defended the thesis of an originary immanence of the ego. At the beginning of his trajectory, he considered the ego as a simple "bundle of lived mental experiences," that is, one empirical reality among others, a transcendent object in the same way that a house or a tree is.[6] His discovery of the method of reduction some years later was not going to modify his position. On the contrary, it favors the ego's exclusion from the field of immanent consciousness: by accomplishing the reduction, "we put the transcendent position of the ego out of play and we remain with what is absolute in it, namely, consciousness in the pure sense." This is then presented as an anonymous consciousness, as a thinking that "belongs to no one."[7] It is only later that Husserl will allow for the existence of a "pure ego" dislodged by the reduction and distinct from the empirical ego.[8] What leads him to this decision? It is first of all the necessity of ensuring the unity of experience, of understanding what holds several differentiated temporal fluxes (for example, two series of memories, one near and the other distant, or a memory and a present impression) together in one same consciousness. One response is imposed: these fluxes are linked together in a unique current of consciousness *because they are mine*; they belong to the unity of my ego.[9] But this is not the only reason: Husserl was finally able to allow for an immanent ego because of an essential tenet of his thought—*his fidelity to experience*, to our most immediate and everyday experience that he had always refused to dismiss as inauthentic. Nothing is excluded from our naive approach to ourselves and to the world; everyday realities are not effaced but subsist "in parenthesis" as enigmas or clues. Yet only one among all the transcendent givens or data is imposed on each of us with an irresistible force— that of being an ego. Certainly this ego has only one empirical reality, that of a human individual among others, but this is no reason to eliminate it. When we undertake the reduction, no aspect of reality is abolished: "we transpose all our natural experiences into phenomenological experiences," including the evidence of being *me*.[10] Following this operation, the empirical ego is consequently doubled with an immanent ego "parallel" to the first. This doubling does not result in a scission or total dissociation, because we are always dealing with *one sole and same ego*, considered from two different points of view. However, it is no longer exactly the same: the reduction changes the status of the ego, modifies some traits of it, gives it a new face in which I am no longer certain to recognize myself. Is this solitary ego without name or body, which is no longer "human" nor lives with others in the world, still *me*? Husserl hesitates between several contradictory responses. He most often claims that it is indeed the same ego, but he also sometimes opposes the two planes and makes of the immanent ego a second ego distinct from the first, even refusing to designate it as an "ego." A particularly sensitive hesitation is seen in this embarrassed passage from the *Crisis*: "the 'I' that I attain in the *epokhè* . . . is called 'I' only by equivocation"—and yet "I can say nothing other than: it is I who practice the *epokhè*."[11] It is in order to do away with this ambiguity that his epigones, with Sartre at the head of the list, will decide to banish the ego from the domain of originary phenomena, determined henceforth as an impersonal consciousness, a "transcendental field without subject." But if the ego is no longer anything but a transcendent object, if it is put out of play by the reduction, then we no longer understand who undertakes the reduction, because there is *no longer anyone to do it.*

What is at stake here is the importance of the reduction, the relation that it allows to be established between the naive experience of the world and the field of immanence. Some people have sometimes accused Husserl of being insufficiently radical, with limiting himself to tracing out a carbon copy of empirical reality, doubling it without ever discovering anything new. But we must nevertheless guard against an excessively radical reduction that would furrow a hollow between the two planes so deep that it risks becoming an unbridgeable abyss. The majority of Husserl's successors are engaged in the path of an always more radical *epokhè*, or a return to an Originary that is always more distant from our experience.[12] With them, one is soon dealing with a Being that is no longer the Being of any being, with a Flesh of the world that is no longer the flesh of any singular body, with an absolute Life that no longer has anything to do with my life, with a Face of an infinite Wholly Other that no longer has anything in common with the visible and mortal figure of the other person. The most common experience—of being an ego, of having a body, of being in the world with others—becomes absolutely opaque and incomprehensible, and we suspect it of betraying the Originary, of being an illusion that has to be dissipated. This is how a radicalized *epokhè* becomes egocidal, working hard to deconstruct the ego or seeking to recognize only an empirical ego in its everyday reality. We then find the same aporia as in psychoanalysis, the same project of deriving the ego from a more originary non-ego—an attempt necessarily destined to fail. This radicalism encloses itself in an impasse for having transgressed the principle of fidelity to experience, but what we must hold onto is the invincible certitude of being *me*, and we have to try to show how this evidence is rooted in the immanent life of the ego.

Is Husserl up to leading us on this path? His position on this decisive question is less certain than it seems: when he hesitated to designate the ego attained by the *epokhè* as a true ego, he had already taken a step toward the anonymous Originary of Sartre or Heidegger; and the "equivocation" that we note here affects all of his thinking, including his conceptions of the ego, immanence, flesh, and temporality. The whole of Husserlian phenomenology is then destabilized, condemned to slip from one equivocation to another and to search for a center of gravity that always slips away. Let us briefly try to retrace the different phases of this destabilization:

1. Husserl ended up admitting that absolute consciousness is not anonymous, that it is always the consciousness of an ego. The ego seemed thus to be anchored in the heart of immanence—but only then to be quickly dislodged from it. At the very moment that he recognized (in paragraph 57 of *Ideas* I) that the "pure ego" necessarily belongs to all of my lived experiences—because I always live them *as mine*—Husserl took two steps back, as if he were afraid of his own audacity. He claimed that the pure ego could not be considered as one of my lived experiences, which amounts to expelling it from my immanent life, throwing it back into the transcendence of the world (as Sartre will do, and as Husserl himself had done just a few years prior). My consciousness and my life will then fall back into an impersonal neutrality. He cannot accept this: unable to decide between—or to situate the ego clearly within—either transcendence or immanence, Husserl came to define the ego as "transcendence in immanence." His entire equivocation is concentrated in this ambiguous notion, which he never tried to clarify. Taken strictly, it means that the ego *does not belong* to immanence but rather that it haunts it like a stranger or a sort of squatter, even though it is indissociable from it. In the end, the ego is *neither immanent nor transcendent*, is in no way sited or situated, and lacks any determinate status.

2. To eliminate this ambiguity, we would have to trace out a precise demarcation between the two planes of immanence and transcendence—but any such delimitation is missing, which leads us to believe that Husserl was unable to determine what is truly immanent. When introducing these notions for the first time, he emphasized that they are themselves equivocal, and that we could therefore understand immanence in a "double sense"—as either *actual* immanence and *real* belongingness to the lived experience of consciousness or as a givenness "in person" within an absolute evidence.[13]

In the first sense, immanence designates the absolute self-givenness of a lived experience that is given to itself without ever leaving itself. In the second sense, immanence is enlarged to include the intentional grasp of transcendent objects, mundane realities, or ideal essences—that is, entities foreign to me and that do not originarily belong to my life. He designates this intentional immanence, however, as the "most authentic," and in this way, Husserl pushes the borders of immanence much farther back: it ceases to be the characteristic trait of my ego or of my always-mine experiences and tends instead toward an anonymous neutrality.

3. According to Husserl, "my [flesh] is what is most originarily mine,"[14] and the ego is itself defined as the *Ichleib*, as an "ego-body," a "flesh of an ego," an ego-flesh. He even goes as far as to present the flesh as *Urleib*, as "originary flesh," the unique source of all incarnation.[15] But the equivocal character of immanence will affect the status of the flesh. He will now say of a thing given in evidence and presented to me in an immanent fashion (in the second sense) that it is given or presented, *leibhaft*, "in the flesh." If we were to go one step further, we would be able to speak, as Merleau-Ponty does, of a flesh of the things or of the world. But the status of the flesh is even more equivocal, and Husserl eventually and totally casts it out of the field of immanence of the ego, arguing that it does not belong to what is properly ego.[16] Henceforth an ego without flesh is opposed to a flesh without ego, and phenomenology falls back into the traditional opposition of soul and body.

4. This collection of difficulties converges on an ultimate aporia, on the most difficult question of temporality. I am not going to try to work my way through the labyrinth of the Husserlian phenomenology of time-consciousness, which was constantly reworked over a period of thirty years. I would merely like to show how the equivocal determination of the ego and the flesh affect the conception of time. When he posits it for the first time in the 1905 *Lectures on the Phenomenology of Internal Time Consciousness*, Husserl seems to believe that the temporal flux constitutes its own unity without any intervention from a constituting ego (hence the fascination this text exercises on those who commit egocide). But he takes himself to task later for "not having spoken then of the ego" or for not having known how to determine the constitutive intentionality of time as a function of the ego or as rooted in the life of an ego that "self-temporalizes."[17] He had not yet developed his theory of the living present and its implications. He had,

however, discovered that the "now-point" or present moment must be defined by "originary sensation," by *an originary impression* that is the absolute source of every temporal flux.[18] Yet this impression is necessarily given "in the flesh" and to my flesh, which means, strictly speaking, that *the flesh gives time*, that it is the condition for the possibility of temporality. And if it is true that my flesh is always mine, always me, then we have to recognize that the originary impression is "issued from the ego": by being given to itself through its carnal impressions, the ego-flesh constitutes the unity of the temporal flux.[19] Husserl hesitates to allow this, probably because of the equivocal status he had given to the flesh as both immanent and transcendent, both originarily mine and foreign to me. The consequences of this hesitation waste no time making themselves known. If the life of my flesh is the first given of time, an ego deprived of flesh would lose all sense of time: by disincarnating itself, the ego detemporalizes itself, while temporality loses all of its anchorage in an ego. Husserl will in the end define the absolute ego as "in-temporal" and the most originary present as *ichlos*, as a "flux without ego."[20] But to what extent would an anonymous flux—a flux that would not be crossed by the carnal self-impression of an ego—still be *one* flux, a unique current of consciousness continuously unfolding itself? Would not a temporality without an ego be condemned to be out of sync, and to sink constantly in a dispersion without return? If we want to avoid this fatal scission of ego and time, we must show how the ego's carnal self-givenness is temporally constituted and how it thereby constitutes time itself through the *Ur-impression*. And we would have to wonder what this impression must be in order to be *truly* originary, to be the origin of time. How, by sliding into the past, is the originary impression able to be continuously tied to itself in the modified form of a retention, through the self-alteration or self-differentiation that constitutes the unity of the living present? Derrida had noted this difficulty and concluded from it that the originary impression is an "auto-affection . . . which produces sameness as self-relation with self-difference; it produces sameness as the nonidentical."[21] The impression is given to itself as different from itself, on the model of an *auto-hetero-givenness*. What, then, is this *heteron*, this mysterious alterity that constantly digs deeper into the present instant? If the living present is nothing other than the living presence of the ego-flesh to itself, the alterity that traverses it must therefore come from the ego. This leads us to confront the enigma of the

First Stranger, of a first transcendence *in* immanence of the ego. To think this, Husserl's admirable analyses will no longer be useful to us: the key to the problem of time is found not in time itself but in the flesh, in the life of the ego-flesh. The moment has thus come to dismiss the phenomenology of temporality and to appeal instead to an egoanalysis.

To "analyze" the ego amounts in a strict sense to *dividing* it, that is, to recognizing that its originary multiplicity is covered over by the appearance of a unity and self-identity. Surely this step is not totally foreign to Husserl's thought. For him, "the life of the ego in activity is absolutely nothing other than the process of constant splitting up," of splintering into multiple, differentiated egos. And he insisted on the multiplicity of acts of consciousness, on the fact that "each act has its particular ego," whose life is exhausted in the completion of the act. There is thus a visual ego and a tactile ego—or, more exactly, an ego that sees this yellow wall, another ego that touches this rough surface, another still that sees that man in front of the wall, and so on—an ego that suffers and an ego that rejoices, one that remembers, another that hopes, one that waits, and so on again. But he underlines immediately that "it is nevertheless the one and the same ego that is divided," that the multiplicity of its manifestations does not in any way affect the essential unity of the ego, this single ego that, through its different acts of consciousness, sees, touches, remembers—"and thus I claim: everywhere I am the same."[22] He presupposes that the ego is one, that its unity precedes its successive divisions and persists, immutable, across the multiplicity of its acts. As the field of immanence is characterized by the irreducible plurality of the flux of consciousnesses, we are led to believe that this Ego-One always identical to itself no longer belongs to my immanent life, that it overhangs it from the outside as a transcendent entity. Descartes did not accept that this ego "that doubts, that understands, and that desires" might not be the same—because for him, it is obvious that I am always one, always the same me. Husserl also ceded to this old prejudice. He could scarcely escape it, since he had introduced the pure ego as the principle link, the unification of my experience: if this principle of unity were not itself unified, how then could we avoid a dislocation of my field of consciousness that would make me sink into a bottomless chaos? By supposing that "I am One," I erect a barrier in front of the abyss: I try to conjure away this mortal risk, this menace of an infinite dispersion where the affirmation of the multiple engages me.

This line of defense is both fragile and immediately thrown into question. We have seen that the Cartesian cogito exists only when I think, and disappears only to arise again at every moment in a continuous re-creation, affirming itself anew countless times. But how can we be sure that it is always *the same ego* that returns? As Kant noted, the self-identity of the *I think* "at every moment" does not necessarily imply that its identity persists "in different times." The temporal unity of my existence risks being dissolved into a multiplicity of ephemeral egos. It thus seems impossible to affirm the multiple without throwing the very existence of the ego into question. The contemporary deconstructions of the ego rest on the same prejudice, the same naive certainty that the ego can be only one unique Subject. Our egocides do not foresee the possibility of an ego that can be shared out or divided without at the same time ceasing to be an ego. When they encounter in our experience a multiplicity of impressions or desires, events or phrases, they decree that this experience no longer belongs to an ego and that this multiplicity makes the ego splinter, thus annihilating the illusion of being me. And so those who, from Descartes to Husserl, consider the ego as a first truth presuppose its unity, while those who, from Hume to Deleuze, contest this unity in the name of the multiple see merely an illusion in it. The ego's defenders and adversaries at least agree on this: that the ego, if it exists, is originarily one. Had there not been One, had there been only the multiple, there would be no ego, no me. This common prejudice must now be questioned. Either we play the One (the originary unity of the ego) against the multiple, or we play an originary multiplicity against the One, that is, against the ego. We must instead imagine the ego as *the unity of the multiple*, as an ego originarily divided yet unified. This unity is not initially given to me: it is the last phase of a genesis, and I always have to reconquer it anew, to renew the unity of my life by battling against all those forces that disperse me in my daily existence into innumerable ego-fragments, none of which is *me*. Most of the time, we barely even perceive this dispersion: each of us lives as an *individual*, as a unique and indivisible ego, always identical to itself, without realizing that its unity, its individuality, is constituted in the course of a history or that it is the result of a process of unification of identification. The sovereign individual against whom our modern epoch defends is only a fiction that dissimulates the division of the ego and its struggle to overcome its initial dispersion. This forgotten genesis is what is rediscovered through the *epokhè*, by suspending the prejudice of the Ego-One, in order finally to let the originary multiplicity, from which I arose, appear.

This gives rise to new difficulties. We have seen that every attempt to derive the ego from a non-ego is doomed to failure. And so the identification constituting the ego would be only a self-identification: these originary elements that are united in order to compose the ego cannot be foreign to it; they are already "me," albeit as fragments or shards of me. The *ego is thus preceded by itself*; it engenders itself, gives itself *from* itself (from multiple fragmentary egos) to itself (while constituting itself as a sole unitary ego). But this self-constitution seems in every respect to be circular. If I am already present at the origin of myself, in each of my constitutive elements, why would I then need to engender or constitute myself as an ego? And if these elements have always preceded me, then is that not proof that they are *not yet me* and will never be able to constitute me? We needed the poetic genius of Plato to be able to tell the story of how Hermes had succeeded in making two separate beings out of the one being that had been divided by Zeus's anger. What divine magician would be able to put together the puzzle of my ego starting from these dispersed fragments of ego? These questions remain without answer, as long as we content ourselves by reasoning in an abstract manner: the moment has come to take the next step, for me to undertake the *epokhè* myself, by trying to describe the ego that I am, such as it is given to me.

5

The Field of Immanence

You think you're alone.
It's not true,
You are a multitude.

—Artaud, *Histoire vécue d'Artaud-Momo*

I undertake the *epokhè*: I have decided to suspend my naive belief in the existence of the world; from now on, I abstain from every judgment about (or attitude that presupposes the reality of) things or the existence of others in the world. I do not deny that there is the world or things and other people in the world, but I do not affirm that any of this really exists: I content myself with describing what is given to me as it is given, considering it no longer as a real object but rather as a simple phenomenon. This is a deliberate decision, a voluntary conversion of the gaze. Let us leave aside the case of "savage" reductions, that is, the suspension of the world that sometimes occurs in the limit-experiences of anxiety, mourning, joy, persecution, or madness, when our familiar world suddenly feels completely strange and foreign. There is a loss of bearings and of natural evidence in this, a disquieting or uncanny strangeness that invades everything, but I could also find another mode of it when I freely chose to undertake the *epokhè*. The real table has consequently disappeared: I lightly touch a cold and smooth surface, and I see the bluish reflection of the glass and the dark wooden grain. A preliminary sketch or outline is first given, wherein an angle stands out in the foreground, then other successive sketches, wherein the contour of the table is modified, or the jutting corner is gradually blurred, fading from my field of vision while my gaze slides further along the edge. None of these sketches is the table as such, yet the table *is given* in each of them, because it does not exist outside of them as a thing in itself, and it is nothing other than the continuous flow of the sketches, a continuous unity of the fragments of perception. What is presented as a single object is endlessly divided and dispersed into many fugitive silhouettes, tactile impressions, and primary sensations of color and sound. The landscape is dissolved into countless colored impressions. The form of the object is dislocated, and splinters into a multiplicity of profiles that overlap and intersect without completely obscuring one another. This splintering or diffraction to infinity is first of all a matter of the perceptual experience in which the table presents itself "in its flesh" through its sketches. But it is also offered otherwise, in other modes of givenness whereby it is merely re-presented. There is an indeterminate halo that surrounds my perception; there is the other side, the reverse that I do not currently see but that is presented indirectly to me by the part of the table that I do see; and there is also the table that I imagine, the table that I remember, and a whole world of memories awakened within my perceptions: Piazza San Marco and all of Venice are resuscitated by the irregular cobblestones in the courtyard of the Guermantes. Each time it is always the same table, and yet it is never the same table: the echoes and resonances are innumerable, and this irreducible diversity of the modes of givenness make the immediate unity of the thing fragment.

Our thinking is moving too quickly toward the one, the same, the identical: it delights in the reassuring unity of things in the world, in the stable identity of human subjects populating the world. This unity must be broken into shards so that we can recuperate it in terms of a genesis. Every unity is formed from out of a primitive multiplicity; every identity (including the ego or the "individual") is constituted through syntheses of identification. What presents itself as an immutable thing is first given in a flux, as a series of fluid sketches [*Abschattungen*] that succeed upon and flow into each other. This splintered and moving dimension that appears when I suspend the transcendence of the world is what immanence is. We were wrong to consider it as a simple point or as a Self closed in on itself, crushing in on itself: immanence is *im-manence*, a *field* always in movement, which is temporally unfurled as an incessant flux and which is spatially extended by constantly displacing its limits. The field of immanence is first presented as a disseminated multiplicity, as chaos, as a *khôra* from which no form or stable identity emerges. This initial chaos springs forth again when our common world is unraveled or when a crisis threatens the unity of existence. Deleuze knew this difficulty well when he situated the plane of immanence at the limit of chaos, as a "sieve" of chaos: "the problem of philosophy is to acquire a consistency without losing the infinite into which thought plunges."[1] But he insisted so much on the divergence of series endlessly increasing their divergences in a limitless becoming-mad that we can see neither how these series could intersect one another nor how the plane of immanence could escape chaos. And yet, *there is the world*, with my ego and the others lodged in it, and we must remain faithful to this experience of the world. The transcendence of the everyday ego, of men and things, must be constituted by showing how they are announced in immanence. This supposes that the field of immanence is not a pure chaos; that regularities and constant concordances come to order the flux of appearances; that different perspectives, series of divergent impressions, may also be able to converge on, intersect with, and cross one another; and that each point of intersection is constituted as a pole of identification, allowing for always larger and more stable unities to be formed. In this way, order will emerge from chaos.

In fact, even if each partial sketch of the table differs from others, they nevertheless possess a common *style*, and they continuously follow upon one another in the unity of one and the same perception. This series of impressions can, moreover, converge with another series: while my hand glides across the table, my gaze runs along its surface, and I see my hand sliding along it; I identify the tactile sensation of this surface and the visual sensation that corresponds to it. A unique table-thing is gradually constituted in this way, as both seen and touched. How are these tactile impressions, which differ profoundly from visual impressions, able to coincide with them as two different perceptions of one unique object? We are constantly accomplishing this sensible synthesis or overlapping of the visible and tactile without thinking about it, but this is by no means obvious. As Aristotle had already noted, it is not possible to feel two sensations coming from two different senses at the same time (for example, white and sweet). We must be able, however, to bring them into relation: "therefore discrimination between the white and sweet cannot be effected by two agencies which remain separate; both the qualities discriminated must be present to something that is one and single."[2] What shall we call this unique principle that is capable both of seeing the whiteness of sugar and of tasting its sweet flavor, of perceiving their difference and of bringing them into unity? We moderns, who come after Descartes and Kant, readily call it the *ego*: it is my unique ego, always identical to itself, that effects the synthesis of the diverse aspects of sensibility—a synthesis of the different perceptual series and the different perceptions within each series. But this is not obvious when we undertake the *epokhè*. Just as the natural thing splinters into a multiplicity of partial sketches and primary sensations, so too is the ego divided into innumerable egos dissociated from one another. To each facet of the world, to each profile of the things, to each intentional aim of each of these profiles, there corresponds a singular ego. And it is no longer sufficient to distinguish an ego that perceives from an ego that imagines or remembers, an ego that loves from another that suffers: there is this ego that sees this sketch of the table, with its corner jutting out into the foreground, and another ego that sees the other sketch; there is another ego that touches the surface and another still that lightly touches the edges, and numerous others remember all these acts, anticipate them, or imagine them, and so forth. The problem, then, is how the unity of my ego arises from all the diffracted egos that follow one upon another during the entirety of my life.

One thing at least must be considered as acquired: the larval egos, fragments of ego, are still and always will be me. If it is impossible to derive the ego from a more originary non-ego—from an unconscious Id or from an impersonal transcendental field—then we must conclude that the ego is always preceded by itself, is originarily given to itself. To those who insist on chasing every trace of the ego from immanence, I would like to say this: if the plane of immanence is something other than a simple abstract construction, if we must have an experience of it in order to describe it, then we will have to find access to this field. How do we access immanence without putting aside all transcendence? And how could this reduction occur were there no one to make it happen? What the reduction effects cannot fall under the reduction, lest this operation annul itself and immanence remain forever inaccessible. But it is me who achieves the reduction, here and now: there is thus a part of my ego that resists the reduction, that continues to live and to think after transcendence has been put out of play, and we could not eliminate it from the field of immanence without prohibiting access to this field. Deleuze wanted to avoid reintroducing the transcendence of an ego into the plane of immanence, but he did not imagine the possibility of an immanent ego. In this perspective, the field of immanence is no longer threatened by the ego, *because it is the ego*, because a multitude of fragmentary egos are disseminated over all its span, coinciding with each area, each stratum of the field—and these egos are mine, they are me.

How can I claim that my field of immanence has merged with me? Among those phenomena that are given to me *leibhaft* or in an "immanent" manner, the majority seem on the contrary to come from the outside or to refer to an experience of the world or to exterior events foreign to me. What are the limits of such a field? Husserl, as we have seen, is barely able to circumscribe the meaning of immanence and its relation to the ego and instead doubles it into a "real" immanence and an "intentional," supposedly more authentic, immanence. It is now time to make a decision about these equivocations in Husserl's thought. I propose to define the core of the field of immanence, its most originary layer, by *the real immanence* of the lived experience of the ego living it. In feeling this anxiety, that joy or pain, I feel nothing other than myself; I am affected only by myself; I am given to myself. Just as much as transcendence is, so too is immanence a manner of being given: what characterizes an immanent givenness is the power to be given from oneself to oneself; and in that it needs nothing else in order to be given, then it is a matter of an absolute givenness. I define immanence, then, as self-givenness [*auto-donation*], as the identity of what gives and what is given, the identity of the origin of givenness (it is given *from* itself) and its destination (it is given *to* itself).[3] Descartes teaches us that such a power can belong only to an ego. Husserl goes astray by making of the "pure ego" a "transcendence in immanence": it is what is most immanent; it is entirely wedded to its field of immanence. No alterity, no exteriority, is interposed here between myself and myself; nothing foreign or strange diverts or disfigures it—which is why my self-givenness is *always* true and is manifested in an immediate manner, *without sketches*. While mundane realities appear to me through a series of changing sketches, my ego is given wholly to myself in each of my lived experiences, and my flesh is presented to me in the same way, in one unique offering.

It now becomes possible to determine the essence of transcendence: it is defined on the contrary by the gap that it opens up between the origin and the destination, by the fact of being given from the Other or toward the Other, by *other-givenness* [*hetero-donation*]. I will therefore call the transcendent (a) that which is given *to me* without coming *from me* and (b) that which is given *from me* without returning *to me.* In the first case, we describe transcendence in the traditional sense, as realities exterior to my consciousness, the immense world that surrounds every part of me, the incessant flux of the phenomena of the world that affect me, and other humans who throng around me. In the second case, the term designates my power to project myself beyond myself in order to give myself to an Other, to expose myself to the Other, identify myself to it, sacrifice myself for it—and it does not matter if this Other to whom I give myself and am devoted is the world or another person, or God, or Being, the Father, the Chief, or a collective entity, since in every instance this givenness or devotion separates me from myself, leads me far from myself. To this second determination belongs one of the variations of the transcendence of Dasein in the Heideggerian sense, namely ek-static transcendence, which as I have already shown alienates existing being and annihilates its singularity. This is true for all the modes of transcendence, which always carry the threat of a radical disindividuation, ripping the ego away from itself in order to submit it to the law of a foreign Other. But this threat must be overcome: because it *has already come* from itself, the ego is also able to *return* to itself. Although transcendence exiles it in the world, its immanence frees it from its alienation. Were such a deliverance possible, it would be because immanence is more originary than transcendence. Whether it comes from me or goes toward me, every transcendent givenness supposes that *there is an ego*, that I am already given to myself, and this *gift of the I* in immanence is what makes all other givenness possible. This does not mean that the ego is able *to be grounded* by itself or to acquire a total mastery of its existence: the power to be given to self has nothing to do with this metaphysical aim of self-grounding, with the self-certainty of the "strong ego," of the conquering subject of modern Times. In my suffering, in my passivity, my most extreme alienation, I am always given to myself. A "collapsed" ego, absolutely broken by the Other, nevertheless continues in its prison, its asylum, or its camp, to be affected by its life, to be given to self; and for this reason, as soon as it will have been freed from the hostile powers that oppose it, it will be possible for it to retrieve itself, to come back to itself.

We begin now to discern the frontiers of the field of immanence. To delimit the field better, we will have to clarify the status of sensible perceptions. I call "immanent" a phenomenon that is given from itself to itself. Yet when I see or touch the table, these sensations that are given to me do not come *from* me: it is what leads me to determine that the table is a transcendent thing foreign to me; and my perception of this table, of all things in the world, is also transcendent. But what I call "my perception" is a composite reality. As soon as I undertake the *epokhè*, my perception will differentiate itself, divide itself into several heterogeneous strata: some of the transcendent sensations put in suspension by the reduction—the cold and white surface *of the table*—are henceforth distinguished from the sensations of the touching-of-the-cold, the seeing-of-the-white, dissociated from all relation to the table-thing. It is a matter of purely immanent impressions whereby I no longer aim at an object exterior to me, where I affect myself only by my own power to feel. Just as with my affects, so too are impressions the same as my consciousness: *I am* my despair; I am an ego-in-despair just as I am this icy sensation. In order to distinguish it from the sensation of objects [*Empfindung*], Husserl calls this type of impression "sensing" [*Empfindnis*],[4] and what is given in such impressions is the primary "material" of all perception, which he calls "hyle." Certainly this whiteness or coldness already points toward the transcendent thing, and they will soon let themselves be swept away by the intentional aim constituting the table-thing outside of me. They differ in this from another type of sensing, those called "kinesthetic," which are primary sensations of movement, effort, and resistance, tension and release that accompany all my perceptions. By moving myself, by anticipating my movements, I am affected only by myself, by my own motility; and the same is true for all my sentiments and all of the affective and instinctual substrata of my life. Freud already foresaw this: the instinctual drive is "indifferent to its objects"; and even if its manifestation can be *occasioned by* a mundane event, it remains without object, coming from myself and being addressed only to me. Of all of my sensings, the affective, instinctual, or motor impressions are the closest to self-givenness. But it would be a grave error to restrain the field of immanence to only these sensings and to exclude those of a perceptual type.[5] Even if these are oriented to the transcendence of things, they are not totally captured by it, and these pure impressions of redness, whiteness, or coldness would remain always mine, always immanent to my flesh, to my life. Husserl said that this hyletic material of perception constitutes the *Ichfremdekern* in me, the "kernel of the foreign in me"—and it is a matter of *an intimate stranger* who "is the same as and is indissociable from" me.[6] Far from being a continuum, a compact and faultless mass, the field of immanence is thus presented as a stratified terrain, divided into several layers that are superimposed on one another. But each of these strata belongs to immanence and manifests in its own way the living presence of the ego to itself: in each one of them, what gives coincides with what is given.

The primordial layer of the field of immanence, the site of my originary impressions, my affects, my sensations of movement, all of my sensings, is *the plane of life*. It is not an anonymous life or a grand undifferentiated current of universal Life (by invoking "Life," we always end up forgetting the living ego), but a singular life, each time my own, *my* life. We can also give it another name, which better expresses the sensible dimension of the ego: *the flesh*. Husserl uses this term to designate the site of immanent sensings; but as soon as he uncovers it, the meaning of the flesh escapes him and he makes of it a transcendent reality, foreign to the pure ego, a synonym for the body. In his last works, Merleau-Ponty took up the same term while trying to free himself from the traditional oppositions of body and soul, matter and spirit, object and subject: the name "flesh" designates for him the very stuff of the visible and the tangible, an Element that "has no name in any philosophy." He thus gave it a universal extension, envisaging it as an anonymous milieu from whence my own flesh emerged by a sort of folding, torsion, or rolling back on itself. But these lovely metaphors deceive us in that they export the flesh into an insensible Outside where no life is ever self-given. In truth, *there is not a flesh of the world*: the things sense nothing and give themselves in the flesh only to *my* flesh; the landscape that I see does not see me, and without the gaze of the painter who lends his own flesh to it, Mount Sainte-Victoire would be only a dead pebble oppressed by the sun. I would say the same for the experience of the other person [*autrui*]: for me, *the other has no flesh*. I never sense this foreign body that I see and touch from within as my own flesh; my look, my caress, glide over it like the surface of a thing. For the other to be able to be incarnated, I will have to identify myself with it by transferring my incarnation to it. Husserl understood this well: there is only one sole primordial flesh, and this *Urleib* is *my* flesh. Let us be careful not to cast this into the transcendence of the world: if the flesh is what is closest to me, or the most originarily mine, if it possesses all the characters of the immanent ego—its power to give itself to itself, its singularity that is always mine, its initial dispersion—it is because my flesh is the same as me. "Flesh," "life," "ego": these terms are perfectly synonymous; the immanent ego is the *Ichleib*, a carnal and living ego, an ego-flesh.

By designating it in this way, I am not adding any determination to it; I am only insisting on its vitality, sensuality, and its spatial dimension, its *spacing*. For there is an essential link between flesh and space: space is constituted in movement, which is above all the movement of the ego-flesh. Even when it seems at rest, it does not stop being moved or experiencing ever new sensations of movement. And yet it does not budge, at least in the sense of a body displacing itself from one point to another in space: no matter where I go, I never distance myself from myself. Like a vigilant sentinel, I am always "here," in an absolute Here, a central "zero-point" around which the things and the world gravitate. Husserl sometimes designates this a "null-region is a spatial hole [*Raumloch*], something not constituted, not intuited, not intuitable."[7] One must wonder how the ego-flesh is able to pull itself out of this hole, to give a spatial meaning or orientation to its Here, or to be a fixed pole allowing it to situate and to localize all that appears in space. This immutable fixity of the I-point is what allows me to constitute space in all its dimensions, and if my flesh is not found in space like a body among other bodies, it is because it *gives place* to it by unfurling space around it. It is not "spatial" but rather "spacious"—the giver of space. None of the terms describing the position of things in space are suitable for it anymore. We must say both that it is always in movement and yet immobile, that it is what is closest but that the difference of "close" and "far" has no meaning for it. How do we qualify this immobile Prime Mover, this place outside of place but from which radiate all places? I propose to designate it as a *mouvance*, as this old word names both the movement and the country or territory delimited by the habitual paths of an animal or a man. This carnal Mouvance opens to me the domain where I can move myself, making possible all my displacements in the world and the impulses that push me toward others and things—but which itself goes nowhere. It is this immobile voyage where I carry myself to myself without ever separating myself from myself.

We wonder how multiple egos divided into fragments can be united in order to form an Ego-One. Since these egos are of the flesh, would not the flesh be the common element capable of assembling and unifying them? But the primordial flesh belongs at every moment to a singular ego and is itself dispersed into innumerable egos, each one of which possesses *its own flesh*, dissociated from the others. By closing each fragment of the ego in on its Mouvance, its flesh separates it from other mouvances, making of it a monad without either doors or windows. Certainly this same carnal movement that isolates it also carries it beyond itself at the same time, inserts it in space, opens it onto the world—but it is a matter of a world cut to size, limited to the field of its sensings; of a world that is itself fragmentary, a unique "ray of the world" incapable of intersecting other rays, of merging with them in one common horizon. The flesh hardly gives us the key to the mystery. It seems that by taking into account the carnal dimension of the ego, we have made it still worse, since we no longer are concerned with only a temporal multiplicity—with the blinking of the cogito, a discontinuous succession of ego-instants—but also with a spatial dispersion. The synthesis that we were looking for will thus have to be effected in both space and time. But in what way? Should I first solder back together my scattered members, which no longer form only one sole flesh, in order to be able to renew the time of my life? Or on the contrary will a temporal synthesis ensure the unification of my flesh?

One might say that such questions have no meaning: unless we are crazy, each one of us is absolutely certain of being *one* ego and of possessing *one* body—"how can I deny that these hands or this body belong to me?" This massive evidence of the Body-One is thrown back into question, because it is valid only in the world, under the gaze of others who perceive me as an objective body similar to all human bodies. As soon as I exercise the *epokhè*, as soon as I suspend the world and others, the body-object fades away at the same time as the world and others. I nevertheless continue to hear my voice, to see my hands or other parts of my body, immobile or in movement—or rather to sense that I hear myself, that I see myself, that I am in movement—but these diverse sensations no longer belong to the unity of one sole body. If there is no longer a world, then I no longer have a body; if there is no longer anything but a whirlwind, a chaotic multitude of impressions arise here and there, enduring for a few seconds, and then are blurred. Certainly it is I who hears this sound, who sees these colors and those forms: no matter how partial or fragmentary they may be, the impressions are mine, but I no longer have the right to say that it is my eyes that see, my ears that hear. When I effect the reduction, my material body disappears with all its organs and physical qualities; what remains is not the body but rather flesh. We are no longer working with a distinction between two mundane entities, like my body and another's body, but rather at the invisible border separating one thing in the world from the enigmatic dimension of my flesh, this X, outside of place, outside of the world, which is the condition of my openness to the world. Despite all this, it is a matter of two planes of my experience, as indissociable as my immanent ego is from my human ego. My flesh never stops passing into this insensible and inert puppet that we call "my body," incarnating itself by giving its movement and its life to itself. We would have to wonder how it manages to encroach on the border between two planes, to be incorporated in objective space, and to become body without ceasing to be flesh.

As I understand it, the flesh is not very different from Deleuze's "body without organs." Borrowed from Artaud, this notion nevertheless has the defect of being purely negative and does not invoke this necessary *reorganization* of the flesh, the "new dance of the organs" of which Artaud also spoke. Even if my flesh never crystallizes into a differentiated organic unity, if it has neither eyes nor hands nor sex organs, it has nevertheless passed through whirlwinds and fluxes, innumerable sensible impressions, each one of which has its singular carnal site—many fluid and mobile micro-organs that open and close constantly and never stop touching, hearing, seeing, desiring, rejoicing, suffering. In order to avoid confusing them with corporal organs, I will henceforth designate them as *poles of the flesh*. There are as many carnal poles as there are impressions, myriad poles separated from other poles; and in each of them is lodged an ego-flesh, a touching, listening, seeing, desiring, or suffering ego dissociated from the others. Each of these poles, each of these egos, lasts as long as its originary impression lasts and then fades away with it. Once the impression has stopped, it continues to affect the poles through a series of retentions, primary memories in which a muffled echo still persists. The ego that perceived it is then modified, becoming an ego that remembers, a retentional ego. In this form, it lives for a while off of itself, and then its "comet's tail" of retentions finally fades; this pole of the singular flesh is always and forever closed in on itself, and the ego that animates it sinks into nothingness.

Each of these fluid, larval egos is already "me," a fragment or a part of me—but none of them is truly me. None of them coincides entirely with the ego that I am, the ego that perceives across all the poles at once, that remains always the same in vision or in listening, in memory or in waiting, love or hatred, sliding constantly from one impression or sentiment to another. So that I exist, a synthesis is therefore necessary, *a synthesis of identification* in which each fragmentary ego rejoins the egos of other poles, recognizes them as other modes of itself, other faces of one and the same me. Without such a synthesis, I would never be myself, there would never be an ego, and egocide would be triumphant. I know now that my ego does not exist outside of my flesh: this synthesis constituting the ego is *a carnal synthesis* whereby each pole of flesh is united to other poles, fusing with them, until they all become one sole flesh. *Wo Ich war, sol Ich werden*: since in a certain way I am already all these egos, all the poles, then it cannot be a matter of simply adding on exterior elements. Rather, it is a matter of a self-givenness in which, starting from myself, from all the parcels of my ego, I give myself to myself, to the unique ego that I am. No transcendent entity—no God, no Being, no mirror image—could bring me to birth. If there is self-givenness, it must be purely immanent, and it is for me alone to join together all the instants of my life, to assemble all the splinters of my flesh. It would not be a question of a voluntary choice, similar to the resolute decision to be authentically itself in which Dasein puts the unity of its existence into play: if this synthesis of self-identification had not *already* taken place, before every project and decision, existing being would be condemned to an irreducible dispersion that no resoluteness could overcome. Our concern is thus for *a passive synthesis* that operates without me; it secretly subtends my project to be me and allows me to remain faithful to myself throughout my life. It is not a matter of an abstract problem, nor am I looking for a purely conceptual solution but rather an actual experience, a singular event that happens to my flesh. We do not have to wonder *if* such an experience is possible but only *how* it happens: if not, if this synthesis did not take place, I would never be myself; I could not situate myself in space nor unfold myself in time; I would not have a body and would not be in the world.

6

The Carnal Synthesis: The Chiasm

The demiurge divides this entire compound into two parts which he joined to one another at the center like the letter χ, and bent them into a circular form . . . he made the one the outer and the other the inner circle. Now the motion of the outer circle he called the motion of the Same, and the motion of the inner circle the motion of the Other.

—Plato, *Timaeus* 36bc

In what does this privileged experience, this synthesis through which I engender myself, consist? In this immense crowd of fragmentary egos, dispersed in my field of immanence, one of them must leave its mouvance, encounter another ego-flesh, and identify itself with it without ceasing to be itself. Of course, the alter ego with which it identifies is not another person [*autrui*], another subject in the world, but another part of me: in my field of immanence, the only "other" I can encounter is myself. We must then wonder *how* this identification is possible and where it may be produced: in what zone, what region of the field, do the two poles join up, recognize each other, and fuse? Through what affective experience does it happen? Suffering? Anxiety? Joy? But the ego that suffers is affected only by itself: stuck on itself, grounded by its own pain, it endures (more so than it manages or achieves) being torn away; it endures leaving its mouvance by forgetting a moment of its suffering in order to be opened to the ego of another pole (and *a fortiori* to another human subject). This is also true for other affects, as well as drives, sensations of movement and effort, and everything comprising the deepest layer of the field of immanence. Is it necessary to pass to the plane of perception for the encounter to be possible? If affectivity oppresses me and pushes me into myself, then perception would, on the contrary, seem to be too "exterior," too distant to allow for an intimate contact between two poles. How could the seeing ego discover, across the entire extension of the body, another seeing ego and recognize itself in it or identify itself with it? Natural experience testifies to this: when I look at a part of my body, I perceive it from the outside, as if it were another's body; and when I see myself in the mirror, I might be able to see my eyes, but I cannot see my gaze, and the eyes I see fixate on me from the outside as if they were a foreign Thing, two glass balls in a waxen head. Husserl was right: "Obviously, it cannot be said that I see my eye in the mirror for my eye, what which sees qua seeing, I do not perceive. I see something that I indirectly judge . . . as identical with my eye as thing [*Ding Auge*] (the one constituted by touch, for example) in the same way that I see the eye of another."[1]

We must therefore turn to this immanent experience that allows me to recognize that this "eye-thing" is mine, that these hands and this body belong to me: we will have to appeal to touching, to a particular mode of touching. In the whole field of my perceptual experience, there is one sole case in which the perceiving ego is able to find in another pole the same perception that it felt within itself: *when I touch myself.* Freud said the same thing when he situated the origin of the ego in touching, in the tactile "double sensations" that are born on the surface of the body. When one of my hands touches the other, it perceives it first as the smooth and inert surface of a thing. But then this hand-thing senses itself being touched, and tactile impressions arise in it. It *becomes flesh*, a hand of living flesh touching the hand touching it. At first divergent, the perceptions of the two poles subsequently converge, intersect, and fit each other in order now to form only one perception with two foci. At the same time and in one single gesture, each of the two poles is given as flesh to itself *and* to the other: what gives—my touching flesh—coincides with what is given. Each pole now recognizes itself in the foreign pole, recognizes it as the flesh of its flesh, as *another* pole of the *same* flesh. Each of the two egos discovers in the other an unknown part of itself; it penetrates into its mouvance, identifies with it, until they together form one flesh, one self-same ego. The synthesis whereby I am carnally given to myself by myself is thus accomplished. And Merleau-Ponty designates this very singular experience of the touching-touched as an "intertwining" or "chiasm," the latter a name of a rhetorical figure implying a crossing-over or crossing-out, with an inversion of terms. Although I prefer the term "knotting," I will preserve the word "chiasm," as it also invokes the asymmetrical Greek letter χ, a schema that allows that divine artisan of the *Timaeus* to create the soul of the world by intertwining the Same and the Other. The carnal chiasm is a foundational event, comparable in the field of immanence to the fashioning of the world by the Demiurge. A precision is necessary: by designating it as an originary event, I mean that the chiasm is *at the origin of* the ego; it is not a matter of an *original* episode that would have taken place in primary infancy. It does not refer to or arise from a psychological genesis (like that which the Freudians present to us); it is situated not in the time of the world but rather in an immanent temporality in which there is neither before nor after. If I happen to say that the chiasm "precedes" the formation of the body or that it "prefigures" the encounter with the other, it is because the chiasm allows the body and the encounter to arise, that is, that it is their condition of possibility. This does not suppose any chronological anteriority: in truth, the carnal chiasm can come forth at any moment and always begin again anew.

Artaud said that "in every lived moment, we precede our own birth."[2] It seems in effect that the ego is always preceded by itself, that a multitude of dispersed egos already exist "in me" before I come to myself through the chiasm. It is like a circle—but this apparent absurdity disappears as soon as I take everyday temporality (and with it, all temporal or causal succession) out of play; for I then understand that the micro-egos do not *really* precede me, that their dispersion had not taken place in some distant past, that it is the always actual and necessary condition of my genesis. These larval egos are not yet myself, and what is needed is the miracle of a chiasm so that they encounter one another, identify with each other, and thereby generate the one concrete ego, my true ego. It is in this sense that the chiasm is *an act of birth*, the source of my entire history: in this singular event, I am revealed to myself, and I am constantly engendering myself. Surely, "before" the chiasm, each fragmentary me already lived as an ego but did not perceive other egos as "mine," as other facets of one same ego. There is thus an originary illusion, a self-dissimulation of the ego-flesh where, in each of its poles, it presents itself to other poles as a foreign thing. The chiasm allows this veiling to be lifted: what appears to me as "other" is henceforth revealed as my own flesh—and this is what it *truly* is. Through the chiasm, my flesh discloses itself, is recognized by itself, explores itself in each of its poles, and its disclosure is an event of truth: *alétheia*. We must then wonder whether it can be disclosed in a total and definitive way, whether a part of my flesh could resist its disclosure, and whether the ego will not necessarily fall back into its initial blindness.

For the moment let us leave this question in suspense and content ourselves with describing what happens in the chiasm. When one tactile pole identifies with another pole, their carnal and scarcely separated mouvances fuse into one single and much larger mouvance. But each of these carnal mouvances does not only define a certain area, a circumscribed region of space: it also supposes a movement that endures, that is prolonged during a certain temporal sequence; it implies each time a knotting, an interlacing of space and time. When the mouvances overlap, their spatio-temporal fields are united in a more ample bundle: through the chiasm, my flesh is unfurled both spatially and temporally. We encounter once again here the redoubtable problem of the temporal constitution of the ego-flesh, up against which both Descartes and Husserl ran afoul. The source of the temporal flux is an originary impression that is each time different but always incarnated: my carnal ego is the element, the initial "milieu" of all impression and givenness. In each of them, it is given anew to itself, and its endlessly iterated self-givenness is what constitutes the unity of the flux. It is in this sense that *the flesh takes precedence over time*, that it gives place to time. But this analysis is still too abstract and superficial; we have to try to show how the ego-flesh temporalizes itself and how its temporality is unfurled on the basis of the chiasm.

Before the polar egos identify with each other, each of them lived isolated in its own mouvance, with its own temporality: in each pole were born originary impressions that immediately give rise to an ego, lasting only a few instants before disappearing with the ephemeral ego that they had affected. Everything will change when these punctual egos are united, when their mouvances blend together and are extended. Between the impressions of each pole, *a community of resonance* is created.[3] I would say that they are "synchronized," that their common resonance *puts them in synchrony*: by bringing them close together, by calling them, by resonating in unison, they bring along with them their temporal horizons, the arrow of their protentions and the comet's tail of their retentions. Finally, their temporal flux comes to be fused in one sole and same flux that is always further unfolded in the past and in the future. It is therefore important to distinguish several modes of originary impressions, which are temporalized at different levels. In each carnal pole, the very singular impression that the ego-flesh feels when it is united with itself in the chiasm is distinguished from the constantly arising micro-impressions. Though the polar micro-impressions are at the origin of more or less brief temporal sequences or simple phases within the flux, the archi-impression wherein these phases are unified is *at the origin of the flux itself.* And so the carnal chiasm gives itself time. As long as my right hand ignores my left hand, my tactile impressions last just as long as my hand runs over the surface of the table; as soon as it reaches the edge, the impressions sink into the past. But here the two hands reveal themselves to be like two poles of one sole flesh— and in my left hand touching the table, I now sense the same sensations of the smooth and the cold that I sensed earlier in my right hand. Though the first series of impressions stopped affecting me and survive only as simple retentions, my left hand still continues to run over the surface of the table, and its present sensations awaken the memory of the past impressions felt in the other hand: they are intertwined with their retentions, and together they comprise a self-same flux that prolongs itself. Through the magic of the chiasm, the ego that was about to sink into nothingness is united with the ego present in the other pole, and this union recalls it to life, allowing it to endure and persist from one moment to the next. It is in this way that I escape the cloture of the moment. We have finally discovered a solution to the Cartesian aporia: through the chiasm, the ego overcomes its impotence and is sustained by itself in time: it overcomes the deficiency that led Descartes to seek a more stable foundation for it in the creative action of God. For the continuity of my duration is based on a *continuous self-givenness* in which I do not stop recalling myself to life or being reborn by the power of the ego-flesh alone, without appealing to a transcendent Other for it.

By uniting the poles of flesh and the egos present in each pole, the chiasm also assures the unification of their temporal fluxes: in being given to itself, in being identified with self, the ego-flesh gives itself time. This does not mean that everything is reabsorbed in a unique and undifferentiated current: between each pole, a gap [*écart*][4] subsists. Their impressions are never exactly the same, and they confer a singular style and rhythm to each flux. By placing all the poles of the flesh in synchrony, all the fluxes of time, the chiasm creates the conditions of a new differentiation within their community, a new melodic variation between the currents that intersect, call, and respond to each other. And what takes place in one sole field of experience is also valid, *a fortiori*, when a more ample synchrony is established between many fields, that is, when I become capable of perceiving the white and the sweet in a single act, in one moment—when I see and I touch the same thing, when I hear this voice while seeing that face, when I feel the joy of recognizing the voice or the pain of remembering the face. These different experiences that each have their own ephemeral ego, their own temporal flux, join up in order to form an always larger community of resonance made up of agreements and disagreements, intertwinings and lags, which become the mouvance of one single ego. What name will we give to this now unified ego-flesh, which is capable of continually passing from one impression to another, of being "self-impressioning" at the same time in each of its poles? The name "subject" could suit it since, well before qualifying the human ego, this word meant for the Greeks the persistent support of all things, the subjacent ground that always sustains the appearing of phenomena. I am no longer afraid that by using this word, I might give it the illusory permanence of a thing or assimilate it to the arrogant Principle of modern metaphysics, for henceforth I know that my "subjectivity" is not initially given to me; that it is conquered in a grand struggle over the course of a history; and that it remains precarious, unstable, at the mercy of a crisis in which I always risk de-subjectifying myself. No ego ever *is* a subject: there is no "subject"; there are only *processes of subjectification*.

Now it is time to explore the other version of the chiasm, its spacing dimension, as the giver of space. The spatial constitution of the ego is more complex still than its temporal constitution. It is oriented in two very different directions, since the chiasm constitutes the flesh both as flesh and as body at the same time, allowing it to unfold itself carnally while inscribing it in the objective space of bodies. This is one of Husserl's most beautiful discoveries: by having the experience of the touching-touched, "hence the [flesh] is originally constituted in a double way: first, it is a physical thing, *matter* . . . Secondly, I find on it, and I *sense* 'on' it and 'in' it"[5]—it appears to me at the same time as flesh and as material thing. For

Husserl, this double appearance seems to be self-evident, and he does not ask by what miracle my flesh becomes body *while remaining flesh.* We have to deepen the analysis, try to elucidate the mystery of this double givenness. What happens when one pole of the flesh embraces another? Each of them discovers that the other is not only a thing but also a sensing and touching flesh like itself, that is, that they are of the same flesh. It is a matter not of an exterior projection, of a transfer of its flesh to the foreign body, but of a true *identification* in which the two initially separated egos fuse in order to form only one single ego. This supposes that each ego-flesh does not remain closed in on its mouvance, that it leaves its field of immanence, transcending itself toward the other pole, crossing the abyss of carnal difference that separates it from the other ego in order to identify with it. I will call this singular knotting in which each pole incarnates the other a "horizontal synthesis." On the basis of this synthesis of *incarnation*, a second knotting can be accomplished: at the heart of the chiasm, each pole of touching flesh is perceived by the other pole as a corporal thing touched by it, discovering that the other is also a body. The ego-flesh is able to overcome the originary difference a second time—but no longer overcomes it from the outside, by jamming up the gap separating it from the other: it crosses it *in itself*, recognizing that it is not only flesh but also itself a body. Let us call this traversing of carnal difference a "transversal synthesis," a synthesis of *incorporation.* If these two syntheses are not able to link up with one another, my flesh can never take on a body, and I will find no place in the world.

Let us try to describe this interlaced double knotting constituting the chiasm in a more precise manner. When the horizontal synthesis is accomplished, each ego-flesh is freed from its initial reclusion, enters into contact with other carnal egos, is united with them. At each point of the encounter, a *pole of identification* is formed, from which other syntheses follow, leading to new encounters and new fusions: a carnal community of monads is in this way formed in me, which will be the matrix of every human community. To the extent that the egos are brought together and enter into resonance and are unified, their perspectives become convergent, their mouvances overlap and fuse: the field of immanence of the ego-flesh is always extended further and is unfurled to form only one carnal surface. This always larger layer, constantly in movement, already begins to wrinkle, to fissure, to differentiate itself: for the rays of each ego, the mouvances of each pole are not exactly the same. Each of them appears both *similar*—issued from the same flesh—and yet *different*, since it radiates from elsewhere, from another site of incarnation. We will have to seek where this distance comes from, this gap that all the power of the chiasm cannot abolish. No matter how complex or differentiated it is, this stratified mass is still not a body: to be such requires another synthesis, a transversal synthesis that allows the flesh to be incorporated. In truth, this incorporation remains still enigmatic, and we must wonder what secret armature sustains the flesh, allowing it to become body while ceasing to be flesh. This knotting does, however, take place: each pole of touching flesh also senses itself touched or felt by the other as a simple thing, as a *body*. Consequently, its relation with other poles takes on another meaning: it will compose the unity of my body with them. On the surface of the flesh is now formed a resistant tissue, a skin that separates the interior of the body from the outside. The orifices are hollowed out on this surface, and from it, protuberances emerge. From then on, there are no longer undifferentiated poles embracing one another or opening unto a world; there are organs differentiated from other organs, hands that palpate or grasp the things, eyes that open in order to see, a mouth that speaks, ears that listen. By giving it the status of a body, the transversal synthesis brings the flesh out of the *Raumloch*, the bottomless hole of its absolute Here, and inserts the flesh in the space of things, an objective space ordered by the difference of the near and the far, the high and the low, the left side and right side. It is as if, by joining the Same with the Other in the form of a χ, a divine artist tirelessly fashioned the initial *khôra*, the moving and plastic material of my flesh, in order to impose a stable figure upon it. I myself am this demiurge, and it is the power of the ego-flesh that is unfurled while differentiating itself, that is given to itself by giving itself a body, and that is incorporated in space just as it is subjectified in time. Its genesis is not achieved in some immemorial past during an obscure fetal gestation; it is never completed and always begins anew in each moment of my life. By throwing it into the transcendence of the world, by dividing it and modeling its poles in order to impress an organic structure upon it, the process of incorporation exerts a great violence on the flesh. We will not be surprised if many myths describe the "creation of the world" as a murder, sacrifice, dismemberment of an immense original flesh—for example, the myths of Purusha, the primordial Man according to the Veda; or of Chaos in Chinese mythology; or of the mother-goddess Tiamat in Babylonian mythology—whose dispersed fragments give birth to different parts of the cosmos and to human society. What is present in the phantasms and myths as a dislocation or a mutilation is the very movement of my incorporation, which transforms my flesh into a thing of the world—a very singular thing that never stops being flesh: my body.

By becoming body and thus inserting itself in the world, the flesh submits to several major modifications. It loses its *reversibility*, it submits to the distinction of *whole* and *parts*, and this metamorphosis would not be possible without passing from the plane of *touching* to that of the *visible*. For there to be a chiasm, my flesh must be Two, divided into at least two carnal poles able to be reciprocally affected. This originary duality is both *asymmetrical*—partitioned into an active pole (affecting the other) and a passive pole (affected by the other)—and nevertheless *reversible*, since in the embrace of the chiasm each pole becomes both active and passive, touching and tangible. There is every time a *point of inversion* where each pole passes into the other and returns from it by turning itself inside out [*se "retourne"*], as one turns a glove inside out. In this way the flesh is properly *an-archic*, knows no hierarchy, no distinction between the pole that commands and the other that obeys. This is probably how this reversibility is—an incessant passage of passivity to activity that, on another plane, will allow the ego to free itself from its passive submission to the Other. Yet this identification becomes impossible only when the poles of flesh change into bodily organs. When the ego-flesh gives itself a body, the carnal relation that united each pole to all the others takes on a new meaning: the poles of flesh henceforth appear as simple members, parts of the totality that is the body, each one of which occupies a well-delimited function and place. By being unified, by becoming body, the flesh is submitted to a schema that was previously unknown to it, to the relation of *whole* and *parts*. Since the Greeks, the interpretation of this relation has given a primacy to the whole over the parts, submitted the parts to the whole—and the representation of the body as organic totality has for a long time served as a model to justify political or religious hierarchies. The reversibility and infinite plasticity of the flesh threatens this metaphysics of the body with a rebellion of the organs, a chaotic indifferentiation that metaphysics must exorcise at all costs. Herder, following a long tradition, asked "whether the body as a whole is destined to see, . . . and if the hand and the foot would prefer to be eye and brain, then would not the whole body be condemned to suffer?" It is for the good of the body, or in the superior interests of the whole, that each member part must accept *remaining in its place*. And one can wonder whether this traditional representation truly corresponds to what our body is; if it is not helpful for understanding our body, then let us put aside the metaphysics of the body.

In what perceptual field is this incorporation carried out? So that the flesh overcomes its anarchic dispersion and constitutes itself as a whole, the carnal poles must be tied together within the chiasm. But this knotting does not suffice for ensuring the formation of a total body—precisely because it is a question of a *tactile* chiasm and because the only dimension of touching does not allow for unifying all the poles in a stable manner or of linking them together in one single body. The tactile impressions are dispersed, intermittent, separated by intervals of emptiness: while my hand moves along the surface of the table toward my other hand, I initially feel a sensation of the smooth and the cold, then an absence of sensations, followed by the entirely different sensation of a warmer and more supple surface, then a new interruption, and so forth. If we want to move beyond this discontinuity, this blinking of tactile sensings, we will have to appeal to another perceptual experience. Of all of our senses, sight is the only one to unfold a homogenous and permanent field, a sort of always already unified tableau or screen: everywhere I look, I encounter only the visible, colors grounded in other colors, figures following upon other figures, and each particular phenomenon stands out against the background as an element on a canvas, a part of a spectacle. Only sight can give us access to unified totalities, and it is not by touching but rather by seeing that the flesh can hope to achieve its incorporation. However, the vision I have of myself remains very limited: my eyes, my face, the total form of my body—all necessarily escape me, unless I am perceiving my reflection in the mirror, recognizing it as my own image. Lacan understood (and Wallon before him) that the experience of the mirror, the specular identification, allows me to overcome this initial breaking up and to access the total grasp of my body. But he did not take into account that this visual identification presupposes another identification or takes support from the more originary knotting of a tactile chiasm. What is present in front of the mirror is an already partially incorporated flesh, a body of flesh on the path to unification, and if the ego-flesh had not already begun to move itself, to be unified, to identify with itself onto the plane of touching, then no mirror, no vision, could reassemble the dispersed members. My hand had to touch my other hand, the two tactile poles had to identify so that I could recognize myself in each of my successive identifications, when I perceive my image, when I hear my voice, or when I respond to the call of my name. For the ego-flesh, the passage from touch to sight, the synthesis of the visual and the tactile is an essential moment of this genesis in which it takes on a body and becomes subject. Nevertheless, this gain in incorporation is paid for immediately with a loss, with an extenuation of the flesh, with a *disincarnation*. For *there is no visual chiasm*: the eye does not see itself seeing, and the seen flesh is not a seeing-visible in the sense that the touched flesh is a touching-tangible. The possibility of this reversion, in which each carnal pole slides into and fuses with the other, will always falter in the realm of vision and of listening as well. Husserl reminds us that "a subject whose only sense was the sense of vision could not at all have an appearing [flesh]."[6] This means that the tactile ego is the only incarnated ego, that the tactile chiasm is the foundational experience subtending all of my incorporation, that it falters or unties itself in one instant, and my body *disincarnates* immediately, ceasing to be a body *of flesh* in order to become a foreign thing, a fleshless specter. We will see that it is a matter here not of a mere hypothesis but of a very real risk that constantly weighs on the fate of my flesh: the threat of becoming fleshless, of *disincorporation*, which coincides with a desubjectification of the Ego.

The incorporation of the ego-flesh thus traverses a series of planes or staggered layers, each one of which appeals to another in order to overcome its own limitations. The primordial layer of touching gives access only to a fragmentary and discontinuous experience: in order to become unified, the flesh must pass from touching to sight, but it will be able to see itself as a body only by ceasing to be flesh. We reach here the limits of a solipsistic self-incorporation: as long as I remain alone, neither my touching flesh nor my seeing flesh will be able to be unified completely in one body. In order to complete my incorporation, I will have to leave my field of immanence, go in search of an encounter with others, recognize that their body resembles mine, try to see myself as they see me, and relate on my own body the various qualities I discover on theirs. Only then will I have a total body, a human body, similar to so many other bodies in the world. I will have become a human individual, a "subject." Should we not have begun here, by first being installed on the plane of intersubjectivity, of social existence, language, communication? But this identification of my body with the other's body, grounding all relations to others [*autrui*], raises unavoidable difficulties, and the passage from an isolated ego to a community is insufficient for achieving the incorporation of my flesh. An indicative allusion of Husserl resonates here as a warning: he notes that "the same [flesh] which serves me as means for all my perception obstructs me in the perception of it itself and is a remarkably imperfectly constituted thing."[7] How are we to understand this strange incompleteness of my flesh? As a provisory limitation that could easily be lifted when we pass from the plane of the flesh to the plane of the body, and then to the other? Or as a more radical limit, the index of an essential failure prohibiting my flesh from being completely constituted as a body? And if my incorporation remains forever incomplete, if I accede only to a partial, shattered, precarious body, how will I then be able to identify it with the bodies of others, or to unite myself to them within a community? We must look for where this obstacle impeding the completion of the genesis of my body comes from. Is it rooted in the same structure of the chiasm, which, at the intersection of two poles, would be opposed to the synthesis that checks it? Or is it a matter of an obstacle totally foreign to my flesh? If we want to respond to these questions, every analysis has to be taken up again. That the carnal chiasm is possible, that it has always already taken place—we have admitted these claims as inscrutable evidence, but without questioning their conditions of possibility. What would happen if the flesh were never able to be joined to flesh or if the ego-flesh did not succeed in totally coinciding with itself?

7

How Touching Touches Itself
Touching: The (Im)Possibility
of the Chiasm

For Husserl, the chiasm did not seem to be a *problem*: he took for granted that the touching hand and the touched hand spontaneously recognize each other as two members of the same body. As he most often considers the flesh as a kind of body, he makes of the carnal chiasm a simple episode of my everyday existence, which in no way concerns the life of the immanent ego. It is as if what is to be constituted (namely, the unity of the lived body, the identity of the flesh and the body, the temporal simultaneity of their givenness) were given in advance. This is because Husserl does not practice the *epokhè* in a sufficiently radical manner here: it suffices to speak, somewhat carelessly, of one "hand" touching "another hand," and the whole analysis is falsified—for it then seems obvious that the same hand can be both touching and touched and that the two hands belong to one sole body. This massive obviousness must now be called into question. We must be more Husserlian than Husserl himself on this point; we must be more faithful than he was to the radicality of the *epokhè*: we must suspend the naive certainty of being in the world and having a body. We must confront both the strangeness of a primordial flesh (which does not yet have eyes and hands, only carnal poles) and the strangeness of an ego (which is not yet a subject or an individual human but is instead dispersed into innumerable ego-splinters). The problems of the unification of poles—of the self-identification of the ego-flesh, of the conditions for the possibility of these syntheses allowing the ego-flesh to be incorporated in space and subjectified in time—are thus posed in all their difficulty. The question of knowing how the chiasm is possible thus emerges as an enigma.

There is another way to sidestep this difficulty—by decreeing that the question is not even posed and that the touching and the touched can never coincide. This would be Levinas's position[1]—but he considers only the contact *with the other*, without ever evoking the possibility of touching oneself touching. More rigorous and attentive to the phenomena of existence, Sartre imagines this possibility but only in order to claim that the chiasm does not happen: "I cannot touch my hand only insofar as it touches," declared Sartre: touching and being-touched are for him "two radically distinct phenomena" that "exist on two incommunicable planes."[2] Sartre thus installs himself in a rigid dualism, an insurmountable opposition between the for-itself and the in-itself, between the body and the flesh, the subject and the object, the self and the other. In order to overcome these cleavages, to retrieve an "interworld" or a milieu common to myself and to others, Merleau-Ponty returns to Husserl. Not only does he recognize that the chiasm is possible, but he even gives it a universal weight: according to Merleau-Ponty, it is no longer just my touching hand and my touched hand that are joined in the chiasm but also my own hand and the other's, when I discover that the hand of the other possesses "the same power to espouse the things that I have touched in my own," so well that the other and myself "function as one unique body."[3] Not only does the chiasm "encroach on" or straddle the difference between myself and the other, but it also traverses the divergences between me and the things and between me and the world. For "my body is made of the same flesh as the world,"[4] and what we call the flesh therefore stops being my singular flesh and becomes the ultimate element of Being, the place of a generalized exchange, of a limitless effusion where all the planes intersect and intermingle, and where I fade away with all others into the immense flesh of the world. For each one of us, this universal intertwining is rooted in an "exemplary sensible," the privileged experience of *one's own* flesh when it touches itself touching: the chiasm of my flesh would be the "measure" of all flesh, the matrix of all the chiasms of the world. But am I *truly* capable of touching myself touching? Merleau-Ponty hesitates to admit it, and he even seems to confirm Sartre's objections when he recognizes that the hand of flesh can never coincide with the hand-thing, that "the right hand as an object is not the same as the touching right hand: the first is an inter-twining of bone, muscle, and flesh squashed into one point of space, the second traverses space like a rocket in order to reveal the exterior object in its place."[5] If this is the case, if the two sides or the two "lips" of my flesh are unable to be rejoined, then the thread of the world comes unraveled, and I will never be able to open myself to others or to Being in the com-mon element of one and the same flesh. Obviously Merleau-Ponty refused to recognize this, as it would mean that his whole philosophy rests on a false hypothesis. He is constrained here to waiver between two opposing points of view, insisting sometimes on coincidence, sometimes on diver-gence, reaffirming that the chiasm is possible while recognizing that it has never occurred.

What impedes my flesh from being joined to itself? It is Time that is lacking from it, because the temporal *simultaneity* of contact is confirmed as impossible: "the two hands are never *simultaneously* related to one an-other as touching and touched," and this reason, their meeting, remains "always imminent" but "is eclipsed at the moment of being realized."[6] We would be dealing here with a *virtual* synthesis, which would never really be accomplished: endlessly delayed and deferred, the chiasm is missed every time. Merleau-Ponty cannot accept this failure. At this moment in his analysis—and in order to get around this difficulty—he invokes "the total Being of my body," its originary unity in which the "hiatus" traversing my flesh would have always been absorbed. Even if he were attentive to the dif-ferences that existed between the senses, between the tactile fields of my two hands or the perspectives of my two eyes, he nevertheless claims that this multitude of divergent experiences is "sustained, subtended by . . . the unity of my body," and that it remains "the experience of one sole body before one sole world."[7] Like Husserl before him, Merleau-Ponty presup-poses what he had to constitute, and his analysis is enclosed in a circle: what would make the chiasm possible would be the unity of my body, whereas the chiasm is supposed to be grounded on this unity. But by what right does he claim that the body is a "total being" or that the body and the world are One? This naive certainty falls apart under the *epokhè*: like the unity of the world or of the self, the unity of the body is splintered into a multitude of dispersed poles. There is no longer any reason to assume that the self and the world would be successfully united in a chiasm. We may suppose that the solution Husserl proposed would not have been satisfactory to Merleau-Ponty, and indeed, some of his working notes show that he was looking for another way out of the problem and that he was oriented outside of the body, toward a "central blind spot" that could serve as a hinge between the two sides of the flesh: "to touch and touch oneself . . . do not coincide in the body . . . something other than the body is needed for the junction to be made: it takes place in the *untouchable*."[8] What might this point X that Merleau-Ponty designates as "the untouchable of touching, the invisible of vision, the unconscious of consciousness" be, and how does it ensure the "juncture," the knotting of the chiasm? Death interrupted Merleau-Ponty's work just as he was trying to elucidate this very enigma.

His incomplete work leaves us with a question to which we should try to respond. Let us consider the principal obstacle he ran into, namely, the Evil Genius of temporality: in his view, the impossibility of a *simultaneous* contact, of a perfect temporal coincidence between touching and being-touched, prohibits the chiasm from being knotted. Posed in these terms, the problem is no doubt unsolvable, because its shifts, its "overhangs," will inevitably persist between the different versions of my experience, impeding the two lips of my flesh from clasping each other in the same moment. By formulating the question in this way, Merleau-Ponty prevented himself from giving an answer. He had not seen that the problem of simultaneity— of the punctual coincidence of two experiences—had meaning only on the plane of the world: only in everyday temporality, in the clock-metered time that regulates our daily lives, can two points of time coincide (e.g., two trains can arrive "punctually," simultaneously in the same station). If I engage in the *epokhè*, the world and the time of the world are put out of play, and I access an immanent temporality where the present appears no longer as a simple point in time but rather as a layer in movement, a fluent phase within a flux, *a field of presence*. What we call simultaneity is already announced in this immanent temporal flux, when several impressions are given "at the same time" to my consciousness, when their fields of presence are superimposed and overlap each other and become *contemporaneous*. And yet as Husserl notes, these originary sensations that constitute simultaneity "are not themselves simultaneous."[9] They do not put isolated events that may or may not coincide into relation; rather, they compose a temporal community, a synchrony within the flux; and this community is in turn based "upstream" in the temporal flux on this side of temporal synthesis, in the depths of carnal *hyle*: in these communities of resonance in which the originary impressions appeal to each other, and associate themselves, and resonate in unison.

By wanting to base the chiasm on a temporal simultaneity, Merleau-Ponty completely inverted the order of constitution: in truth, it is the carnal synthesis that grounds the temporal synthesis. The carnal chiasm makes the synchrony of the temporal flux possible, and so there is no reason to claim that this synchrony can never happen or that the different fields of experience (that of the touched hand and that of the touching hand) are unable to be unified in an immanent manner. The aporia in which Merleau-Ponty got stuck is alleviated: the chiasm is possible, or at least temporality is not an obstacle for it. But this does not mean that it really happens: another obstacle could well prevent the touching hand from totally being identified with the touched hand. If it is true that my flesh remains "incompletely constituted," that the two poles cannot be touching and touched at the same time, that a counter-time bars them from joining up, then we must see here the clue to a more radical discrepancy. Here also the flesh takes precedence over time and it is not a disjunction of time that impedes the flesh from being united with itself: rather, an internal divergence of the flesh breaks the temporal synchrony. What, then, bars the ego-flesh from traversing the divergence that splits it, from recognizing itself in this unknown entity, this non-ego, this non-flesh that is nevertheless its own flesh?

One of the greatest contemporary philosophers has recently confronted this question. In one of his last works, Derrida confronts the "metaphysics of the touch," which, according to him, still reigns in Husserl: a "haptocentrism" based on the traditional opposition between touching as a sense of proximity, of contact without distance, and the exteriority of vision. We would have to recognize on the contrary that the "*I* self-touches spacing itself out, losing contact with itself," that is, that *I touch myself without touching myself.*[10] I am never given to myself in a pure auto-affection miraculously protected against all alterity. By conceiving the chiasm as the immediate coincidence of two hands, we misunderstand both that "a certain *exteriority . . . must* even partake of the experience of the touching-touched,"[11] and that an absolutely exterior element must insinuate itself between the two sides of my flesh, an element "foreign to both the touching versant and the touched versant of the impression," a "parasite," an "intruder," that would nevertheless be the condition of the chiasm—the condition of its possibility but also (and *above all*) of its impossibility. Certainly, Derrida never simply claims that the chiasm is impossible but rather that it occurs without occurring, that it "happens without happening," that the flesh "is touched without being touched," and so forth. But I fear that these "undecidable" formulations that he so cherishes have only a purely rhetorical value here: they allow him to maintain an apparent equilibrium between the possible and the impossible and between coincidence and divergence, whereas the balance always tips to the same side, namely, that of the impossible. The draconian conditions that he imposes on it prevent the carnal synthesis from becoming knotted up: destabilized, dislodged by this foreign outside, this intruder that separates it from itself, the experience of self-coincidence "succeeds in interrupting itself," that is, it occurs only by interrupting itself, by immediately cancelling itself. The chiasm thus does not occur; it happens only by failing; like every event, *it happens only by not happening*.[12]

Just like Sartre, but for very different reasons, Derrida contests that a meeting or identification between the two disjoined poles of my flesh is possible. But why does he refuse to allow the possibility of a carnal synthesis? Why implant this exterior Other in the flesh, this Outside that impedes it from rejoining itself? For reasons that belong to fundamental motifs of his thought. According to Derrida, there can never be *pure* auto-affection or a purely immanent givenness, because "every auto-affection is traversed by an inner alterity" and reverts to a "hetero-affection." We would thus be concerned with a philosophy of auto-*hetero*-affection in which an irreducible alterity (which is stated in multiple ways as "trace," "rest," "specter," etc.) always comes to trouble the closure of the Same, prohibiting it from closing in on itself. And here again, the balance is not equal: in this knotting of the same and the other, the *heteron* in fact takes precedence over the *auton*. For Derrida, the Same (presence and self-identity, appropriation, coincidence, adequation, truth, meaning, etc.) can only be an effect of the Other (of *différance*, non-presence, interruption), and this alterity contaminates and destabilizes the Same that claims to erase it. Derrida applies this schema to the question of the touch, and this leads him to maintain that carnal contact (auto-affection) presupposes the "hiatus of non-contact" and that a hetero-affection inevitably interrupts the chiasm. I wonder whether this schema does violence to the phenomenon of touching. Perhaps it can be imagined differently, by inverting the primacy that Derrida confers on the *heteron*, and by considering carnal auto-affection, on the contrary, as the originary condition of the alterity haunting it. Certainly I am affected by myself *as an other*, but this alterity is purely apparent, and it is still me who affects me in this way. If this is indeed the case, the Derridean objection falls away, and nothing prohibits the flesh from embracing itself in a chiasm.

How do we decide *in truth* between these two conceptions of the touch, these two versions of auto-hetero-affection? It is precisely the truth that will make all the difference: we must wonder if this Other, this foreign Outside, is truly foreign to the ego-flesh or whether it is instead a matter of self-blindness, of a self-dissimulation of the flesh, of an *internal* fold or withdrawal, of a part of my flesh that forgets itself and is presented in an illusory manner, as if it came from the Outside and from the Other. Derrida could not accept this, first of all because he refuses to distinguish truth and nontruth: for him, "truth is phantasm itself." He thus risks mistaking a phantom for the truth, of letting himself get trapped by the *apparent* exteriority of element X that emerges in the heart of the chiasm, without perceiving that this Stranger is the flesh of my flesh. What is this phantom, this untouchable that haunts the touch, and where does it come from? He gives us a rather disappointing response to this question. According to Derrida, this heterogeneous element proceeds simply from the *visibility* of the tactile surface: it is because "of the possibility of the hand being seen" that the gesture of touching "cannot be reduced to a pure experience of the purely proper body."[13] No alterity, no self-divergence, would characterize the touch *as such*: they would affect it only from the outside, in the radical exteriority of vision. We too quickly conclude from this strange analysis of the possibility of my flesh seeing itself that my flesh touching itself is impossible. This strange turn leads us to the classical position opposing the immanence of the touch to the exteriority of sight: in this way, Derrida falls back into the "haptocentrism" that he had criticized in Husserl. The deconstruction of the metaphysics of the touch comes up short. This is no doubt the consequence of an analysis that puts such a strong emphasis on the Outside, on hetero-affection: it no longer succeeds in finding *in* the tactile field the alterity that affects it and can only attribute it to a radically foreign element. By insisting at this point on the "conditions of impossibility" of the chiasm and by rejecting outside of the flesh the heterogeneous element haunting it, Derrida bars us from reconciling with it and from freeing ourselves of the phantom assailing us. In order to understand how the chiasm is possible and how we could overcome this haunting, we must be more Derridean than Derrida himself: instead of attributing it to vision, we must try to locate the birthplace of the Untouchable *in touch*.

8

In Contact with the Untouchable:
The Remainder

The Residue of Sacrifice containeth name, and form, and world:
... Real, non-real, both are there, ... and Death, and strength:
... All things that breathe the breath of life, all creatures that have eyes to see,
... Inbreath and outbreath, eye and ear, decay and freedom from decay,
All the celestial Gods whose home is heaven sprang from the Residue.

—*Atharva-Veda*, book XII, hymn VII

Philosophers who have approached the question of the tactile chiasm fall into an antinomy: either they (like Husserl) presuppose that the chiasm is possible yet neither inquire *how* it is produced nor take account of the divergence or hiatus that breaks it apart, or they take note of this divergence only then to conclude (with Sartre and Derrida) that the chiasm is impossible or "only interrupts itself," or (like Merleau-Ponty) they oscillate between the two terms of the alternative, emphasizing sometimes the coincidence and sometimes the divergence. One thing, though, is certain in all these cases: if there is indeed an aporia of the chiasm, if it is true that some still unknown element is an obstacle for it, this results neither from a temporal disjunction nor from the exteriority of the visible, but rather from a carnal divergence internal to touching itself. In tactile experience, each pole of flesh attains the other pole only *from the outside*, perceiving it as a foreign thing with which it collides without ever joining. It seems absolutely impossible that my touching flesh *recognizes itself* in my touched flesh: how could the ego-flesh join this insensible and inert thing without renouncing its singularity, its carnality, its life? It is a matter here of an essential impossibility or a radical demarcation separating the ego from the non-ego, the flesh from the non-flesh. And this insurmountable separation of the egological difference is a major obstacle for the chiasm.

Yet the chiasm takes place—and it would therefore be absurd to inquire indefinitely about its possibility or its impossibility. It is a fact that *there is the chiasm*, for otherwise, I would not have a body. There would be no other and no world for me, and the whole of my experience would sink into a bottomless chaos. What defines an event is openness to *the possibility of impossibility*: there is an event when what appeared to be impossible, that is, what seemed never able to happen, nonetheless happens. This is above all true for the originary event that is the chiasm: it seems impossible that my immanent flesh could identify with what is given to it as a transcendent thing, but this impossibility is exactly what happens in each case. The desire to explain or constitute everything here reaches its limit: *that* the chiasm is possible, *that* my dispersed flesh unifies itself and makes itself into a body in the world—this is an event that no anterior condition or superior principle could provide a ground—a grace, a miracle, a gift that is given by the flesh to itself. But nothing justifies the claim that the abyss of the carnal difference can be entirely filled in: that two poles of the ego-flesh could recognize one another and be united does not imply that they are perfectly identified with one another. Let us risk a hypothesis here: it may be that the chiasm is brought about only by a *partial* and *precarious* identification, endlessly put into question by some element X, a divergence or gap that destabilizes it. Though Merleau-Ponty was not wrong to speak of "success in failure," this failure does not have the meaning he thought it did: rather than seeing in this failure the *imminence* of a virtual and always deferred synthesis, we must instead see the *irregularity* [*intermittence*] of a real but always failing synthesis. Despite its apparent "failure," the double synthesis is able to ground itself; my flesh is able to be united to my flesh and to give birth to my body. My incorporation and my subjectification will certainly remain fragile, punctuated by regressions and crises; and yet from the chaos of the primordial flesh, from the Diaspora of my fragmented egos, the outlines of a body and of a subject emerge in the world. I want to describe this very genesis, in which the nascent figure of my body is sketched out, then confused, only then to be fixed once again.

Here is the hypothesis I propose: if the identification brought about in the chiasm remains precarious, discontinuous, blinking, it is because it is partial and because each time it generates a leftover or a residue of non-flesh that is indissociable from my flesh. From now on, I will call this foreign element within the flesh the "remainder." No philosopher who has confronted the experience of the touch has been able to unravel this phenomenon completely. Aristotle had already noticed that despite appearances, tactile contact is never immediate: between that which touches and that which is touched is interposed a "milieu" [*metaxu*], which is the flesh, as if it were a hymen or a sort of "membrane" enveloping our body. Unlike sight, in which the distance between the seer and the seen is obvious, the unsensible divergence opening up between the touching and the touched is dissimulated and eludes contact: the flesh would be this untouchable condition of touching.[1] But the Greek philosopher neither took into account the particular experience of being touched nor gave tactility (and the sensible in general) the possibility of sensing itself, preventing him from noticing the phenomenon of the remainder. Conversely, by evoking the "hiatus" that impedes the two lips or leaves of my flesh from joining up, Merleau-Ponty had glimpsed the remainder but wrongly interpreted it as the effect of a temporal divergence. As for Husserl, he came very close to recognizing it when he remarked that in the experience of the touching-touched, the two initially separated tactile surfaces "can still overlap one another, and in certain manner, fuse, but do not merge." We are thus dealing with a partial fusion that allows discontinuous zones of the tactile field to "enter into a sort of continuity" and to "constitute one and the same surface," even though their "localities remain separate." And this, he adds, is "an altogether unique event on the phenomenological plane."[2] But he did not sufficiently deepen the analysis and was instead content to describe the partial overlapping without wondering what opposed a total fusion. Let us go one step further: if the two surfaces are identified without ever merging, then there must be a heterogeneous element that resists complete identification. This element X, which is an obstacle between the two poles within the chiasm, is the remainder. We begin now to understand why the flesh remains incompletely constituted: the synthesis that unites it to itself generates a remainder. In being given to itself, the ego-flesh opens a divergence within itself, marking a certain relation to alterity; and like the temporal synthesis constituting the field of presence, the originary carnal synthesis has the structure of an *auto-hetero-givenness*.

How do we understand this "entirely unique" phenomenon? The remainder is the untouchable of my touch as well as the invisible of my vision and the inaudible of my hearing; it can never be intuitively understood, nor will I ever encounter it in the world as one element among others in my daily experience. We will soon see that certain phenomena can provide us with an indirect access to the remainder and that although hatred, love, or dying can be seen as its "effects," they are never confused with it. It is a matter of an always fleeing limit-phenomenon: like the tactile phenomenon of which Aristotle spoke, it is always dissimulated in the experience that makes it possible; and like Plato's *khôra*, it is an "ever fleeting shadow of some other," and can come into being only in something else.[3] A theory of the remainder is clearly quite difficult to elaborate: it is related to what Heidegger called a "phenomenology of the inapparent." If the remainder is evasive, it is because it is constantly covered over by the chiasm and masked by the syntheses that unify and give body to the ego-flesh. In order to approach it, we must attempt a radical reduction: we must first put out of play the blinding certainties of being only one flesh, of having one body, and of being a unique ego. And then we must uncover the field of immanence of the ego-flesh in its originary multiplicity and try to *construct* the elementary phenomena given in this field, namely, the chiasm and the remainder.

An objection immediately arises. Because the remainder is not immediately accessible, it must be the object of a construction. What will protect it against drifting into the speculative? Can the genesis I am here sketching be anything other than an arbitrary fiction? I have reproached Husserl's successors for undertaking an excessive reduction that makes them lose contact with everyday experience, and I have criticized the Flesh of the world or absolute Life as no longer having any relation to my flesh or my life. But is not the always evasive remainder a still more abstract entity? There is only one answer to this kind of objection: there is a functional fecundity to such a construction, a capacity to take account of our experience and to respond to our most fundamental questioning—and this fecundity is quickly proven through concrete analyses. Were it not capable of throwing new light on the phenomena of love and hatred, dying and faith, madness and sovereignty, persecution and sacrifice, and so many others, the analysis of the remainder would not be worth our time. Husserl proposed a method, a sort of safeguard protecting us against drifting too far and juggling pure concepts. By undertaking a series of "free variations of the imagination," by freely forging new possibilities of thought, we end up encountering a radical possibility that brings the variation to a halt. We can thus determine the essence of a phenomenon (its *eidos*), prove its resistances to diverse variations, and circumscribe its limits. Husserl calls this method an "eidetic analysis." When I claim that the carnal chiasm engenders a remainder, this is not an arbitrary postulate but rather is a necessity of essence, a necessity of the eidetic order. Let us carry out a free variation of the imagination and ask what would happen if no divergence and no remainder subsisted between the poles of flesh. What would happen if each pole were able to identify with the other pole *without remainder*? Each pole would become absolutely identical to the other: the flesh of the other pole would merge with its own flesh; the site of the other would become confused with its own site. Each would become *the same* or a sort of "double" for the other, indiscernible from it. The carnal poles would stick to one another; they would be mixed and integrally fused together with nothing distinguishing them anymore. The flesh would fold back on itself, sink into itself. It would implode without ever successfully giving itself a body with differentiated organs. At the limit, there would be neither flesh nor ego but only an anonymous and unformed mass, a magma.

The chiasm therefore has to "fail," at least partially, because its "success"—the absolute fusion of carnal poles—would be a disaster that would throw the ego-flesh into a blind chaos. I will call this collapse or catastrophe that destroys the ego-flesh by the name the Greeks used to designate destruction, death, disappearance, the impossibility of appearing or of becoming manifest as phenomenon: *aphanisis*. The psychoanalyst Ernst Jones had used this term to qualify the object of fundamental anxiety, the fear of the total disappearance of sexual desire, whose derivative forms are castration anxiety and the fear of death. But I see things differently: this primordial anxiety is aroused by the possibility of self-annihilation, of the implosion of the ego-flesh. This eventuality is not simply a fiction or the result of a free variation of the imagination but is an always present threat: the conditions of the chiasm make this disaster possible, and the very same synthesis that allows my flesh to give itself a body also risks annihilating it. This terrifying possibility stands out in certain psychoses, when the subject becomes anxiety-ridden about a *black hole* threatening to suck him in and swallow him up. Autism also testifies to an attempt to construct a kind of "shell," a barrier in front of this abyss in order to try to save the ego and its flesh from their sinking into the abyss of *aphanisis*.[4] Remember that Husserl designated the "zero point" or absolute Here that is the site of my flesh as a *Raumloch* or a "hole of space." The chiasm allows the flesh to tear itself away from this gaping, endless, bottomless hole by inserting itself in the objective space of bodies. But this implies that the *Raumloch* is also inscribed in space and is thus transformed into a localized opening or interval between my flesh and my flesh, between the "here" of this pole and the "here" of the other pole. If this interval is unable to be maintained, the ego-flesh would risk falling back into the initial gaping pit, the hole of the *Raumloch*: this collapse is exactly what stands out in the anxiety of *aphanisis*. For the ego-flesh to escape from the Black Hole, for it to take on a body, it must be able to be united to itself by differentiating itself. Each of the poles must be distinguished from the others, perceiving them as *other* poles of the *same* flesh. This supposes that the fusion of poles is not complete in the chiasm and that some part of each pole resists identification—hence it supposes that there is a remainder that maintains the divergence, preventing the flesh from imploding and from sinking into the bottomless abyss. It is a matter of an eidetic necessity: if there were no remainder, there would be neither flesh nor ego. What I call the remainder is therefore defined above all by this openness: it guards my flesh against disaster, offering it a mouvance, a playing field in which it can appear and unfold itself. However ambivalent or threatening it may be, however mortifying it may become, the remainder is above all what protects the ego-flesh and makes its genesis possible—it is my ultimate condition of possibility.

The eidetic analysis has shown us that the existence of the ego flesh is indissociable from a remainder—but we do not yet see what this term means and what its relation to the ego is. A more concrete approach is necessary. Since the remainder is first given in a tactile experience, we must once again take up the analysis of sensible perception and apply it to the singular experience of the chiasm. What happens when I touch myself? I am at first dealing with two different perceptions, situated in two distinct poles, which fuse together and become one single, yet doubled, perception, a single flesh that is at once both touching and touched. Each of these initial perceptions is itself divided: I have the sensation of a transcendent object (for example, the smooth warm surface of the other hand I touch), and at the same time, I feel in the touching hand a pure sensation-of-smoothness, an immanent sensing. If I suspend every transcendent sensation and thus center the analysis on just one sensing, I discover that it, too, is divided: the primary content of perception (the smoothness or the warmth I sense), which already points at an exterior thing, is distinguished from a second layer (of motor sensings, affects, originary impressions) in which my flesh is affected only by itself, its own mouvance, its life. When I sense my hand moving, when I feel the tension or relaxation of my flesh, its effort, pleasure, suffering, I am dealing only with myself—and so what gives coincides with what is given. This second stratum belongs entirely to the flesh of the ego: I sense it as "mine," as "of my flesh." It implies the *consciousness of being mine*—even though the stratum of primary perceptual data is accompanied by *a consciousness of foreignness*. But these data themselves are not absolutely foreign to me: it is the smoothness or warmth that *I sense in my flesh*—and all these sensings, whether they are perceptual, affective, or motor, belong to my field of immanence and to my self-givenness. Among them, perceptual sensings are *both* mine *and* foreign *at the same time*: they form the nucleus of the foreign in me.

Thus, in the perception of each pole, I am dealing with a double apprehension, wherein the consciousness of being-mine is inseparably intertwined with a consciousness of foreignness. In the chiasm, this double apprehension present in each pole fuses with the double apprehension proper to the other pole—or more exactly, each of the two layers in one pole fuses with what properly corresponds to it in the other pole. The consciousnesses of being-mine and of being my flesh unify to form the singular consciousness of being one sole flesh and one sole ego, while the consciousnesses of foreignness also unify and are subsequently presented as the aim of a Thing foreign to, yet indissociable from, my flesh—that is, as a remainder. When the other pole joins with and shares its sensations with the first, each pole collides with the perception of this resistant surface that it senses as foreign. It continues to be conscious of a foreignness that persists in the other pole but no longer perceives it as *totally* foreign, because it recognizes the other pole as the flesh of its flesh. The meaning of alterity is thus modified through the experience of the chiasm: the other pole is qualified no longer as a transcendent thing but rather as an internal "other"; it is interiorized in me, encrusted in my flesh but without ceasing to be foreign to it. This is how the consciousness of an *intimate stranger* emerges in me—as the obsessive presence of the remainder. It is therefore not a matter of an originary phenomenon, because it does not precede the chiasm: it arises from it and helps it to be established. Issued from the chiasm, it becomes an obstacle to it and thus at the same time safeguards it, preventing it from sinking into *aphanisis*. By resisting it, it allows it to happen.

Certain essential traits flow from the genesis I have just described. It thus appears that (1) it is a synthetic phenomenon; (2) it is transcendent in immanence; (3) it produces a cleavage within the ego, an unconscious effect, a haunting; (4) it is foreign to the world and to Being; and (5) it is only an appearance, a mode of nontruth. Born of a synthesis, the remainder results from the fusion of several layers, several currents of consciousness hitherto distinct, and we will see that it has totally opposed functions, that it has more than one face, that it elicits hatred or disgust just as much as fascination, desire, or love. Its hybrid character and ambivalence are once again emphasized if we move from the tactile field to other fields of experience, where other effects (visual, auditory, intersubjective), based and superimposed on the primordial tactile remainder, are formed. If the remainder is always in solidarity with my flesh, its unfurling and crises, it is because *it is of my flesh*, rooted in the immanence of my tactile sensings, and because it is issued from this originary synthesis whereby I am self-given. And yet it continually resists this synthesis: it is what is given in my flesh as foreign to my flesh. Though it belongs to my field of immanence, it appears to me as a transcendent Thing affecting me from the outside, as a *transcendence in immanence*—an Other in the Same, a stranger hidden in the most intimate folds of my flesh. Husserl tried several times to think transcendence in immanence, but he never clearly defined it, sometimes assimilating it to consciousness of the past, sometimes to the pure ego, sometimes to the alter ego. He did not uncover the phenomenon of the remainder, which is present as the First Stranger, the originary transcendence that I encounter within my immanent life. The intrigues that I will tie together with other transcendences (those of the body, the other, the world, Being, or God) are already prefigured in my initial relation to the remainder. How do we qualify this paradoxical situation? In homage to Freud's *fort-da*—the game his grandson played by throwing a little toy top far (*fort*) and then bringing it back here (*da*)—, I will call this by the name *Fort-Dasein*. The notion of "extimity" (that is, exterior intimacy) created by Lacan in order to define the place of the object of phantasm, is entirely suitable here. But the best name given it was thought of by an ingenious novelist: we will baptize this invisible Other—this clandestine Double that obsesses and devours me, this strange *Outside* that reemerges in a frightening proximity—the *Horla*.

In the chiasm, the ego-flesh gives itself to itself. Formerly dispersed among different poles of flesh, the consciousnesses of being-mine are unified in order to form one consciousness of one unique ego. At the same time, the consciousnesses of foreignness also unify themselves and constitute another, distinct, consciousness of the Other-in-me, which is the remainder. When it emerges from the chiasm, the ego-flesh discovers that it is divided, torn apart by the doubling of consciousnesses, which is the work of the remainder. We have seen that the major function of the ego is to ensure the unification of the currents of consciousness and to integrate a unitary field of consciousness of the present and the past, of the consciousness that perceives and that which imagines, of my consciousness of myself and one of the other, and so forth. Its synthetic activity encounters its limit, however, when it runs up against a foreignness that it is never able to overcome, namely, the irreducible alterity of the remainder. This other-consciousness intertwined with mine is presented as foreign to my consciousness—that is, as *of the unconscious*. Merleau-Ponty was not wrong to say that the untouchable of my touch, the invisible of my vision, is also "the unconscious of my consciousness."[5] This does not mean that the remainder would come from a mysterious Unconscious anterior to it. On the contrary, the cleavage of the ego provoked by the remainder prevents it from appearing in my consciousness, and this is what grounds the possibility of phenomena that do not appear to me—which is to say, unconscious phenomena. The remainder is thus not an offshoot of the unconscious, but rather the unconscious is an effect of the remainder. And so the science of the unconscious entity, psychoanalysis, must be connected to a more radical theory capable of describing this originary scene wherein the remainder unfolds its phantasms—namely, an egoanalysis. It is time to end the dogmatic demarcation between the ego and a more ancient "unconscious Id" from which it issues: in truth, this other scene is the unconscious *of my consciousness* and remains inseparable from the ego. Even if it seems to come from the outside or to impose itself on me as an Other, the remainder is born of my flesh, of my carnal sensings. It is a part of myself presented as other than me, as a crypt dissimulated in me. No matter how far or distant it may seem, it nevertheless belongs to my flesh and to my life. It is mine. It is me.

The remainder is a *inapparent* phenomenon (or if you prefer, an "unconscious" phenomenon)—and yet it is still a *phenomenon*, which means above all else that it appears, that it *is given* to me. Like the fugitive phantom in the *Timaeus* or the ghost of which Descartes spoke—a phantasm "which suddenly appears to me and just as quickly disappears," without me seeing where it came from or where it goes—it affects and obsesses me without ever presenting itself "in person" in the light of my consciousness. How are we to qualify this apparition that assails me while escaping my grasp, this manner of being offered to me while also evading me, of giving itself in me as foreign to me? I will call this a *haunting*. There are different sorts of haunting and each of them is singular, as are the remainder and the ego that it haunts. It is always accompanied by a more or less intense anxiety, but haunting is sometimes also colored by disgust, hatred, or horror, or on the contrary is sometimes presented as a fascinated attraction with all the characteristics of desire or amorous passion. It is closely akin to the "obsession" and "traumatism" Levinas described, which is awakened not only in the encounter with the other person considered as a "total object": most often, it is attached to a *partial* mark, a physical detail, a sign, a look, a voice, and it may also aim at a simple thing, a fetish object or an object of horror at the heart of a phobia. Everything thus leads us to believe that my obsessive relation with others in fact derives from a primordial haunting addressed to an Other without face. Its most characteristic trait is probably its apparent absurdity: it suddenly emerges in the universe and reassures our everyday existence, irrationally released by a simple word, an insignificant gesture, an unimportant detail. As soon as it irrupts, everything that appears, all the realities of the world, awaken and revive it, as if the entire world endlessly recalled us to our haunting. And when it breaks away from and overwhelms the ego, no ordinary reality seems able to resist it. Its indetermination and apparent indifference to every empirical "object" are signs that haunting *does not belong to the world*, is not the effect of a real cause—not even a psychical unconscious cause—but rather attests to a more originary phenomenon, namely, that it is rooted in the immanent life of the ego. The factor releasing it operates as a hanging point, a random element X that allows for a punctual encounter, an intersection of the ego's plane of immanence and the transcendence of the world. This element enjoys no privilege and possesses no particular value: it is merely a point of passage between two planes. And it will be immediately abandoned if another element fills this function better than the first. What reveals such a phenomenon to us is the fragility of our world—and what its "reasons" and "causes" are worth when a haunting emerges from the most profound layers of our life.

One of the most remarkable characteristics of the haunting is its temporal style. It possesses its own temporality, which does not at all resemble everyday temporality. Although ordinary phenomena of our existence appear and then slip away into the past, thus losing their living force and are soon forgotten, the haunting does not disappear or sink into a past but constantly comes back, reappearing at any moment and in every new impression, as if a past impossible to overcome has contaminated the living present, encrusted itself in it. The phenomenon of the haunting thus seems to transgress a fundamental law of temporality: it interferes with the *fluidity* of the temporal flow, with the incessant eviction of the present impression into the past by another impression. The time of haunting is given as a petrified, immobile time, a *contretemps* or *setback* in which death arises in the life of the living present and paralyzes it. Like every true event, the haunting is *without a why*, appears without motivation, and disappears without reason. What is presented in the analysis as its unconscious mental "cause" is probably only an occasion, a pretext allowing it to be manifested. My haunting does not necessarily come from a distant past, from an infantile trauma, or a returning "repressed" conflict: it reveals the nagging insistence of a present impression that is repeated from one moment to the next and clings to every present moment by refusing to let it flow into its past. The haunting is the remainder's mode of givenness, its always singular manner of giving itself to my consciousness, and we know that the remainder resists the chiasm and the carnal synthesis that engendered it. The chiasm gives time: by synchronizing the temporality of the different poles of flesh and fusing their mouvances, it allows each temporal sequence to link itself to others within the same unitary flux. But the remainder breaks this synchrony. It thus introduces a temporal interval or discrepancy in the heart of the living present and widens the divergence between the originary impression and its retention. From then on, instead of being rooted in subsequent phases, a certain temporal sequence persists and is encrusted as a block of frozen time unable to pass. The obsessive temporality of haunting would be the index of a rupture of synchrony, of a crisis of the chiasm wherein my flesh, uniting itself to my flesh, becomes a gift of its duration.

How is the irruption of the remainder manifested in the ego's life? It is inseparable from an affect that gives its somber tonality to the moments of the haunting. This affect is anxiety: it invades me at the moment when the Other, the stranger from the outside, suddenly reemerges very close to me, in me. Certainly, the remainder stands most often beyond my consciousness, separated from the conscious ego by a cleavage, but the border is not absolutely impervious, and the remainder sometimes crosses it in order to penetrate me. This crossing gives birth to anxiety. By underlining that it does not have a determinate object, that it is awakened by the Nothing—the nothingness of death, of Being, or of freedom—the philosophies of existence have emphasized an essential characteristic of anxiety. And yet, as Lacan clearly saw, anxiety is "not without object," even if its paradoxical "object" is nothing determinate, not a thing in the world. In haunting, and in the anxiety that it provokes, the remainder of my flesh is suddenly revealed to me. It is the *affect of the remainder*: in the originary phenomenon of anxiety, the truth of the remainder is disclosed when I discover this stranger who has always haunted the most intimate parts of my life. Such a discovery calls into question everything I thought I knew about myself, everything that allowed me to situate myself as a determinate "subject" and to differentiate myself and the other, the proper and the foreign. The Question is awakened in the burning of anxiety. This is a matter not of philosophical interrogation but of *the question that I myself am*, a question concerning my relation to the remainder. It is no doubt different for each of us, but some of its formulations are regularly encountered in experience. It most often takes the form of a choice between two possible options, an agonizing alternative concerning the very identity of the subject. Lacan had sketched out the typical and the clinical forms of the question; he looked for which interrogation characterized each type of neurosis or psychosis. "Am I a man or am I a woman?" would be the question for the hysteric, while the obsessive would wonder whether he were living or dead. This classifications seems too rigid and static to me: such questions secretly traverse all existence and are not situated on the same plane or in the same phase of our genesis. "Am I living or dead?"—this, for a living ego, is a "crazy" question and yet also one of the most decisive. "Am I myself, or another?" Am I myself or a foreign thing? All of these questions reveal a fundamental haunting, and essentially ask whether I am an ego of flesh or its remainder. Other questions will be posed later on another level: I must encounter other humans, define myself by myself as a "man," subject like others to the Law, so that I may then ask the question already posed by Dora, Gregor Samsa, and Joseph K: "am I a man or a woman? An animal or a human? Innocent or guilty?" These alternatives—and above all the most originary—are the consequence of a cleavage within the ego-flesh, a scission between what is mine and what appears to me as an Other, between a living part of my flesh and another that seems dead, foreign, or filthy [*immonde*] to me. Is it possible to get beyond this cleavage? Why does the remainder so often present itself in this way as a mortal menace, a specter, an unnamable thing? Could the ego overcome its haunting; could it engage in a different relation with the remainder and perhaps be reconciled with it? Such questions designate the ultimate horizon of this research, and in order to approach them, still more radical analyses will be necessary.

What, then, is the remainder? Could it be nothing at all, neither a being nor the Being of a being? Could it not belong to the plane of Being? But how would this be possible, since it *is* precisely the remainder of my flesh? What philosophy has called *Being* since the Greeks is the luminous horizon of the world, wherein all that is comes to appear. The world is the horizon of the visible, and its thread is woven of symbols, articulated by the Logos, by language, which is the "house of Being." The transcendence of Being, of the world, is situated at the intersection of the visible and the sayable, and we must wonder whether the remainder can appear in these two dimensions, whether it is given to sight in the spectacle of the world, and whether it lets itself be said in the order of the Logos. As Husserl noted, there is not a visual chiasm, and I will never be able to see myself seeing: where the visible reigns there is neither chiasm nor flesh, and therefore, there will not be a remainder. Born of a tactile synthesis, the remainder eludes sight and never appears in the horizon of the world. Even though its different corporeal figurations populate our phantasms, the remainder never shows itself "in person" in the imaginary scenarios that awaken our anxiety or sustain our desires. The remainder *remains invisible* in every image—and this also means that it is inscribed there *as* invisible, as the most secret vanishing point of the picture. What is true for vision is also true for language: the name *remainder* itself designates an Unnamable beyond the reach of the Logos, which all words try in vain to name. It is the invisible of my vision, the unsayable of my speech, the unhearable of my hearing, the blind point of the spectacle, the outside-of-language, the *Horla*, the nonworldly [*im-monde*],[6] the foreign of Being. If we try to approach the mystery of the remainder, we would need the audacity of a Meister Eckhart or an Antonin Artaud, of those who tried to think beyond Being. We have to look for it where Rodez's solitary figure dreaded it, in the unsayable cruelty of a *life without Being*, of a flesh that "cannot suffer being," and which is *me*. In *Glas* and other writings, Derrida questioned a "leftover" [*un reste*] or a "remaindering" [*une restance*] that had escaped Being. What I call the "remainder" is obviously not without relation to this motif. But Derrida does not relate it to the touch, to the tactile chiasm—a chiasm, moreover, that he judges impossible, that "would only fail"—and these terms always qualify for him *a general function* (the "remaindering" of the text insofar as it resists interpretations or of the trace of writing insofar as it survives its "author," etc.), whereas the remainder that I am trying to thematize here is the *always singular effect* of an equally singular event.

This much at least has been gained: the remainder is not *truly* foreign to me. When it breaks into my life, it is still my flesh that is given to me; I am anxious about myself, about an unknown part of my ego. Relentlessly stalked by this phantom, overwhelmed by its haunting, the ego is affected only by itself. Before the carnal synthesis is effected, my flesh is initially given to itself in the touch as an exterior thing, similar to other things in the world, and its poles do not recognize one another as parts of the same flesh. The chiasm is able to dispel this originary dissimulation by revealing the ego-flesh to itself in each of its poles. It works actively for the truth and is a major mode of *alétheia*. But this discovery is never integral, and the flesh refuses to let itself be entirely stripped bare. The part of my flesh that in each pole persists in giving itself to the other pole as nonflesh is the remainder. In other words, it has no consistency of its own, is only an appearance, an inevitable illusion, *a counter-truth* that is an obstacle to the disclosure of the ego-flesh. We would mistake this phenomenon if we considered it as a totally exterior element, an "intruder" or a "prosthesis" artificially implanted in my flesh. Certainly the remainder is presented in this way, as the traits of an Other assaulting me from the outside, but only because it dissimulates its true identity: in truth, it is the flesh of my flesh. It is because the ego-flesh has forgotten itself, is blinded to itself, that a remainder arises and I must be able to free myself, at least in part, from the illusion that traps me. What I call the haunting is not reduced to a simple appearance or apparition: it is the remainder itself that is manifested in this manner, as a *Horla*, a menacing Double that surges forth in me and disrupts my life. There is thus a truth of the haunting: it reveals the *place of the remainder* to me, the true site of this phenomenon that had wrongly appeared to me as a transcendent Other. And yet it is only a matter of a *partial* discovery: if this Other intruding in my life arouses my anxiety or my hatred, it is because I continue to dread it as an Other and because it moves about and is encrusted most deeply in my flesh while keeping all of its initial strangeness. Is a more radical disclosure possible, one that would not be limited to a simple displacement but would concern the very essence of the remainder? How could it be given in another mode, revealing its true face to me, which is another face of myself? And what would happen if the ego finally stopped repressing this accursed share?[7] If there were no longer a remainder, nothing would prevent the carnal poles from merging into one another and becoming indiscernible. The ego-flesh would be liberated from its haunting only in order to sink into the bottomlessness of *aphanisis*. How will the remainder be able to maintain itself *as remainder*—as this third party, this divergence preventing my flesh from imploding, from disappearing into its own abyss, while also recognizing that it is a part of my life, that it is *me*?

In the haunting of the remainder, truth and nontruth are intertwined, and only a more radical truth, a more authentic disclosure, can free me of my haunting. My flesh is thus the place of and the stake in a conflict between truth and nontruth, chiasm and remainder, and this combat will rarely cease in my life. Each synthesis, each unfolding of the ego-flesh, is accompanied by a new uncovering, an advance of the carnal truth. From each failure of the synthesis and every crisis of the chiasm, new illusions emerge, new phantasms that profoundly mark my relation to my body, the world, and others. Through these phantasms, I dread the remainder in the anxiety of death by anticipating my becoming-corpse; the abjection of the remainder becomes the target of my hatred while its transfiguration constitutes it as my first object of love. It is the Persecutor with which delirium is obsessed, and it is probably also what the mystic hopes to attain in that breakthrough that we strangely call "ecstasy." Our concern now is to sketch out a few characteristics of this intrigue of the flesh and the remainder that weaves the thread of our life, and to describe what becomes of the remainder in the process of incorporation through the encounter with others and the crises of the chiasm. Surely such a genesis does not take place in the time of the world: it happens in an originary temporal flux that knows neither succession nor simultaneity. Names fail to describe this immanent temporality. We can figure it out for ourselves only on the basis of our ordinary experience, present it as a story, a process whose different phases succeed one another. Such a presentation is not false and is probably the only one possible, even if it necessarily deforms what it exposes. We do, of course, have the right to consider all this as a fable, a simple fiction destined to figure the infigurable, but "fiction is the source that feeds the knowledge of 'eternal truths.'"[8] This story tries to tell the drama of our life. If by respecting the limits that the eidetic analysis prescribes, the story brings an answer to the fundamental questions of our existence, if it permits the disclosure of the originary configurations of the ego-flesh, it is because this fiction is true.

9

This Is (Not) My Body: The
Remainder of Incorporation

And if I did not see myself in the glass . . . I did not dare advance . . . feeling certain nevertheless that He was there, but that He would never escape me again, He whose imperceptible body had absorbed my reflection.

—Guy de Maupassant, "Horla"

Wherever I look, I see only bodies near and far, some immobile, others in movement. Among these bodies, there is one that possesses very particular qualities. It is the only one that is never far from me. A faithful companion, it goes everywhere with me, as if we were soldered together. It is the only body that never appears facing me in its entirety, the only one that I cannot walk around and that I cannot have in front of me as my object. It is the only visible and tangible body that seems to coincide with the very source of my touching and my vision, and is one with my opening to the world—my body. It is similar to other bodies, exposed like them to sight and to contact, attracted or repulsed by them, brushed against, impacted, moved, or stopped by them. And yet it is not identical to all the others: Husserl said that it is "the only body that is not only a body [*Körper*], but also flesh [*Leib*]." Have we sufficiently taken account of this paradox? How does my body manage to straddle this carnal difference, that is, to be neither entirely *Leib* nor entirely *Körper* and yet both body and flesh? There is nothing in common between the flesh and bodies,

between this immanent flesh that is my flesh, that is me, and those foreign bodies arising "over there" in the transcendence of the world, then
slipping out of my perceptual field. My flesh is not of this world, and none
of the categories that apply to the things of the world would be suitable to
it. Neither full nor empty, it has neither a front nor a back, neither an inside nor an outside. Since it is always here, in this absolute Here that will
never be over there, nothing can move it or displace it elsewhere in space;
and as it has neither "interior" nor "exterior"—nothing can penetrate or
come out of it. Inviolable, intangible, invisible, deprived of center, of contour, of differentiated organs, it is unfurled in itself as a *khôra*, an unformed
and limitless spacing.

By a strange paradox, this flesh subtending all my perceptions does
not see, hear, or touch. Descartes taught us this—*videor videre*: it seems
that I see, I *sense myself* seeing, hearing, or touching. In being affected by
my carnal impressions, I affect only myself and never leave myself. But this
solipsistic flesh is also what opens me to the things and to Being: I sense
myself seeing the brightness of the visible, I sense myself hearing the deep
rumblings of the world, and my flesh diffuses itself beyond itself, as far as
my experience extends, up to the ultimate confines of Being. It is this non-
limitation that most differentiates the flesh from bodies, which are always
delimited, surrounded by other bodies or bordered by empty beaches
within a unique and homogenous space wherein all spaces are distributed.
Insofar as it is situated in space, in the horizon of the visible, my body is
exposed [*exposé*] there in every sense of this word: exhibited, delivered to
sight but also to contact, to shocks, to multiple pressures exerted on it by
other bodies. It makes itself vulnerable to [*s'expose à*] the overwhelming
transcendence of the world in the same way that one experiences danger
or a mortal risk. It lays itself out [*s'ex-pose*], finally, by situating [*se posant*]
outside of itself, by ceaselessly diverging from itself in order to devote itself
to others and to things.[1] This exposition defining the corporeity of the
body destines it to alienation, to diverse political and technical manipula-
tions, to "disciplines" and training of all kinds—and we may wonder
whether the flesh is able to be incorporated without at the same time letting itself be subjugated by the dominant images of the body. But we must
above all examine how this incorporation is possible, how the limitless
chaos of my flesh is able to delimit itself, to organize itself into the form of
a body. A complex intrigue is played out here between the one and the

multiple. For the originary multiplicity of my flesh is infinitely diffracted, and its incorporation supposes a series of chiasms in which its innumerable poles encounter and unite with one another, and in which their mouvances recognize one another and are wedded. This synthesis, however, only reveals the unity of what was *already* originarily one. This unique element, this homogenous milieu, must be divided and differentiated so that corporal organs and distinct parts articulated within a whole can appear. When the anonymous poles indifferently unfold their mouvances, a right hand comes to be distinguished from a left hand, an eye from a mouth, a sexual orifice from some other orifice. And so, incorporation consists not merely in leading the multiple back to the one but also in engendering a plurality on the basis of an indeterminate unity.

The great mystery is not Incarnation but rather incorporation, and it is less a matter of knowing how the Word becomes flesh than it is of understanding how the flesh becomes body—and in becoming body, how it could invoke the Word. Husserl tried to respond to this question. He described the "self-objectification" of the flesh, its transformation into a "corporeal thing," as a complex processes in which several different experiences intervene, especially the experience of the passivity of my flesh (my hand is bumped by the other, pushed like a thing), the experience of the coincidence of vision and touch (I discover that the hand I see is the same as the hand I touch), and finally the relation to others who perceive me from the outside as a material body. This analysis does not seem convincing to me. The passivity of my flesh is differentiated from the inertia of things because it is always reversible—because this hand, displaced or manipulated like an inanimate object, can at any moment turn back against whatever is manipulating it in order to move it in its turn. This reversibility should prevent one hand of flesh from being assimilated to a simple thing. Though they are very subtle, Husserl's analyses nevertheless end up at the same difficulty: we do not see how a moving multiplicity of undifferentiated poles can be transformed into a human organism; or how this unique flesh that is mine, an absolutely singular flesh foreign to the world, can nevertheless appear in the world as a body similar to other bodies; or how my flesh can become a thing without at the same time ceasing to be flesh.

We will have to look for the key to this enigma in the originary event by which the ego-flesh is given to itself: the possibility of my incorporation is rooted in the carnal chiasm. This is effected, as we have seen, through a double synthesis: to the horizontal synthesis of incarnation, by which each pole incarnates and identifies with the other pole, is linked a second synthesis, in which each pole senses itself touched by the other, as if by a thing. Prior to the primordial synthesis, such a perception would have remained foreign to it—but the other pole is now revealed to it as its own flesh. Henceforth, it senses "with" or "through" this other pole; it perceives *itself* as the other pole perceives it, as a touched thing with the smooth and warm surface of an exterior body. This perception-of-thing is superimposed on its perception-of-flesh, on its own feeling of being flesh; the two impressions overlap, thus engendering a new impression—that of being both touching and touched, both flesh and body. In the horizontal synthesis, each pole leaving itself straddles the abyss in order to give its flesh to the other pole; in this new synthesis, each of them *in itself traverses* the difference of the flesh and the body. It is for this reason that I designate it as a *transversal* synthesis, and this synthesis is what grounds the possibility of incorporation. The horizontal synthesis allows the ego-flesh to be unfolded as a field of immanence, to be extended as a surface by passing from one simple pole to a plane; this new synthesis, based on the first, gives another dimension to the ego-flesh, the opening of a transcendence, allowing it to overflow itself into the depths of the world.

Is this sufficient to elucidate the mystery of incorporation? How does the transversal synthesis cross the abyss that separates my immanent flesh from the transcendence of bodies? Even if it happens that my perception-of-thing and my perception-of-flesh overlap or intersect in the same experience, these two impressions could well succeed one another without being confused. Instead of living *in the same time*, in one same field of presence as flesh and body, the ego would perceive these impressions *alternatively* opposed in each of its poles: the being-flesh and the being-thing would coexist exteriorly without ever fusing in one unique body of flesh—as with the hemiplegics who are no longer able to recognize their paralyzed limb and understand it as a dead thing, a cadaver's leg implanted in their flesh. So that my flesh becomes body while remaining flesh, there must be a passage, a hinge between the two planes, an *entre-deux*, a *metaxu* that is neither merely flesh nor totally body. We already know this third element, this part of the ego-flesh that is given like a stranger to my flesh: it is the remainder. Transcendent but immersed in immanence, both mine and other, flesh and thing, the remainder belongs to neither of the two planes but traverses them both, thus allowing them to be joined. It is in this sense that I understand Merleau-Ponty's obscure indication that there must be something other than the body for the junction to occur, that it takes place "in the untouchable." How is this joining effected? We have seen that the chiasm results in an interiorization, an *injection* of the remainder in the flesh: when the two poles are identified, the remainder of the other pole no longer appears to me as an absolutely foreign entity but rather as an intimate alterity; it penetrates into the deepest parts of my flesh, is more and more narrowly intertwined with it, and ends up merging with it. As the remainder is not really foreign to my flesh, a synthesis remains possible. Even if it is only a matter of a partial identification, even if the remainder is never completely reabsorbed in the flesh, they are nevertheless able to be united. Incorporation thus consists in *incarnating the remainder*, conferring on it certain traits of flesh, while the flesh appropriates some of the remainder's determinations for itself. The ego-flesh crosses the border separating it from the remainder, offers its carnation to the residue of nonflesh, giving it the meaning of being a living flesh. This rebel foreignness that I integrate into my flesh gives it all the qualities of a thing, allowing it to be delimited, to be inserted in space, to be put at risk of the transcendence of the world, like a body among other bodies, and to be exposed to the contacts and shocks, making it infinitely vulnerable; but I also recognize this foreignness as my own. A new reality then appears, possessing properties of the ego-flesh and of the remainder at the same time (in the same manner as, in the platonic myth of Eros, the son of Resource and Poverty participating in the double nature of its parents). This hybrid entity, this bizarre mix of flesh and thing—both immanent and transcendent, one and multiple, invisible and visible, always mine and exposed to the Other—is what I call *my body*. The carnal synthesis is what gives birth to it when the flesh fecundates the remainder, recognizes itself in it, frees it (at least in part) from the foreign appearance that had dissimulated it to itself.

What allows my flesh to be incorporated is thus the mediation of the remainder—and this function is revealed *a contrario* when it is unable to guarantee the mediation or to form the hinge between the two planes: instead of being joined, they are pushed apart and diverge. Flesh and body are opposed, then, as two hostile entities, and the very possibility of an encounter, of a passage from one to the other, will be feared as a terrifying threat. This is why incorporation is so often presented in fantasy or myth as an intolerable violence inflicted on the flesh. Artaud thus denounces the appearance of the visible body, of the organic body, as the result of an "abject operation," a mutilation that dissociates the "true body"—the invisible flesh without organs—and destines it to death. He imagined this antagonism only from the point of view of the flesh, but it is also possible to understand it from the opposite point of view by considering the flesh as a threat to the body. "The essence of flesh is decomposition," wrote Mishima, and he tried to counter this decline of his flesh by *disincarnating* his body, by fashioning himself a powerful and perfect body, a body-work-of-art whose every muscle would be like a "ray of light." Yet this ascetic and glorious "sun-body" succeeds in overcoming the ignoble collapse of the flesh only by hastening it toward its self-destruction, by mobilizing all its energy in the ritualized staging of its death—because "the thing that ultimately saves the flesh from being ridiculous is the element of death that resides in the healthy, vigorous body."[2] When all mediation fails, when only a reciprocal *repulsion* subsists between the two planes, the coming-into-the-world of the flesh, the coming-into-life of the body, becomes impossible: either the flesh is unincorporated and collapses into the ignoble chaos that Artaud spoke of, or the body is disincarnated by ceding to the element of death that haunts it and ends by annihilating it. The transversal synthesis allows this double disaster to be conjured away by offering to my flesh a body in the world and by giving to this body the gift of its movement and of life.

Born of the happy union of flesh and the remainder, this body is not a mere thing in the universe of things. It is not a question here of "this machinery of organs that we observe in the cadaver," of the objective body studied by the sciences, x-rayed, scanned, dissected, provided with mechanical prostheses and grafts. It is a matter of the *Leibkörper* evoked by Husserl, *a body of flesh*, of one sole body that is also flesh, a unique body in the world that I feel as mine, that is not merely visible and tangible but also touching, seeing, desiring, suffering, and living. This body in its endless movement—of pleasure, pain, and joy, traversed by fantasies, drives, and affects—is the body that Freud discovered when he listened to the speech of hysterics. It is an already divided body, parceled out in zones of suffering or pleasure, an "organic" body in a certain sense, but whose phantasmatic anatomy differs profoundly from the anatomy described by medicine and biology—because it is composed only of fluid, unstable semi-organs, displacing and connecting them together, and of orifices and protrusions, any one of which can be substituted for any other, just as Dora's painful throat is identified with her vagina or Anna's paralyzed arm with an erect penis. By its plasticity and its unending metamorphoses, such a body still remains quite close to the initial chaos of the flesh and its limit-less mouvance, its reversibility, its infinite plasticity that allows each of its poles to pass into other poles and be identified with them. It is on the surface of this body that Freud thought he had found the origin of the ego, and this *Körper-Ich* issuing from the double tactile sensations is, in fact, a modification of the primordial ego-flesh, the first phase of its incorporation. And it is likewise on the surface of the ego-body that we have to look for the traces of the remainder. It is the support of my incorporation, and my entire existence is sustained by this phantom, traversed by its haunting; and yet certain traits of the body of flesh bear its mark more than others do.

The remainder is above all what ensures a gap, maintains an openness between the two poles of the chiasm, by preventing the ego-flesh from imploding in the abyss of *aphanisis*. The more the flesh draws near to itself, the more it tries to take hold of and fuse with itself, the more it runs up against the remainder that rejects it, and the more it diverges from itself. It thus exercises a sort of *repulsion* on the flesh, which we must understand in an affectively neutral way, without abjection or disgust, as a placing at a distance or a pushing away, a primordial rejection. Everything leads us to believe that it persists during the incorporation, despite the new alliance of the flesh and the remainder, as if the threat of *aphanisis*, the terror of chaos, of indifferentiation, were never truly dissipated. How and where is it inscribed in the body? In everything that traces out a *limit*, that delimits the body by exposing it to the outside: right on the skin and the corporeal orifices. When I palpate the surface of my body, I always end up on a sort of screen enveloping all of its parts, opposing penetration. During incorporation, the resistant envelope of a skin unfolds itself and extends over the entire surface of the body of flesh, drawing a border between an inside and an outside, containing my body within itself, protecting it against any aggression coming from the outside and against any intrusion by a foreign body. The corporeal ego is an *ego-skin*: it is constituted as both a surface of inscription and a protective barrier while ensuring what had been the remainder's function of rejection. When this fails, "the pathologies of the envelope" described by psychoanalysis appear, the masochist's envelope of suffering, autism's ego-shell, or the broken ego-strainer of certain psychoses, whereby the outside violently erupts inside the body.

This function of opening up a divergence also works in another manner: it does not merely demarcate the body from its outside, but it also imprints itself on the body's surface by hollowing out lines of fracture, cavities, orifices. We have seen that the flesh is able to insert itself in space by emerging from the gaping hole of a *Raumloch*. This "hole of space" is then inscribed right on the flesh, is shared out in a series of intervals localized between the carnal poles, which makes them appear as different poles of one sole flesh. By separating the poles from one another, the remainder allows intervals to be opened and introduces a first differentiation into the chaos of the primordial flesh. Zhuang-zhi says that during the creation of the world, the gods noticed that Chaos had no face. So they decided to drill through its skin the Seven Openings that allow for seeing, hearing, breathing, and eating. When the seventh hole was opened, Chaos died, but from its dispersed flesh was born the sun and the moon, rivers, mountains, and humans. The myth tells the truth: without these openings that the remainder cuts into the flesh, we would not have a body, and there would be no world and no other humans in the world. This function will be maintained during the entire process of incorporation: these spacings, intervals, or holes will henceforth be inserted in certain delimited zones of the body, like orificial vents through which the gaze, speech, nourishment, excrement, and joy all pass. The corporeal envelope is thus presented as a perforated surface and the ego-body as an ego-hole. Fragments of the body transition through these points of passage, these tears in the envelope, haunting our fantasies, awakening desire, anxiety, or disgust. Freud had already noticed that "'Faeces,' 'baby' and 'penis' thus form a unity, an unconscious concept (*sit venia verbo*)— the concept, namely, of 'a little one' that can become separated from one's body."[3] Lacan will add the breast, the gaze, and the voice to this list, and he will conceptualize these "little things" as modes of the object of desire, that is, *object-a*—those partial objects detached from the body of the Other. We know, however, that the child considers the mother's breast a part of his own body, and *a fortiori* this is also true for excrement, the penis, and even the voice. These erratic fragments are not *objects-a*, that is, "little others," and come not from the Other but rather from my own flesh: they are *corporeal figurations of the remainder*.

By letting itself be traversed and divided by the remainder in this way, the body of flesh is opened to sexual desire. The primordial flesh was too undifferentiated—both too disseminated and too homogenous—to be able to arrange a place for the Two of sexual difference. For sexuation to take place, a sectioning is necessary, an originary tearing distributed over the entire surface of the ego-skin in a series of local openings and differentiated orifices, thus making contact possible with different zones, on which desire is fixated; it makes possible displacements that let it migrate from one zone to another, distances, penetrations, ejections, and spasms—the unsettling intrigue of desire and of jouissance. Is this not what is described in the famous myth in the *Symposium*, when the origin of desire is situated in a division, an initial wound, followed by the complex work of a fashioning, cutting up, folding over, and a permutation of organs that will give birth to a sexed body? There is also an essential relation between these corporeal orifices in which the body's erotic dimension finds its anchorage and the *effects of the cutting up of the remainder*. Because it hollows out a gap between my flesh and itself, impeding the two poles from joining up or from adhering to one another without distance, the flesh is incorporated in the form of a sexed and sectioned body with its organs opening outwards, its cavities, its folds, intercellular spaces, and orificial crevices. Certainly physiology or embryology determine the origin and the functions of our anatomy differently—but I am not telling the same story, nor am I looking for physical causes and universal determinations of the material thing called a "body": I want to describe the immanent genesis that allows an individual human to have the experience of its own body.

I find evidence that this is not a matter of the simple abstract construction one finds in both the clinical view of psychoses and in anthropology—in those disciplines that in one way or another suspend the immediate evidence of being in the world and of having a body. Let us consider the example of "symbolic wounds," rituals that mark the body, including tattooing and scarification, or ritual operations like circumcision, excision, and even castration. Ethnologists teach us that these practices are integrated in the rites of passage that mark one as belonging to an age group, a clan, or a cast; they are often accompanied by a staging of the "death" and "rebirth" of the subject. Incisions allow the initiates to be distinguished from non-initiates by preserving a trace of the ritual. Thus in an African ceremony of initiation, young boys are supposedly devoured by a "crocodile spirit," then return to life and rejoin their village after having been circumcised or having had engraved on their skin incision marks representing the marks of the Great Crocodile's jaws.[4] In all these rites, I see attempts to figure the process of incorporation by replaying a decisive phase of these dramas, namely, the expulsion of the remainder. This is not merely considered as impure trash or a threat to the body: the ritual also takes into account its function of opening up a divergence, which allows the ego-flesh to be reborn while avoiding disappearing into the jaws of the monster, the black hole of *aphanisis*. After having cut away the part of the body symbolically representing the remainder, the rites try to keep a track of it, to reinscribe its divergence right on the body in the form of a scar or an incision, all while venerating the residue of this operation (blood, pieces of flesh, skin) as sacred offerings. This ambivalence subsists in an attenuated manner after the disappearance of initiation rites and confers a signification on corporeal marks that is sometimes infamous (such as the stigmata of slaves or the condemned) and sometimes aesthetically or erotically valorized (as the current trend for tattoos and piercings indicates). These practices that seek to delimit the remainder in order to expel or annihilate it, all while preserving a trace of it in its corporeal remains, are also found in another major rite: *sacrifice*. As the anthropologists teach us, ritual sacrifice can be defined as *a cuisine of the remainder*: after putting the victim to death, the body is chopped up, and part of it is served up to the gods as a sacred offering, a sacred part most often destroyed by fire, in which all the ambivalence of the remainder is concentrated.[5]

We begin to understand why the "little things separated from the body" are both infinitely desirable and objects of disgust and horror. Bataille was interested in this "elementary *subjective* identity between types of excrement (sperm, menstrual blood, urine, fecal matter) and everything that can be seen as sacred, divine, or marvelous."[6] He sought to elaborate a theory of this *heterogeneous element* present in sexual obscenity, death, the cadaver, sacrifice, or religious ecstasy by relating it to the fundamental process of *excretion*. He insisted on the fact that "this element itself remains indefinable and can be fixed only by negations." He tried to find, in a situation marked by the rise of fascism, a political application for his heterology while pinpointing the "heterogeneous forces" liberated by the crises of homogenous society and the different modes of attraction orienting them to the "imperative sovereignty" of fascism or to a politics of emancipation. Bataille was ahead of the curve on all these points, and admirably, he was able to describe certain traits of the remainder. But his analysis is situated only on the plane of constituted bodies, of organic bodies already demarcated from their outside and thus capable of appropriating or rejecting the remainder. He did not see that the ambivalent attitude that bodily waste provokes is rooted on this side of the world of bodies, in a more radical but nevertheless *reversible* exclusion. Because he did not grasp this reversibility, this initial kinship between the flesh and its remainder, he enclosed himself in rigid alternatives (homogenous and heterogeneous, appropriation and excretion, production and expense, etc.) that prevented him from imagining the different destinies of the heterogeneous element and the possibility of an ultimate synthesis between the flesh and the element that it excludes.

All these questions arising from Bataille's heterology can be elucidated only by analyzing the crisis of the chiasm and this other side of the synthesis where the remainder dominates the ego-flesh. We will then discover why the remainder is presented sometimes in the mode of the *abject* (i.e., as a threatening blemish or stain) and sometimes in the mode of the *sublime* (which awakens fascination, desire, and love)—and how this oscillation could be overcome. At the moment, I would like to outline a first response: the remainder is most often manifest as a sort of waste arousing repulsion or disgust because *there is no place for it* in the body. Incorporation would not be possible if the ego-flesh were unable to absorb the remainder, to reabsorb this heterogeneous element in the synthesis that constitutes my body. By becoming body, the flesh thus seems capable, at least for a time, of overcoming the old conflict, the primordial duality that traversed the plane of immanence. When it gathers the dispersed carnal poles, fashioning them into parts of the totality that is body, the synthesis creates homogeneity. As complex and differentiated as it appears, my body is woven out of unique stuff: by passing from the other side of the skin, by exploring the depths of the organism, we will never encounter anything but "a darkness filled with organs," that is, nothing other than the body. The body tries to reject this strange Thing encysted within my flesh, and when this intimate Stranger reappears in our haunting, it necessarily takes on the appearance of a dissociated part of the whole, an errant fragment of the body outside of the body—a gaze without a face, an eye without a gaze, a shard of voice, a sliced member, excremental waste, and so on. Though it supports all incorporation, the remainder becomes intolerable for the constituted body, as if its function of opening up a divergence were turned against it, pushing it always further away from the body, making it the object of insurmountable aversion.

For my body to emerge, the remainder must be narrowly united with the ego-flesh—and yet the body succeeds in constituting itself only by expelling the remainder that had engendered it. How does the body of flesh manage both to integrate and exclude it at the same time? It is because it is not a matter of the same mode or the same face of the remainder. It is probably too "corporeal," too foreign to my flesh and to myself to be inserted harmoniously in the body, which is mine, which is the body of *my flesh*. When it is intertwined or identified with the flesh, there is only a partial synthesis: in the course of incorporation, a part of the remainder lets itself be absorbed by the flesh, *becomes body* with it, while the other part is maintained as remainder. This division repeats the primitive scission on another plane whereby one part of my flesh was separated from my flesh, like a heterogeneous element resisting all incarnation. It therefore seems that the primordial syntheses fail, at least in part, to ally the remainder with the flesh, and that incorporation will never be done with it and will not be able to reabsorb it entirely in the body. Whether it arouses anxiety, desire, or hatred, it ceaselessly reappears in our fantasies and in our nightmares, our jouissance and our delirium, like a vestige more originary than the body, the ultimate witness of an originary foreignness. So it is not merely my flesh, as Husserl thought, but also my body that remains "an incompletely constituted thing"; if this incompleteness persists throughout existence, then we must see it as an effect of the remainder that eats away at me, ruining my attempts to give myself a body. The becoming-body of my flesh is thus not a continuous advance but a complex process, regulated by fallbacks and by crises. Phases of dislocation and *disincorporation* in which the resistance of the remainder triumphs are succeeded each time by phases of *reincorporation* and reconstruction of the corporeal unity in which the ego is once again able to break down the remainder and partially integrate it in the body while tossing its irreducible part outside of it.

This continues until the synthesis is irrevocably reversed, when the influence of the remainder totally destabilizes the body, turning against its defenses and exhausting its resistance: it is this final defeat that we call aging and dying.

To those who would like to see in the theory of the remainder only groundless speculation, I ask them to reflect on the role that this motif plays in the traditional concept of the body, which continues to impregnate modern science and philosophy. Since the Greeks, our body has been determined as a whole, governed by a well-determined conception of totality and of the relation of the parts to the whole. In this perspective, the whole is considered as anterior and superior to its parts, as the sovereign power that lets them exist, unifying them, and attributing a function and rank to each one. Certainly these parts are needed to exist, and while the body can easily survive their disappearance, no part could subsist outside of the whole. This is what Aristotle emphasizes: in being separated from the whole, the part loses its life, its being, and the real sense of its name. Yet the example that Aristotle gives is always that of a part *of the body*, a mutilated member. Between my living organs and the detached fragment, there would no longer be any community of essence, nothing but a nominal identity without true signification—because the parts "cannot even exist if severed from the whole; for it is not a finger in any and every state that is the finger of a living thing, but a dead finger is a finger only in name."[7] A dead finger, a blind eye, a cadaver's hand—they furtively traverse all of Aristotle's work, as, for example, in this decisive passage from the *Politics* where he tries to ground the primacy of the City on the individual: "the whole is of necessity prior to the part; for example, if the whole body be destroyed, there will be no foot or hand, except in an equivocal sense, as we might speak of a stone hand . . . And thus it is obvious that the City exists by nature and that it is prior to the individual."[8] These motifs return with such insistence, not as simple "examples" or images chosen by chance but as a true haunting: how can one not spot in these detached fragments of the body the corporeal figurations of the remainder? By defining the body as a whole, by determining this whole by the exclusion of the remainder, Aristotle tries to free the body from this haunting. He postulates that the disincarnated fragment *cannot belong* to the flesh and to the body, has no kinship with them, and is deprived of all ontological consistency—in brief, that it is nothing of the Whole (absolutely nothing:

rien du Tout). He thus grounds a theory of the body and a politics, even a metaphysics, on a denial of the remainder.

Aristotle's philosophy thus confirms a gesture of exclusion that was already accomplished in the depths of the flesh. By being incorporated, the ego-flesh constitutes a domain in which there is no longer any place for the remainder: it can take on a body only by expelling the remainder as waste and by constantly repeating this expulsion. The term *retranchement* (which in English can mean "entrenchment" or "refuge" but also "removal" or "taking away") is altogether fitting to designate such an operation, if one hears in it both a reiterated cutting (the action of cutting anew, *re-trancher*) and *a folding back on itself* of the body as it closes in on itself. There would probably have never been an individual or collective body without the *retranchement* of a remainder. We find another testimony for it in Plato, but there the operation takes on a more violent form, closer to the originary process of incorporation. Whereas the body appears in Aristotle as a harmonious totality composed of parts in solidarity, from which every trace of a remainder has been eliminated, Plato presents it as a divided and unstable reality, endlessly threatened by the rebellion of a heterogeneous element. In the myth of the *Timaeus*, he describes the creation of the body as a divine surgery, a work of division and exclusion, an *internal retranchement*: after having put aside the immortal part of the soul by separating the head from the trunk, the Demiurge's auxiliaries carry out a new scission between the noble element of courage lodged in the heart and the vile desires arising in the groin by "dividing the cavity of the thorax into two parts, as the women's and men's apartments are divided in houses, and placed the midriff to be a wall of partition between them."[9] These many cleavages have the goal of isolating the wild savage element of desire, of taming and enchaining this "multi-headed beast" in which we effortlessly recognize a figure of the remainder. We find this motif again in Plato's political theory, this time in the form of an *external retranchement*, a true mutilation, when the master of the City who governs according to science is presented as the doctor of the social body, destined to purge it, to amputate its sick limbs for its greater good.[10] We know the fate of this metaphor, enduring in modern times up until the Jacobin Terror and the "purges" of totalitarian states, justifying the persecution and extermination of "parasites," "foreign agents," and "gangrene" that corrupt the social body. For this Great Body is able to be constituted only by excluding those who are designated as subversives of the remainder, and experience teaches us that this foundational exclusion is found in less extreme forms in all political communities, including the most "liberal" and "democratic." Whether they are grounded on a violent *retranchement* or a simple denial, the traditional conceptions of the body always imply the decision to eliminate the remainder, to eliminate this heterogeneous element that compromises its unity and its identity. The philosophical concept of body thus appears as a *defensive formation* destined to protect real bodies against the threat of the remainder.

But it is insufficient to denounce the metaphysics of the Total Body as an illusion: we must still locate the primordial experience in which it is rooted, while also disfiguring it. We now know that the originary tactile syntheses remain partial and unstable and are incapable by themselves of completing the incorporation of the ego-flesh, of constituting a One-Body, a body-object in the world. Sight is the only sense that gives us the experience of an absolutely homogenous field, a unified totality: it is not by touching myself in a chiasm but by seeing myself in the mirror that I have access to the total form of my body. It is not merely because of the discontinuity or irregularity of tactile impressions, but rather because the touching hand is squashed on the surface of the touched hand without ever rejoining it, and because the experience of touching is confronted with the resistance of the remainder that separates it from itself, prohibiting it from forming a continuous surface, making every part of the corporeal envelope crack and tear. This resistance disappears on the plane of vision, for the remainder is never given to sight, does not appear in the horizon of the visible. By appealing to sight, by identifying myself with my image, I have access to a world from which every trace of the remainder seems to have disappeared. On this basis, metaphysics grants a privilege to vision: the body that it exhibits is an entirely exposed specular body, that is, a body without remainder, both seeing and visible, capable of *being integrally reflected*, of fixing its image by seeing itself seeing. And all this leads us to believe that the modern determination of the subject as a thought that thinks itself or that constitutes itself in its self-reflection finds its origin in this representation.

We have, however, discovered that the ordeal of the mirror encounters its limit in the scission between the visible eye and the seeing gaze. It is not true that I see myself seeing: I do not see my eye seeing me in the same sense that I can touch my hand touching me, and my vision is never able to be knotted together with itself in a chiasm. Whenever I see my body, it immediately stops appearing to me as an incarnated and living body, and a hole emerges in the center of my image: I am able to see this eye of flesh from which my gaze arises in the mirror only as a *Ding-Auge*, a strange "eye-thing"—and I thus endlessly witness the blinding of my gaze. If there is no visual chiasm, if no identification is involved on this plane, there would not be any resistance to this identification: there would not be a remainder. But is it really so certain? Since I recognize these iridescent blind globes as *my eyes seeing me*, there must indeed be an identification effected between the seeing eye and the visible eye, at least in an indirect manner, by drawing on support, as Husserl suggested, from the primordial tactile self-identification. I "indirectly judge" the "eye-thing" that I scrutinize in the mirror as "identical to the eye-thing that is mine," identical to what "is constituted as mine by the touch."[11] It is this face that I palpate, and those are my tangible eyes on the surface of my face that allow me to appropriate my visible eye and to recognize myself in the face that I see. My touching flesh is diffused in my vision while breathing life into it and is also what contaminates it, transmitting its haunting to it by making its remainder pass into the world of gazes and faces. Certainly no chiasm will have ever taken place on the plane of sight—and yet in my vision of myself, a *quasi-chiasm* is initiated, replaying the experience of the tactile chiasm and exciting a similar resistance. I henceforth recognize this *Ding-Auge* as mine; it belongs to my body, to myself, but is at the same time presented as a foreign thing: it has all the traits of the remainder. A *visual remainder* can thus appear on the blind spot of my gaze, but it comes from another field of experience, from the only perceptual field in which a true identification can be produced. We have discovered this primacy of touching, of tactile mouvance, by analyzing the mirror stage—the real experience of it, not the deformed reconstruction of it given by Lacan. For a child to recognize itself in its image, passively contemplating the image while letting itself be fascinated with its own reflection, is insufficient: the child must move itself in front of the mirror, play with its image while projecting the nascent form of its body on the plane of the visible; the tactile and motor experience of the body has already offered a first sketch to the child. Without the tactile synthesis subtending and animating all of my experience, without this originary identification whereby I give myself to myself, I will never be able to identify my eyes, my hands, my face, or my voice, nor distinguish them from the gaze, the face, or the voice of another.

The lesson of the myth of Narcissus is indeed that my relation to my image is not enough to allow for a self-identification. Far from falling in love with his image, as we too often represent the myth, Narcissus lets himself be captivated to death by this figure given to him as the image *of an other*. Recognizing it *as his own* reflection would have allowed him to detach himself from it and not succumb to this mortal captivation. What condemns Narcissus is his lack of narcissism. One will say the same about all these little Narcissuses that we are: the screens of the phantasm or of the spectacle are many *invisible mirrors* in which we are reflected to ourselves without perceiving ourselves. In this sense, we are never "narcissistic" enough: we never sufficiently recognize these images that fascinate us as our own, as projections of our own flesh, and this is why our desire is captivated by the desire of the Other, and why we identify ourselves with it while forgetting ourselves. When it happens, the specular recognition remains always partial and precarious: this is because it prevails over a non-recognition, an initial foreignness that never entirely disappears. It runs up against *a point of resistance*, a scission between the eye and the gaze, an unbridgeable gap separating my seeing eye from my eye-thing, opposing a complete identification. Should the tactile synthesis sustaining it fail, my visible eye will be immediately disincarnated, becoming once again this blind Thing that fixates me like Medusa's face. I have already evoked those psychotics who avoid the gaze of others in order to avoid sinking into those "death eyes," that gaping "black hole" found at the source of vision. All human cultures know the haunting of the evil eye that brings bad luck, this "great eye at the bottom of the horizon" that follows the guilty to the grave. This eye without a gaze, this gaze without a face, these are my own disincarnated seeing eyes that contemplate me from the outside like the eyes of an Other, in a petrifying vision that presents an image of my death. These effects of the remainder are not limited to the gaze alone: when the narcissistic identification is interrupted, the entire image is altered, presented with the traits of a Double both foreign and familiar, an *unheimlich* or uncanny figure that arises in the place of my image, like the "pale face" that terrifies Anna. Most often this strangeness, this alteration of the proper, is barely perceptible—and thus all the more threatening. Sartre evokes this experience in these terms:

Imagine going up to a mirror; an image appears in it: your nose, your eyes, your mouth, your suit. It's you; or, rather, it *should* be you. Yet there is something in the reflection—something that is not exactly the green of the eyes, or the shape of the lips, or the cut of the suit—something that makes you exclaim: there is *another* person in the mirror, in place of my reflection.[12]

When a remainder appears in the breach of my image, I only repeat a more radical experience: the invisible of my vision is first and above all the untouchable of my touch, which is transposed on another plane. By thus changing register, it is profoundly modified—for the tactile remainder remains the remainder *of my flesh*, of a flesh that adheres to itself by recognizing itself in each of its poles. Nothing like this happens in the visual field and the exteriority of sight; the always partial and incomplete character of the specular chiasm can only accentuate the foreignness of the remainder, making it both more distant and more obsessive. Is this why the remainder invests the appearance of a threatening rival on this plane? Transferred from my own image to the look of the other, the remainder will nourish a major haunting, the anxiety or shame of being seen, of *falling under the gaze* while becoming myself a thing, an ego-object, ego-waste; and this leads the seeing subject to reject this mode of the remainder in the Other, to turn toward it its gaze in order to try to degrade it in its turn. It is not sight as such, nor is it the prestige of the imaginary; rather, it is the impossibility of seeing oneself seeing, of being both "subject" and "object" of the vision that gives its infernal dimension to the space of the look. In the closed field of the mortal joust, I am always exposed; I am the object of the look of an endlessly elusive Other. Much more foreign to me than familiar, the specular Double is not merely my fraternal rival, this nagging presence that obsesses me—it is also the Absent of the mirror, the Invisible that devours my image, the *Horla*.[13] Even though his work offers glimpses of other versions of the remainder—carrion floating in the stream, a mummified hand, the hair of a dead lady—Guy de Maupassant knew that the worst haunting eludes sight, that it makes itself seen as invisible, as if the impossibility of seeing oneself, of grasping one's own gaze, could sometimes be extended to the perception of the whole body, in this horrible moment when "a sort of opaque transparence" is interposed between the narrator and his reflection, breaking the identification with the image and dispossessing the subject of itself. This *effect of the Horla*, this defection of the imaginary, could indeed be, in the horizon of the visible, the principle mode of appearing of the remainder. In a world that increasingly coincides with the universe of vision, in an era in which the production of images—what we call the Spectacle—has become a major focus of alienating identifications, this trait is a decisive stake—politically, aesthetically, and on the plane of thought. Nothing today resists the becoming-image of the Spectacle—neither sex, nor death, nor the worst abjection, with the exception of this blind stain that bores holes in the most narcissistic of all the spectacles. Whatever escapes its grasp still has to be inscribed *in* the image itself. The greatest painters had long ago understood this: a picture has value only because of the place that it allows for the trace of the Invisible. Only in this way can the painter displace the narcissism of vision while showing us, as with the Burgkmairs, this point of death, the empty place of our image.

Is it only on the plane of sight that we will meet these offshoots of the remainder, or do they also appear in other perceptual fields? Will we find them, for example, in the auditory field? For this, a chiasm would have to be knotted—and also a part of my hearing would irremediably have to escape me and return to haunt me. When I let the clamor of the world rise up toward me, in this confused mixture of rumors and voices, one of them is detached: I hear myself speak. It is indeed my voice that I discern, it is a part of myself, of my flesh, that is given to me, and this gift is also fulfilled in a chiasm, a *vocal-auditory synthesis*. We are so accustomed to considering language as a "means of communication," so persuaded that our speech is destined to the Other, that we have ended up forgetting that it is above all addressed to ourselves: to speak is first of all to hear oneself speak. It is not just in the "call of conscience" or the uttering of the *ego sum* but already in the least phrase, the least significant statement by which I call myself to myself, and this primordial call is one of the modes of my self-givenness. Even before saying the world or naming things, my word is a cry of my life that is affected of itself. Experimental research teaches us, moreover, that phonation is regulated by audition, that the emission of our voices depends on a sort of auto-affection, a "self-listening." With the help of a technical apparatus, it is sufficient to disturb the auditory control so that the voice is altered, discarded, loses its timbre, its rhythm, and clarity of elocution: by no longer hearing myself, or by *attuning myself* to my listening, my speech becomes totally inaudible. This appeal that I endlessly address to myself echoes more intensely in certain words, namely, when I name myself or when I speak *in my own name*, in the first person. Even if language necessarily betrays the singularity of the ego, the proper name and the pronoun "I" remain its essential points of anchorage. The Latin languages bear witness to this, because "to call one-self" [*s'appeller, se chiamare, se llamar*] is synonymous with *being named*. I propose to designate this privileged statement whereby my self-givenness manifests itself as an *invocation*, and we will have to distinguish it from all other language situations in which I am convoked by another and from those *interpellations* by which the Other appeals to me and assigns me my identity in order to submit me to its law. Althusser taught that the "ideo-logical apparatuses" like Religion, Family, Media, and School—"call individuals into subjects," subject them to [or subjugate them through] ideological rituals of recognition.[14] He had not understood that for me to be able to let myself be called by and respond to the Other "here I am," I must first be able to say "I" and already be constituted as a singular indi-vidual. The invocation of the ego, its call to itself, is what makes all inter-pellations by the Other possible—and it is also what allows it to dissent or rebel, to resist the power of these apparatuses that subjugate it, normalize it, strip it of its singularity.

Every invocation of myself would be impossible without this chiasm in which I hear myself speaking. But the synthesis of the voice and listen-ing remains necessarily imperfect, deprived of the immanent unity, of the reversibility that characterizes the tactile synthesis. The site of speech does not coincide with the site of listening, and my voice always reaches me from the outside like the voice of another, a transcendent *voice-thing* simi-lar to any of the noises of the world: as in the case of sight, we are merely dealing with a quasi-chiasm. What allows me to distinguish it from the others and to recognize it as *my own voice*? It is, once again, the originary dimension of touching: the immanent tactile sensing, the perception of internal vibrations accompanying phonation, gives me the *signature* of my voice and allows me to constitute it as mine. When these vibrations are absent, the sound does not come from me. Husserl had recognized the im-portance of these primary motor sensings ("kinesthesia"): the belonging of the voice, its appropriation by the ego, is grounded for him in the "origi-nally given kinestheses of the vocal muscles" in "vocalization."[15] Factual science both confirms and unexpectedly extends this analysis: as the work of Tomatis has shown,[16] it is not merely the throat but the whole skin that is sensitive to the resonance of the voice and to the variations in pressure provoked by "verbal flow." These diffused tactile impressions, this "cutaneous keyboard," play an essential role in the control of phonic emission, and if we break this sonorous flow by isolating certain zones of the body, the voice will no longer be able to raise itself and will become monotonous, staccato, imprecise. It is with all my flesh, with my entire body that I speak, that I sing, that I call myself; and in the same manner that my touching flesh is identified with my visible body, the sonorous envelope of my voice also coincides with the tactile envelope of my skin. The layer of touching is confirmed as the bedrock of all the other perceptual layers, and the tactile chiasm sustains these quasi-chiasms that are knotted between my look and the image of my body, between my speech and my hearing, between my body and the bodies of others.

We could thus expect to encounter effects of the remainder in this field, made inevitable by the very conditions of the vocal-auditory synthesis—the separation of mouth and ear, of speaking and listening. It suffices that its tactile nucleus slips always, that there is a failure of the primordial chiasm, for my voice to detach itself from my flesh. It will then come back to me as a foreign voice that seems to come from an Other and yet resonates in my depths—as the voice of the remainder. The call of conscience is also presented in this manner, as a call that "resounds from the far to the far" in order to recall Dasein to itself, whereas it is in truth a matter of a call that is addressed by Dasein to itself. We could regret that Heidegger was scarcely interested in the carnal bedrock of the call. He neither wondered why it is altered to the point of being presented "initially and for the most part" in a false manner as the call of an Other, nor did he explain how an existing being alienated in the world and to others, absorbed in its own inauthenticity, could recognize its own call in this foreign voice. Psychoanalysis encountered the same difficulty. We know that Freud insisted on the role of acoustic traces in the genesis of the *superego*. By this term, he designates an *inneres Ausland*, a sort of "interior foreign county," "a part of the ego that is opposed to the rest" of the ego:[17] the differentiation of the superego and the ego leads us back to the mystery of the voice, of a foreign voice that would have been "introjected" in the ego and that would have become mine while remaining other. But Freud did not seek to know how these fragments of voice at the origin of the superego could be linked with the tactile sensations constituting the ego. For this, he would have had to question the knotting of touching and listening, as well as the possibility for a corporal ego to experience its own body and its own voice, as an unknown Thing.

But psychoanalysis encounters the ordeal of madness, the hallucinatory experience of "hearing voices" coming from nowhere—and it is here that we will find the key to the enigma. Gisela Pankow tells us the story of a woman who constantly hears the "voice of a policeman" coming from the neighbor's house, a voice that "repeated like an echo all that she did" and that "always said: 'nothing.' "[18] This voice appeared for the first time when the sick woman had a piece of furniture that did not belong to her taken out of her house. As Pankow notes, the house is here a projection of her body, a body she lives "as if it were composed of two heterogeneous parts," so finely intricate "that no separation was possible anymore." This attempt to expel the foreign part from the self provokes the appearance of the Voice, as if it were merely a substitute for the little thing cut from the body, an auditory redoubling of the carnal remainder—no doubt because the intricacy of the flesh and the remainder was too strong for her to tolerate its separation without immediately compensating for it on another plane, making it return in the form of auditory remainder. Neither integrated in the body nor totally expelled outside of it, the remainder persists *at the limit*, on the imprecise border between the same and the other, like an "echo" coming from the neighbor's house. The very term itself reveals that the voice haunting her is not the voice of an Other but merely an echo, a sonorous reflection, a resonance of her own voice returning to her from the outside, when she no longer is able to recognize it while hearing herself speak and identifying it as an *internal* resonance of her flesh. Like the Cartesian deceiver, like the call that recalls to Dasein its nullity, like the mortifying injunction of the superego, this persecutor is a part of the ego that it does not recognize as its own. By always calling out to itself "nothing!" the voice cries out to the ego the Nothingness in which its life has sunk; it cries to it that by thus doubling it, by substituting itself for its invocation, it reduces the ego to nothing (*ut nihil it*); and perhaps this foreign voice also cries to it that the voice itself is nothing—nothing but its own voice detached from it and illusorily projected on the Other. This nullity of his persecuting voices was highly astonishing to President Schreber: a cultivated mind like his could only be outraged by this "monotonous and fastidious blabbering," in which he saw a new proof of the unfathomable stupidity of God.

The haunting of the voice is thus not originary: it is rooted in a carnal tear, a *crisis of the chiasm* in which the ego-flesh is no longer able to reabsorb its remainder by integrating it in the unity of its body. This failure of the tactile synthesis affects the relation of the remainder to the ego-flesh but also its mode of figuration, its manner of appearing in experience: since it can no longer be manifested on the plane of touching, it is transposed on to another plane, emerging as a voice without flesh or a look without a face. By losing its anchorage in the tactile field, the remainder is modified, ceases to be reversible, and is ever more detached from the ego. This crisis affects the reversibility of the chiasm, the incessant exchange between the touching and the touched poles of my flesh. When the chiasm is broken, this rupture increases my haunting: I could never address myself to this Voice that hassles me and impose silence on it; I will never succeed in turning back on this Look that fixates and petrifies me and fixate it in turn. I am thus exposed without recourse to the influence of the Other—because my vision and my hearing are related to touch and rooted in the tactile field, they are given flesh, allowing me to perceive them as mine. Deprived of the "keyboard" of vocal vibrations and tactile impressions that help it be attuned and recognize itself, the voice loses its feeling of belonging, loses the signature of the ego that identified it as *my* voice. It is then floating in a no-man's-land, an "internal foreign country" where it resonates like the voice of no one, neither altogether mine nor absolutely other. With this failure of the limit—of the interval function that was the remainder's—the border separating the ego and the other collapses: sometimes my own voice reaches me as if it were foreign to me, and sometimes it is the voice of another that reverberates in me as if it were my own. Whether it is the call that penetrates Dasein, or vocal traces from which the superego issues, or the hallucinated voice of the policeman, we witness each time *a crisis of belonging* wherein the same and the other, the outside and the insider, the proper and the foreign, become indiscernible. This situation defines the most extreme alienation, the moment when the injunction of the Other, its call, is substituted for the invocation that I address to myself, the moment when the desire of the Other is imposed on me as if it were my own desire. All my relations with Others will bear the mark of this alienation, and I will no longer even be able to discern *to whom* my desire, hatred, shame, respect, or love are destined. Nor will I be able to discern whether these sentiments are truly addressed to other egos or to this "other" in me who seems to me more me than myself. We evaluate the naiveté of those pious moralists who summon us to renounce our "egoism" in order to open us to the call of the Other. How do they not see that in order to be able to respond to this call, the ego must first of all find itself and find its voice? It is only on this condition, when I mark the difference between the Other and myself, between his speech and mine, that I will be able to recognize it as Other, to address myself to it in truth. The path leading me toward others first passes by myself, and only an ego freed of its haunting can hope to discover the true face of the Other.

But how will an ego—alienated to the point of no longer being able to discern its own voice and of letting itself be dispossessed of its flesh, its image, and its desire—be able to reconquer what has escaped from it? Even if its concrete forms still remain obscure, this deliverance must be possible: it originates in this continued creation whereby I make a gift of myself to myself. It is *because* I am always already revealed to myself that I can *also* dissimulate myself to myself, identify myself with an other, be submitted to its law as if it were my own. It is because I call myself that my invocation can let itself be diverted and captivated by a figure of the remainder, to the point of calling out to me as if it came from an other. The self-givenness of the ego is more originary than its alienation and its haunting and should allow it to overcome them. But in what way? An ancient legend tells the story of the son of a king exiled far from his homeland. He had forgotten his high birth and his name, until one day a messenger brought him a letter from his father, reminding him who he was, and the son then returned to his native land. In one of his tales, Kafka recounts a more somber and ironic version of this story. The king's messenger is unable to get out of the castle, and the prince waits forever to receive the letter. His situation would be more desperate still if the royal messenger were also the prince: if the author of the call and its receiver were the same. How would an ego that had forgotten itself still be able to address the message of freedom? For my deliverance to occur, I would have to be able to modify profoundly my relation to the remainder, stop rejecting it away like a foreign thing, and finally recognize it as my own flesh. Would it be sufficient to pursue the incorporation by trying to re-absorb the remainder in the body? In going from the plane of touching to the plane of sight, I thought that I had access to a world in which the remainder had disappeared. But it does not happen, since the remainder reappears in the haunting of the Gaze, and the same is true on the plane of listening. There is no dimension of my experience, no phase of my genesis that does not bear its mark; the whole process of incorporation is thus affected by the effects of the remainder that destabilize it. In order to resist it, the ego must pass from one plane to another, by building always more complex and precarious configurations. The body that is mine, the subject that I am, would only be defensive formations destined to overcome the haunting of the remainder—and that will never be able to prevent its return. This should at least be the case, when we abide by a solipsistic self-constitution: when I encounter the other and enter into dialogue with it, I gradually learn to see myself as it sees me, to consider my body as a human body similar to all others, a material thing situated in objective space, a total body in which there is no longer any trace of a foreign element. Does not this grant too much to the Other? How would a transcendent entity, foreign to my life, be able to free me from my haunting, from this remainder that is one with my flesh? And how could an ego that has not yet discovered itself in truth be able to encounter the Other without letting itself be captivated and alienated by it? In order to know whether the encounter with the other could free me from the grip of the remainder, or whether my phantasms and my alienation will reappear on the plane of the community, we will have to try to understand what kind of intrigue there is between the ego and the alter ego and how this falsely familiar phenomenon that we call the other is constituted.

10

Beyond the Other

My consciousness, like a circle, returns to itself by passing through the foreign
that is opened up within me.

—Edmund Husserl, *Husserliana XV*

How is the ego able to constitute the meaning of being an ego other
than itself—of being an "other" [*autrui*]? This question already posed by
Husserl seems to have become inaudible, buried under the common evidence that the ego is necessarily preceded by the other, determined from
its birth and throughout its life by the place that others assign to it in the
world. Husserl sought to understand how a solipsistic ego is able to constitute the alter ego by itself. None of his successors followed him on this
path. They all succumbed, in one form or another, to the egocidal temptation: by refusing to allow that the ego is originarily self-given, they barred
themselves from imagining that it could originarily give itself an other-
than-itself or constitute in itself the alterity of the other. But even if they
all agree in rejecting the primacy of the ego, they find themselves at odds
with each other as soon as it is a matter of a more precise determination of
its relation to the other: whereas some suppose an original indifferentiation or indistinction of the ego and others, others claim on the contrary
that an infinite distance separates them. Yet in the two cases, significant
difficulties are present. When we claim that I am always already with
others, alienated to them, merged in them in the indistinct mixture of the
They in which "each is the other and no one is itself," it becomes very

difficult to understand how the existing being that I am could be able to resist the tyranny of the They and finally exist as an authentic Self. Will we have more luck by insisting on the transcendence of the Other and on the infinite distance that separates it from the ego? We hope to preserve the possibility for an ethical relation to the face of the other—but it comes at the price of a debasement of the ego, stigmatized as the unique source of injustice and of evil and summoned to submit itself to the sovereign authority of the Other, to devote itself to it, to sacrifice itself for it. When, between the other and me, such a profound divergence is opened up, it becomes impossible to understand this simple fact: the other is, like myself, always designated by saying "I." This means that it also is lived as an ego, that it is given every time as an *other me* similar to me—an alter ego. The thesis of originary alienation does not allow for thinking the separation of the ego and the Other, their *disidentification*; but conversely, those who posit an absolute distance between them will not be able to think the possibility of their *identification*, of a community between myself and others. In fact, these two rival theses rest on the same prejudice: they both postulate that the ego is always defined on the basis of the Other, that is, by transcendence. They both suppose that transcendence takes precedence over immanence and that ego's relation to the Other is what constitutes it. I want to call this prejudice into question: by starting from the Other, one is barred from reaching the truth of the ego, and one attains instead only an ego already disfigured by its alienating identifications. I thus propose to return to Husserl's orientation and explore once again the Cartesian path abandoned by his unfaithful disciples. Perhaps it will finally give us access to *the phenomenon of others [autrui]*.

By a radical *epokhè*, I place the existence of the Other and all it implies out of play: I seek to attain what is originarily mine, my ego's primordial field of belonging from which every trace of a relation to the other has been separated. The other, of course, is not annihilated: it subsists as a "simple phenomenon," as this foreign body that suddenly emerges in my field of experiences, momentarily gesticulates, then fades away. It is on the basis of my perception of this body that I will constitute the phenomenon of the alter ego. And yet this body is not presented as a flesh similar to my own flesh and does not offer me any direct presentation of an ego similar to mine. This body that I perceive over there is presented first as a simple thing, and it is not just in the hallucinatory visions of a

Francis Bacon but also in our own experience that the body of the other is given to sight or to touch as a "corporeity similar to meat."[1] How is this "meat" constituted into a body of flesh, the living body of the other? By conferring on it the meaning of being flesh, by making a gift to it of the only flesh whereby I originarily have the experience—that is, mine. This carnal gift is designated by Husserl as a *transference* in which I project my own carnation on the other's body. In each of my gazes, each of my caresses, my flesh is transfused in the body-thing, giving life to it. What makes this transposition possible? It is our resemblance, the similitude that I discover between this foreign body and my own body, between my hand here and his hand over there, between his aggressive or joyous mimicries and those accompanying my anger or my joy.

But it is not a question of a mere resemblance or of a purely exterior relation between two bodies that remain forever foreign to one another. The projection that transfers my flesh to the other's body does not imply a total identification or a communion that absolutely fuses it with the other's. Between my ego and the alter ego there always subsists an irreducible gap or divergence, and if it disappeared, "if what belongs to the other's own essence were directly accessible, it would be merely a moment of my own essence, and ultimately he himself and I myself would be the same."[2] This is why Husserl insists so much on the "unbridgeable abyss" that separates my experience from the other's. The body of the other presents to me an unknown ego that animates it, but presents it only indirectly, in the same way that the surface of the table that I perceived indirectly presents its hidden other side to me. I will never be able to understand the other ego, the other body *in its flesh*, to suffer its pain, to feel its anxiety or joy. Far from *truly* transferring my flesh in the body of the other, I attribute it to him "merely by analogy on the basis of my flesh," which means that we are dealing here only with an exterior association, an analogical transposition that ultimately cannot abolish the distance separating us. And yet the transfer takes place: by projecting my flesh on the foreign body, I am able to cross the abyss, to recognize in this body a flesh similar to my own, a same suffering, a same joy, an other ego similar to yet different from me. Its alterity, its foreignness, does not fade away but henceforth receives a new signification—that, precisely, of being an alter ego. This gives all of its meaning to this capital claim: "the intrinsically first other (the first 'non-Ego') is the other ego" (*CM*, 107). Revealed by its body of flesh, the other appears in the world, and its appearance is similar to a second birth—because "each foreign flesh must be given in the exteriority according to its first birth, like an exterior thing," before "having the experience of a second birth, of being apprehended as flesh."[3] This rebirth endlessly recommences: in every moment, body-things are presented to me so that I transfigure them into many bodies of flesh. From transference to transference, these innumerable bodies are intertwined and weave a unique texture, a community of monads born of one sole flesh, endlessly gravitating around the same center, the primordial monad that I am. This is a very remarkable analysis, which possesses the sober beauty of the great classical theses of philosophy. Husserl could have apparently avoided the impasses in which his successors got trapped: he succeeded in maintaining the primacy of the ego without sacrificing the alterity of the other, taking account of both the separation of monads and their community. But is this indeed the case? Despite the rigor and radicality of his analyses, is he really able to constitute the phenomenon of the other? Was he right to identify the "first foreigner" and the other ego? Does this not do violence to both the alterity of the other and the singularity of the ego?

The Eleatic Stranger had put us on guard: resemblance is "a very slippery sort of thing."[4] By rooting the constitution of the other in the perception of a resemblance between our two bodies, Husserl gave a rather fragile basis to his theory. We could easily object that the grasping of resemblance is never primary in human experience, that men are above all sensitive to dissemblance, to the foreignness of others, to physical differences—racial, sexual, linguistic—that prevent them from recognizing them as other men, as their similars. As Levi-Strauss noted, the members of a tribe or ethnicity tend most often to consider themselves as the only "true men" and reject other groups as inhuman, often designating them as "earth apes" or "phantoms." And we know that one of the most brilliant civilizations was for millennia built on the claim of a radical dissemblance between men, distributing them into numerous well-defined and hierarchical castes, the lowest of which are rejected to the limits of humanity. Such a common situation in human experience must have its source on a transcendental plane: it must be rooted in this initial intrigue wherein my first encounter with the other is played out. The feeling of strangeness taking hold of us when faced with a body and the presence of the other originates here. At this level, it can no longer be a question of resemblance. How could a body similar to every other body in the world resemble this singular, incomparable entity foreign to the world, my flesh? If it is true that "my flesh has still nothing that is similar to it,"[5] then it cannot have the experience of things resembling it except by ceasing to be flesh, by becoming a corporeal thing like the body of the other. I must already be lost in the world, identified with the other, alienated, for me to be able to measure myself against it and discover characteristics of resemblance in its body. It seems that Husserl's analysis inverts the meaning of experience: it is not the perception of a resemblance to the body of the other that allows me to identify myself with it—it is my identification with it that makes possible the perception of a resemblance between our two bodies. The primordial identification that must be undertaken "blind," prior to all perception of a visible form that could resemble me or not. My flesh resembles nothing in the world, and yet a trait or a pole of this flesh is blindly identified with a singular trait of the foreign body to the point of transferring its carnation to it, of making a gift of its life to it.

A new difficulty then appears. We do not see how such an identification could ground the transference or give to the other body the meaning of being a flesh—because the other does not have flesh. Certainly the other feels his own flesh like I feel mine, as a body of flesh. But his flesh does not give itself *as flesh* to my flesh: my perception will never coincide with his, and I will never feel his flesh touching or being touched as I touch myself touching. For me, my flesh remains *Urleib*, the sole and unique flesh, and this should prevent it in principle for letting itself be transferred to a transcendent body. Let us suppose that my flesh is, despite it all, able to pass into the body of the other: as soon as it stops being mine, it immediately stops being flesh—and the other's body remains what it was, a simple thing deprived of flesh. Let us admit conversely that the transference has indeed happened: by some unknown magic, this other body is able to be incarnated. As soon as the other takes on flesh, as soon as it receives this flesh that is always mine, it stops being other in order to become a part of myself, my simulacrum or my double. These difficulties had not escaped Husserl. He wondered why the transfer is not immediately annulled (*CM*, 114) and how it happens that "I do not apperceive the other ego simply as a duplicate of myself" (*CM*, 117), as a second version of my own ego. Yet, barely imagined, these disturbing eventualities are eliminated. Not only does he underestimate the *resistance* to the transference and the force of dissemblance—which, in the other, resists letting itself be incarnated—but he also misconstrues everything that leads the ego to be identified with the other, to consider the other as a double of itself or to let itself be captivated by or absorbed in the other. All of our experience shows, on the contrary, the power of these alienating identifications, the threat that they make weigh on the singularity of the ego. For men do not stop identifying themselves with the dominating figures of the Other, or subjecting themselves to their human or divine Sovereign, to the glorious images and idols of the epoch; and they are probably just repeating on another plane the more archaic identifications that since their childhoods have allowed them to become subjects. We must now try to think the possibility of such identifications if we want to understand how the ego-flesh is also able to separate itself and to free itself from the overpowering grip of the Other.

We must therefore wonder how my flesh can be identified with the non-flesh, with this foreign thing that is for me the body of the other, without consequently ceasing to be flesh. Can a synthesis of flesh and non-flesh bridge the gap that separates them? My preceding analyses allow for a response to these questions: not only is this synthesis possible, but it has *already taken place*. Prior to being identified with an other in the world, the ego-flesh was already identified with itself in the carnal chiasm, when each pole of my flesh recognizes the other pole as the flesh of its flesh—and it is this primordial self-identification that makes all identification with an other-than-me possible. For my flesh to be able to recognize itself in this meat that it palpates from the outside, it has first of all to undergo the ordeal of its own foreignness, recognize itself in this piece of meat that it also is for itself. Every encounter, every community with the other is based on this first encounter, this archi-community of my poles of flesh. What led Husserl astray was the prejudice of the Ego-one, the certainty that the ego is originarily identical with itself. The constitution of the other was then presented as the passage from the One to the Multiple, from an isolated ego to a community, and we do not see clearly how this solitary ego would succeed in finding in itself a path toward others. The aporia is dissipated as soon as we abandon this naive belief in the originary unity of the ego. I do not have to tear myself away from myself in order to have access to the community; I need only pass from one mode of community to another: I thought myself alone, but I was a multitude.

The first non-ego, the first stranger to me, is thus not the *other me* but the *other in me*, this adverse pole that my flesh brushes against and immediately recognizes as another pole of the same flesh. The enigma of transference and of the identification of my flesh with the other's body is thus clarified: it repeats the originary identification of my flesh with my flesh on another plane. I try to replay this synthesis of incarnation on the other's body, in the gaze and in speech, contact, caress, or embrace. Sometimes the miracle seems to happen, and I think I recognize in the other the same gift that I feel in me: and thus this insensitive thing, this packet of meat, is reborn as a body of living flesh. The constitution of the alter ego is thus possible because it repeats the solipsistic self-constitution of the ego-flesh. In what way is it a repetition? Will all the traits of the initial synthesis be found in this new synthesis constituting the other? By making a gift of my flesh, will I also transfer the remainder that corrodes my body to the other's body? This hypothesis allows for the elucidation of two otherwise inexplicable phenomena, for a taking account of the always *partial* character of identifications with the Other and for the representation of the human community in the form of a *collective body*. By putting the Ego-One out of play, I also set aside the Body-One, the total form of the body as it appears in the visible: in my field of immanence, only presubjective, precorporeal singularities, which I call poles of flesh, exist with the blinking, dispersed, larval egos that live in each of these poles. On the basis of these carnal poles, the most original identifications are effected, directed toward other poles of my flesh or toward the body of an other. These are always partial identifications with traits that are themselves partial, purely affective and blind identifications that precede all perception of an image or a total form: and remember, these are what Freud designated as "the most originary mode of connection with the other." On this plane, neither resemblance nor dissemblance are yet possible; only attraction and repulsion, couplings and uncouplings, resonances and dissonances, are possible. In the chaos of the flesh, some singular traits are configured—marks, orifices, and protuberances are constituted as many of the *poles of identification*, while others are presented on the contrary as poles of resistance to identification, as hints of sexual or "racial" difference, which, by prohibiting the consideration of the other as a *similar*, awaken anxiety, disgust, or hatred in mankind. This explains why our phantasmatic identifications are always aimed at partial objects or at fragments detached from the body, for the "subject" of these identifications is itself a fragmentary ego disseminated in innumerable poles of flesh, each of which was already identified with other fragments of its flesh.

What allows for overcoming the initial diffraction of the ego-flesh is this other synthesis that unifies my flesh as a body, the synthesis whereby the dispersed poles of my flesh are united together in order henceforth to be lived as the parts of a whole, the members of one single body. Just as the originary synthesis of incarnation is replayed when I transfer my flesh to the other's body, so too is this synthesis of incorporation repeated on the intersubjective plane, embracing each individual body and uniting it with all the others within a total body. Our carnal community is then transformed into an immense Body, whose limbs are my body and the bodies of others, indissociably united, hierarchically submitted to superior organs and to the visible or invisible Chief that is in the head. In a text of admirable audacity, La Boétie wondered how men could renounce their freedom and submit without reserve to a master. At the root of this *voluntary servitude*, he discovered the mystery of carnal givenness, of a transference where they let themselves be dispossessed of their flesh in order to project it onto a collective body, on the Body-One of their master: "where has he acquired enough eyes to spy upon you, if you do not provide them yourselves? How does he have so many arms to beat you with, if he does not borrow them from you? . . . How does he have any power over you, except through you?"[6] Nothing justifies this subjugation of men to the "great colossus" that crushes them, nothing explains the persistence of such a representation or its tendency to reconstitute itself wherever it seemed to be undone—except that it is rooted in the deepest depths of ourselves, in those immanent syntheses that give us body and make subjects of us.

On the psychical plane as on the political plane, the relations established between the ego and the others replay an intrigue that was already knotted between me and myself. The other is thus presented as *a derivative phenomenon*, constituted on the basis of a more originary alterity, all the determinations of which it reproduces by transposing them on a transcendent plane. This fundamental rule is thus confirmed: what arises in transcendence of the world is already *prefigured* in immanence, sketched out in advance by the elementary phenomena manifested in the field of immanence of the ego. All that happens to me in the world, every encounter with a transcendent Other, affects me only *after the fact*, by coming to be inscribed in an already constituted configuration. Certainly this "advance" or this "delay" does not arise from a linear succession in the time of the world but rather from a continued self-givenness that begins again in every moment. We are, however, constrained to describe this immanent genesis as a history whose phases succeed one another. In the course of this history, the other is like the strange messiah evoked by Kafka: he comes only when it is too late. To where does this prefiguring extend? Are *all* our concrete relations with others necessarily pre-sketched in immanence? Do we not throughout our existence simply repeat in a theatre of shadows a drama that has already played out elsewhere? We would then have to allow that all our desires and affects are originarily "narcissistic"— this love, hatred, fraternal rivalry, the whole range of feelings that I experience would first of all be addressed only to myself or to this other in me, which is the first stranger to the ego. But if they are not originarily addressed to the other, if they merely transfer a primordial auto-affection to it, to what extent would it still truly be a question of hatred or love? In what sense can we say that my relation to the other derives from my originary relation to myself? Is the phenomenon of the other entirely constituted on the basis of my ego?

One of Husserl's indications can serve as a guiding clue. When he evoked the "coupling" of my body with a foreign body that makes the carnal transfer possible, he specified that it is a question not of an identification in the strict sense but merely of an association (*CM*, 112), that is, a passive synthesis in which a couple of phenomena form a community of resonance; in which they "mutually call each other," "are recovered by reciprocally passing their elements," all while maintaining their initial duality—unlike identification, where the phenomena fuse in order to be one. What is decisive for distinguishing these different syntheses is not their partial or total character: we know that there are only partial identifications. It is instead a matter of knowing whether the synthesis implies an identity of essence (an "eidetic" identity) between its constitutive elements. When, in the chiasm, each pole intertwines with another pole, it does not transfer to the other *a flesh that does not belong to it*: both discover that they are one same and unique flesh. The alter ego will always lack this originary community. Merleau-Ponty wondered if by touching the hand of another I could touch "the same power to espouse the things that I had touched in mine"[7]—but nothing of this kind can be revealed in this transcendent thing, this body similar to meat. Zeus's anger a long time ago tore the androgyne apart, and the monads palpate or track each other in the caress, the look, or listening, only in vain: they remain without windows or doors, and our two foreign fleshes brush up against and embrace one another without me ever sensing the same carnal impression awakened in me dawning in the other.

Husserl had got it right: the other is never originarily given to me in its flesh, and the transference incarnating it only effects an exterior association without allowing for a true identification. But that does not mean that there is never any identification, or that the ego never identifies itself with the other or with a partial trait of its body—on the contrary, these identifications model us, sustain us throughout existence. And yet, whether they are affective, imaginary, or symbolic, whether they constitute an isolated subject or a political body, does not matter, because such identifications are in fact illusory: all of these are just phantasms blinding the ego to itself and the other. In truth, the I is not yet an Other, I am not the breast of my mother, nor my reflection in the mirror, nor the name or the phallus of my father, nor any of those heroes with whom I thought I had identified myself. In our relations with others, we are never dealing with anything but a transference by association that is *falsely* presented as an identification. The synthesis of incarnation constituting the alter ego repeats the originary synthesis of the chiasm in which each pole of flesh is identified with the other pole in order to make with it one sole flesh. I try to reproduce this primordial identification on the plane of transcendence by seeking to identify myself with this other body that I encounter outside of me. But what is true in immanence is no longer true on this plane: when it is no longer a matter of the other pole of a same flesh, then I am dealing with a transcendent body separated from mine by an insurmountable gap. The repetition of the originary synthesis falsifies the meaning of the transfer by presenting this purely exterior association as a true identification, which creates the appearance of a carnal identity with the other. As "real" as it may seem when it envelopes me and intertwines with mine, the flesh of our community is in fact only a *quasi-flesh*, and the collective bodies in which this community is figured merely have the consistency—albeit an overwhelming one—of a phantasm. Husserl did not notice this disfiguration of experience. He may have recognized that the carnal trans-

ference is not an identification, but he did not perceive that this transference is linked to an illusory identification. He had understood that no
real link exists between monads, only an "intentional community," an
"'irreal' intentional reaching of the other into my primordiality" (*CM*,
122). He did not see that this community necessarily takes on the appearance of a real unity, of a real intrusion of the other in my life, and that
such a representation traps the ego, alienates it to this Other with which it
identifies itself. When I encounter the other, I am victim of an illusion
that consists in projecting my own flesh on the other, as if my flesh likewise belonged to it, as if the other and I had always been of one sole flesh.
Is this not the same phantasm that had already blinded the first Man
when, awaking from the torpor into which he had been plunged by the
Elohim, he hailed the companion coming out of his flank as "the flesh of
his flesh"? It is Adam's illusion, and his first sin.

Why speak here of a phantasm? Because this term already designates in Plato a fundamental illusion, a mode of *nontruth*—a simulacrum,
a shadow cast on the wall of the Cave, that is, an effect of an illusive
projection—and also because, as Freud taught us, the phantasm implies
an erasing of the ego and is presented as an anonymous scenario ("a child
is being beaten") in which the singular position of the ego is totally
hidden (I do not perceive that I am the child beaten), and where every
difference between the ego and the Other disappears. In order to mark
the difference between conscious or unconscious psychical fantasies that
appear in the horizon of the world and always presuppose a relation to the
Other (for example, the fantasies of castration or incest discovered by Freud)
and the *archi-phantasms* formed in the field of immanence of the ego, I will
designate the latter as *phantasms*. They stage the purely solipsistic relation
of the ego to itself and to the remainder of the flesh: they are phantasms
of intrusion and autophagia, fragmentation and fusion, necrosis and resurrection, and so forth, that egoanalysis will have the task of describing. I
see here the most originary matrix of the psychical fantasies that impregnate our relations with other men. This supposes that these immanent
phantasms are able to be projected in the transcendence of the world, on
the plane of being-with-other. Through this projection, they maintain
their initial mouvance and the elementary impressions accompanying it
(the feeling of being dislocated, of dying, of letting oneself be penetrated
or devoured by a foreign Thing), but their meaning is profoundly altered,

and they are presented now as if they came from another or were addressed to it. In the place of the remainder, mundane figures appear, populating our unconscious fantasies, figures such as the mother, father—or rather the breast of the mother, the phallus of the father—and the innumerable faces of the Other that we endlessly cross in the course of our existence.

If this hypothesis is correct, the intrigues and the dramas of my daily life are subtended by a *projective identification* in which I transpose the play of my flesh with itself on the other. But to what end? Would every relation to others be phantasmatic? Or is there a part of the other that resists identification? Husserl's successors are divided between those who insist on the distance that separates the ego and the other and those who affirm their originary indifferentiation. In fact, their opposition is merely apparent, and the adversarial theses are both true at different levels. If we want to move beyond this antinomy, we must distinguish two modes of the givenness of the other and mark out the difference between the other as an *object of identification*, constituted by a phantasmatic projection, and *the other as Other*, beyond every projection and all identification. Just as the ego-flesh was dissociated from its remainder, so too is the other split in two, and one of its elements lets itself be identified with the ego and be constituted as another myself, while the other part remains foreign to me and is maintained as a transcendent thing. Freud came close to this phenomenon in an astonishing passage in his 1895 *Project* in which he described the original division of the experience of the other in two components, one that the subject can assimilate or identify with a "message emanating from its own body" and the other that remains exterior as a thing.[8]

How are these two dimensions of the other named? The French term for "other" [*autrui*] comes from the Latin expression *alter huic* and designates this other that is here, that is present to me in the greatest proximity. I will henceforth use this term "other" to name this part of the other that is constituted nearest to me by projective identification, while reserving the name "Other" [*l'Autre*] for the second, more distant and more foreign, layer. These two modes of the other are not really distinct, are not situated on two totally different planes (as it was with Lacan with his imaginary *petit autre* and the symbolic *grand Autre*). The other is the *first giving*, the first phase of the Other: it is nothing other than the Other such as it appears to me in its first birth, still covered by the projections of my ego; and the Other is only another face of the other, such as it could be revealed

during a second birth. What I call "other" is the other ego insofar as it derives from me, the transcendence of the Other *in* the immanence of the
ego, the Other-in-me, disfigured by the ego. Understood in this way, the
other is a phantasm, the effect of a phantasmatic projection. It is a *surface*
for the ego's *projection*, a *plane of identification* wherein the carnal transfer
can be achieved while disfiguring itself. From its first appearance, the phenomenon of the other unfolds as a sort of envelope that redoubles outside
the primordial surface of my skin, a screen on which simulacra and detached fragments of my flesh are projected. In a sense, I am never dealing
with anything other than myself, my own flesh, my affects and refracted
phantasms on this screen: the constitution of the other rests on an auto-
affection deceptively presented as a hetero-affection. It is a narcissistic
projection that we take for the marvel of an encounter, an epiphany of the
Other. We can say the same thing about the other that Marion says about
the idol: it is a matter of *an invisible mirror* that "turns my gaze back on
itself," in which I am reflected to myself *without noticing myself in it.*[9] This
does not mean that in this experience, there is *nothing of the Other,* no
trace of the Other in the other. The phenomenon of the other is constituted through a synthesis between a foreign body and my own flesh, between some transcendent elements that I perceive on the outside—this
silhouette, this gaze, this face, this voice I hear, this skin I touch—and an
auto-figuration whereby my flesh refracts itself on its surface of projection.
These transcendent givens, these sketches, fragments of the body of the
Other, come to be inscribed on this surface, where they are identified with
projections issuing from my flesh. Thus my figuration of the other, my
phantasm of the other, is a phagocyte of the Other, devours it, absorbs it in
me, and all my attempts to rejoin the Other will come to be broken on
this figure-screen.

There is a plane where this phantasmatic dimension of the Other is
manifested in a privileged manner—that of vision. The other's mode of
appearing in the visible is by what we call its *face.* It is by offering me its
face—and the advanced point of the face that is the gaze—that the phantasm of the other is presented to me, attracts and seduces me, or turns me
toward it. The face, Sartre said, is "visible transcendence." It is also disfigured transcendence, frozen in a grimace, when *the madness of vision* takes
hold of it and makes it come into the visible. *Sembianza*, an Italian term
that designates the face, tells us what it is, the mirage that is for each of us

the face of the other: it is a *semblance*, a mask that dissimulates the truth of the Other to me and dissimulates me to myself—the very figure of the Evil Genius.[10] The visible transcendence of the face is the major focus of those projective identifications in which the difference between the ego and the other is blurred, in which an entire part of me—my desires, affects, and flesh—lets itself be captivated and absorbed by the phantasm of the other. The other is a highly paradoxical phenomenon: like the Cartesian deceiver, it is a part of me that I wrongly take for an other—and yet it is indeed presented each time as an other really distinct from me. It is an immanent phenomenon that is given as transcendent, a pure auto-affection manifesting itself as hetero-affection. If it does not appear as foreign to me, then it would be only my double, a simple reflection of myself—but it is never presented in this way, and this appearance "as an other," this apparent alterity, also constitutes the phenomenon of the other. From where does it come? From transcendent givens issuing from the body of the Other? But they can appear to me only by ceasing to be *of the Other*, that is, by becoming inscribed in my phantasm in which their initial foreignness disappears. Since the phenomenon of the other is born of a projection of my ego, the response is clear: what makes the other appear to me as an "other" can only come from myself. There must be an *internal alterity* in me—an archi-transcendence in immanence, an other = X within the ego-flesh—that I project on my plane of identification, where it serves me as a matrix or schema to constitute the other. At first sight, nothing in my own experience announces the alterity of the other: I am thoroughly my flesh, and I continually experience it as mine. Yet this self-identification is not completed in a total fusion: the synthesis of incarnation always leaves a residue, an inassimilable leftover, which I have called the remainder. The first transcendence is situated there, the first non-ego, the first foreigner in me. In fact, the remainder is not truly foreign to me: it is a part of my flesh given as different from me, *as if* it were foreign to me. This internal alterity that allows me to constitute the other is the remainder of my flesh that I project on the body of the Other.

The becoming-body of my flesh leaves no place for the remainder: for the ego-flesh achieves its incorporation; it must eliminate this waste outside of itself. We will therefore not be astonished if the remainder, expelled from my body, reappears in a foreign body, on this surface of projection that we call the other. We have already seen this in the phenomenon of haunting, when my own gaze fixates on and paralyzes me or when my own voice calls out to me as if it came from an other. What seemed to be a "pathological" phenomenon is thus found in our everyday experience of the other. More astonishing is the role that the remainder plays in the constitution of the alter ego, as a factor of differentiation or alteration that succeeds in giving the appearance of a real "other" to a narcissistic phantasm. Let us remember, however, its initial function in the chiasm: when it slides between my flesh and my flesh, it prohibits the carnal poles from fusing together, from completely identifying in a mortal implosion. In being an obstacle for the synthesis, it allows it to be maintained as a *synthesis*, a partial unity of differentiated elements. We have found this function of openness in the course of the process of incorporation, in this gap, this limit that it traces between the inside and the outside of my body, these orifices that hollow out its surface. We will now encounter it on another plane, in this internal alterity that I project on the other and that impedes me from being totally identified with it. Without this, its constitution as alter ego, as another me different from me, would be altogether impossible. This alterity that I lend it is certainly only a projection of my ego— but the appearance of being "an other" is at the heart of the phantasm that the other is. If it did not appear to me in this way, I would no longer be able to avoid a total identification, a deadly fusion with my double: for me, there would never be others in the world.

How is this projection possible? What allows me to transpose the remainder *of my flesh* on an "other"? There is a remarkable analogy between the remainder and the body of the Other: in both cases, we are dealing with a flesh that is not originarily self-given as flesh and does not let itself be incarnated by my flesh. When I transfer it on to a foreign body, I find this buttress in it, this part of the *untouchable* that I had already encountered in my own flesh. This kinship between the two phenomena allows the remainder to be projected onto its body. By making a gift of my flesh to another, I contaminate it by transmitting the remainder that haunts me to it—and from then on, I find in my relations with the other those affects that call forth the haunting of the remainder in me. For our relation to the remainder is steeped in affects, anxiety, hatred, disgust, and probably also desire and love. They are the same feelings that I experience anew when I rediscover this remainder corroding my flesh *in the place of the Other*. It thus falls to another person, to some foreigner I encounter, to fixate on my haunting, to give it a face and a name by capturing the affects that are initially addressed only to me and to what is foreign in me. A new screen is interposed between the ego and the Other, and a new projection overlays those that already obscure the traits of the face. It is no longer only my flesh that I transfuse in it but also the remainder, with the phantasms that it arouses. It is not to Odette that Swann's love and mad jealousy are addressed, but to a phantom, a mirage forged within him and by him, to the haunting of the remainder that slips away, of an object of love that was always lacking: he loves her *because* she does not stop betraying or eluding him—and he is ready to ruin his life for a woman "who was not even his type." This is how the phantasm of the other is formed in us, on the basis of a nucleus constituted by our relation to the remainder: it operates like a matrix, an a priori schema orienting all of our relations to others. When an other appears in our life, we project on it a schema that decides the style of our relations, prefiguring our experience of the foreigner, governed each time by an always different intrigue—marked in some by a feeling of persecution or rivalry or jealousy, and in others by the anxiety of absence, and in still others by a limitless devotion and a desire for sacrifice, or by a desire to dominate and be dominated, and finally in others by more complex forms that are even more difficult to describe. What we most often take for the "encounter" with the Other is in fact only an encounter with our own haunting. This is why some men always fall in love with the same woman hidden behind multiple masks or are confronted with the same "enemy" constantly reappearing in new identities. But these innumerable figures of the other are only figurings, the *linings* of an intimate alterity, of the First Stranger in me who marks all the others whom I meet with its imprint.

Here we are at the heart of the paradox of the other, of this unstable synthesis of the same and the other, immanence and transcendence, identity and difference, which constitutes the phenomenon of the other: it is an always identical schema; it is the *same* remainder that *lets the other be*— and an other who is different each time. How do we become incapable of recognizing the influence of the remainder under these numerous masks? It is as if the prefiguring of the other had to remain veiled: at the moment when it makes a gift of its alterity, the remainder is totally erased in front of it, allowing it to appear as other by taking on the appearance of an always new alterity. Most often dissimulated, this operation is sometimes revealed in certain psychoses. Psychiatry has noted a particular trouble in the relation to the other in what it calls "Fregoli's delusion." The name comes from a famous Italian actor and quick-change artist who could incarnate several dozen different characters in one play. Those suffering from it believe they recognize the obsessive presence of the same Persecutor in the various characters they encounter; the Persecutor is able to borrow and put on numerous different faces and guises. The delusion consists here in tracking a secret "resemblance" allowing for the identification of dissimilar individuals as one. But this delusion has some truth to it: by everywhere disclosing the traits of one sole and same person—a unique remainder—it dissipates the apparent alterity of the "other" and reveals the *function of the mask*, the figure-screen, that assures the phenomenon of the other. Thus, one sick woman recognizes her persecutors "by certain characteristic traits" despite their many disguises: "They always change clothes and hairstyles, but I know it's them . . . it is like an actor and actress preparing for different scenes," and they wear "what she takes initially to be horrible masks with brilliant eyes staring at her."[11] Then, she discovered that these masks were their own faces. The limit-experience of delirium reveals the truth of the other: what is most "other" about it, what constitutes its alterity, comes from me, from the remainder of my flesh that I project back on it. But then we would no longer discern the limits of projection from what, in the phenomenon of the other, could refer to the Other and not to the ego: in other words, we no longer see how the alter ego could be anything other than my reflection or my double.

Is it possible to go *beyond the other*, to pierce the screen of the phantasm and finally discover the true face of the Other beneath this mask that my projections and my identifications have glued on its skin? How can I encounter this enigmatic Other at which I always aim but without ever really reaching it? Such an encounter should *be an event*, undoing the prefiguration that determines in advance my relations with others—and nothing is more difficult. For me to be able to encounter the Other, it must respond to my expectation, take hold of my phantasm by becoming inscribed on my surface of projection: otherwise, I could not even encounter it, and it would escape from me into total indifference. And despite all this, for the meeting to take place, this surface must be torn, the Other must reach me *as Other*, beyond the phantasm, beyond all prefiguration and identification. For the messiah to come, he must be betrayed, denied as messiah, such that even that which allows him to come also prevents him from being revealed and thus forever defers his coming. My projective identifications and the figure-screens issuing from them become obstacles to the revelation of the Other. We must therefore see whether it is possible for the ego to be liberated from its identifications and thus to escape the phantasm of the other. How is it possible to cross the screen of the phantasm, this surface of projection that envelopes me like a second skin and is an obstacle to every encounter with the Other? How could these figure-screens that predetermine all my relations with others be blurred and disappear? In a sense, nothing is more common that this defection of the phantasm: not only is the other an illusory phenomenon, but it is also a matter of an unstable phenomenon, always menaced with decomposition. This instability that finds its source in the conditions of the carnal transference takes on the form of an oscillation or of a dramatic alternation. Either the transference is successfully achieved and is then accompanied by an alienating identification that makes the other into my reflection and my double or makes of me a double of it; or this identification fails, in which case the barely initiated transference is interrupted, and the other, ceasing to be my reflection, is degraded, with its flesh once again becoming a thing "similar to meat."

A very remarkable phenomenon is then produced. With the rupture of the transference, my relation to the other should leave place for the pure indifference I ordinarily feel toward exterior things. Yet experience shows that it does not happen like this, that instead the degradation of the other awakens a feeling of disgust or horror that strikes me in my deepest depths. From the Saragossa manuscript to Lovecraft's writings and Bacon's portraits, the greatest artists have often depicted this failure of the body of the other, its metamorphosis into an unclean and terrifying leftover. Psychoanalysis tried to make a theory out of it by characterizing the disgust arising when the object of desire is desexualized as a major symptom of hysteria,[12] or by taking account of the anxiety seizing the subject when it discovers the gaping wound of maternal castration. But Freud and his disciples do not explain why the discovery of the absence of a penis on the body *of the Other* rebounds on to the subject itself awakening in it the anxiety of *its own castration*. What psychoanalysis lacks is a more rigorous understanding of the constitution of the other: only a radical phenomenology of the ego-flesh—an egoanalysis—allows for an understanding of this backlash whereby the encounter with the other violently reverberates on the ego's own body. For my flesh would remain incompletely constituted, and my body of flesh could not have followed its own genesis had I not had the encounter with another body or had the discovery of our common resemblance not helped me complete my incorporation. What I have given to my alter ego by transferring my carnation to it is returned to me through a sort of *countertransference* allowing me to represent my body to myself by analogy with it. It sometimes happens that this return transference is brutally interrupted when I perceive the marks of a difference on this other body—for example, a sexual or "racial" difference—that prevents me from identifying immediately with it. The color of his skin, the characteristics of his face, the absence of a penis, or the sonorities of an unknown language are some of the many clues to the foreignness of the Other, the many points of resistance that undo identification. When I discover them, our nascent community is undone, the surface of projection is torn, and the very possibility of achieving my incorporation is compromised. Since my body was intertwined with this other body, and since I had constituted my subjective identity by identifying myself with this other subject, the encounter with the Foreign, the discovery of the irreducible difference of the Other, affects me in my deepest depths: it leads my body of flesh back to its first instability, to the "chaos" from whence it came. This dissemblance separating me from the other awakens a more ancient wound, a feeling of incompleteness, of a tear or rip within my flesh, and my own body is under threat of becoming disaggregated.

We begin to understand why men react with such violence to the perception of difference in the other, and even more violently when this difference arises in closer proximity—in my brother, my neighbor, my friend, my *prochain*—interrupting a process of identification in the midst of being achieved. As dramatic as it may be, this crisis nonetheless carries a promise with it, allowing us to glimpse the possibility of a disidentification, a *catharsis* that could liberate my relation to the Other of the projections that falsify it. If men were able to go through the screen of their phantasms, to overcome the disgust and horror inspired in them by the perception of dissemblance (but how could they?) in this ordeal of the Stranger, they would discover the promise of an authentic community able to welcome difference, to take on its divisions without being broken apart. And if, beyond the other, the hidden face of the Other could finally appear, it would then be appropriate to speak of a *second birth*: because the Other would have to be born a first time and disfigured by the phantasm in order to be reborn as transfigured beyond all identification. How is this rebirth possible? The alterity of the alter ego is not constituted merely by the projection of the remainder or of an immanent alterity projected beyond; there are also points of resistance that I discover on its body—singular traits, gestures, words that reveal to me his foreignness. We will need to be careful not to confuse them and not to assimilate what is resistant *in* immanence to what is resistant *to* immanence, this intimate stranger that is the remainder with the external points of resistance in which are manifested the transcendence of the Other. In the haunting of the remainder, it was still only with myself that I was dealing; in this resistance to identification, it is the truth of the Other that points through the phantasm. In each of my encounters, a gesture or a word that interrupts the projection can arise from the unforeseeable, undoing my prefiguring of the other but carrying the promise of the coming of the Other: each new encounter is this "narrow door" by which the Other can break into my life.

Is the experience of dissemblance sufficient to reveal the Other to me *in truth*? Doubtful. The example of sexual difference shows this clearly enough: the dissemblance I perceive in another body does not prevent me from identifying with certain traits of it or from projecting myself on it, integrating it in my phantasms, degrading it to a new version of the other. All our experience attests to it: we cannot tolerate the radical alterity of the Other, and the possibility of its revelation always meets the resistance of the phantasm recomposed in new forms. The interruption of the transference-in-return provokes an intense anxiety that awakens my hauntings. I react immediately to the perception of a dissemblance by a new projection: once I stop identifying the other *with myself*, I identify it *with the remainder*. The ordeal of the Stranger—of the other as Other—is rebuilt on this first foreigner in me; and the traces of a difference in its body, these signatures of its alterity, become points of anchorage for the remainder, traits that arouse my fear, disgust, or hatred. It is thus suiting to distinguish two modes of projective identification, two very different manners of transferring the remainder. In the first case, I project on another body the pure alterity of the remainder, its a priori and affectively neutral form, and this projection that is produced every time constitutes the phenomenon of the other. In the second, rarer, case, it is a partial trait (an *einziger Zug*, as Freud would say), that is, a singular mode of the remainder that I project on the body of the other, with the particular affects that it arouses. In this kind of projection, the other is no longer simply constituted as "other" in a neutral and indeterminate fashion: it identifies with the remainder of my flesh such as it is manifested in my worst hauntings, as this repugnant, threatening, detestable Thing that I reject far from me and try to destroy. This is not an academic hypothesis; men and women have historically been the targets of such projections, stigmatized as figures of abjection, as henchmen of the remainder. It is thus that a theologian of the Middle Ages stigmatized women: "if men saw that which is beneath the skin . . . a single view of women would nauseate them. The feminine grace is but phlegm and blood and humor and bile . . . filth everywhere. And we who find it repulsive to touch vomit or manure even with a fingertip, how could we wish to hold in our arms a bag of excrement?"[13] There is but one step from this repulsion to persecution and murder, and we know that during the witch trials the inquisitors hunted for the "devil's mark" on the tortured bodies of their victims, a secret trace that would attest to their allegiance to the Beast—the index of their foreignness, the corporeal inscription of the remainder. Most often it is not a physical difference but a symbolic criterion (language, religion, culture, politics) that favors the projection of the remainder—and even in this case, the foreignness tends to be phantasmatically materialized in corporeal marks. This is the case for pariahs, Jews, heretics, the insane, the proletariat, dissidents, and all those who were persecuted, locked up, tossed aside, banished, exterminated for having historically represented a figure of the remainder. By placing in crisis the communitarian identifications, by testifying to the hatred of the Stranger who cemented human societies, they incarnate "the eternal irony of the community" and its hidden truth.

I nevertheless obscurely perceive this Other-waste, this threatening intruder, as a part of my flesh. Even when it provokes hatred or disgust, the perception of difference is not fundamentally opposed to identification. Freud imagined the possibility of a *negative identification* that could happen in hatred but not in love[14]—but *all* our identifications are ambivalent; all our relations with the other suppose both repulsion and attraction: even that which distances me from an other, that which I find more repulsive in an other, is often that which captivates me and that with which I identify. The more I am identified with it or feel that *I am of it*, the more violently I reject it. When Kant examined the most intense feeling of repulsion, namely, disgust, he defined it as an affect in which "the object is presented as if it insisted, as it were, *on our enjoying* it even though that is just what we are forcefully resisting."[15] He recognized that the abject is still an object of enjoyment [*jouissance*], that our efforts to resist it are accompanied by a secret fascination. Clinical evidence confirms this. Consider, for example, the case of phobias: the object of anxiety that the phobic tries desperately to avoid is also what captivates his gaze—but which he *cannot* not see. It then becomes very difficult to oppose the tendency to identification to the experience of the difference of the Other, its resistance to identification. Not only do we continue to identify ourselves ("negatively") with the object of our hatred, but this "bad object" can also appear as a pole of positive identification, an object of desire or love. In most of our affective relations, we oscillate in this way between love and hate, desire and disgust, merely substituting one alienating identification for another.

Is it possible despite all this to cross the plane of identification and find an access to the truth of the Other? What still unheard-of figure of the community could emerge from such an encounter? We have admitted that the carnal transference is linked every time to an identification and that these identifications are necessarily alienating. Is this an arbitrary postulate? Can I give flesh to the other's body without losing myself immediately in his flesh or absorbing him in mine? We could very well conceive that a transference took place without turning into an identification or that I am identified with another without being alienated in it. If identifications always rest on a fundamental illusion—they transgress the egological difference—this does not mean that they are all of the same nature. It is important to distinguish fusional, alienating identifications from an *identification at a distance* that could respect the alterity of the Other, allowing me to recognize the foreigner as my similar and enter into community with it, but without ceding to the phantasms of fusion within a Unique Body. For such an identification to be achieved, it would have to inscribe a gap or divergence, a limit between the ego and the alter ego—an element of alterity would have to be inscribed *in* the very process of identification. The remainder is characterized precisely by its function of openness and by differentiation. When I project it on the body of the Other, the border that it traces between each pole of my flesh is displaced to the outside, between my flesh and the foreign flesh, preventing me from being merged into this other flesh. But the first stranger in me is never foreign or different enough from me to open itself to a true alterity: the remainder's immanent resistance to identification must be sustained and reinforced by another resistance that comes no longer from myself but rather from the transcendence of the Other, increasing the distance that the remainder hollowed out. This double resistance would make an identification possible, which would no longer be alienating—a community in divergence, a love that could escape from the fusional madness of love. Between the Other and myself, there must be *both* identification *and* a limit to identification, attraction and rejection, or, to describe it as Kant does, a *synthesis of respect and love.*

He defined respect as a "principle of repulsion" obliging men to "keep their distance from each other" and thus opposed it to love as a force of attraction; and he concluded from this that "if one of the two great moral forces declined," "nothingness would engulf in its abyss the whole realm of beings like . . . a drop of water in the ocean."[16] Where does this force resisting the fusional attraction of love come from? According to the *Critique of Practical Reason*, respect comes from and is addressed to the Law. It *is* the ethical Law itself when it is manifested as subjective motive for action, as a "moral feeling" that mobilizes our will. Kant nevertheless underlines that this feeling is accompanied by suffering, by a sort of terror, as if it exerted an extreme violence on the subject. Its function is to keep the forbidden object of desire, this "object of aversion" that Kant calls evil, at a distance, to keep it away from our faculty of desire and hold it in respect. It is high time to be done with the humanistic and moralistic interpretations of respect and the Law. Such a feeling has nothing "moral" or "human" about it, and respect for the other person is not the most originary mode of respect: it is rooted in a primordial repulsion, the distancing of the simultaneously terrifying and fascinating, monstrous and sublime object=X that is situated on this side of every relation to the other. At the origin of respect, we recognize the action of the remainder, this diverging that safeguards the ego by preventing it from sinking in its own flesh—and which allows it to constitute the other as Other without sinking into its flesh. The question then is to understand how the remainder *becomes law*, how the affects of terror or disgust characterizing the relation to the remainder can be neutralized, and leave room for the pure affect of the interval, a pure feeling of respect for the other person.

The law prohibiting me from fusing with or absorbing the Other, or letting me be absorbed in it, is the "law" of the remainder: it is the remainder itself insofar as it is abject, insofar as I have *ab-jected* it, thrown it far away from my flesh, projected it on the body of the Other where it is transformed into an unclean Thing, a "bad object." This projection supposes that I am already distinguished from the Other or at least that I have noticed the traits of dissemblance, obstacles to complete identification, on its body: they are the marks that serve as hanging points or targets for the projection of the remainder. When this "abjected" part of my flesh is projected on it, our difference is increased and changed into an intense repulsion. It seems to me possible to reinterpret the Freudian theory of castration anxiety in this light. The discovery of the absence of the penis of the mother provokes such a feeling of horror in the child because the child feels this discovery in its own body, awakening castration anxiety and a fear of forever remaining an incompletely constituted flesh, a body mutilated by the removal of its remainder. This anxiety excited by maternal castration pries the child away from the maternal body and inscribes the incest prohibition in its desire: before any intervention of the symbolic Other or of the father as representative of the Oedipal law, an uncoupling or a disidentification allowing the subject to escape from its captivation by the mother's desire is effected. To tell the truth, the mere perception of sexual difference is insufficient to complete this dissociation, this rupture of an original identification: I must still project the remainder of the flesh on the mother's body. The maternal body is subsequently presented no longer as just a pole of attraction or an object of identification and love but also as a pole of repulsion. By awakening feelings of anxiety and disgust, it will henceforth incarnate the remainder in the mode of the abject. In the perspective of egoanalysis, castration fantasy and the Oedipal law can no longer be considered originary phenomena, because they only reinscribe what had already been played out in my field of immanence in the relation to the Other. This is how castration anxiety repeats the primordial anxiety born of the breaking of the chiasm, the exclusion of the remainder, on another plane; whereas the incest prohibition—of sexual fusion with the mother's body—finds its source in the threat of *aphanisis*, a deadly fusion of my flesh with itself, which had been kept apart by the resistance of the remainder. The "desire of the Other" is not what initially structures the subject; it is instead my relation to myself and to the remainder of my flesh that decides my relation to the Other.

This projection of the remainder on the foreign body can, moreover, be manifested in a different mode, such as when it is not entirely transferred on this body, instead taking the form of a partial object, an "organ" projected on it. As we learn from clinical studies, the castration of the mother is so intolerable that the subject can only deny it by imagining a penis attributed to the mother, the absence of which terrifies the patient. The fantasy of the phallic mother is thus born, and it plays a big role in certain pathologies. Neither Freud nor any of his epigones clearly explain where it comes from. I see here again an effect of the remainder: I project outside of me a fragment of my own body—the fragment in which castration anxiety is crystallized—onto the other's body as a surface of projection, where it is manifested as an object of desire (in fetishism) or as an object of horror (in phobia). How can the child project its penis on his mother's body, or on those horses that terrified little Hans, or on the shoes, the lingerie, the pubic hair that arouses the desire of the fetishist, on any object *whatsoever* in the world? For this, the ego-flesh must already be divided, even before taking on body, and a part of my flesh must have already been dissociated from me for it to come back to haunt me as a "little thing" detached from my body, an entrenched organ that I find on another body. Is it possible to go past these projections and partial identifications and knot a relation to the Other, that is, to the mother, as a "total object"? And how is it possible to overcome this incessant oscillation between attraction and repulsion, this ambivalence of the relation to the remainder that is transferred on the foreign body? Repulsion was no doubt necessary to maintain a gap between the mother and the child's desire. For it to be overcome, this gap must be reinscribed differently: a third element must be interposed to pacify the relation by giving the force of a law to the incest prohibition—and this, we are assured, is the very function of the father in the Oedipal complex. Yet the concrete experience of the Oedipal conflict contradicts this reassuring "solution": it is as if the initial ambivalence of the relation to the mother was, on the contrary, placed on the father who, by becoming an object of identification, also arouses hatred or love. To escape this conflict, the child should, according to Freud, pass through a rivalrous and hateful identification with his father to another form of identification that preserves a certain distance, which "is not exhausted by the precept: 'you *ought to be* like this (like your father).' It also comprises the prohibition: 'you *may not be* like this (like your father).'"[17] But Freud does not tell us how one passes from one to the other or how this identification at a distance could bring an end to the Oedipal ambivalence and rivalry. It is analogous to a difficulty confronted by Kantian ethics. Whether it is a matter of the Law of practical reason or the Oedipal law, what makes the law for the ego originates in the operation of the remainder. This is manifested at first by an alternation of attraction and repulsion, and it is only when this oscillation is eased, when the affects accompanying it let themselves be neutralized, that it can be revealed in its pure interval function. How is this affective neutralization possible? In what way can a "pathological" feeling of suffering or terror be changed into an ethical feeling of respect? By what magic is a subject able to pass from the imaginary to the symbolic, to assume castration as the law of its desire while overcoming the horror that it inspires in him? Psychoanalysis gives just as few answers to these questions, as does the Kantian *Critique*, because both these theories are initially situated in the transcendence of the world, whereas our affects are rooted in the immanent life of the ego: their mutations are the index of a modification of the ego's relation to the remainder—and our concern now is to describe this.

The time has now come to make the point. I wanted to understand the origin of identification, which leads the ego to alienate itself to diverse figures of the other, to take them as models, to submit to their influence. I thought I had found the answer: the originary identification of the ego with itself is repeated in its relations with the other and incites it to fuse with it as if they were but one sole flesh. I wonder whether this analysis is sufficient, whether it manages to take account of the persistence of our alienating identifications, of those phantasms of fusion that are endlessly reborn in the desire for servitude and the madness of love. In a sense, everything is opposed to such identifications—these physical and symbolic differences that distinguish us from other men, the double resistance of the remainder and the Other—but despite this, we do not stop identifying ourselves with others. Is this the clue to a crisis of the remainder, a failure of its interval function? Would it be itself ambivalent, a factor of separation and openness, but also of identification and alienation?

To try to respond, we will have to deepen the analysis of the originary synthesis from which the remainder comes. This will perhaps allow for an elucidation of another enigma, namely, understanding why the ruptures of identification are most often accompanied by anxiety, hatred, disgust—even though they preserve the ego-flesh, prevent it from totally alienating itself to the other. I tried to understand *the birth of hatred*: it is the discovery of a dissemblance between an other and myself that interrupts the transfer-in-return and threatens to break the precarious unity of my body. The ego-flesh reacts to this danger by projecting all the abjection of the remainder on a foreign body. But how can an empirical difference between two bodies in the world compromise to this degree my most originary identifications? In my field of immanence, there is neither resemblance nor dissemblance—only the elementary phenomena of attraction and repulsion, coupling and uncoupling. The allure of the other, the form of its face, the color of its skin, its manner of speaking and behaving, should never suffice to break our identification. For me to refuse to consider it as another man, my "similar," a more radical divergence must have already opened, interrupting this blind identification by which my flesh had been linked to its. My initial relation to the remainder must already be modified, and repulsion must subsequently take precedence over attraction, so that this inversion of meaning is reflected to the outside of the foreign body. This is how the perception of our dissemblance becomes intolerable, and the tiniest difference appears as a terrifying threat.

This inversion of the relation to the remainder that engenders disgust and hatred must also be able to be reversed. An identification at a distance, a synthesis of respect and love, must be possible; otherwise, human communities would have long ago sunk into the jouissance of hatred and the madness of love, "like a drop of water in the ocean." The question now is to uncover this true relation to the remainder and to the Other. Because my projective identifications disfigure my relation to the Other, we must be able to interrupt them, to stop projecting my remainder on the foreign body. But such a projection is probably inevitable—which constitutes the stranger as an alter ego. It is thus a question not of stopping the projection but of disarming its affective charge. The affects of hatred, anxiety, and envy must let themselves be neutralized if they are finally to cede their place to respect; my relation to the remainder must lose its ambivalence by being reduced to the most neutral affect, to the pure sentiment of divergence we call respect. It is only in this way that the remainder can *become law* for the ego. How could my relation to the remainder be reversed once again or be modified in this sense? And what would be the consequences of it for my experience of the other, of the phantasm that I interpose between me and the Other? The phenomenon of the other is an unstable synthesis of transcendence and immanence, a mixture in which elements detached from another body are mixed with the remainder of my flesh that I project outside of me. Projection that must necessarily remain hidden: if it is not dissimulated, the grimace of the remainder would resurge endlessly in masks of otherness. It is this projection that parasitizes and fogs my relation to the Other. I constantly attribute to it intentions and affects that come from me: I thought myself to be the target of its hatred, whereas it was a matter of my own hatred refracted onto the screen of my phantasm; or I imagine that these feelings are addressed to it, even though they are aimed only at me, and it is me that I love when I declare my love for it. I inevitably replay the same intrigue with every foreigner that I meet, and I imprint on all our relations the mark of my relation to the remainder.

For this projection to stop being an illusion, it must appear in the light of day, and I must be able to sort out, in the phantasm of the other, what comes to me from the other and what is issued from myself. If the remainder is no longer dissimulated, if it finally appears to me as remainder, then it would at the same time make the other appear as Other. The *truth of the remainder* must be revealed to me for the Other to unveil its true face to me; only then could I join myself to it in the divergence of respect and perhaps love it with true love. Only the truth can still save us, give us the chance for a community beyond the phantasm. This supposes a radical mutation of my relation to the remainder, whereby it is no longer presented as a foreign Thing and whereby I finally recognize it as the flesh of my flesh, a part of myself that I have projected out of myself. Am I the one to make this mutation happen? I am left at this point captivated by and so profoundly identified with the remainder that it is not at all clear how I could free myself by myself from such captivity. Should I expect it from the Other, from a chance encounter with the Stranger? But how could it be revealed to me given that the projection of the remainder has always already falsified our relations? How do we get out of this impasse? Let us hold on for a moment to this fundamental rule: everything presented to me in the transcendence of the world was already prefigured in my field of immanence; what decides my relation to the Other is my originary relation to myself, to what is foreign in me. For a "second birth" of the Other to be possible, beyond the other, my own rebirth must have already begun. I who am born a first time under the domination of the remainder must now be reborn by delivering myself from its influence. We must now examine the conditions of this resurrection, if I want to understand how my ego "like a circle, returns to itself by passing through the foreign that is opened up within me."[18]

11

The Crisis of the Chiasm

Following the eternal act of self-revelation, the world as we now behold it, is all rule, order and form; but the unruly lies ever in the depths as though it might again break through, and order and form nowhere appear to have been original, but it seems as though what had initially been unruly had been brought to order. This is the incomprehensible basis of reality in things, the irreducible remainder which cannot be resolved into reason by the greatest exertion but always remains in the depths.

—F. W. J. Schelling, *Of Human Freedom*

What does the ego desire? It desires its freedom, its *deliverance*—the Great Health that Nietzsche spoke of, which will come forth when the Earth has become a place of healing. It desires to overcome its hauntings, its alienating identifications that subject it to the innumerable figures of the Other. It wants to find an authentic access to itself and to the Other and "to throw the anxiety of the Earth far away from itself." What are the conditions of its deliverance? *There must, above all, be an ego*, a singular ego that has the power to give itself to itself, to reveal itself to itself, to call itself to itself; and its self-givenness, self-revelation, and invocation must be more originary than its alienation and its fallenness. The ego must be able to *be recalled to itself*, to come back to itself "by passing by the foreign that is open in it." Apparently this third condition follows from the first two: only an ego that has already been called back to itself can also possess the power to be recalled to itself, to find itself. If my self-givenness makes my return to myself possible, then how do I let myself become exiled in the world and captivated by others, without being able to address the royal letter to myself, the call that could free me? What is the obstacle to my deliverance? Is it the facticity of my existence, my letting-be, my being thrown in the world? But my facticity still belongs to my life: this situation, this epoch, and this body are *mine*, and I have to assume them freely. If I do not do so, if I do not decide for myself, I am entirely responsible for my indecision. In order to take account of my alienation, I no longer have the right to invoke the overwhelming domination of the world and of others: my self-givenness is originary, and what comes forth to me on the plane of transcendence was already announced in the immanence of my life. Each of my ordinary defeats refers to a more radical disaster; and the decision to submit myself to the powers of this world, or to resist them, is rooted in an archi-decision, a first alienation or resistance, in those *immanent events* that are the weave of my life. At bottom, this is good news. What happens to me is thus not the fault of the Other, and I do not have to accuse it or blame it entirely—for the Evil Genius who tries to deceive me is in me. And it is in me that I must look for the principal impediment to my deliverance, in an initial self-blindness, a self-forgetting, and it must be in my power to deliver me from it.

It could be, however, that voluntary servitude is the worst of all, from which it is the most difficult to be freed—precisely because it is grounded on a free decision. This is what Kierkegaard claims: whoever holds himself captive will not be able to free himself by himself—"he uses the power of freedom in the service of unfreedom . . . no one is so dreadfully imprisoned, and no captivity is so impossible to break out of as that in which the individual holds himself captive!"[1] The "freest" and most "autonomous" ego will be in truth the most alienated. Its deliverance cannot come to it except from the Other, from a Savior who "saves it from itself," from a divine Redeemer. If we do not accept this conclusion, we must wonder how an ego that has forgotten itself could be recalled to itself, free itself, *without* the help of an Other. But could I forget the ego that I am? Being can withdraw itself, God can turn away from me, because at the outset a distance separates us and because they are given to me from the outside in the interval of their transcendence. How else can an ego that is constantly revealed to itself also be dissimulated to itself and thus lose itself, except by admitting that I am not always given to myself as myself?

In the movement of my self-givenness, a part of me is dissociated from me, and I am no longer able to recognize it as mine. This First Foreigner that is opened in me, this archi-transcendence within immanence, is what I have called the remainder. This is what, by sliding between each of the poles of my flesh, distances me from myself and makes me opaque to myself: it is the target of my primordial identifications, and it is by identifying myself with it that I alienate and forget myself. My deliverance will be possible only if I am able to modify radically my relation to it—and only if it is itself modified in its relation to the ego. How could this happen? How could the remainder save me from itself?

For this, it would have to be able to divide itself, turn back against itself. As Descartes' strange God—sovereign source of truth that first presents Himself with the traits of a great Deceiver—what alienates me must also be my liberator. We have seen that the remainder possesses several faces. Issuing from a synthesis, from the partial recovery of several currents of consciousness, the remainder remains a synthetic and unstable phenomenon, a *metaxu*, a hybrid, a Proteus. It is above all distinguished by its function of making an opening: by maintaining a gap or divergence between my carnal poles, it prevents me from sinking in the chaos of my flesh; by tracing a limit between the inside and the outside of my body, between my flesh and the foreign body, it helps me resist the phantasms of fusion and the mortifying identifications with the other. As an agent of differentiation and disidentification, it is an essential condition of my freedom. And yet, the very remainder that protects me also appears to me as a threat, an unclean Thing, a petrifying Gaze, a Voice that obsesses me, and its appearance is most often accompanied by anxiety, hatred, disgust. But we know that these feelings of repulsion can be mixed with completely opposite affects, so we must also imagine the possibility of an attraction of the ego by the remainder, of its identification with the remainder. Paradoxically this phenomenon that was first manifest as a factor of separation or resistance to identification is now presented as a focus of alienating identification. Which of these two opposed facets is the most originary? Which best reveals the truth of the remainder? Do they coexist simultaneously, or is there a passage from one to the other? And if this is the case, is this movement reversible? How can we pass from repulsion to attraction or, inversely, from a fusional identification to the divergence of respect? How is our relation to the remainder modified?

It is difficult to respond to such questions, because the remainder is never manifested "in person." Similar to the *khôra* of the *Timaeus* and to Aristotle's "prime subject," this limit phenomenon appears only "as an other in an other," as the "fugitive phantom of something else." This other that it haunts is me—because the remainder exists only in its synthesis with the ego-flesh, and there are different versions of this synthesis, its transformations and its crises, that we must now examine. What happens to the originary synthesis so that the remainder that it produces becomes threatening to the ego-flesh? The analysis of haunting gave us some elements of a response. What allows me to recognize this "eye thing" that I perceive in the mirror as my eye of flesh, what helps me to identify this voice I hear as my own voice, is the tactile experience that subtends these perceptions, that is, when I palpate my face, when I feel the vibrations of my vocal chords, the "sonorous flow" of my voice over my skin. If the tactile chiasm subtending them fails, my vision and my voice lose their anchorage in my flesh, and they then reappear outside of me as an unknown Voice that calls to me, a strange Gaze that petrifies me. This experience of a loss of belonging, of an alteration of the proper, is rooted in a failure of the tactile synthesis, in a *crisis of the chiasm*. Does it concern only the extreme phenomena of obsession, hallucination, delirium? Or do its effects make themselves felt throughout our life—in our anxieties, our loves and our hatreds, our despair, our fear of death?

Let us briefly recall the results of the preceding analyses. For my flesh to become body, three syntheses are required: a horizontal synthesis of incarnation, a transversal synthesis of incorporation in which the flesh intertwines with itself, and a *new synthesis of incorporation* in which it unites itself with the remainder engendered by the previous two syntheses. The most originary of these three syntheses is the horizontal: it grounds the other two, and its failure is what we will first of all have to approach. In fact, even if the analysis allows them to be distinguished, these syntheses are nevertheless inseparable; and if there is a crisis of the chiasm, it will affect all three of them. But how can a primordial intertwining whereby my flesh is knotted up with my flesh be undone? Precisely because it is a matter of a *syn-thesis* and because it puts differentiated elements in relation in order to unite them and identify them with one another. If the ego-flesh were not originarily divided and dispersed in innumerable poles, no chiasm could have taken place: for there to be a synthesis, there must be an initial differentiation, an alterity, a divergence of the constituent elements—of the poles of flesh for the first two syntheses and of the flesh and the remainder for the third—and this very divergence is also what threatens to destroy them. We have seen that primordial self-identifications always remain partial, that incorporation is not able to reabsorb the remainder entirely into the unity of the total body. In each phase, a distance is maintained: there is some "play" between the elements of the synthesis, and as they are not perfectly adjoined, it is always possible for them to be dissociated. This eventuality is all the more threatening when some forces oppose a complete unification: in the process of incorporation, then in the constitution of the other, we have seen *a resistance of the remainder* to identification. All this allows us to think that this resistance experiences fluctuations in intensity and can either decrease or reinforce itself. When it is weakened, the remainder's function of creating an opening is compromised, and the ego-flesh risks collapsing on itself, imploding in the abyss of *aphanisis*. When, on the contrary, it exceeds a certain threshold of intensity, repulsion prevails over attraction, the primordial identifications are effected with increasing difficulty, and the carnal syntheses enter into crisis, threatening to interrupt.

How is such a crisis manifested? By the most extreme anxiety or a feeling of absolute distress, or by phantasms that see the light of day only in certain psychoses. As soon as the synthesis of incarnation fails, each pole of the flesh is violently separated from other poles instead of uniting with them: the texture of my flesh is torn apart, its nascent unity is undone, and I become anxious about being dismembered or infinitely cut to pieces. When the syntheses of incorporation fail, my flesh is no longer able to be lived as a body. No passage, no mediation, is possible anymore between these two dimensions of my experience: either the flesh experiences its incorporation as an atrocious mutilation (as with Artaud's phantasm), or the body feels its carnal dimension as an abject decomposition (as with Mishima or Céline). All the demarcations between the edges of my corporeal orifices, between my different organs, between the inside and the outside of my body, then collapse. A splintered ego, a body torn to pieces, a reciprocal double abjection of the flesh and the body, a ripping apart of the corporeal surface—the crises of the carnal syntheses are manifested first by a disincorporation of my body, a disincarnation of my flesh, a desubjectificating panic that lets the ego pass the limits of madness. What puts the ego-flesh in peril is thus not merely the abyss of *aphanisis* but also the inverse and equally terrifying threat of a dissociation or rupture of the chiasm. Throughout my existence, I remain confronted by this double threat that presents the two faces of my death to me.

As long as I am alive, it will only be a matter of a threat, a simple and endlessly invoked possibility of an imminent "death." Because dissociation is never absolute, a total interruption of the chiasm would immediately result in the disappearance of the ego-flesh, its annihilation. It must therefore be allowed that the dissociated elements remain in contact and that a certain attraction, a tendency toward unity, is maintained within the most extreme repulsion. The dislocation of the synthesis can therefore be succeeded—if the ego is not totally annihilated—by a phase of recomposition, a resubjectification of the ego, a reincorporation of its flesh. Does not this simply bring us back to the initial situation? Or will the crisis have left traces, wounds that no longer become scars? Is it indeed the same body, the same ego, that is reconstituted once the crisis has passed? It does not suffice to oppose the happy unity of the synthesis to the tragedy of its dissociation—because the synthesis could indeed be recomposed in an entirely other mode, producing new phantasms and new threats. In the third synthesis, which completes the process, the ego-flesh is united with the remainder in order to engender this very singular phenomenon that is my body. This is how I define incorporation, the movement whereby the ego incarnates the remainder, gives it flesh, while receiving certain characteristics of the remainder in return. During the process, the ego-flesh overcomes the resistance of the remainder, penetrating it in order to offer its life to it: I am the "subject" of the synthesis, the agent of this metamorphosis—and the synthesis of the ego and the remainder is here effected *under the dominance of the ego*. Is this primacy of the ego-flesh always assured? Is the chiasm re-knotted every time in this manner? The phenomenon of haunting obliges us to imagine the possibility of *an inversion of dominance* in which the synthesis would be recomposed under the primacy of the remainder.

It is not the separation of forces that constitutes disharmony in itself, Schelling said, but rather their false unity. He tried to take account of the real possibility of evil—of an evil that would not be a mere fault, privation, or limitation of the good—without attributing it to an evil

Principle. Evil would come not from a diabolical will opposed to the good but from a "division of the whole" and from a "reversal of principles"; and we must indeed see that "the identical elements which existed in the unified whole are in the divided whole; the matter in both is the same—from this aspect evil is no more limited or worse than good; but the formal aspect of the two is totally different and it is the very form."[2] The elements that are in accord or torn apart are *Existenz*—the manifestation or coming to light of the phenomena—and *Grund*—the condition of all manifestation that, in itself, is not manifested. There is at the root of the phenomena an "absolutely irreducible residue" that resists "the lightning of life" and "remains eternally in the Ground." By seeking to discern this "remainder that can never be resolved," Schelling came closest to what I call the remainder. I will not retrace the grandiose theogony wherein he sketches the conflict of Ground and Existence within God itself and within the movement of Creation. What interests me here is the possibility of an inverted and false unity, of *a perverse synthesis* in which the dissociated totality is reconstituted under the primacy of the Ground (that is, the remainder) while unleashing the highest power of illusion, evil, madness, and death.

Schelling teaches us to think in terms of attraction and disjunction, a battle between primordial powers, relations of forces, and reversals of relations. If we want to understand the relation of the remainder to the ego, we must no longer limit ourselves to a static description but also take into account their dynamic, drive-based dimension, their mouvance. In such a perspective, the remainder is no longer merely an inert residue that passively resists incarnation: it exerts an attraction on the flesh, tries to captivate it, to absorb it in itself, just as the ego-flesh also tries to attract the remainder in its own mouvance. A double-crossed attraction in which each tries to capture the other and imprint its mark upon it, reabsorb it in itself. When they meet and fuse, their union keeps the trace of this combat, and so we would then be dealing with two opposed modes of synthesis, one in which the remainder dominates the flesh and the other in which the flesh dominates the remainder. I have up until now examined only the mode that presides over our incorporation. How will the inversion, the perversion, of this synthesis present itself? As a new knotting of the ego and the remainder wherein, this time, the remainder imposes its essential character on the ego—the character of being a foreign Thing, deprived of flesh and life. Instead of letting itself be revived by the ego, the remainder penetrates into it and devours its flesh. It does not totally annihilate it but fuses with it in a different manner, altering all its traits, provoking a *disfiguration* of the ego-flesh. New phenomena thus appear *in the place of* the Ego, its body, its temporality. It seems that my fragmented ego finds a certain unity; a re-subjectification seems to be initiated, but it is a Double, a foreign rival, who has taken my place—an *Horla*. We do indeed witness here a reincorporation, but in the form of a monstrous body, an Anti-Body. Instead of a flux, an incessant passage, my lifetime is contracted in a unique and frozen moment, the obsessive Counter-Time of the haunting that is repeated and incrusted without ever fading.

Why designate this as a "disfiguration"? Because the inversion of the synthesis results in a series of distortions that deform and dissimulate the ego-flesh. When the remainder becomes an intrusion in my life and is confused with me, the truth of my ego lets itself be hidden by a countertruth, a deceiver who is substituted for me. It is not just the ego but also an essential trait of the remainder—its interval function, its power of differentiation—that is covered over and annihilated when it resurges in me as the abject Thing *that I am*. There is an erasure of the difference between the ego and the other, a confusion between the ego and the remainder—and we recognize this as what defines the phantasm. Certainly all my identifications are accompanied by phantasms, including those that constitute my body or the alter ego; but in this case, I can be identified with the remainder or with the other without the risk of losing myself in them. This is no longer the case when the remainder devours my life. The part of me that I no longer recognize as mine penetrates into me and tears me away from myself: it *becomes me* while remaining foreign to me. An Horla, an Anti-Body, a Counter-Time—how are such phantasms constituted? the originary carnal syntheses are what make incorporation possible and give it its meaning: we must try to discern at this level the disfiguration affecting the ego-flesh. Through the horizontal synthesis, each pole recognized the other pole as its own flesh and identified with it. At the instant that the chiasm is reversed, a foreign Thing suddenly emerges in the place of the other pole. From then on, instead of tending toward the other pole in order to be united with it, the ego-flesh pushes it far away from it: it is this repulsion that we will have to describe. What happens to the other synthesis when the ego and the remainder are re-identified under the dominance of the remainder? Through the transversal synthesis, each carnal pole senses itself touched by the other as a body, is lived *both* as flesh *and* as body *at once*. If this synthesis is undone, it will be lived sometimes as flesh and sometimes as body; it will feel its living flesh being changed into a corporeal thing. This time, I feel the remainder devouring my flesh *in myself* and not in the other pole. What in my own experiences corresponds to this disincarnation, this tearing apart of the ego-flesh? And could I take the same path in the reverse direction, passing from the thing to flesh, thus reincarnating myself? Would it be equally possible to reincarnate *the other pole*, to recognize it anew as my own flesh? Here a deepened analysis of the crisis of the syntheses is imposed, on both the horizontal and transversal planes.

I wondered how deliverance is possible. The analysis of the crisis of the chiasm allows determining its conditions in a more precise manner. From the formal point of view, nothing is opposed to that which an inverted synthesis recovers or reconstitutes in the initial mode; for we find in the "false unity" these same elements—the ego, the remainder, their knotting, and their divergence—that had made the disfiguration possible. To overcome this distortion, it would be sufficient to dissociate them again, then recompose them by once again changing the dominance. Things would be quite different were we dealing not with the inversion of one relation but rather with the total destruction of an element by an other: barring a miracle, it would be impossible to come back from this to the initial situation. It seems to me, however, that this formal condition is still insufficient: for deliverance to be possible, there must also be *a point of resistance*. A singular ego must persist within its deepest alienation or disfiguration, and it has to be able to be called back to itself by freeing itself from the influence of the remainder. This second condition corresponds to Descartes' discovery: if I err, I am; the more the great deceiver tries to negate me, the more he confirms me in my existence. But this, too, does not suffice, and Descartes indeed knew it. He had understood that the deceiver himself must change faces, that the focus of illusion must be revealed as a source of truth: only then will a true relation to the Other be possible. This lesson from the *Meditations* we can make our own on the condition that we recognize that the surname "God"—an apparently deceptive but in fact truthful god—is a marker for the phenomenon that I call the remainder. The remainder must be modified so that my relation to it can change and so that I am able to overcome alienation, rivalry, hatred, and envy. Only the truth can save me. The truth of the remainder will heal me of my haunting when I will finally recognize it as the flesh of my flesh. All three formal conditions—of inversion, of resistance, and of truth—are required for deliverance to occur.

12

From Hatred to Love

> At one time it grew to be only one from many, at another it divided again to be many from one. There is a double coming into being of mortal things and a double passing away. One is brought about, and again destroyed, by the coming together of all things, the other grows up and is scattered as things are again divided. And these things never cease from continual shifting, at one time all coming together, through Love, into one, at another each borne apart from the others through Strife.
>
> —Empedocles, *On Nature*, Fragment B 17.6–10

> Hatred . . . is older than Love.
>
> —Freud, "Instincts and Their Vicissitudes"

How do we describe the crisis of the chiasm? How do we apprehend the phenomena unfolding themselves in the field of immanence, phenomena that never appear in the horizon of the world? If we want to orient ourselves in the labyrinth of immanence, we will have to follow Ariadne's thread of affectivity: my affects weave the fabric of my existence—feelings of love, hatred, joy, sadness, fatigue, anxiety, despair. They seem to be produced by exterior causes—events that happen to me within the world or in my relations with others. But these transcendent causes are most often merely occasions that allow the affects to show themselves: my affects belong to the mouvance of my flesh and are rooted in the immanence of my life, in those "sensations of energetic tension and relaxation, sensations of inner restraint, paralysis, liberation, etc.," which are the "hyletic" bedrock of the ego-flesh.[1] By being self-moved and self-given, the ego is affected by itself, its mobility, and its life; its auto-affection is originarily "affective." Each movement of its flesh, each phase of its mouvance—its fluxes and refluxes, blockages, discharges, and withdrawals—is accompanied by singular affective tonalities, purely immanent affections arising without any external cause, which "bloom because they bloom" and then fade away. All sensations I feel toward others are prefigured in these *archi-affects*. The other is only a surface for the projection of the ego, a screen on which I project the affects, which are in fact addressed to me (or to a part of myself): for me to be able to feel love or hatred toward an other, I must first of all have loved or hated myself. In what elementary configurations of my flesh does this strange self-loathing, this archi-love, find their source?

To take account of certain phenomena—hatred, alienating identification, and the loss of a sense of belonging that characterizes them—I had put forward the hypothesis of a crisis of the chiasm that would affect the whole of the constituting syntheses. At the origin, each carnal pole experienced the other pole as a foreign thing; they then had to be identified in a horizontal synthesis, knotted up together, making a gift of their flesh to each other so they could finally recognize themselves as two poles of one sole flesh. If this synthesis were undone, each pole would become foreign to the other again, appearing to it as a transcendent body, exterior to its flesh. But we have not simply returned to the initial situation: each of the two poles was intimately united to the other and had recognized it as its own flesh. Such an impression does not let itself be easily erased: it lingers while the chiasm is unknotted, and it is intertwined with new impressions. Psychologists speak of "residual sensations" to designate those sensations persisting after the disappearance of the initial stimulus (the illusion of the "phantom limb" experienced by amputees is an example of this). I will henceforth designate the persistence of carnal impressions as a *residual effect* [*effet de rémanence*]—while also letting the meaning that Artaud gives to it be heard, namely, the sense of a leftover, a persistent remaining residue, that "rises up" in returning.[2] These phantom impressions will profoundly modify the new impressions provoked by the crisis: when they become foreign to each other, the two poles still continue to perceive each other in a residual manner as two parts of one same flesh. They will thus indifferently oppose each other from the outside; yet each will dread its relation to the other as an internal relation threatening the deepest depths of itself as an unknown Thing suddenly appearing so close to me, even within my flesh, to devour my flesh. It is a question not of an exterior body like any other body in the world but rather of an Anti-Body, a Double that seems absolutely foreign and hostile to me, yet which appears to be more intimate to me than I am to myself. This "extimate" object, this *Horla*, is the remainder—more precisely, it is a mixture, a bastard synthesis of the remainder and the other pole of flesh. We have seen that the crisis of the chiasm is not limited to one dissociation and that dissociated elements tie themselves back together in other modes and are recomposed in an inverse synthesis under the dominance of the remainder. The meaning of the synthesis is thus perverted: instead of the ego-flesh incarnating the remainder by giving life to it, it is now the remainder that disincarnates the flesh, transforming it into a fleshless Thing. And yet, the remainder is only a part of my flesh, still opaque and blind to itself: in this perverse synthesis, this chiasm of death, the unflagging mouvance of my flesh is always unfurled, dissociated from me and turned back against me.

The principal function of the remainder consisted in opening up a divergence within the chiasm, thus preventing a total fusion between the poles of flesh. Here again we find this function, but now with a completely different meaning. In their originary separation, the remainder and the flesh pushed each other without hatred or disgust, while coming to buttress each other as exterior obstacles. Now, the remainder is presented as a danger, an enemy arising *in the place of my flesh*. An intense feeling of *repulsion* is substituted for the initial, affectively neutral opposition: this *Hors-là* [outside-there], this stranger from the outside reappearing in the heart of my flesh, must be rejected at all costs and expelled far from me. The mouvance of the ego-flesh takes on a new form: it is henceforth concentrated in the gesture of throwing-far-away, in a movement of *abjection*—a term understood here in its active sense, as when Artaud speaks of an "abjecting god" or the "abjected limbs of the body." Why does the remainder, which belongs to my flesh, become intolerable for it, to the point of relentlessly rejecting and excluding it? I see here the effect of a distortion affecting the initial relation of the flesh to the non-flesh. With the phenomenon of abjection, the perverse synthesis of the flesh and the remainder is spatially disposed in a *dislocation* or distortion of the relation between the proper and the foreign, the Here and the There. If the site of my flesh is this absolute Here "that will never be over there," then, conversely, the Over There is apprehended as the domain of the non-flesh: in its most originary experience, the ego always associates its own with the nearby, the distant with the foreign. The crisis of the chiasm overturns this topology by making the non-flesh appear in the Here *in place of* the ego-flesh. When it tries to expulse this Thing out of itself, to "abject" it, it is simply an attempt to reestablish the initial disposition, to return the foreignness in its native place, over there. What Plato said of the soul is also suiting for the flesh: "whatever the thing it takes hold of, it comes always towards it by bringing life to it," and this is why "the soul does not admit death."[3] When the flesh encounters in itself a remainder of non-flesh, it has to extirpate it from the self and reject it far away from it.

This distortion or displacement of the border between the proper (or my own) and the foreign is not a mere illusion. When it arises in the most intimate parts of my flesh, the remainder contrarily unveils its true nature: it reveals that it is *of it*, that it belongs to the ego-flesh. The crisis of the chiasm thus becomes a work of truth, not only because it makes this remainder reappear, which had been allowed to be absorbed and incorporated into my body, but above all because it reappears closest to me, dislodges me from myself, *as if it were me*. The ego's attitude toward it, its propensity to reject it as a heterogeneous element, shows, however, that the unveiling remains partial, that it coexists with new illusions, that my relation to the remainder continues to be falsified by phantasms, projections, residuals, more profoundly now than previously. We find the trace of this disfiguration in each of the primary affects awakened by the crisis and above all in the affect initially accompanying the gesture of abjection—namely, *disgust*. To approach this archi-affect, let us start from the ordinary feeling of disgust, such as when we are overtaken by nausea provoked by certain exterior phenomena. One of the few authors to be interested in this determined the *contiguity* between the subject and the object of its disgust as its principal character. It is not simply a matter of a spatial proximity (in the sense that the disgusting "sticks to my skin" or adheres to me so that I cannot unstick myself from it); we also see here an essential *affinity*. Unlike fear, mistrust, or other feelings of aversion, "disgust is turned back not only on its object, but also on a presumed attraction of the subject for it."[4] This characteristic is associated with another fundamental trait—namely, its relation to death or, more specifically, an effacement of the limits between the living and the dead, a decomposition of life paradoxically presented in the case of sexual obscenity, vermin, or rotting trash as a proliferating overabundance of life. Such an analysis remains purely descriptive and considers only the psychological phenomenon of disgust of things in the world. But despite this, it puts us on the path of the immanent affect, of this archi-disgust that the ego feels when confronted by the remainder, this dead thing that "lives off of" the life of its flesh, corroding it from the inside. We will discover the ultimate meaning of this attraction or affinity that I feel toward the object of my disgust: it is the clue to *a possible identification*, revealing the hidden and intolerable truth of disgust—the originary identity of the ego-flesh and the remainder. Barely glimpsed, this identity is immediately and violently denied, and the feeling of a proximity to or a secret kinship with the remainder increases the disgust that it inspires. The spatial distortion, the installation of the Stranger in me, is therefore not sufficient to disclose its true essence. At the very moment it reappears in me, the remainder remains still foreign to me, and this internal alterity is lived as an intrusion that threatens to destroy me—becoming more threatening the closer and more intimate it is to me. Such a situation necessarily provokes an anxiety that will persist in the heart of disgust, hatred, love, and all the affects issuing from the crisis.

What allows me to claim all this? Do we encounter this immanent disgust toward the flesh or a part of the flesh in experience? Clinical experience gives factual attestations of it—for example, in the case of hysteria, the neurosis where disgust is substituted for sexual excitation. By analyzing a young hysterical woman, Freud discovers that her repugnance to sexuality has its origin in the disgust she feels for certain parts of her body, notably for her "white waste," the vaginal and urinary secretions. But this affect could also have another, very different cause: Dora's disgust for sex could come from her resistance to the incestuous and perverse desires that she feels toward her father. The feeling of disgust is thus presented in her as a "combination of contrary tendencies"—both auto- and allo- erotic—and Freud recognizes that he is hardly able to elucidate it.[5] Other clinical examples will allow us to discern this phenomenon more clearly, because they uniquely concern the relation of the subject to his own body. Neurological accidents frequently provoke a hemiplegia, paralyzing and rendering numb the limbs of one side of the body; what happens in the crisis of the chiasm on the plane of the world is equivalent to what I am trying to describe on the immanent plane of the flesh. Now, numerous testimonies show that hemiplegics no longer recognize their paralyzed limb, that it seems like a foreign entity to them ("I don't know where that comes from, it's long, it's dead, and it feels slimy like a snake"),[6] which excites a strong repulsion and the desire in them to eliminate it ("just cut this arm off . . . give it to the Maccabees, for all it's worth"). This aversion to a part of the body also occurs in the absence of any cerebro-vascular lesion, and in certain psychoses where it is conjoined with phantasms of intrusion or persecution, and can go as far as self-mutilation. A psychotic thus complains about a "change in his body," certain parts of which have "been substituted for others": "my hand is not completely mine—had these fat, disgusting women already taken over? It is as if their dirty limbs were there in place of mine . . . I rub myself trying to find my parts, so that the parts of that fat lady will go away."[7]

One of these clinical observations in particular has helped me to understand how our carnal mouvance and the archi-affects accompanying it are modified—namely, that of the hemiplegic who thought that a "leg cut from a cadaver" had been attached to his body in the place of his left leg. He tried in vain to tear it off and throw it away, fell out of bed with it, and hit it with an extreme violence, without ever identifying it as his own leg. This is what aroused horror, then rage, in him. When he had thrown this dead leg "out of bed, he followed it—and *now it was stuck to him*"; "have you ever seen anything so horrible? I thought that a cadaver was just dead, but it fact it is more strange and even horrifying: one might say that it is stuck to me!"[8] We recognize here the mouvance at the origin of disgust—but it now appears that this gesture of abjection is not sufficient to "unstick" the remainder from the flesh, since it *is of it*, is nothing other than this flesh when it apprehends and dreads itself as a foreign Thing. And the gesture must be endlessly repeated in an always more violent rejection that always fails—the more the ego tries to chase the abject outside of it, the more it comes to be encrusted in it, until the ego must finally admit the failure of all its attempts to expulse the remainder. Abjection is then changed into another mode of mouvance that I propose to designate as a *rejection*. It is no longer a matter of getting rid of the remainder but rather of simply destroying it, and it is manifested by the appearance of a specific affect. It is no longer a matter of disgust, which always implies a devaluing of the object and the possibility of keeping it aside. On the contrary, this new affect takes very seriously the menace that the remainder inflicts on the ego, a threat that is impossible to escape as long as its "cause" continues to exist. Such an affect aims now at only one thing, namely, the elimination of its object, its annihilation—and it is this feeling that we call *hatred*.

We doubly mistake hatred if we assimilate it to aggressivity or the death drive of the Freudians. This is the case because, first, at the root of a hatred there is no "hate" in the current sense of the term, no "originary sadism" or desire for destruction, but instead only the ego's desperate effort to separate itself from the remainder haunting it. Next, aggressivity is indifferent to its objects, whereas hatred aims at a singular object, or rather at a certain situation of the object, namely, the distortion that constructs it as an intimate stranger. Descartes had best observed the primary character of hatred: he defined it, without any reference to the will to destroy, as a passion that incites us to "consider ourselves alone as a whole entirely separated from the thing for which we have an aversion"; whereas love, on the contrary, leads us to represent ourselves as part of the whole, the other part of which is the loved object.[9] Its second character, its relation to the "extimacy" of the object, is frequently misconstrued. It is difficult to admit that of all our sentiments, hatred is the most *fraternal*—and yet nothing is more hate-worthy than my twin or my double, this foreignness that *almost nothing* distinguishes from me. Because this foreignness is always a secret part of himself (his femininity or repressed homosexuality, the Jewish part of his origins or culture, his fear of becoming insane, and so many other modes of his foreignness), the hater inevitably looks for it in the Other. The nearly indiscernible proximity to the object of his hatred only reinforces the hater's panicked fear of "being of it," which augments his hatred. If an ontology of the remainder were possible, it would be grounded on an analytic not of being-there but of *being-of-it*, in all senses—topological or trivial—of the expression. Consider, for example, Proust's narrator's description of the "two evil races," the Jews and the homosexuals, wherein he indicates that he now understood why he had thought Monsieur de Charlus seemed to have the air of a woman when leaving Madame de Villeparasis' house the other day: "because he was *one of them*."[10] In our hatred for the other, a strange complicity is sketched out, and this secret complicity reveals an essential characteristic of originary hatred, of the *archi-hatred* that the ego feels for the remainder: it allows us to see that what separates them is almost nothing and that in my hatred I always take aim at a part of myself. As in the case of disgust, of which hatred is a modification, the discovery of this proximity or hidden affinity is intolerable: at the moment it is discovered, the identity of the ego and the remainder is immediately thrown out ("rejected," annihilated) with the most extreme violence. Just as there is a truth of disgust— the obscure intuition of the *Fleisch* that is also at the bottom of all flesh—so too does hatred have its share of truth. But it cannot tolerate it: when it tries to harm the other, it is its own truth that it is trying to annihilate.

But by claiming that there is nothing "bad" at the origin of hatred, or that its mouvance merely tries to defend the ego against the intrusion of the remainder, do we not risk justifying hatred? We must not confuse this hateful repulsion with the authentic resistance of the ego: the truth is what makes all the difference between them or, rather, the relation of the affect to the truth. The ego tries to resist its alienating identifications, to separate itself from the Other to which it is alienated, because it desires to return to itself, to be *truly* itself by giving itself to itself; and it will be able to do so only by recognizing the remainder as the flesh of its flesh. Even though hatred hardens the scission of the ego and the remainder to the extreme, by trying desperately to expulse the remainder, it reinforces this primordial illusion wherein the ego sees itself torn apart: it unleashes the highest power of the *countertruth*. For my hatred is never addressed to an "other" but only to myself, to a part of my ego: this is what hatred denies by projecting itself outside of me, and this projection completely falsifies my relation to both the remainder and to the Other. When I constitute the remainder as an object of hatred, I project this hatred on it as if it were the cause of it, as if it were a dastardly power, a *deceiver* trying to destroy me. The same operation is repeated when I transfer the remainder on to the other, that is, when I constitute my alter ego as a menacing rival: I am not content to hate it—I must also disfigure it. By making of the Other the cause of its hatred, the persecutor is perceived as if it were the persecuted and as if he were merely defending himself: he thus succeeds in hating "in all innocence." When the persecuted responds to his hatred with more hatred, the persecutor triumphs and his rage to destroy is finally "justified." Born of an illusion, of an originary phantasm, hatred can endure only by propagating new phantasms, by provoking new disfigurations: it engenders always more hatred, endlessly feeding off it.

Here is why hatred is profoundly bad: it is the source of all the *unhappy passions* and a major figure of *radical evil*. The imperative to be free of hatred defines for each of us an unconditional obligation. But how could I overcome hatred if it is rooted in the most intimate folds of my flesh? How would a *remission* of hatred be possible? If it is true that the hater is enslaved by a phantasm or victim of an originary illusion, then it could seem that he does not depend on it in order to disengage himself from it. And yet the blindest and most alienated ego still continues to be freely self-given, to submit itself freely to the Other that alienates it, and freely renounces its freedom: when the hater lets himself be submerged in hatred, it is because *he has opted for nontruth*. A new decision should thus be possible, annulling the effects of the first. It would not be grounded on a moral norm or abstract Idea of "duty" or the "good"; it would be decided *for the truth*. Since it is grounded on a countertruth, then only the truth can cure us of hatred; only the disclosure of the truth of the remainder would allow us to be done with the disfigurations and projections that make it the target of our hatred. But how could the remainder be revealed in truth? What subtends the disfiguration is the crisis of the chiasm, the perverse synthesis whereby the ego-flesh is submitted to the power of the remainder. In this "false unity," the originary elements remain the same, and for this reason, the inversion of the primordial syntheses can in turn be inverted by reestablishing the primacy of the ego over the remainder. In theory, this inversion is always possible, but its formal possibility does not suffice for it really to arise, and its concrete conditions, the manner by which it will be carried out, are different every time. We know that it calls for both the ego and the Other, demands a modification of my relation to the remainder and the encounter with an Other who successfully undid my phantasm, breaking the logic of hatred. But even if the transformation of my relation to the remainder does indeed depend on me, even partially, neither the Other's arrival nor my endless waiting depends on me.

I will limit myself here to describing the essential traits of this inversion. As to the real possibility of its effectuation, let us leave it to its freedom and its luck in each singular history. Let us suppose that the ego is finally able to overcome the crisis, that the encounter with an Other had made this possible, that the horizontal synthesis had been reknotted, that the unfolding of the flesh prevails over the resistance of the remainder, that it begins to incarnate it and to give life to it. The illusion that it is a foreign entity penetrating and devouring my flesh dissipates, along with the deadly affects that accompanied it. I now recognize this unclean Thing that I had tried to annihilate as a part of myself. When the flesh begins to take hold of itself again, the meaning of its mouvance is radically inverted: repulsion and abjection are succeeded by an opposed movement, an attraction of the flesh to itself, and this carnal attraction will awaken a new affect. What name can be given to this sentiment that emerges as the reversal of hatred other than *love*? It is a strange love that occurs in all relations with the Other, a self-idolatry, an absolutely narcissistic self-love that the ego-flesh feels for its own flesh; and this *archi-love* prefigures all the feelings of desire and love that I could feel toward other subjects when I project the remainder of my flesh on their bodies. Taken strictly, the Freudian notions of narcissism and auto-eroticism are no longer suitable to qualify this archi-affect. On my plane of immanence, all difference disappears between desire and identification (on this level, *to have* the object and *to be* the object are one and the same), between self-love and the desire for the Other (*I am* this "other" that I desire), between narcissistic love and "true" love (archi-love is all the *more true* when it is addressed to myself). It is thus convenient to limit the concept of narcissism to the relation that will be established during the mirror stage between the ego and *its image* and thus to distinguish it from what I call archi-love.[11]

We must see that it is indeed *the same* object that provoked disgust, hatred, and now love. I would willingly say that it becomes sublime, in the precise sense that Kant gives to this term when defining the feeling of the sublime as a "rapid alternation of repulsion from, and attraction to, one and the same object."[12] This inversion of affects and of the carnal mouvance must have its source in the object itself, in a radical modification of this object and of its relation to the ego-flesh that aims at it: its *disfiguration*, which makes an object of hatred out of it, is succeeded by a *transfiguration*. This sublime and transfigured object is the remainder—more exactly, it is a synthesis of the remainder and the flesh. The other pole of my flesh lets itself be dissimulated and disfigured by the remainder and henceforth reappears with its true face, is reincarnated and recommences to incarnate the remainder. "To find the object," Freud said, "is to find it again": this other part of myself that seemed to have disappeared, I recognize anew such as it was before the crisis and its reappearance awakens my joy and love. Plato was not wrong to attach love to the memory of an original whole—but this nostalgic desire is not addressed to the primordial Great Body torn apart by the gods nor to the archaic fusion with the body of the mother, as the Freudians believe: it aims at a lost and found part of my own flesh. In each of our embraces, we celebrate reunion, this second birth—and a new victory is won over hatred. It is no longer sufficient to claim that hatred is "more ancient" than love: we must say that hatred is the *condition* of love (which does not mean that it is the "cause" of it or that it precedes it every time in the empirical history of the subject). Thus the mystery of affective ambivalence, the indissociable node of love and hate, is clarified: these two opposed affects are rooted in two successive modes of carnal auto-affection and are addressed to the same phenomenon, but to different phases of its manifestation. If the disfigured remainder unleashes my hatred, in being transfigured it becomes the first unique love of my life. Freud moved in this direction by discovering that in the most primitive phases, love "can barely be distinguished from hatred." He very correctly concludes from this that when love is changed into hatred—for example, following a breakup—it is in fact a *regression* from love to the anterior stage. Despite this, he refused to allow their identity or to recognize that in hatred is the originary condition of love: he claims on the contrary that love and hatred "do not originate in a cleavage of any common primal element, but sprang from different sources and underwent each its own development before the influence of the pleasure-pain relation constituted them antitheses to each other";[13] and he would make increasing misuse of his theory of "pulsional dualism," the mythical opposition of the life and death drives, as the two heterogeneous sources of love and hatred. But Freud was misguided: in truth, *there is no death drive.* Every drive is a pulsation of the ego-flesh, just as my love and my hatred belong to my life—to a life that can be torn apart, turned back against itself, seeking to destroy itself, yet also healing itself of its wounds, converting its hatred into love.

It is precisely this co-belonging, this essential identity that allows for the hope of a remission of hatred: if these two affects are rooted in two opposed drives, we do not see by what miracle hatred could be transformed into love. It could well be possible to repress it, or to project it outside (as in paranoid projection), or to sublimate it by modifying its object—but not to overcome it. On this point, Spinoza is a better guide than Freud. The *Ethics* insists, of course, on the opposition of the joyful passions, which are good in themselves, and the unhappy passions, first among which we find hatred. It would be a question, however, not of a real opposition but only of a difference of degree: these two kinds of passions differ according to the intensity of our power to act. An increase of intensity gives rise to the joyful passions, whereas the unhappy passions become manifest through a decrease in intensity. Spinoza's refusal of all dualism allows him to take account without difficulty of the coexistence of love and hatred toward the same object, of the conversion of love into hatred and hatred into love. But love and hatred do remain *passions*, passive affections provoked by an exterior cause, and it must be possible to imagine the passage to the active, purely joyous affections in which the soul by adequately knowing itself will affect itself only by itself, by its own power to act. Here again, this distinction between two manners of being affected does not rest on a real opposition and the transition from one to the other will be able to be effected, when the unhappy affection will be "separated from the thought of an exterior cause and is joined to true thoughts."[14] Spinoza thus teaches us two different ways of extirpating hatred, either by changing it into love or, more radically, by submitting it to the power of truth. He understood that truth could save us from hatred and from the unhappy passion it engenders, that is, that it is the path of deliverance. But he defined truth classically as adequation, as an adequate knowledge of its object—and not as disclosure. He could thus allow neither that the truth is intertwined with an equally originary nontruth, nor that its disclosure could coincide with a concealment that would compromise the chances for our deliverance, nor that we are at odds with the affections of sadness, hatred, or envy that no adequate knowledge would be able to overcome. Because, in his view, our active affections come from our adequate ideas, because they augment our power to be, the affects in question will necessarily be desire and joy: Spinoza could not conceive the possibility of "active" hatred, of an immanent archi-hatred that would erupt without any exterior cause and that could no longer be so easily changed into love. He could not imagine the possibility of a shameful joy born of hatred, this *jouissance* of death that is radical evil.

The admirable analyses of the *Ethics* remain a clarifying help in trying to understand the inversion of affects. When Spinoza remarks that "Hatred which is entirely conquered by love passes over into love, and the love is greater on this account than if hatred had not preceded it," he allows us to understand better the birth of archi-love.[15] We must indeed see that at the moment when its meaning is reversed, the affect preserves all its intensity, which is why the repulsion of hatred or of disgust gives way to an equally intense attraction: the limit between the most violent hatred and the most extreme love is barely perceptible. But there is nevertheless a capital difference between these two affects and the mouvances subtending them. Not only is hatred more originary, but its relation to the truth is not the same: if hatred misconstrues the relation of the ego and the remainder—or recognizes it only in order to deny it—love is, on the contrary, grounded on their identification. What motivates disgust and hatred is the disincarnation of the flesh, the disincarnation of the remainder, the forgetfulness of its carnal dimension, which awakens love and is their reincarnation. In love, I rediscover a forgotten part of my flesh; I glimpse the truth of the remainder: even though it is reborn of its disfiguration, the ego-flesh retrieves itself, becoming once again what it truly was. We thus do not consider transfiguration as a phantasm or a mere illusion: in being transfigured, the ego and the remainder are revealed in truth, and what I call archi-love is not a mere consequence of the truth (as joy is in Spinoza), nor is it one of its "generic conditions" among others: love is *the affect of truth*.

How then does this power of unveiling immediately produce new phantasms, new illusions? And why does love so often fall back into hatred? In order to understand the phenomenon of love, we must refer to *the logic of hatred*. My hatred is so intolerable for me that I constantly try to reject it, to project it on the remainder, and thus on the other. In my phantasm, then, the other seems to be the cause of this hatred (as if it were by itself hate-worthy) or its initial source (as if it were it that hated me and in returned provoked my hatred for it). This paradoxical relation to the object of hatred persists when hatred is transfigured and inverted into love: I also project the amorous attraction whereby my flesh captivates my flesh onto the remainder, as if my love were only responding to its lover, as if it were itself the cause of my desire. I then believe that I desire it because of its own qualities, because it would be desirable *in itself*. During the conversion of affects, the most intense hatred is entirely changed into love, and rather than worthy of hatred, the remainder becomes all the more fascinating and sublime. This metamorphosis is repeated in my relation to the other: by projecting the transfigured remainder on it, I erect it as a glorious idol whose brilliance subjugates me without me being able to perceive the invisible mirror, the figure-screen on which my image is projected. We can see here the origin of several essential determinations of love, of its "narcissistic" dimension (believing that it loves another, it is an image of myself that I adore), its fixation on *a partial trait* (it is a singular part of my flesh that I project on the other), its tendency *to idealize* its object by projecting the transfiguration of my flesh on it.

This could perhaps permit an elucidation of one of the greatest mysteries of love. *Who* is this other I love? What in the Other takes hold of my desire and my love? The grace of an image may be what charms and attracts me, but in truth, it is not what awakens my desire: it is a certain *je ne sais quoi*, an allure or gesture, the brilliance of the gaze, the grain of a voice, a singular and most often dissimulated element masked by the fullness and beauty of the image. It is this "non-imagined residue of the body" that Lacan designates as "the object-cause of desire," the object-a— of desire, but not of love, which according to him obeys another logic. Freud already insisted on the difference between the relations of love and hatred, which would be "relations of the total ego" to a "total object," and the relation of the drive to its objects, always partial, that would be presented as so many "little things" separated from a body. Lacan radicalizes this theory by renouncing the very notion of a total object: the other as object of my desire would never be an other but only "the addition of a heap of partial objects."[16] He is thus prevented from thinking the possibility of *true love*, of a love that would be addressed to the other as Other, beyond the fantasy that disparages the Other as a little thing, an object-a. Surely he was right to claim that desire is first attached to a partial trait—to Plato's *agalma* or Freud's *einziger Zug*—that is, to the remainder of my flesh projected on the other. But this heterogeneous element does not remain isolated: in the course of the process of incorporation, it will be identified with my flesh, fuse with it in order to give birth to a total body. This synthesis of identification is repeated when I transfer it on another body; in being transfigured, it fuses with other traits, other partial zones of the foreign body. Radiating from an initial source-point, it is diffused over the entire surface of the body, propagated to the other's whole person. By a simple addition of objects of desire, the other is transfigured in a unique object of love. At the heart of this amorous transfiguration, the initial hooking point persists, like a final vestige of disfiguration, of abjection that preceded desire and made it possible. We have often noted that the idealization of the loved object is attached to a particular mark that is given first as a fault in order to make of it an infinitely desirable quality. Lucretius perfectly described this phenomenon: in the eyes of lovers, "such swarthy skin is 'honey-gold,' a slovenly slut is 'beauty unadorned,' . . . the dumpy and dwarfish is 'one of the Graces' . . . a huge, hulking giantess is a 'sheer marvel, the embodiment of majesty,' the stammerer who cannot speak a word 'has a lisp,'" and so forth.[17] It is a miracle of crystallization in which we recognize the trace of the remainder, the visible sign of its transfiguration.

Will idealization limit the amorous fusion or reintroduce a distance between the ego and the object? It seems on the contrary that this gap is constantly transgressed. The more I judge the object of my passion to be sublime, the more I am considered unworthy, inferior to it—and the more I come, paradoxically, to identify myself with it: in the state of amorous subjection, Freud said, "the object has, so to speak, absorbed the ego." This fusional identification is already discovered in the relation of the drive to its partial objects: when the masochist inflicts pain on himself or treats himself like trash, when the voyeur makes himself into the gaze, the ego melts into the object of his phantasm, and his unspeakable and blind enjoyment [*jouissance*] leaves him no place to escape the Other or to separate himself from it. The phantasm is characterized by its anonymity and erases every trace of a singular ego: by being identified with the object of my phantasm, I fade away into it; I am annihilated. It is this hypnotic fascination, this "sacrifice of the ego," its self-dissolution in the object, that defines amorous captivation for Freud, but he is also able to describe it, on the contrary, as a state in which the ego would have completely absorbed the object, would have "introjected" it into it.[18] Is the lover then identified with the beloved, or the contrary? Is the ego lost in the object of its love, or does the object let itself be devoured by the ego? These paradoxes are clarified if we put all relation to otherness out of play, if we return to this archi-love where the entirety of our lives is pre-sketched. When the synthesis is recomposed, when the flesh is reincarnated, each carnal pole tends to fuse once again with the other. What had previously prevented them from totally identifying with each other was the resistance of the remainder—but here it, too, tends to be reincarnated as well, increasingly appearing to me as a part of my flesh. At the limit, there is no longer any difference subsisting between the remainder and the other pole: both are transfigured into objects of desire and love. Consequently, no obstacle impedes the poles of flesh from embracing or melting into each other; no foreign element is opposed any longer to this murderous confusion, this implosion that I call *aphanisis*. If the lovers' dream is to become one sole body, then the ideal of the archi-love is one body without organs or openings, the body-shell of autism: it is a flesh without differentiated poles, folded back on itself, collapsing ever more into itself, to the point of dissolving in a magma, in the gaping Black Hole. If there is a nontruth of hatred, a blindness pushing it to reject the remainder as a foreign body, there is also *a madness of love* that is no less dangerous, since it tends on the contrary to deny the foreignness of the remainder and reabsorb its alterity. In hatred, the remainder devoured the flesh; in love, the ego-flesh absorbs the remainder. In a sense, the threat from love seems more serious: unlike hatred, which cedes before the truth, no disclosure can save us from love, because it is its very truth (its power of unveiling, of reincarnation) that conditions its madness. It would no doubt assign a limit to it, requiring it to respect the alterity of the remainder—but what limit, what law, would be able to contain the madness of love, if, as Augustine claims, "the only measure of love is to love without measure"?

At first sight, this danger concerns only archi-love, and it should disappear as soon as we pass to the plane of the world and bodies. Certainly the madness of love persists at this level. It can lead the ego to alienate itself totally to an other, to be subjugated by it, to sacrifice itself for it, and it is what pushes humans to submit to a Chief and to commit the worst crimes in order to earn his love. But we no longer encounter the terrifying menace of *aphanisis* on this plane. The demiurge probably took pity on our distress: while fashioning our body, he took care to provide openings on its surface, orifices that would never close up. He made sure that the resultant disgust can change into desire, and he constrained desire to take this path, to pass through the holes of another body so that it could overflow. Concerned to avoid a total fusion of two bodies, he fixed a term on their embrace, condemning them to enjoy only a restricted part of the other body and only for a short time. When the limit of their enjoyment is reached, their union is undone, and they are again separated. No body is thus able to lose itself entirely in the other. None is able to scar over the wound, the initial separation that made it be a body. In his great goodness and his irony, God inflicted this punishment on us in order to heal us of our madness: to save us from love, he gave us sexuality.

There is, however, an equivalent phantasm in the order of sexuality to match *aphanisis* on the plane of flesh. It is the fantasy of an absolute enjoyment, in which the limits of the ego and the Other are abolished, a fusion with the primordial body from which my body has issued—the desire for incest. Freud had indeed seen that Dora's sexual disgust resulted from both a disgust of her own body and a resistance to her sexual desires. Anna manifests the same resistance, the paralysis that strikes her hand and prevents her from touching her father's body, and it is likewise true for the anxiety of the phobic or for the behavior of the obsessive-compulsive. All major symptoms of neurosis are screens and defenses against the joy of incest: they are constructed as a last resort, when the law that prohibits this joy fails. I have nothing to say back to this psychoanalytic thesis. It seems to me, however, that, as with Dora's disgust, these symptoms are rooted first of all in the relation of the ego to its own flesh and that they resist a threat more radical than incest, that of *aphanisis*. Without this resistance, the ego would have already sunk into the bottomless pit long ago. On the plane of the flesh, there is nothing equivalent to the distance between two bodies or the gaping pit of the sexual orifices. If the remainder stopped ensuring its function to open up a divergence, nothing could protect the ego anymore from a self-destructive fusion of its flesh with itself. The only possible defense would then consist in separating the other pole of flesh, abjecting the remainder with which it is identified. We recognize this mouvance: it is what brings disgust to birth, then hatred. We understand then why love seems impotent to prevent the return of hatred. As soon as it passes a certain limit, it becomes a danger for the ego and necessarily generates hatred, a hatred as violent as love is strong. Here, then, is the ultimate meaning of hatred: it helps the ego resist the madness of love.

This does not mean that the synthesis is immediately inverted or that the disfiguration of hatred prevails again over the transfiguration of love and entirely supplants it. It may be that old hatreds re-erupt *in* the very movement of the amorous transfiguration. It suffices for this that the gap is reopened between the ego and the remainder, that the feeling of an irreducible distance is imposed on me, while I tend with all my forces to the object of my desire. This appears to me to be out of reach, as if it refused my love. In this impotent tension, love is modified and charged with a sort of anger, a ressentiment toward the object, a desire to force its reserve, to take hold of what it refused me: it is transformed into *envy*. If another ego intervenes in the affair, or if an object of my desire seems confiscated by this other, then my envy becomes *jealousy*—but it is only a matter of a derivative phenomenon that always refers to an immanent archi-envy, that which the ego feels toward the transfigured remainder. Melanie Klein was astonished that original envy is addressed equally to the positive and to the negative object (objects she identified a little too quickly with the maternal breast); but the logic of envy undoes such an opposition: the more the object is "good," the more the remainder seems to me sublime and desirable—and the more it eludes my grasp, the more it excites my envy and seems "bad" to me.[19] I then seek to avenge myself of it, to take hold of it in order to destroy it, and what remains of love cedes its place to hatred. Here again, Spinoza saw things correctly: envy is nothing other than hatred itself.[20] More exactly, it is the particular form hatred takes when it re-erupts within love, and this hateful envy is the sign of a new distortion in which the transfigured remainder is once again disfigured.

Thus the ego-flesh seems condemned to oscillate endlessly between phases of disfiguration and transfiguration, disincarnation and reincarnation, threat of dissociation and threat of deadly fusion, the repulsion of hatred and the attraction of love. One of the oldest texts of the West bears witness to this strange history, the history of our life. Certain fragments of Empedocles' lost poem describe a double genesis in which elements "never cease from continual shifting, at one time all coming together, through Love, into one, at another each borne apart from the others through Strife." [21] It is a double movement that is the effect of a struggle between two primordial powers, namely, *philia*, the love that brings together the elements into a unity, and *neikos*, the strife that "divides" and "scatters" what love had united. The entire cosmos is their battlefield, but it is indeed a process of incorporation that Empedocles makes us witness, the genesis of our body on the basis of a chiasm that is unknotted and reknotted: "deprived of bodies, the disjoined parts wander, desirous to be reunited." This incessant alternating, this combat or play of elements, is endlessly pursued to the point of a sort of *aphanisis*, until "One is brought about, and again destroyed, by the coming together of all things, the other grows up and is scattered."[22]

We wanted to know whether it was possible to break the infernal logic of disgust and hatred by appealing to the truth of love. It now appears that the transfiguration of the remainder hardly suffices to overcome hatred, that it is merely the reverse of disfiguration, its precarious and always reversible inversion. It lets us hope only for a mere *remission*, a provisional healing that love offers us, before it slips back into envy and hatred. Love cannot save us from the eternal return of hatred as long as our relation to the remainder has not been modified. Before seeking whether this mutation is possible, it is appropriate to analyze the consequences of the crisis for the transversal synthesis. What modifications of the carnal mouvance will result from it? What new disfiguration, what transfiguration, will it impose on the remainder and on the ego?

13

From Archi-Agony to Resurrection

> We pay dearly for being immortal: one must die several times while one is alive.
>
> —Nietzsche, *Ecce Homo*

What happens when the synthesis of incorporation fails or when the knotting of the flesh and the body is undone? In *the transversal synthesis*, each pole of flesh shares its impressions with the other pole, experiences itself through the other, senses itself touched by the other as a corporeal thing: from then on, it is lived as a body, as a part of my body, while also remaining flesh. Just as with the horizontal synthesis, this transversal synthesis is marked by the combat of the ego-flesh and the remainder: if their relation is inverted, it too enters into crisis, and the nascent unity of my body is disaggregated. This disincorporation can lead the chiasm to be inverted, to be reknotted under the primacy of the remainder. Then it is no longer the flesh that gives life to the remainder but the remainder that disincarnates the flesh, devouring each of its poles. The effects of this inversion will be all the more dramatic: when it was a matter of the horizontal synthesis, this disincarnation concerned only the other pole, and the ego-flesh could try to reject or destroy it in the repulsion of disgust and hatred. In the case of the transversal synthesis, it directly affects the ego-flesh, without possibility of it fleeing from or expelling this Thing haunting it. By letting itself be absorbed by the remainder, the ego-flesh in some sense stops being a living ego, stops feeling what is happening to it. The phenomenon affecting it will be properly insensible and thus all the more difficult to discern—a limit-phenomenon, more profoundly dissimulated than anxiety, hatred, love, envy, and all the other affective manifestations of the remainder. This does not mean that it just erupts in certain extreme situations: it could be that it constantly affects us, without our being able to perceive it ourselves. How can we, despite all this, succeed in describing it or even in naming it?

When such a phenomenon is produced, what is given to me as *both* flesh *and* body will be decomposed, appearing sometimes as my living flesh and sometimes as an inert thing: I feel my flesh disincarnated, and I sense myself slipping into nonflesh. But how could the ego perceive itself in such a manner, sense that it is passing outside of itself and becoming foreign to its own flesh? The ego-flesh is originarily dispersed in innumerable fragmentary egos. The life of one of these ego-fragments lasts only a few moments, just long enough for a sensible impression and its wake of retentions to be prolonged. The ego fades as soon as this wake is erased, but another ego appears with each new impression—other yet the same. The primordial flesh endlessly unfolds and refolds itself, loses itself and finds itself again without ever giving itself the time to be born and to die. By initiating its incorporation, the ego-flesh overcomes its initial dispersion and flickering; it is unfolded in its duration and is continually constituted in the unity of a history, and so the feeling of its identity will not entirely be erased during the crisis. As in the appearance of disgust and hatred, the residual phantom impressions modify the perception of this crisis. Even when it slides into the nonflesh, the ego still keeps the memory of its past life, which is what prevents it from instantly sinking into nothingness. It no longer fades away in an instant: it dreads its next disappearance; it lives on the brink of ceasing to live—it *senses itself dying*. What name other than *death* is appropriate for the passage from my living flesh to the nonflesh, to nonlife? The crisis of the chiasm produces an Anti-Body every time; and if it is presented in the genesis of hatred as the "bad object," the abject, then subsequently it appears to me in another mode: by experiencing its disincarnation of my flesh, I anticipate the moment when my body becomes a cadaver. My body's disincorporation results in a *mortification* of the ego-flesh, a *necrosis*, and this originates in the crisis of the tactile chiasm—because I no longer am able to touch myself touching, I live as if I were already dead. As a psychotic who never stops touching his own body declares: "I have to touch myself all the time to know how I am . . .

No, I am no longer a body, I am like a dead person."[1] But is the name "death" truly appropriate to designate such a phenomenon? What we usually call death concerns a transcendent body, a subject in the world, marking its definitive disappearance, its passage from life to an inanimate state, whereas the limit-phenomenon that I try to describe here affects *only my flesh*—and nothing proves that it is irreversible, that it coincides with its total annihilation. Is this immanent "death" in life, this "death" that is never manifested in the world, still a matter of *death as such*? And what relation is there between this phenomenon and death in the ordinary sense of the word?

Perhaps the problem has been poorly posed: instead of wondering whether such a phenomenon merits the name "death" or questioning its relation to what we ordinarily understand by death, we must first question the common meaning of death. From where does the meaning that we attribute to it come? Is what we naively take to be "death" indeed death *as such*, the truth of death? Heidegger taught us that the determination of death as an anonymous and distant end is based on an inauthentic understanding of this phenomenon. The existing being that I am is confronted at every moment by the possibility of its death; it anticipates its death in anxiety and is carried toward it by constantly running ahead of itself, which makes it a being-toward-death. We have to distinguish death in the ordinary sense (*Tod*), imagined as the "end-yet-to-come" of our life, and *Sterben*, the always present possibility of dying; every authentic relation to death originates in this phenomenon of *Sterben*. We may still wonder whether Heidegger was truly able to differentiate the two and strictly determine the essence of dying. By seeing dying as the present anticipation of a death to come, he makes it a mere prelude, a modality of death, which continues to be understood as a future expiration or an indefinitely delayed "end." Heidegger thus did not overcome the traditional understanding of death because he did not sufficiently mark the difference between dying and death and so could not think of dying on the basis of itself without immediately reducing it to a mere anticipation of death. If *Sterben* is indeed an originary phenomenon, then it must be a matter of an immanent event *of my life*, of a mode of givenness of the ego, in which a living ego is given as *ego moribundus*, as if it had lived its death. This phenomenon is impossible to elucidate without questioning the relation of life and death or what allows a life to be lived as dead, to "give itself" its death [*se donner la mort*: to kill oneself]. Heidegger did not allow this, because he refused to determine existence on the basis of life and because he opens an abyss between Dasein and its living reality. Will we have more luck by turning to psychoanalysis and by no longer considering death as a mere possibility but instead as a real force, a drive that is opposed to the life-drives? But the relation between these two antagonistic forces remains totally obscure, and at Freud's behest, the pulsional "dualism" remains a "mythology," an abstract speculation that does not at all allow us to understand how, in singular existence, life comes to be bound up with death, to let itself be captivated by it, to desire its death and the death of others—or, on the contrary, to resist it.[2]

In order to approach the truth of my death, we would have to go beyond ontology and psychoanalysis. We must refuse to dissociate the sources of life and death and, on the contrary, consider death as an immanent possibility of life, an adventure of life. And we must go a step further by no longer imagining death as a possibility yet to come but rather as a singular event that *takes place* in my life. For the possibility of my death to have a meaning for me, I must have already had the experience of dying while remaining alive, and I must have apprehended and dreaded my death at work in my life, that is, understood my life itself *as mortified*. I have the experience of an adverse power threatening to destroy me; I feel a dead Thing in the heart of my flesh corrupting and killing me—but this Thing is just a part of myself that has separated from and turned back against me. It is the good fortune of our language that we find in it an expression that manifests both the "reflected" character—of dying as being-self-mortified—and its temporal dimension—of an event, passage, agony. "Madame is dying! Madame is dead!": in this terrible cry that Bossuet evoked is expressed all the distress of a life that feels itself sinking into death. This is what the ego experiences when the synthesis is inverted: it senses that *it is dying*. A living ego that is dying is nearer to its death, has more authentic "experience" of death, than does a Dasein *moribundus*, which exists only as a being-toward-death in the anxious anticipation of a death yet to come. For it is a question here no longer of an imminent and always deferred possibility but rather of a true agony. This nonflesh into which I sense myself sliding *is nothing for me*: when the remainder mortifies me, it annihilates me. The experience of dying is not a momentary syncope or a provisional fading-away that we would have wrongly assimilated to death: nothing about this ordeal of nothingness guarantees that the ego could return. It is thus not "derived" from "true" death as a sort of metaphor; it is on the contrary our common notion of death, the anticipation of our end, that is prefigured in the nothingness of this immanent death and draws its meaning from it.

Thus I would be dead, always already dead; I would have already undergone dying long before my death in the strange experience of an antecedent death; and without this *self-mourning* accompanying me throughout my life, I would never be able to anticipate the possibility of my death to come. Another paradox is added to this temporal paradox: when the ego is dying, its death seems to come to it from the outside, from a foreign power. The disincarnation of my flesh, its reabsorption in the remainder, is a putting to death, a transcendental murder prefiguring all the murders flooding human history. We know, moreover, that certain cultures and some psychotics consider every death, even the most natural, an assassination. During funeral rituals, the Diolas of Senegal question the deceased for a long time in order to discover the name of the "witch who eats souls," who supposedly trapped the dead. Likewise, certain Melanesian tribes exhume cadavers in order to examine their skin for supposed traces of the signature of an evil power that caused their death. Wherever desire, envy, and hatred are involved, it is most often a question of erotic markings, which I call the *corporeal inscription of the remainder*.[3] We may judge this conception to be "primitive" (or "delirious"), but it comes closer to the truth of the remainder than do our modern sciences of ethnology and psychiatry—and better than any ontology, it points to that paradox wherein the possibility of dying is grounded on an originary murder.

If there is a share of truth in the phenomenon of dying, it is indissociable from a nontruth, a radical dissimulation. For this foreign Thing that gives me death in fact belongs to my flesh, to my life: it is my own flesh that devours itself or gives itself the illusion of passing into the nonflesh. This co-belonging of life and death, this complicity of the ego and the remainder, always remains as profoundly masked as it was in hatred. My flesh is therefore blinded to itself, to the point of living as if dead—but as with Poe's Valdemar, it must remain alive in order to be able to live its death. I had thought I was dying, but I was not really dying: my flesh merely gave itself the appearance of dying. There is indeed here a disfiguration analogous to that which had elsewhere engendered disgust and hatred: as "real" and frightening as it seems, the experience of dying is nothing other than a phantasm—but it is in this phantasm that each of us finds the meaning of his death. Could what we call "death" be only an illusion? If the ego-flesh seems to die without really dying, would this mean that it is not mortal? If the analysis that I have just sketched is not reduced to a speculative construction or the dream of a visionary, then it must be possible to find an *attestation* for it in existence. To be decisive, this should testify that certain living beings happen to live as if they were dead but also that this experience of an antecedent death *prefigures* that of the "real" death and provides it with its meaning. Sticking just with the first condition, we can quickly find significant instances of it, for example, in contemporary literature, from Mallarmé to Kafka and Blanchot, which examines all the declinations and tones of the motif "I am dead." We could also find it in mental illness: whether it is a matter of the obsessive's tortured questioning ("am I living or dead?"), or of the paralysis striking Anna's hand and transforming her fingertips into faces of death, or of Schreber's hallucinations of being changed into a "leprous cadaver," or even of the melancholic's complaint that it is "as if I were dead, as if I were floating in my skin, like the impression of no longer having any bodily weight"[4]—every time we are dealing with an intrusion of death in life, where the subject feels in his own body the distress of dying or, rather, of being already dead.

Not only clinical cases but also our everyday existence allows us to have such an experience, which is manifested by a singular feeling—not anxiety but despair: if I am anxious about my death to come, I despair over a death already there or a dying without end. Kierkegaard understood this: despair is the sickness unto death in which the ego submits to the torment of "dying without dying, dying death"; but "to die death means to live death." Thus, "in despair, dying is continually changed into living," and this impossibility of being finished with it—of truly dying—only increases despair.[5] We have often noted that the despairing individual at the height of distress never imagines suicide, because he is no longer capable of actively projecting himself toward death, of living as if he were *already dead*, always already in self-mourning. He is no longer able to open himself to the future, because he can no longer welcome what arises in every moment: it is his living present that is dying. On one of the capitals of the basilica at Vézélay, despair is figured as a grimacing demon whose head is turned backward to the past. This torsion does not mean that the despairing individual would live solely in the past or in the nostalgia of a lost happiness: by turning back on itself, the gaze of the demon contaminates the whole past. For despair *leaves me no time*; it flows back from my future on my present and my past, and consequently each instant of my life causes me to despair. This is why this sickness unto death is also, as Kierkegaard said, "a sickness of the self." The self is always led back to the "despair of not being a self," to the desperate will to be *truly me*: the despairing individual lets himself be dispossessed of his duration, of his living ego; he is no longer able to be self-given—or is self-given only by eluding himself, endlessly mortifying himself: *he gives himself as dead*.

None of these experiences—literature, madness, or despair—offers us the confirmation we were seeking, because none satisfies the second condition: none of them allows for an understanding of how the common meaning of death could be prefigured in the very singular feeling of dying or how the delirious or desperate certainty of being *already* dead could be projected toward the future by giving its meaning to the anxious awaiting of a death *yet to come*. I have, however, discovered confirmation in a psychoanalyst. Winnicott advances the hypothesis that "clinical fear of collapse is the fear of a collapse that *has already taken place*." It would find its source in the experience of a "primitive agony" that would have taken place in the past of the subject. To the extent that this has not been integrated into the subject's history or is not recognized as past, it constantly returns to haunt him like a menace still to come.[6] The compulsive fear of death would be a privileged example of it: "here again, death takes place but has not been experienced as the subject seeks." Anxiety over imminent death is rooted in this *originary* agony that he obscurely describes as a "failure of the residence in the body," a fall into primordial emptiness. Winnicott comes very close here to what I describe as the experience of dying. Even though his analysis is drawn from a psychological perspective and limited to the history of a human subject in the world, it allows for a better discernment of the immanent phenomenon of dying and for a better understanding of what way my death precedes me and is announced to me always *after the fact*, like the haunting of an Impossible that would have already taken place. To give his hypothesis its due, we should consider this archi-agony no longer as an original trauma going back to childhood but instead as an originary condition and an always present haunting, thus no longer reducing it to a pathological phenomenon—imagining it, on the contrary, as a universal condition of existence, alone able to give meaning to the possibility of dying.

Whereas despair, in the distress of being always already dead, precipitated dying in the past, this strange projection transposes it into the future by awakening the anxiety of a death yet to come. In the two cases, the present experience of archi-agony is obscured—as if it were so intolerable that the ego always had to get away from it, either by rejecting it into the distant past or by projecting it into a blind future. We can see here two different modes of Countertime, the temporal distortion provoked by the crisis of the chiasm. When the carnal syntheses fail, their crises affect the synchrony of temporal fluxes subtended by these syntheses: it breaks the quasi-simultaneous conjunction of sensing and being-sensed, of touching and being-touched; it introduces into the living present a dead time, a temporal interval or discrepancy, *a death lapse*, between the impression of each pole. The ego-flesh can subsequently miss itself only whenever it tries to take hold of itself. I always arrive ahead of or behind myself, too early or too late to sense myself living in the present instant; and this present that escapes me, that is dying, flees toward the horizon of the past or of the future. In my archi-agony, I feel my flesh *as already dead*, as if it had always been dead (the temporality of despair). And yet I feel myself dying, I live myself dying, which means that I am *not yet dead*: the instant of my archi-agony is indefinitely stretched out by ever further delaying the date of my death, like an imminent and endlessly deferred threat (the temporality of anxiety).[7]

In the face of death, as Epicurus said, we are "like a defenseless city." At least we are able to anticipate it and heal ourselves of the fear it inspires. This is not how it is when one is dying, which does not even allow the time to expect and prepare for it, because it has always preceded us and traverses us in every moment. If it is impossible to flee from or reject it like an object of hatred, we can at least temporally project it into the future or past—but this projection fails, since it reemerges in the heart of the living present and comes back to haunt us in anxiety and despair. And the ego most often replies by denying it, refusing to recognize the death corroding it. This denial is not its only possible defense against the haunting of archi-agony: it tends also to project it "spatially" on that screen onto which it also rejects the remainder of its flesh—that is, on others. Certainly the ordeal of dying is not a "drive," a sort of destructive energy that could be indifferently directed to an exterior object or turned back against the ego: always singular, always my own, it could not be deferred onto an other without disfiguring itself. As illusory and disfiguring as it is, such a projection may, however, be produced: because it constantly projects itself on others, the ego can also transfer its phantasm of dying onto others. This is why Anna discovers in the mirror her father's face with death's head instead of her face, as if she had rejected into the mirror the necrosis paralyzing her. But this phenomenon is not manifested here in its purest form: Anna's father *really* is dying, whereas she only feels herself dying; she identifies with him by anticipating his death in her own flesh. This dying that she projects *on* the Other already comes *from* the Other in an exchange where father and daughter trade hauntings and where each gives to the other the death that they refuse. It is very difficult to see a projection of dying that has not already been contaminated by the death of others. Even if the singularity of a dying that is always mine has nothing to do with the disappearance of another in the world, I am constantly identified with others in my fantasies, and their death recalls me to the distress of my archi-agony. This is the strange experience we call *mourning*. Each time another dies, the death awakens my anxiety about dying in me. In bearing the mourning of the other, I am at the same time in mourning for myself; and I could never mourn for others were I not ceaselessly mourning myself, that is, if I were not always already "dead."[8] Following Freud, certain psychoanalysts distinguish two very different versions of the "work of mourning": first, a normal mourning in which the ego effects an introjection of the dead object, assimilating and digesting it so that the ego can better detach itself from the dead, after which the ego "decides to remain alive"; and then there are these "pathologies of mourning" in which the "shadow of the object falls on the ego," where the mourning subject "incorporates" the dead other, keeps it like a specter by letting itself sink into melancholy.[9] Each time, the style of mourning is determined by the ego's relation to a singular object, which is both internal and external at once, which it tries to reject outside of itself, but which can come back to haunt it forever, incrusting itself in its depths. We recognize this "object" of haunting as the disfigured remainder, that dead part of my flesh, a necrosis that I experience in my archi-agony. When I am confronted with the death of others, I project on it—on the figure-screen, the surface of projection that others are—this remainder for which I have always been in mourning. Thus, the "normal" and the "pathological" issue of my mourning for the other depends on my relation to the remainder: only a transfiguration of the remainder, a rebirth of the ego-flesh, could deliver me from this phantom and allow me *to mourn mourning*.

There is probably another way to carry out the projection of dying. When, in the intolerable vision of her own death, Anna substitutes the fleshless face of her father, it is as if she sent him to death in her place, as if she could not be content to anticipate her own death but instead *desired* that he be dead. Her refusal to assume her dying in herself is tied together here with the desire for the death of the other. One step further and it would be changed into a desire for *murder*. Hegel taught us that "each consciousness desires the death of the other"—but it is not by reason of an ontological "negativity" that would be appropriate to the human subject: this desire for murder is grounded above all on a projection by which I desperately try to escape my dying. The more I project my death on the Other, the more I desire its death, and the more I think I free myself from mine; and this murderous projection hopes to be cured of the dying that haunts it; it confusedly aspires to immortality. This clarifies in a new way Freud's lucid affirmation: in the unconscious, each of us is "an assassin who thinks he is immortal"—incapable of representing to ourselves our own death while endlessly desiring to inflict death on others.[10] To understand this dark alchemy, there is no need to invoke a "death drive": this confused notion leads us astray by too quickly assimilating dying with hatred, my desire to destroy the Other with my relation to my own death. In truth, hatred and dying do not have the same source and are not born of the same carnal synthesis; and if the horizontal synthesis grounds the other syntheses, we must admit that hatred is "more ancient than love" and more originary than dying: it initially has no relation to death and does not so much seek the destruction of the Other as the rejection of the remainder beyond the limits of the ego. Likewise, dying has no essential relation to hatred, and originally its projection onto others does not aim at killing the other, only at discarding my death onto it, interposing this other between my death and myself. But there is a point where these two mouvances end up joining together and fusing. How does dying come to be bound up with hatred? Under the influence of the remainder, the flesh is blinded to itself, is lived as the nonflesh both *in each pole* (in the haunting of dying) and *in the adverse pole* (its hatred of the foreigner). It perceives itself and perceives the other—first the other carnal pole, then an other ego—as a specter, a carcass, an abject and threatening waste. This phantasm awakens both the anxiety of dying and the hatred of the Other, and these two affects feed off one another: I fear others as a mortal threat, an enemy bent on destroying me, which I then try to get away from or eliminate; and the more I project my dying and my hatred on it, the more I figure that it is what hates me and desires my death. Thus my hateful repulsion reinforces my anxiety of death, while my anxiety augments my hatred. As long as the remainder exercises its influence, I remain captive to this infernal circle.

Is another fate possible, another relation to dying that would no longer amount to denying it or to projecting it on others? As dissimulated as it is, experiencing oneself dying runs throughout our life. It is absolutely real for each of us—but its "reality" is entirely that of a phantasm: in experiencing myself dying, I do *not yet* die, not *truly*. By undergoing its archi-agony, the ego-flesh thus reveals that it is capable of resisting its death. Must we conclude from this that it will *always* resist it? Would death then be but a mere appearance for it? If it is true that the ego-flesh's dying originates in the inversion of a synthesis, why would it not be reversible? If it is a matter of a disfiguration, why would it not be followed by a transfiguration, similar to what made us pass from hatred to love? How does this other version succeed in approaching it *in philosophy* without appealing to a religious Revelation? "Nevertheless we sense and experience that we are eternal."[11] In what dimension of the ego-flesh is this experience of a life more powerful than death, which Spinoza situated in a "third genre" of theoretical knowledge, rooted? All the evidence of common sense and all the certitudes of philosophers and wise men are opposed to such a possibility—in the same way that in Dreyer's admirable *Ordet*, the doctor and the pastor agree to deny the perspective of resurrection in order to reduce to silence the Word that favors it. Is it not obvious that death is equivalent to a definitive annihilation of the subject? Who today would still dare to plead for immortality at the risk of being viewed a fool or a madman?

I wonder whether this evidence of the final disappearance of the ego does not rest on a prejudice, which has thus disfigured our experience of dying. Let us consider Heidegger's case one last time. His whole philosophy is grounded on the determination of existence as being-toward-death, that is, as *being-toward-an-end*: the radically *finite* existence of a Dasein that would merely have the power of anticipating its death in anxiety. He thus assigns to death the sense of being an "end," that is, an absolute limit beyond which *there is nothing*. He defines it as the possibility for Dasein "to be no longer there," to be nothing, and later he designates it as "the *arche* of the Nothing." In his effort to demarcate himself from any theological speculation about the beyond and the immortality of the soul, he claimed to stay down to earth, to remain strictly on this side of the Limit. But he immediately transgresses this rule, defining death as a total annihilation, which supposes specifically a certain knowledge, albeit negative, about the beyond. I fear that our philosopher let himself be led astray by the naive "evidence" of everyday existence, for which the world is everything and which can imagine a retreat from the world only as a fall into nothingness. The very meaning of dying is falsified when we define death by limiting it to the single possibility of no longer living, of disappearing forever without taking account of this other possibility that nothing prohibits us from imagining living again, of being revived anew.

"Death will not easily accept Heidegger's astonishing and penetrating high-wire act with it." Such is Husserl's ironic observation about his student's "acrobatics," his un-self-conscious way of treating death.[12] For want of having carried out the *epokhè*, the author of *Being and Time* would have confused the ego-in-the-world—the finite ego destined to death that he calls Dasein—and the immanent ego. Can this ego die as the ordinary ego dies? Can the originary flux of my immanent life be stopped? But such a stoppage "supposes a non-stoppage, that is, a consciousness that would be aware of this stop." For Husserl, every phenomenon finds its meaning and its truth in the life of the ego, constituting it as phenomenon. For the limit-phenomenon of my death to have meaning, I must be able to be aware of being dead; I must *live my death* in my living present. But that would mean that at the moment that I am lived as "dead," I am still alive—and this awareness of my death is purely illusory. Husserl concludes from this that the immanent ego that I am in the *epokhè* would not be able to die.[13] More exactly, he would have to say that I am *immortal*, not mortal in a negative or restrictive sense: incapable of living my death, of living myself dead, and thus of giving my death to myself, of constituting myself as mortal. In this perspective, what we call "death" would consist only in "separating the transcendental ego from its self-objectification as man," as if the originary ego could withdraw itself from the world, break all its relations with the mundane ego and nevertheless continue to live, in the same way that I always remain living in retreat from the world, as when I am plunged into a sleep without dreams. Will death be able to accept this "astonishing" demonstration? Just when he affirms the nonmortality of our immanent life, Husserl must indeed recognize that we are also men existing in the world into which we were born and in which we will one day die. The whole difficulty consists, then, in understanding how the immanent ego that is not born and does not die can nevertheless be manifested as a mortal ego in the world: how can this Immortal that I am *give itself death*—a death that I would, however, never encounter and that is nothing for me?

If Heidegger fails to think life—and thereby to think dying authentically—his teacher is not able to take account of death: neither of these two are able to understand death as an event immanent to life, a life that experiences itself dying and does not stop dying and being reborn. Of all the philosophers, there is maybe one alone who was able to think of my lifetime as a continual rebirth, *a continuous creation*, because he had understood that the ego cogito is always confronted by the possibility of its disappearance and must always be recreated anew. However, by denying that an effective destruction precedes each new creation, that an interval of nothingness can slip in between creation and re-creation, Descartes misconstrued experiencing oneself dying, and this continuous creation leads back to a simple conservation, which, moreover, he confides to the sovereign goodness of God. We must go further and recognize that I must *truly* die in order to be able to be reborn, that my life must find in itself the force to undergo death in order to come back to itself endlessly in an *eternal return*. This is how I would like to understand Nietzsche's "most abyssal thought," which he sometimes presents as the announcement of the eternal return of life, "the triumphant Yes to life beyond all death."[14] He has to think the eternal return as an event immanent to each singular life, to each ego, instead of making of it a law of the world, of universal Life, or the credo of a new God, as is too often the case with Nietzsche. He knew well that to be affirmed as immortal—to reach the eternal return—it was necessary to "die several times while one is alive," to traverse the phases of distress and of extreme despair to be able to be reborn in a higher joy. In such an experience is also sketched in the proximity of madness that had allowed him to experience in his own life the always more ample oscillation of the Return, until it finally led him to the abyss.[15]

This thought that I am here trying to approach seems mad. I nevertheless feel and experience that my "death" is not irreversible, that dying and being reborn can happen to me. What name can we give to this experience that our philosophical tradition has had so much difficulty imagining? It is a matter of an essential possibility of the ego-flesh, namely, that of its *resurrection*. Faith certainly gives us the promise of resurrection engraved in the tympanum of cathedrals but while also profoundly deforming it, since it attributes it to the action of a transcendent God and situates it in a distant future "at the end of time." This theological dogma disfigures the experience: in every moment I experience that I am immortal; any moment could be that of my resurrection, and I do not have to await it from the good will of an Other, but I am myself this gift of life that I offer to myself. For the resurrection of the flesh does not arise from metaphysical speculation or acts of faith: an inversion of the synthesis can happen at any moment, when beyond the nothingness of its death the ego-flesh comes back to life, reincarnates itself, and recommences to incarnate the remainder, unfolding all the power of life in it. By giving itself anew as living, it reveals itself; it overcomes its disfiguration, the illusion of experiencing oneself dying: it is transfigured. Thus, its resurrection reveals it in truth as an ego of the living flesh, and it reveals *the truth of life* to it, namely, that life itself cannot be understood without resurrection and that this event testifies to the most originary mode of givenness of life, of this disclosure in which a renascent life tears away the veil of death and forgetfulness that dissimulated it to itself.

"Yes, I will raise doubts about the mortal character of my existence as long as my connection with the rays endures." President Schreber may have been persuaded of his immortality at this point because he relived his resurrection every day and because he felt in his flesh the "miracle of the rays," which, after having devoured his lungs, stomach, and brain and made of him a rotting cadaver, sucked the "impure substances" from his body and reconstituted his destroyed organs.[16] None of the psychoanalysts who have weighed in on Schreber's case has been interested in this kind of hallucination. Otherwise, they might have avoided considering psychoses only from the perspective of death, as Lacan did, without perceiving that experiencing oneself dying is the prelude of a resurrection. Psychotics are not the only people to confront this ordeal of having to die in order to be reborn: numerous human cultures have made it into one of the pivots of social existence. During the rites of passage to adulthood, and in some initiatory rituals, neophytes are treated as if they were dead or had been swallowed by a monster; then they are reborn, sometimes behaving as little babies, receiving another name and a new identity with diverse corporeal markings. In the Sara tribe in Chad, the future initiates leave the village to go "see death," while their mothers lament and go into mourning. Thrown naked in a pit, they hear around the enclosure a terrifying voice of "the Thing that eats the Thing," which reclaims them to devour them. Their initiators give them a certain food to eat while stating: "let the food I have just given remain alive so that he who eats also remains living." Then, having absorbed Life, they are reborn and can return to the village after receiving ritual incisions.[17] All these rites stage the process of incorporation, the genesis of our body, our subjective identity. They play out on the plane of collective existence the ordeal of death and resurrection that each singular ego secretly undergoes on its plane of immanence. They make visible and tangible the relation of the ego-flesh to the remainder, to the devouring Thing that threatens to annihilate it but is also presented as a principle of Life.

For those of us who no longer live in delirium and for whom the old initiation rites no longer have any meaning, how can this resurrection be manifested? It transpires indirectly in our affective life, when the affects of anxiety, despair, and all the unhappy passions are effaced in order to make way for the opposite sentiments. It is then that the very tonality of existence is modified, while our deadly phantasms gradually blur. The capacity to overcome the effects of the worst trauma (which certain psychologists call "resilience") originates in the power to be reborn from the ego-flesh. When an ego totally alienated to the desire and discourse of the Other, that no longer speaks except in the name of the Other, and that has only ever responded to the Other's call, finally finds the power to call itself, to speak in its own name, we can see in this *invocation* one of the surest clues of its resurrection. By giving birth to itself again, the ego is freed from the alienating identifications that subjected it to an always identical figure of otherness. It is dislodged from these phantasms born of the disfiguration that constantly returned to haunt it in always similar forms. It finds a new path to the world and the other, to the always new irruption of originary impressions, events, encounters. In being self-given in truth, the ego was able to break the circle, to overcome the eternal return of hatred and death. Could this renaissance be reversible? Will the ego be finally able to cure its hauntings, to break with its bad destiny, or will it merely be a provisional remission? Will every return-to-life necessarily be followed by a fall back into dying? Words fail to describe the manner by which the immanent events of dying and being reborn are intertwined with one another. In originary temporality, there is neither a before nor an after, and on this plane, there would be no sense in saying that these events succeed one another or that they happen simultaneously. As to knowing how they are translated in the time of daily existence, only a concrete analysis of each singular history would allow us to say. We can only say that some existences endlessly seem to experience their dying in the interminable wait for a renaissance that never happens and that some others seem carried by the incessant joy of their resurrection, while the majority oscillate more or less quickly between these two poles. One thing alone is clear: not only is the resurrection of the flesh always possible, but it has already taken place in our life. To tell the truth, the influence of the remainder is so powerful, the weight of the world and for others so overwhelming, that the ego would have already long ago succumbed to it were it not for its capacity to tolerate the ordeal of its death, to traverse it in order to give birth to itself again. We have seen an essential trait of the Cartesian cogito in this resistance to the threat of death that the Evil Genius makes weigh on the ego, namely, the initial experience that gives the ego access to itself (*si me faillit ego sum*). We will discover now that its capacity to resist the great Persecutor is rooted in its continued re-creation, in the originary event of its resurrection.

What is the importance of such an experience? If am able to be reborn at least once, it is because a victory over death is possible. And yet, even if this rebirth occurred numerous times, would that mean that I can live forever? An objection is immediately announced: when I determine dying as phantasm, an illusion that could be dissipated, it is not death *as such*, the final end, the absolute Limit of life that I aim at; it is only *a quasi-death* that does not truly interrupt the course of existence, a parenthesis analogous to sleep, to a syncope, to the "little death" of the orgasm. I can always be awakened from these "deaths," but it is not at all the same with the true death in which nothing would be able to guarantee for me the possibility of resurrection. Socrates had already dealt with a similar argument. The evening before drinking the hemlock, the old master tried to prove the immortality of the soul to his disciples by showing them that dying and living are reciprocally engendered and that we endlessly pass from one to the other. He then comes up against Cebes' objection: even if the soul could survive the death of the body several times and each time be reborn in a new body, nothing assures us that this transfiguration had no term limit and that none "of these 'deaths' or separations from the body proved fatal to the soul." Its *athanasia*, its nonmortality, that is, its aptitude to be reborn after an apparent death, does not mean that it is eternal, forever preserved from death, "unless he can prove that the soul is absolutely immortal and indestructible."[18] This is a redoubtable objection, and the silence that follows Cebes' exposition—as well as the very aporetic style of the last part of the *Phaedo*—suggests that it is not easy to refute. Socrates indeed tries to respond by claiming that the converse does not tolerate becoming its own converse: as soon as this is advanced, "either it flees it, or it perishes," just as snow melts when fire is near. The soul is what brings life to the body; the body participates in the idea of Life, and thus, it is impossible that it receives death within it, so that "it will never be a dead soul." But the argument is insufficient: it only showed that the soul, *as long as it remains living*, cannot be lived in truth as "dead." It still has to be proven that it absolutely cannot be annihilated. Yet this demonstration dramatically fails: the *Phaedo* is not able to conclude from the nonmortality of the soul that it is therefore immortal in an affirmative sense, that is, eternal. Plato perhaps wanted to make us understand that faith in immortality could not be grounded on a theoretical knowledge and that it is a matter of a sort of bet, an "incantation" that is addressed to "the child in us," to "persuade him not to be afraid of death like a bogeyman."[19]

Cebes' objection not only calls into question the ancient belief in an eternal transmigration of souls. It is also goes against Husserl's position, assimilating death to a profound sleep in which the flux of life is not stopped—and against my own hypothesis of a resurrection of the ego-flesh. This immanent "death" that I can overcome would not truly be death: it remains an event of life, a passing experience in which my life is given the appearance of experiencing itself dying. But nothing prevents us from imagining another way of dying, another death, totally foreign to my life, irrevocably interrupting it. Let us designate this destruction without return, this ulti-mate *aphanisis*, with a term borrowed from the Bible: *the second death*.[20] Experiencing oneself dying would only be a deformed and misleading prefiguration of it: there would be nothing in common between these two versions of death. My analysis in fact concerned only an illusory quasi-death, and it would not be right for me to apply it to the only truly menac-ing death, which is not be followed by any resurrection. The objection is strong—but from where do we get this knowledge that so surely distin-guishes a "real" death from a merely "apparent" death? What allows the de-cree that the second death is the only "true" death? If I undertake the *epokhè*, all transcendence is put out of play, including that of the second death: from now on this appears as a mere presumption, an arbitrary construction corresponding to nothing in my experience. If the limit-phenomenon of my death has meaning, I would not find this meaning in a terminal pseu-dodeath that is never given to me, save in the immanence of experiencing oneself dying. This always already past dying—which never stops passing or letting itself be passed over by life in renascent moment of my flesh—is certainly only a phantasm but is nonetheless what grounds the possibility of every relation to my death. Like every representation of a death yet to come, the anticipation of a second death without resurrection finds its origin in the haunting of my archi-agony. I misconstrue and disfigure this primordial experience by mixing it up with the experience I can have of others' deaths, of their total disappearance from the world, and by defer-ring it to an indeterminate future. What I naively call "my death," the final end of my life, would then be only the projection of phantasm, the disfigu-ration of an already disfigured appearance.

Does this mean that all the characters of originary dying are found unchanged when I reject them in the future, in the phantasm of the sec-ond death? And notably, is this decisive trait of being only apparently dead, incapable of definitively interrupting the flux of life, also unchanged? If this were the case, the second death would be *nothing more* than my imma-nent death, a phase of my life that I traverse in order to be reborn: the immortality of the ego and the resurrection of the flesh would be grounded in truth. Nothing justifies such a claim. Nothing proves that the phenom-enon of the second death is absolutely identical to that of the archi-agony or that the archi-agony could project itself in an indeterminate future. Nothing proves that the power to be reborn, which allows the flesh to overcome its archi-agony, could also vanquish this other unsayable, un-thinkable agony still to come. Cebes' objection is still not refuted. And yet nothing obliges us to follow it, to dissociate totally experiencing oneself dying and the second death, identifying this with a pure and simple annihilation. Death remains a limit-phenomenon that escapes our grasp, and I will never be able to understand what intrigue is bound up with these two figures of my death. Two possibilities thus remain open: that of an eternal return of my life or of a continued resurrection and that of a second death whereby I would forever disappear. Here we touch the limits of philosophy, and it is not a question of going beyond them. As there is a madness of love, there is also *a madness of faith* that goes beyond the limits of what we can know, claiming with an absolute certainty the final vic-tory over the second death. Just as love tended to deny the alterity of the remainder, so too does faith refuse to recognize the radical alteration that the remainder inflicts on the flesh, this extreme disfiguration that we call death. In the two cases, the transfiguration of the remainder seems irre-versible, because we empty out the possibility that the remainder may be disfigured again, that love falls back into hatred and life into death. And yet such a possibility can no longer be spared: if a disfigured synthesis can always be reversed by transfiguring itself, nothing formally prevents a transfigured synthesis from being reversed *in the other direction* or from letting the ego-flesh be disfigured again by falling back into the grasp of the remainder. Neither love nor resurrection will be sufficient to set us free. As we approach the end of this inquiry, it is time to wonder whether such a deliverance can happen and how it could be achieved. Within the limits of philosophy, we have at least discovered that a resurrection of the ego-flesh is possible. A poet like Artaud becomes the messenger of it. He had to traverse the night of asylum and the death throes of agony to dis-cover that it is possible "to exceed death, somber death, through life" and to return to the world in order to announce the good news: "my body is remade / despite it all / and through a thousand assaults of evil / and ha-tred / which has always deteriorated it / and left me for dead / and so by dying / I end up gaining true immortality."[21]

14

Toward Deliverance (*Instasy*)

Your breath is mixed with mine just as amber is blended with fragrant musk, whoever touches you, also touches me: you are me, there is no separation.

—Hallaj, *Diwan*

The presentation of the tragic rests primarily on the tremendous—how the god and man mate and how natural force and man's innermost boundlessly unite in wrath—conceiving of itself, on the boundless union purifying itself through boundless separation.

—Hölderlin, "Remarks on Oedipus"

As we arrive at the conclusion of this research, the possibility of a deliverance for the ego-flesh still remains obscure. At least this much has been gained: disfiguration is not its only fate. A transfiguration can undo, at least for a time, the knotting up of hatred and death. What makes this possible is the maintenance of its initial elements in the inversion of the synthesis: the ego's resistance persists in the heart of its disfiguration. This, more than anything, is the originary identity of the ego and the remainder. Were it not a matter of a fragment of the ego-flesh, I could not identify with the remainder without being forever alienated to it, and the perspective of its transfiguration would be a mere phantasm. But *I am* this shameful part, this accursed share, of my flesh: when the remainder is transfigured, when I recognize it as mine, it is revealed to me in truth. Nothing, however, guarantees that this disclosure is irreversible or that it is sufficient to conjure away the threat of a new disfiguration—and the transfiguration itself seems to engender new phantasms and a new alienation. In disgust and hatred, in the madness of love, the sometimes abject and sometimes sublime remainder is not yet done haunting me. Are these oscillations inevitable? Is it possible to escape the endless cycle of disfigurations and transfigurations? Perhaps we will have to recognize that the crisis of the chiasm provokes a series of distortions, projections, residuals that aggravate this disfiguration to the point of making it insurmountable.

We have seen that projections totally falsify the relation to the alter ego and constitute otherness as a phantasm or a figure-screen that bars all access to the Other. These are not merely my affects that I project on this invisible mirror; they are also the remainder of my flesh that I transfer on the body of others, where it becomes an object of desire or anxiety and where, unbeknownst to me, I reproduce my relation to the remainder in all of my relations with others. These projections oriented toward others supposed a more originary and immanent projection whereby I transfer my affects onto the remainder: I then imagine that when the remainder directs its hatred or love toward me, this remainder is already disfigured by the first projection that I projected on the Other. In every case, such projections erase the difference between the ego and what is foreign to it, between the inside and the outside, immanence and transcendence. They annul the egological difference; they are at the root of the alienating identifications whereby the ego lets itself be dispossessed of its singularity, dispersed in the world, and subjected to others. As long as they have not been overcome, the truth of the Other, the truth of the remainder, and *my own truth* are dissimulated for me. What is the origin of these projections? If we were to believe Freud, the ego is "purified" of its hatred by rejecting it onto an exterior object so effectively that the "the external world, objects and that which was hated were one and the same thing." And "the ego has extracted from itself an integral part that it rejects into the exterior world and views as hostile"; this projection *constitutes* the excluded part of ego as the hated object.[1] Projection thus initially concerns this hatred that I can no longer tolerate feeling in me and that I transfer onto an "other" as if it were its source—and this First Foreign Thing that becomes the object of my hatred is the remainder of my flesh. But I feel such hatred toward it *because* it is manifested to me in a disfigured manner, as an unknown Thing intruding on me and devouring my flesh. The remainder's disfiguration leads me to hate it and to project my hatred on it; and this projection, which presents itself as a desirous Persecutor eager to destroy to me, increases my hatred toward it, thereby disfiguring it all the more profoundly.

How can we break this cycle of death? It is probably impossible to eliminate projections entirely: they are too tightly woven into the fabric of my existence, and they subtend my experience of others. To what extent would it be possible to neutralize the disfiguring projections and prevent them from creating a screen between the ego and the foreign? We find once again the essential structure of *transcendence*—that ecstatic movement that throws me out of myself toward the world—in this gesture of projecting itself or of transferring a part of itself onto an exterior object (or "extimate"). If transcendence were originary, if I were always outside of myself, then I would be unable to return to myself, and my projections would therefore be insurmountable. But this is not how it is: before projecting myself on another, I must have first been self-given. Transcendence finds its truth in the immanence, and the being-outside-of-itself of the ego—that is, this ecstasy subtending its alienations, identifications, and projections—is grounded in its self-givenness. This is what allows hope for a return to self, beyond the alienating projections. And yet, to overcome disfiguration, it is not sufficient to reappropriate what had been transferred onto the remainder or onto others or to reinject it in the ego, because this interiorization of the disfigured remainder coincides with the worst haunting. I have already evoked this moment of extreme anxiety where the Thing that penetrates me dislodges me from myself and where the foreign injunction reverberates in my interior as if it were my own voice. As much as the truth of the remainder remains hidden, its return to immanence appears to me as a threatening intrusion that I will do everything to expel once again. It is therefore insufficient that the remainder merely come back to me—it must also still be represented *as remainder*, as a foreign Thing, and I must recognize it as a part of my flesh.

Projection implies a spatial distortion, an effacement of limits between the inside and the outside, the here and the there, but it is also accompanied by other temporal lapses. We have seen that the appearance of the remainder results in a rupture of synchrony within the living present. During the crisis, this discrepancy increases, disjoining temporal fluxes from different poles and then impeding them from crossing and fusing again. When its living present is torn away, the ego-flesh is no longer able to be contemporary with itself: this is how the Countertime of the haunt-ing, the disfigured temporality of the remainder, is constituted. Another phenomenon reinforces this disfiguration: phantom impressions, residu-als that persist after the inversion of the synthesis, are intercalated with new impressions. In my haunting, I come up against a *present* impression that obsesses me and that is incrusted in every moment by refusing to be effaced or to slip away into the past. With the residual, I am instead deal-ing with a *past* impression that latches on to my present, superimposing itself on it while blurring its traits. In the two cases, we bear witness to a *blockage* of the temporal flux, to a *deadly standstill* wherein certain im-pressions no longer let themselves be overcome or repressed in the past by the incessant eruption of new impressions—and to the same deficiency of the living present, incapable of welcoming the newness of the instant. We know that residuals play a decisive role in the formation of funda-mental phantasms. Without these phantom impressions, the fleshless pole of my flesh would be perceived as a mere exterior object without ever arousing disgust or hatred; and the phases of disincarnation and reincar-nation succeed one another but without any continuity and without me ever having the feeling of dying or being reborn. In a sense, these residu-als are even more dangerous than the projections, because they allow the affects of hatred and death to reerupt at any moment and be mixed with the love or joy of being reborn. Thus, my past disfiguration continues to haunt my transfiguration, threatening to reverse it again: through the residuals, the whole weight of the past burdens my present and compro-mises my future. The only way to be free of these phantoms is to go back to the origin, to the source-point of genesis, before the crisis of the chi-asm, before any disfiguration—but we do not see what miracle could lead the ego-flesh back to the source of its history, the early-hour instant of its first givenness. If temporality were the ultimate horizon of our life, deliv-erance would be strictly impossible. In this book, I have maintained the opposite thesis: I have tried to show that the flesh takes priority over time, that the carnal chiasm *gives me time*, that the unity and continuity of my lifetime are constituted on the basis of the chiasm, when the poles of flesh synchronize their temporal fluxes by uniting with each other. Even if the unity of this temporal flux can tear itself apart in the crisis, the re-knotted chiasm will be able to repair this tear: in being transfig-ured, the ego-flesh once again weaves the fabric of a single duration. The primacy of immanence over transcendence, the primacy of the flesh over time, thus makes deliverance possible.

A last obstacle still remains, which is much more difficult to escape, since it is no longer a matter of an external obstacle but rather of the very movement of transfiguration that puts the ego in peril by going beyond a certain limit. When the transfigured remainder is revealed in love as the flesh of my flesh, nothing prevents the poles from totally fusing, becoming confused, or imploding by hastening the ego-flesh into the bottomless and groundless. To protect the ego-flesh, to resist the madness of love, the abjection of disgust and rejection of hatred reappear again; and this condemns us to oscillate endlessly between the reigns of *philia* and *neikos*. I have been claiming that only the truth can set us free—but the truth of the remainder can also be a mortal threat. What should save me is also what kills me. We must therefore allow that deliverance does not coincide with transfiguration, the re-identification of the ego, and the remainder. More exactly, transfiguration is only a necessary but *not yet sufficient condition* of deliverance. To the extent that we go forward, its preliminary conditions appear always more numerous and more difficult to satisfy. What more than the transfiguration and the disclosure of the truth would be necessary for my deliverance to be possible?

Nothing other than this: in transfiguration, a gap or divergence must persist between the remainder and the flesh. In being disclosed, the remainder must safeguard its major function, which maintains an opening or a distance between each carnal pole. The resistance of the remainder is most often manifested in feelings of disgust, repulsion, or horror. But it is only a matter of derivative manifestations that have already been worked over by disfiguration: in its origin, the function of the remainder consists merely in tracing a limit, marking the gap of a difference, and it is this initial, affectively neutral operation that must be reinscribed in the process of transfiguration. In other words, the concern is to *neutralize* the intense charge of affects that falsify our relation to the remainder, to stop constructing it as an object of hatred or love, a persecuting rival or sublime idol, and to recognize its neutrality and absolute indifference. Like the Justice of which the Abbot speaks at the end of *The Trial*, the remainder "wants nothing of me" at the outset, takes me when I come and leaves me when I go. Is it possible to retrieve this "disaffected" relation to the remainder, this originary neutrality beyond all disfigurations? Kant recognized an analogous problem when he examined the subject's relation to the ethical Law, which is manifested in the feeling of respect. He saw in it a "principle of repulsion" that preserves a distance between men and is thus opposed to the attractive force of love. It is in this strange affect, this repulsion without aversion or this rejection without repulsion, that allows the remainder *to make the ego into law*. When the ego is able to neutralize its relation to the remainder while maintaining of its past abjection only the tracing of a gap—then, beyond disgust and hatred, beyond love, respect emerges.

Despite all this, respect alone is not sufficient. It is not enough to trace a limit between the ego and the Other, between the subject and the Law—and Kant understood this near the end of his life. He feared that if it reigned without sharing, the force of repulsion of respect would make the human community disappear like a drop of water in the ocean. This is why he appealed to a synthesis of love and respect, so that the two opposed principles could be compensated and balanced. This is also true for the ego's relation to the remainder, where a total dissociation without synthesis would precipitate the ego-flesh in the groundlessness of madness. The gesture that reopens the divergence must be reinscribed in the movement of transfiguration, in this affect of truth that we call love. He must make a new form of identification with the remainder and the Other possible, a form that would be neither fusional nor alienating. A paradoxical synthesis where attraction would not foreclose the gap, where distance would not prevent identification, where respect would accompany desire and love—this *identification at a distance* seems very difficult to accomplish. It runs up against a double contradictory constraint, since the concern is to preserve the remainder's function of opening an interval at the very moment I identify with it and to maintain the remainder *as remainder*, in its alterity or its irreducible strangeness, while also recognizing it as the flesh of my flesh. Only on this double condition will I be able to avoid the threats of a mortal fusion (*aphanisis*) and of a dissociation that would annihilate the unity of the ego-flesh. If the identity of the ego and the remainder is the ultimate truth, then it is necessary both that this truth be revealed and that a part of the shadow persist in this revelation as the veiling, the *lethe* at the heart of *alétheia*, a nontruth that would no longer be the countertruth of the phantasm but instead the clue to a mystery, the reserve of a secret. It is subsequently suiting both to renounce the utopia of an integral unveiling of the remainder, the epiphany of an Absolute

Knowing or of a final reconciliation in which "the wounds of the spirit disappear without leaving any scars," and to allow the persistence of a blind spot, an opacity impossible to dissipate—that is, to accept the maintenance of a difference, a discordance between the ego and the remainder: to mourn the Total Body and the Ego-One. "One day," prophesized Novalis, "all will be flesh, one single flesh." It is time to say adieu to this mirage of a single flesh, a love without limits, a chiasm without remainder.

A deliverance is thus possible on the condition of tying together a very singular relation with the remainder, namely, by rediscovering its primary identity, its originary unity with the ego-flesh, while preserving a divergence within this identity. This requires a double movement of disidentification—disalienation, a separation from the remainder—and of reidentification with it. Deliverance therefore implies a new knotting of the ego and the remainder, a *fourth synthesis* that completes the work of the syntheses of incarnation and incorporation. What makes it possible is the internal division of the remainder, which is presented both as the focus of alienating identifications and a force of resistance to these identifications. Between the part of the remainder that devours me and the part that saves me, the relation of forces must be able to be reversed: the ego must be able to base itself on its primordial function of opening up a divergence, of differentiation, in order to introduce difference within identity and go beyond the fusional identifications to another mode of identification. In this ultimate synthesis, I return to myself "by passing through the foreignness opened in me." I am given to myself *as an other*, which is *me*; and in this way alone am I given to myself *in truth*. What name will we give to this knotting that unties? To name the entry whereby the soul discovers its unity with the *Gottheit*, the deity in God, Eckhart spoke of a *Durchbruch*, a piercing or breakthrough. To define the relation of the *Atman* (the universal Self) and the individual ego, Sankara, the great Indian thinker, invented the concept of *advaita*, a nonduality that would be neither One nor Two. I will call the divided unity of the ego and the remainder, such as it is woven in the fourth synthesis, an *instasy*. By this term I designate a return to immanence, the exact opposite of the ecstatic transcendence that throws us outside of ourselves. Here again the *in-* must be understood in an active sense: *in-stasy* is a mouvance that reinserts the remainder into my field of immanence while marking an irreducible divergence between the ego and it. Understood in this sense, it is not opposed to transfiguration but is instead the extreme point of it, its most radical mode, which achieves the promise of resurrection and love. It is not a question of demanding a new condition of possibility: *instasy* is not a condition of deliverance; it *is* my deliverance itself.

"Do not ask 'what is the way?'—you are yourself the way." Zarathustra's words are also true for the hidden road that leads me back to myself: it follows no predrawn plan, and each of us must blaze it anew for ourselves. *Instasy* is more difficult to describe than the play of disfiguration and transfiguration, because it imposes a limit on disclosure and always keeps a share of mystery and also because it is absolutely singular, putting what is most singular in every ego—its relation to the remainder of its flesh— into play, and it modifies this relation in a different manner each time. It is thus impossible to enclose it in a preestablished formula, and it cannot be described, only experienced, undergone, in a trajectory that is singular every time. There is nothing to say about *instasy*. We can nonetheless approach it indirectly through certain limit-phenomena and try to give a name to that which all names fail to name. What makes transfiguration fall back into new disfigurations is *the madness of truth*, the excess of love that erases every difference between the ego and the remainder. By marking this divergence between them, *instasy* saves the truth of love. It allows transfiguration to be maintained, at least for a time, and if, in our daily existence, the oscillations do not necessarily disappear, do they at least decrease in frequency and intensity? Could transfiguration become irreversible? As long as the relation between the ego-flesh's immanent temporality and the time of daily existence remains unclear, it will be impossible to respond to these questions. As with continual self-givenness, the chiasm and its crisis, the archi-agony and the resurrection, *instasis* is inscribed in an originary temporality that does not obey the same laws as the time of the world. It is presented in a paradoxical manner both as an always deferred promise—the utopia of our deliverance—and as an archi-event that would already have taken place in our life: if *instasis* had not already occurred, if the ego, in being transfigured, had not already marked out a distance from the remainder, we would have long ago succumbed to the incessant return of hatred and the madness of love. But it may not be a matter of a permanent state similar to Epicurus' *ataraxia* or to the beatitude that supposedly confers a "knowledge of the third kind." A negative sense must also be given to the prefix *in-* so as to take account of the precarity, the *instability* that affects *instasis*. As a random conjunction of several heterogeneous conditions, it could always not happen, or it could fail as soon as it happens; the synthesis constituting it can be undone or reversed—but nonetheless, it has taken place. For it is a matter of an immanent event, just as ephemeral as all other events, exposed like them to disaster and forgetting and yet able to mark a caesura, *a point of no return*, in existence.

We can designate this instant of *instasis*, this libratory event capable of breaking the cycle of disfiguration, as *a messianic time*, but only on the condition of understanding it as the "messianism without a messiah"—without a proper name and without an assigned face—of which Derrida spoke. We would be largely wrong to assimilate messianic hope to the interminable wait for an "end of time" situated in an indeterminate future: as Benjamin claimed, "each moment is the narrow door through which the Messiah can come." This means that his coming is always possible at any moment, that it may occur as *an exceptional instant* interrupting the course of history. But it also means that it can pass through the door of the Moment without necessarily passing away or that it can remain always imminent and deferred. Kafka said that the messiah will arrive when it is too late. But it could also be, as the Talmud suggests, that he had already come long ago without anyone recognizing him. Torn between the immemorial of the always-already-past, the promise of a future-yet-to-come, and the irruption of the Instant, the time of the messiah is plied with the same paradoxes as the immanent temporality of *instasis*, which is why I designate it as a messianic event.[2] Would this mean that *instasis* would be granted to us by an Other? That we merely have to wait passively for our deliverance? A Talmudic master denounced a similar misinterpretation: "if the messiah belongs to the living," declared Rav Nachman, "then it's me." Commenting on this sentence, Levinas concludes that "to be Me is to be the messiah" and that "each must act as if he were the messiah."[3] This formulation seems too abstract for me: it reduces the ego's messianism to an "as if," a mere fiction without truth—even though the coming of the messiah puts me in play in my essential self-relation, offers me the chance to return to myself by revealing myself as this stranger that I also am for myself. At the moment when the ego discovers its identity with the remainder and the difference traversing their identity, the imperative of *welcoming the stranger* and the imperative of *becoming oneself* coincide. I am my truth, my path, my life. I free myself from the haunting of the remainder, I become my own liberator, the messiah who makes a gift of myself to myself. This is how I want to understand this lesson from our old masters—that the coming of the messiah depends on me at every moment.

Taken strictly, this means that the possibility of *instasis* depends not merely on the Other but also on my free decision. How must we understand this? If it never happens, or happens only by failing, am I therefore responsible for this failure? How can we take account of such a responsibility? When an event in the world reaches me, I have the choice of welcoming or of turning away from it, denying it, forgetting it: and this decision necessarily comes after the fact, in response to the impact of the event. The field of immanence is itself traversed by singular events—reversals and crises, disfigurations, transfigurations, *instases*—and each of them demands a decision. But on this plane, the event does not precede the decision, because there is no longer any difference between its coming and the emergence of a "subject" that would decide whether to welcome it. Here, what gives and what is given are one and the same, and nothing lets us distinguish the giver, the gift, and the receiver of the gift. In being self-given, I decide freely for myself, for the event that I am: the *truth* of the event coincides with its *freedom*, with my free decisions to be revealed to myself. Such a radical decision has nothing in common with the empirical choices made by a subject when it opts for this or that object in the world. On my plane of immanence, I do not exist before deciding for myself: it is a question of an archi-decision, the stakes of which are me and which calls me to myself, convokes me to my freedom—and this is repeated at every moment through continual creation. As Descartes had clearly seen, because my decision is free, I can also freely decide *against the truth*, manifest "this positive power which we have of following the worst although we see the better,"[4] by becoming my own deceiver. This is what happens when the synthesis is inverted: disfiguration also supposes a decision, and so does transfiguration. Because the ego can decide for both the truth and the nontruth at the same time, it oscillates between phases of dissimulation and disclosure, between hatred and love, death and rebirth. The archi-decision thus does not consist merely in welcoming the event that I am—it also concretely engages the style of my existence, my singular way of revealing myself or of being blinded to myself, ceding to phantasms that lead me astray or, on the contrary, resisting them. To put it in Kantian terms, it makes a stake of the "act of freedom," "the choice of the supreme maxim" by which I decide for radical evil or, conversely, decide to free myself from evil by an "ethical revolution" that is like *a second birth.*

How is this liberatory decision possible? How will an ego, rooted in evil, captive to phantasms, alienated to the remainder, succeed in freeing itself? How will it decide not only for transfiguration but also for *instasis*? How will the remainder be played against itself, taking support from its force of openness in order to counter its force of identification by making the divergence of *instasis* come to pass *within the remainder itself*? Am I able to come by myself to myself without the help of the Other, without the chance of those encounters in which the Other comes out of its withdrawal? A certain relation to the Other—to a community freed of its own alienation—should be able to help the ego in disidentifying itself from the remainder. But how can I have access to such a community as long as my phantasms and my projections prevent all access to the Other? Let us underline once more that the Other of which I am speaking here is neither another name for God nor is it the symbolic Big Other of psychoanalysis. It is not really distinct from others, those singular subjects that I encounter in the course of my existence: with this name I designate the other version of the alter ego, that which could be given in truth, beyond all phantasm. This revelation of the other as Other is what is most difficult: it supposes that the disfigured remainder ceases to constitute a screen between us, that the truth of the remainder was revealed—but as we know, the remainder stops being disfigured only at the moment when the Other will have unveiled to me its true face. It is the circle that each ego must undergo when it comes back to itself by passing by the foreign opening up in it. How can we get out of such an impasse? How could the breakthrough of *instasis* break into my life? In what limit-experiences of existence will we have to look for the immanent events of disfiguration, transfiguration, or *instases* that have finally become readable?

And Moses said unto God, "Who am I, that I should go unto Pharaoh, and that I should bring forth the children of Israel out of Egypt?" / And he said, "Certainly I will be with thee; and this shall be a token unto thee, that I have sent thee: When thou hast brought forth the people out of Egypt, ye shall serve God upon this mountain." / And Moses said unto God, "Behold, when I come unto the children of Israel, and shall say unto them, The God of your fathers hath sent me unto you; and they shall say to me, "What is his name? what shall I say unto them?" / And God said unto Moses, "I AM THAT I AM": and he said, "Thus shalt thou say unto the children of Israel, I AM hath sent me unto you."[5]

The interpretation of this speech emerging from flames of the burning bush has never been exhausted after centuries of exegetical effort. By translating it as "I am that which is," that is, "I am Being itself," the dominant current of Christian theology forced it in the direction of an identity of God and Being. The biblical phrase can be understood at first as a nonstarter, a conversation stopper—"I am that I am . . . and don't ask more"—which would refer God and the ego back to their common mystery,[6] before Elohim cedes to Moses' prayer and finally reveals His true Name to him. And above all, the theologians did not know that this speech articulated in Hebrew in an imperfect mode, like a sort of future. The least bad translation of this untranslatable sentence would therefore be "I will be who I will be," which gives it the sense of an anticipation, a promise: it appears to the coming of the future, the yet-to-come [*à-venir*], which is messianic time. What comes from this promise that I will be? Nothing other perhaps than the possibility of saying "I." We have already seen this, at the heart of the second *Meditation*, when Descartes lets us glimpse an enigmatic proximity between the Word on Sinai and the enunciation of the cogito, between the ego's saying-I and God's saying-I. It seems possible to me to understand it as a call inviting the ego to reappropriate to itself the power it had let be taken away from it by the Other, by all the dominating figures of the Other. Is this libratory injunction at bottom so different from what the voice of Elohim states? Far from keeping the privilege of the I for itself, on the contrary, it calls upon Moses to speak, to dare to address the pharaoh. It promises Moses that as long as he says "I" before the tyrants of this world, then *the I will be with him*.[7] This amounts to giving to the "I will be who I will be" the capital meaning of stating this power of saying "I" offered to every ego. If we have to attempt to translate the untranslatable, we could therefore prefer Lacan's proposed version: "I am what the I is"—by placing it in the future, in the time of the promise (and by marking "being" with invisible scare-marks). In my *instasis, I will be this I that I am to be*. Such speech accompanies us every time we say "I" in truth, because this saying manifests in language the force of invocation of the ego, its power to be called to itself as a living and singular ego.

I do not mean that the Word of Sinai concerns only this self-givenness and self-invocation of the ego, because that would constitute an impasse for the revelation immediately following from the utterance of the "I will be," namely, the revelation of another name of Elohim, his singular and unpronounceable Name, YHVH. And yet, even if all the names of the Name were not reduced to the one single name of ego, the first phase of its revelation does indeed concern the possibility of saying "I," stages the gift of the I, its self-givenness that precedes the revelation of the Other name and that of the Law.[8] How is this gift of the I manifested? It appears in a visible and tangible manner in the element of the flesh, a living flesh that takes hold of itself, a carnal remainder that is disfigured and transfigured. This is what is taught to us by that well-known text, too well-known to be understood. When he is invested with his mission by Elohim, Moses refuses at first to take responsibility for it, asking for a "sign" that would prove to the people that he is indeed the messenger. The answer:

"That they may believe that the LORD God of their fathers, . . . [YHVH, Elohim of their fathers], hath appeared unto thee." / And the LORD said furthermore unto him, "Put now thine hand into thy bosom." And he [Moses] put his hand into his bosom: and when he took it out, behold, his hand was leprous as snow. / And he said, "Put thine hand into thy bosom again." And he put his hand into his bosom again; and plucked it out of his bosom, and, behold, it was turned again as his other flesh.[9]

This is not to force the interpretation that recognizes in it a precise description of the crisis of the tactile chiasm, with the disfiguration of the remainder that results—leprosy, major abjection for the mosaic law—and the marvel of a flesh restored to itself, transfigured. This is what the sign consists in, the visible trace of the invisible, and the revelation of Elohim coincides with this reincarnation as if the name of "God" designated here the transfiguring power of the ego-flesh. If we go from here to look at another text, foundational for another tradition of faith, we will find the same schema, the same passage from disfiguration to transfiguration—but this time it will no longer merely be reinscribed in the body of an individual human: it is the invisible Life itself that passes into the visible in which it experiences the abjection of death before gaining the glory of its resurrection:

Who, being in the form of God, thought it not robbery to be equal with God / But made himself of no reputation, and took upon him the form of a servant, and was made in the likeness of men: / And being found in fashion as a man, he humbled himself, and became obedient unto death, even the death of the cross. / Wherefore God also hath highly exalted him, and given him a name which is above every name.[10]

God's "emptying-out," which the theologians have named his *kenosis*, his descent in flesh and his death on the Cross, are the condition of this invocation allowing him to call him by his Name. It is indeed the same story that the two books of the Alliance tell, that of a living flesh that is disfigured and transfigured, that dies and is resuscitated—and it is the story of *our* flesh, our life, the intrigue of the ego and the remainder.

Could what humans invoke with the name "God" thus be the remainder? How are we to go from there to identify the genesis of the remainder with the Passion of an incarnated God? When the chiasm overcomes its crisis, when the inverted synthesis is put back upright, the repulsion provoked by the remainder gives way to an intense attraction, and it becomes all the more fascinating and sublime than it had been formerly abject. Its reincarnation is then presented as the possibility of the impossible, the miracle of a victory over evil and death. How would this marvel be the fact of this moral existing being that I am in the world? The work of an immanent life lives in my flesh, this invisible life that humans represent as a transcendent power they call God. The transfigured remainder also appears to them as the sign of divine election, the glorious body of a resuscitated God. Does this mean that "God" would be *nothing other* than the remainder? That *all* openness to the divine merely leads me back to myself, to the remainder of my flesh? Nothing allows us to say this. I do not suffer from the exorbitant pretension of reducing God to a part of the ego, of denying what in the name of God could signal to a more foreign alterity. The remainder is not the hidden truth of God—but it is our relation to the remainder that most often gives us access to the divine: the immanent experience of its disfiguration and transfiguration subtends the madness of faith.

At the bottom of this obscure night, the soul-seeking God feels the distress of agony and all the other torments of hell—and this, said Saint John of the Cross, has as its cause "the fact that two other extremes meet here in one, namely, the Divine and the human." When the divine invades the soul, it "destroys and consumes it . . . as if it had been swallowed by a beast and felt itself being devoured in the darkness of its belly . . . for in this sepulcher of dark death it must needs abide until the spiritual resurrection which it hopes for."[11] Because it aspires, at the end of this ordeal, to a "union of love," these espousals are completed on *the plane of touching*, as a "touch of God" in which he fills the soul "with a taste for everlasting life" that is felt throughout the body.[12] In the Christian faith, the schema of incarnation and of *kenosis* allows the believer to identify with God the Crucified, to relive in his own flesh the stigmata of the Passion and the glory of resurrection—and also to discover the traces of the divine in what seems the most abject in the flesh, such as the remains of cadavers or the sores of a leper. But this jouissance and torment of being united in the divine is found in other beliefs without such a support: from the *Rubayyat* of the Rumi to the *Gita Govinda*, the revelation of ultimate identity between the ego and God is presented each time as an amorous embrace, a carnal fusion. "I have become what I love and what I've loved has become me," sang Hallaj, the crucified poet of Islam, and here too these mystical espousals blossom on the plane of touching, in the miracle of a chiasm without remainder: "If someone touches you, they touch me, you are me, there is no separation."[13] In this extreme experience of the madness of love—sustained by so many men and women to the point of torture and death—what seemed the most transcendent and foreign suddenly erupts on the plane of immanence and is now one with me. How do we not recognize the remainder in this "wholly Other" that appears more intimately to me than myself, this "god" that is manifested in the abjection of the flesh and in amorous enjoyment, both as a devouring Thing and as the Well-Loved? Its most secret truth—its originary identity with ego—is revealed in what we call "mystical ecstasy."

Will the way of the mystics be the path of *instasis* and thus the key to our deliverance? As I understand it, *instasis* certainly implies the revelation of the identity between the ego and the remainder, but it does so in order to reintroduce a limit, a gap within this identity. This mark of a difference is lacking in an amorous union with God: here every law is lifted and all singularity disappears when the ego is annihilated in the embrace of love—in the fusion without distance of an *aphanisis*. Except, perhaps, in one of the most audacious of these adventurers. Eckhart may have never stopped proclaiming the undivided unity of the ego and of the deity in God; he also dared to claim that in my highest breakthrough, I am "delivered from God himself"; in this ultimate point, "I am neither God nor creature, but I am what I was"—absolutely One with God and absolutely distinct from him.[14] But it is not by luck if the strongest affirmation of this divergence, of this radical separation of God and man in their becoming-One, is encountered not in a mystical theologian but rather in one of the greatest poets, just as he was sinking into madness. No doubt because the adventure of madness also engages a disclosure of the remainder and may thus support—in its own way obscure and infinitely exposed—the work of truth of the work. This would confirm Plato's provocative thesis that a poet who is not mad is not a true poet. By meditating on the proper character of poetry in modern times, and thereby on the fate of Western man, Hölderlin was able to think the *Ungeheure* (the monstrous, the intolerable at the center of Greek tragedy) as a "coupling" or mating of the divine and the human in which every limit is abolished, revealing "how natural force and man's innermost boundlessly unite in wrath." This union with the divine can be completed only by annihilating the tragic hero, and therefore "[G]od is present in the figure of death." We should specify that the God in question refers to no established religion and is identified with the "conditions of time or space," with the pure carnal and temporal form of our sensibility. In this "eccentric enthusiasm" that tears man away from his center, his Self, his finitude, in order to win out over the Absolute, the poet discovers the fundamental tendency of modern humanity (our art, philosophy, politics, and so forth) haunted by the nostalgia for a fusion with the One-Whole. This "panicked exuberance" and the threat that it imposes on us has to be countered by effecting what Hölderlin called the natal reversion [*retourne-ment*]. It is a return to the earth, to the respect of the limit, to a more sober piety and poetry, which supposes a certain forgetting, a reciprocal betrayal in which God and man henceforth "speak to each other in the wholly forgetful figure of infidelity."

The return of man to his native earth must correspond to a perversion or turning away [*détournement*] *of God himself,* who is withdrawn and lets himself be forgotten. This tracing of another limit in the very experience of fusion is designated by the poet as a catharsis by which "the boundless union purif[ies] itself through boundless separation."[15] Such a gesture has nothing abstract nor speculative about it and does not merely concern the status of the work of art; the mark of divergence must be inscribed in existence in the form of a caesura dividing it from itself. We wanted to see in this an allusion to the "ethical revolution" of which Kant spoke, but we are left thinking that the poet also evokes in this text the imminent menace of delirium from which he desperately tried to escape. This caesura "suspends" for a time the "rhythmic sequence of representations," the oscillation between the divine and the human, the near and the far, the native and the foreign—the vertiginous cycle of disfigurations and transfigurations from which the incessant alternation of the moorings of madness results. No one could describe the essential traits of *instasis* better than Hölderlin, probably because, unlike the theologians and mystics, he had to confront *the failure of God*, the distress of an epoch when "the Father turned his face away from us." It is in the void opened by this retreat that is discovered another version of the divine, this "immediate god," "whole-One with man," which devours it in a mortal fusion or frees it by separating itself from it: we recognize without hesitation another version of the remainder. When he evokes the "categorical turn" in which God and man both do a turnabout or cause each other to detour yet continue to address each other and thus to maintain a relation throughout their double infidelity, his meditation comes close to the ultimate mystery of *instasis*—the *reversal of the remainder* that would respond to the natal reversion of the ego to itself. He therefore leaves us the task of thinking what relation can be tied together between the torn ego, interrupted by its own return, and this divine remainder, which, within myself, is turned away from me. He invites us to look for how modern humanity could still have the experience of the remainder, experience anew the furor of becoming-One, the infidelity of the caesura and of the double reversal.

In what other field of experience could the fate of the remainder be revealed today, an epoch that endures more profoundly still the mourning and the withdrawal of God? Even though mystical transports have become foreign to us, even though we are perhaps witnessing the "end of the age of the poets" and the stifling of all the voices of madness, the irruption of the remainder, the ordeal of its disfiguration and transfiguration, are still at stake in the political domain. With the same threat of an "unlimited becoming-One," the same utopia of a remainderless chiasm will, during the twentieth century, have taken on the form of a murderous fusion in the total body of the One-People. This imposes the task of looking for what caesura, what turn, what new figure of the community, could make deliverance possible. How can an egoanalysis, a process centered on a solipsistic ego, claim to clarify the collective dimension of existence, its properly political dimension? Because it shows how our relations with others repeat on another plane the originary relation wherein our ego is self-given. If in all human societies, the political community tends to be figured in the form of a collective body, as the *corpus mysticum* of the Church, the Kingdom, the Republic, or the Party, it is because this figuration is grounded in the immanent syntheses that give body to my flesh. By carrying out the *epokhè*, I separate the evidence that is attached to such representations; I suspend my certainty of being a simple member of the community, a fragment of the Great Body. I then discover that this "colossal" power that crushes us is, in fact, only a *quasi-body*, a projection issued from my flesh, from the innumerable singular bodies of flesh projected on a figure-screen, allowing themselves to be captivated by and identified with an image. This is why we find phantasms on this plane affecting the individual body, the same anxieties about intrusion, fragmentation, dislocation, the same fear of falling back into chaos—and the same exclusion of a heterogeneous element, an intimate stranger. The haunting of the remainder reappears on the plane of the community by being fixated on an individual or particular group, on a "caste" or class, a "racial" or religious, political or sexual minority. Every time, the community takes on a body by excluding, persecuting, or exterminating those who seem to it to be dangerous henchmen of the remainder, without perceiving that it is a part of itself that it is trying to annihilate. Freud claimed that human societies find their origins in a collective murder of the father of the primitive horde. I will say instead that the "political body" is grounded, like my own body, on the exclusion of the remainder.[16] Certainly all the modes of exclusion are not equivalent—but political communities, as different as they are, are constituted in the same manner. Each of them is represented as if it formed only one body, even though its unity is not originary, supposing a more ancient division or the rejection of a heterogeneous element and the denial of foundational violence. If we want to be free of this blindness, of the illusion of the One-Body, we must look for the division that grounds it, the trace of the remainder that it excludes. Only then could we undertake a radical *epokhè* of the communitarian illusions: only what was dissociated from the Great Body can hope to disclose its hidden truth. For this, we would have to try to situate *in the place of the remainder* the place of the pariah, the *pharmakôs*, the *homo sacer*, the witch, the heretic, the insane, the proletariat, the *zek*, and all those excluded from the community. More exactly, it would be a matter of making the place of *truth*—wherever the exclusion of the remainder is revealed—coincide with the place of *resistance*, of the subject of action. Today when the classical representations of the body politic are erased, when the heroic figure of the Proletariat, which for more than a century had given body to the remainder, is disappearing from our horizon, it is a matter of determining the new modes of division and exclusion that constitute the community, of spotting which new figures could give a name to the resistance of the remainder. For this resistance never stops, but it most often remains anonymous and silent. The possibility of naming it gives its possibility to an epoch: it would allow the grounding of a project of emancipation and the search both for how to overcome the exclusion of the remainder without abolishing any difference in the unity of a total body and for how to give its possibility to this "power of the powerless" that Merleau-Ponty evoked. Nothing proves that the exclusion of the remainder is irreversible or that human communities are necessarily destined to injustice and violence: if a reconciliation with the remainder—an *instasis*—can arise in the life of the ego, it should also be possible on the plane of the community. As Benjamin soberly wrote, it must be possible to "free the future from everything that disfigures it today."

"Moses and Pharaoh are in you, it is in you that you must seek these two adversaries." Yet we keep forgetting Rumi's speech: because the caesura of *instasis* must at first be inscribed in the life of each ego. Whatever will appear in the transcendence of the world is already announced in my field of immanence; it is here that the fact of being a body, of excluding a part of its flesh or of being reconciled with it, of being alienated to another or desiring being free of it, all take on their full meaning. We know that the body politic is only a quasi-body; that the "flesh" of the community originates in a transfer of my own flesh; that the First Stranger I encounter—and with whom I identify myself or from whom I dissociated myself, my first object of hatred, love, or respect—is the remainder of my flesh. If incorporation, disfiguration, transfiguration, or deliverance were impossible on the plane of the ego, they could never take place on the plane of the community. Only by suspending the certainty of being in the world, of being embodied, of being with others, and finally of "being" or "existing," only by suspending these everyday evidences can the ego find itself, retrieve its vital source of its self-givenness, recognize in the remainder the flesh of its flesh and within its own self-reconciled flesh trace out the divergence of a difference. Then I will be in truth this "I" that I have "to be." Then will this originary affirmation, this always singular event, this promise made each time in a different manner, the gift of the I, be achieved. Because I "am," I "exist," and even if one deceives me, I "am"; I live; I am living. And I will be what I will be; I will be with whom I will be. I am I, I am what this I is. I am the path, the truth, the life; before Abraham ever was, I am. In my breakthrough, I am one with God, I am the God of God, and I am neither God nor creature, but I am what I was. There where it was, I must arise. I am ego prior to the birth of my father and my mother; I am my father, my mother, my son, and me. In the end, all the names of history are me, the ego. I tell you that I am dead, that I have been dead forever; I am a dead man who sees himself in the mirror. I was dead and here now I am living. In every moment, I precede my own birth.

REFERENCE MATTER

Notes

Translator's emendations appear in brackets.

1. *EGO SUM MORIBUNDUS*, OR HEIDEGGER'S CALL

1. Heidegger, *Nietzsche IV: Nihilism*, tr. D. F. Krell, in *Nietzsche*, vols. 3 and 4 (New York: HarperOne, 1991), 130.

2. Heidegger, "The Age of the World Picture," in *Off the Beaten Track*, tr. J. Young and K. Haynes (Cambridge: Cambridge University Press, 2002), 84.

3. On this question, the most specific analysis is by Jean-Luc Marion, "Ego and Dasein," in *Reduction and Givenness: Investigations of Husserl, Heidegger, and Phenomenology*, tr. T. Carlson (Evanston, IL: Northwestern University Press, 1998), 77–107.

4. Heidegger, "The Age of the World Picture," 70.

5. [Here, at the author's preference, we follow the old convention of capitalizing the word "Being" when it is a matter of Heidegger's special use of the verbal noun (or nominal verb) *Sein* (which is usually rendered as *l'être* in French, sometimes capitalized, sometimes not) and using the lowercase "being" or "beings" when it is a matter of *seiendes* (which in French is usually rendered as *étants*, and sometimes in English as "entities").]

6. [Rogozinski appears to be "violating" one of Heidegger's express wishes to leave the word Dasein untranslated, but he does not adhere rigorously to this rule throughout his analyses in this chapter, frequently using the phrase "existing being" and sometimes leaving it as "Dasein." It is worth noting in advance that Rogozinski is proposing this translation for a philosophical purpose: by the end of the chapter, he will have shown that Dasein, existing being, is profoundly equivocal, "both mine and not mine, me yet not me," and this equivocation is a central element to his argument about egocide.]

7. Heidegger, *Being and Time*, tr. J. Macquarrie and E. Robinson (New York: Harper and Row, 1962), 78. Hereafter, citations for *Being and Time* will be given parenthetically in the text, using the abbreviation *BT*, followed by the page number. [The newer Stambaugh translation was likewise consulted, and we have sometimes imported some of the changes and improvements made in that edition

into the citations made here, often without signaling them. We also note that the author referred to an unpublished translation of *Being and Time* by Emmanuel Martineau, generally considered superior than the published translation in French but unavailable due to copyright restrictions. This situation has sometimes posed some challenges for rendering the author's interpretation of the Heideggerian text in English, since he is sometimes exploiting the richness of the French idiom, which is not always necessarily heard in or resonant with the English.]

8. Heidegger, *Fundamental Problems of Phenomenology*, tr. A. Hofstadter (Bloomington: Indiana University Press, 1988), 130.

9. Ibid., 159. See also *Being and Time*, section 10. "But these formal determinations, which provide the framework for idealism's dialectic of consciousness, are nevertheless very far from an interpretation of the phenomenal circumstances of the Dasein, from *how* this being shows itself to itself in its factual existence, if violence is not practised on Dasein by preconceived notions of *ego* and subject drawn from the theory of knowledge."

10. Heidegger, "Introduction to 'What Is Metaphysics?' (1949)," tr. W. Kaufmann, in Heidegger, *Pathmarks*, ed. W. McNeill (Cambridge: Cambridge University Press, 1998), 283.

11. [The phrase that we here translate as "being-ego or being-mine" is, in French, *être-(à)-moi* and is found in the Martineau translation. If something is *à moi*, it is mine; it belongs "to me" and even "for me." *Etre-moi*, in contrast, refers to "being-me" but also "being-ego," in that *moi* is both an ordinary word for "me" and the technical word for "ego" in French. Hence, operating in the background here is the notion of "mineness," that is, Dasein's character of being "in every case my own." Rogozinski exploits the ambivalence or equivocation of the Martineau rendering of the Heideggerian notion as *être-(à)-moi* effectively in this chapter and throughout the book.]

12. We find here, in the relation of existing being to the ego, the same ambiguity that characterizes its relation to man: this leads Derrida to say "that Dasein, though *not* man, is nevertheless *nothing other* than man . . . it is a repetition of the essence of man." See J. Derrida, "The Ends of Man," in *Margins: Of Philosophy*, tr. A. Bass (Chicago: University of Chicago Press, 1982), 127.

13. Heidegger, "On the Essence of Ground," tr. W. McNeill, in *Pathmarks*, 135.

14. Such an endorsement is explicit in Levinas, for whom "the position of the self is dis-position of the Ego," or in Ricoeur, who intends "to overcome the Cogito" in a "hermeneutics of the self," in which the I "is deposed."

15. Heidegger, "On the Essence of Ground," 122. On this "neutrality" of the existing being, see also the 1928 course on *The Metaphysical Foundations of Logic*, tr. M. Heim (Bloomington: Indiana University Press, 1984), 136.

16. Heidegger, "The Age of the World Picture," 79.

17. That Dasein "is 'in every case mine': this means neither 'posited through me' nor 'apportioned to a singular ego.' [Dasein] is itself by virtue of its essential relation to being in general." Heidegger, *Introduction to Metaphysics*, tr. G. Fried and R. Polt (New Haven, CT: Yale University Press, 2000), 28–29. I admit to not understanding how the always-mine character could occur in any relation to my singular ego; on this question, we can refer to the work of Francois Raffoul, *Heidegger and the Subject*, tr. D. Pettigrew and G. Recco (New York: Humanity Books, 1998).

18. Heidegger, *The Concept of Time*, tr. W. McNeill (Oxford: Blackwell Publishers, 1992), 10e.

19. As works of historians—such as M. Detienne's *Les Maitres de vérité dans la Grèce archaique* (Maspero, 1967)—have shown, it is indeed in this way that the earliest Greeks understood it: for them, "true" speech [*alethes*] is first that of the poet, for it saves the names of the heroes from Lethe, the darkness of Forgetfulness that threatens to obscure them.

20. Heidegger himself determines the essential structure of the "I think" as an "auto-affection"; see Heidegger, *Kant and the Problem of Metaphysics*, tr. R. Taft (Bloomington: Indiana University Press, 1990), 129ff.

21. Heidegger, *The History of the Concept of Time: Prolegomena*, tr. T. Kisiel (Bloomington: Indiana University Press, 1992), 318.

22. Derrida notes this in *Aporias*, tr. T. Dutoit (Stanford, CA: Stanford University Press, 1993), 44–47.

23. Edgar Allan Poe, "The Facts in the Case of M. Valdemar," in *The Portable Edgar Allan Poe*, ed. J. G. Kennedy (New York: Penguin Books, 2006), 71–80.

24. By analyzing this story, I tried to show that Poe fools himself or fools us about Valdemar's "case": in truth, only a living ego is able to say "I," even if it can delude itself into believing that it is already dead. See Jacob Rogozinski, *Faire-part—cryptes de Derrida* (Lignes-Leo Scheer: Paris, 2005), 79–80. This lesson is equally valid for Heideggerian being-toward-death.

25. Heidegger, *The History of the Concept of Time*, 317. "If such pointed formulations mean anything at all, then the appropriate statement pertaining to Dasein in its being would have to be *sum moribundus* ["I am dying"], *moribundus* not as someone gravely ill or wounded, but insofar as I am, I am *moribundus*."

26. Deleuze, *The Logic of Sense*, tr. M. Lester and C. Stivale, ed. C. Boundas (New York: Columbia University Press, 1990), 150.

27. Levinas, "Dying for . . . ," in *Entre Nous*, tr. M. B. Smith and B. Harshw (New York: Columbia University Press, 2000), 209.

28. Heidegger, "Call to German Students," Freiburg, 3 November 1933, in *The Heidegger Controversy: A Critical Reader*, ed. R. Wolin (Cambridge, MA: MIT Press, 1993), 47.

29. See my "Chasser les héros de notre âme," in the collection *Penser après Heidegger* (Paris: L'Harmattan, 1992).

30. See Heidegger's "Call to the Students," a memorial to a Freiburg student on the tenth anniversary of his death, given 26 May 1933 and published in *The Heidegger Controversy*, 40.

31. Heidegger, *Gesamtausgabe 39: Hölderlins Hymnen "Germanien" und "Der-Rhein,"* 1934, section 7 (g). One is right to see in this seminar the most consequential exposition of Heideggerian politics in the 1930s. The English translation, forthcoming, was not yet available at the time of this translation. The citation appears at the very outset of the subsection.

32. In the 1933 "Rectoral Address," this reference to "the Dasein of the people" is made about twenty times. In this context, it becomes impossible to continue to translate Dasein as "existing being."

33. This, as we know, is one of the critiques Levinas addresses to him.

34. Cited by Hugo Ott in *Heidegger: A Political Life*, tr. A. Blunden (New York: Basic Books, 1993), 246.

35. "The German people has been summoned by the Führer to vote. The Führer, however, is asking nothing from the people. Rather he is giving the people the possibility of making, directly, the highest free decision of all." Heidegger, "German Men, German Women," discourse pronounced in Leipzig on 11 November 1933, and published in *The Heidegger Controversy*, 47. It goes without saying that this submission to the will of the Guide is imposed much more strongly on the individual Dasein.

36. Heidegger, "Postscript to 'What Is Metaphysics?'" tr. W. McNeill, in *Pathmarks*, 236. The 1936 lecture "The Origin of the Work of Art" already made sacrifice one of the essential modes of the unveiling of the truth of Being.

37. Heidegger, *Nietzsche IV: Nihilism*, 141.

38. On this subject, one can refer to Dominique Janicaud, *The Shadow of That Thought*, tr. M. Gendre (Evanston, IL: Northwestern University Press, 1996), as well as to the works of Michel Haar.

39. Heidegger, *Nietzsche II: The Eternal Recurrence of the Same*, tr. D. F. Krell, in *Nietzsche*, vols. 3 and 4, 81.

40. Heidegger, *Metaphysical Foundations of Logic*, 160: "Here the subject is thought of as a sort of box with an interior, with the walls of a box, and with an exterior. Of course the crude view is not put forth that consciousness is in fact a box, but what is essential to the analogy and what belongs to the very conception of the transcendent is that a barrier between inner and outer must be crossed." He comes back to this again a half-century later when confronting his teacher one last time in the Zähringen seminar: "With Husserl, the sphere of consciousness is not challenged, much less shattered . . . the ego cogito is an enclosed space. The idea of 'exiting' this enclosed space is itself contradictory. This is why one needs to

start from something other than the ego cogito . . . It was this other domain that was called Da-sein . . . In contrast with the immanence to consciousness expressed by 'being' in consciousness, being in Da-sein says 'being-outside-of.'" See Heidegger, *Four Seminars*, tr. A. Mitchell and F. Raffoul (Bloomington: Indiana University Press, 2003), 70–71.

41. Here I once again find, in a different context, Michel Henry's fundamental thesis.

42. Heidegger, *Nietzsche III: The Will to Power as Knowledge*, tr. D. F. Krell in *Nietzsche*, vols. 3 and 4, tr. D. F. Krell (New York: Harper and Row, 1991), 230.

43. Heidegger, "Letter on Humanism," tr. F. Capuzzi, in *Pathmarks*, 246.

44. Husserl, *The Idea of Phenomenology*, tr. L. Hardy (Dordrecht: Kluwer Academic Publishers, 1999), 52. Translation slightly modified.

45. ["Mouvance" is an old feudal and courtly word in English, and the author will be using it as a conceptual category in Part III of this work. It refers to both those who travel with or in the company of a central actor, and the space in which they travel. For example, in the feudal ages, a noble would have had influence over a mouvance, the territory on which his serfs labored (everything in this territory would have "moved" according to his wishes); when the noble himself moved about to inspect his territory, his various lieges accompanying him would likewise be his mouvance, though today we might call this his entourage. Both the area over which and the underlings over whom the noble has influence comprise his mouvance. When the noble approaches, the peasants might back up and "make way" for his eminence, clearing a space for him to show himself and command a deference from his subjects; this phenomenon would also be a part of the noble's mouvance.]

46. In his philosophical testament, Deleuze underlined, however, that "all transcendence is constituted solely in the current of immanence proper to this plane." See Gilles Deleuze, *Immanence—A Life*, tr. A. Boyman (New York: Zone Books, 2005). He thus legates to us the task of understanding this constitution, of situating the genesis of transcendence in the plane of immanence.

47. Heidegger, *Kant and the Problem of Metaphysics*, 69–74 and 82–85. In these pages, Heidegger proposes an interpretation of what Kant called "the transcendental object = X," which grounds the possibility of objective knowledge.

48. [Macquarrie and Robinson frequently render this idea as "Being is transcendence pure and simple."]

49. Descartes, *Principles of Philosophy*, vol. 1, section 10, in *The Philosophical Writings of Descartes*, ed. and tr. J. Cottingham, R. Stroothoff, and D. Murdoch (Cambridge: Cambridge University Press, 1985), 1:195–96.

50. Husserl, *Husserliana XV: Zur Phänomenologie der Intersubjektivität. Texte aus dem Nachlass. Dritter Teil: 1929–1935*, ed. I. Kern (Dordrecht: Springer-Verlag, 1973), 583–87. Translation mine.

51. I will soon return to this in another book, where I try to explain it through Artaud's thought. For a first approach, see my study "Sans je ni lieu: la vie sans être d'Antonin Artaud," in the collection *Michel Henry, l'épreuve de la vie* (Paris: Editions du Cerf, 2000).

2. I AM THE DEAD PERSON I SEE IN THE MIRROR, OR LACAN'S SUBJECT

1. This painting was also reproduced in J. Baltrustratis, *Le Miroir* (Paris: Seuil, 1978), 78. It would be interesting to compare it to Holbein's *Ambassadors*, among others. [This oil painting by Lukas Furtenagel is entitled *Der Maler Hans Burgkmair und seine Frau Anna geb. Allerlai* and dates from 1529. It is part of the permanent collection of the Kunsthistorische Museum in Vienna, where it typically hangs in the Gemaldegalerie.]

2. See Josef Breuer and Sigmund Freud, *Studies on Hysteria (1895)*, tr. and ed. J. Strachey with the collaboration of A. Freud (New York: Basic Books, 2000), 37.

3. Jacques Lacan, *Seminar II: The Ego in Freud's Theory and in the Techniques of Psychoanalysis 1954–55*, ed. J.-A. Miller, tr. S. Tomaselli (New York: W. W. Norton, 1991), 232–33; and *Ecrits*, tr. B. Fink (New York: W. W. Norton, 2007), 411. On Lacan's references to Valdemar, see Jacob Rogozinski, *Faire part*, 49–50. Henceforward, the *Seminar*s will be designated as S, and *Ecrits* as E, within the body of the text. In addition to *Seminar II*, the seminars most frequently cited are *Seminar III: The Psychoses 1955–56*, ed. J.-A. Miller, tr. R. Grigg (New York: W. W. Norton, 1997); and *Seminar XI: The Four Fundamental Concepts of Psychoanalysis*, ed. J.-A. Miller, tr. A. Sheridan (New York: W. W. Norton, 1998).

4. "Where the id was, I must go" (or rather, "the ego must go"): this statement is found at the end of the thirty-first lecture in Freud, *New Introductory Lectures on Psychoanalysis (1933)*, ed. J. Strachey (New York: W. W. Norton, 1990), 99.

5. [The title of this section in French is "Le stade du mouroir," which blends the mirror stage—*le stade de miroir*—together with the mortuary—*le mouroir*—a wordplay that cannot properly be rendered in English. "Le stade du mouroir" could be translated as the "dying stage" or even the "arena of death," but Rogozinski's intention here is to link the mirror image and the identification that it makes possible to death and to the impossibility of seeing oneself dead.]

6. Freud, *New Introductory Lectures*, 80.

7. S, II:167. He will later speak of an "acephalic subjectivation." Could this be a discreet homage to his friend Bataille and to the secret society linked to the journal *Acéphale*, in which both participated?

8. Jacques Lacan, *Seminar I: Freud's Papers on Technique 1954–55,* ed. J.-A. Miller, tr. J. Forrester (New York: W. W. Norton, 1992), 149. It is from Hegel that Lacan borrows this determination of death as the "absolute Master."

9. See the rich material gathered by F. Tustin in *Autisme et psychose chez l'enfant* (Paris: Seuil, 1982), 29 (for the pupil as "black hole"), 45–46 (on the construction of a monster-object and its "eyes of death"). In the last part of this book, I will try to discern the origin of this haunting.

10. See A. Cordiés, *Un enfant psychotique* (Paris: Seuil, 1993), 165–69. On the therapeutic use of the mirror to help psychotics "to discern their failure" in the image of their body and to "restructure" it, see the rich work of G. Pankow, *L'homme et sa psychose* (Paris: Aubier-Montaigne, 1969).

11. H. Wallon, *Les origins du caractère chez l'enfant* (1932) (Paris: PUF, 1983), 218–37 (recall that this is the principal source of the Lacanian theory of the mirror stage).

12. Sami Ali, *Corps réel, corps imaginaire* (1977) (Paris: Dunod, 1994), 150.

13. Ibid., 143. We know that in a slightly different context, Winnicott defined the face of the mother as the "first mirror" for the child.

14. See chapter 9, "Identification," in Freud, *Group Psychology and the Analysis of the Ego* (New York: W. W. Norton, 1922), 37–49; and *New Introductory Lectures*, 63.

15. Freud, "Findings, Ideas, Problems (1941)," in *The Standard Edition of the Complete Psychological Works of Sigmund Freud* [*SE*], ed. J. Strachey et. al. (London: Hogarth Press, 1953), 23:299–300.

16. Lacan, "Réponses à des étudiants en philosophie," in *Cahiers pour l'analyse 3*, ed. Alain Badiou et al. (Paris: Publiés par le Cercle d'Epistémologie de l'Ecole Normale Supérieure, 1966), 6.

17. Edgar Allan Poe, "William Wilson," in *The Portable Edgar Allan Poe*, ed. J. G. Kennedy (New York: Penguin Books, 2006), 85–86:

A large mirror—so at first it seemed to me in my confusion—now stood where none had been perceptible before; and, as I stepped up to it in extremity of terror, mine own image, but with features all pale and dabbled in blood, advanced to meet me with a feeble and tottering gait. Thus it appeared, I say, but was not. It was my antagonist—it was Wilson, who then stood before me in the agonies of his dissolution. His mask and cloak lay, where he had thrown them, upon the floor. Not a thread in all his raiment—not a line in all the marked and singular lineaments of his face which was not, even in the most absolute identity, *mine own!* It was Wilson; but he spoke no longer in a whisper, and I could have fancied that I myself was speaking while he said: *"You have conquered, and I yield. Yet, henceforward art thou also dead—dead to the World, to Heaven, and to hope! In me didst thou exist—and, in my death, see by this image, which is thine own, how utterly thou hast murdered thyself."*

18. It is this function that will fail in psychosis. See S, III:204–5.

19. See E, 690, and especially the Lacan's *Séminaire VII: Le Transfert (1960–61)*, ed. J.-A. Miller (Paris: Seuil, 2001), 410–14.

20. S, III:287. Several times, Lacan will try to retranslate this enigmatic claim, moving from "I am that which I am" to "I am what I am" before finally arriving at the inspired translation: "I am what is the I," in *Séminaire XVI: D'un Autre à l'autre*, ed. J.-A. Miller (Paris: Seuil, 2006).

21. Merleau-Ponty, *The Visible and the Invisible*, tr. A. Lingis (Evanston, IL: Northwestern University Press, 1968), 144.

22. Lacan, *Séminaire IX: L'Identification*, ed. J.-A. Miller (Paris: Piranha, 1990), session of 10 January 1962 [translation mine].

23. Lacan, *Séminaire XIV: La logique du fantasme* (Paris: Schamans, 1981), session of 1 February 1967 [translation mine].

24. This is just as the clarifying study by F. Balmès shows: see *Ce que Lacan dit de l'être* (Paris: Presses Universitaires de France, 1999).

25. See E, 694, or S, XI:206–9.

26. Freud, *The Ego and the Id*, tr. Joan Rivière, ed. James Strachey (New York: W. W. Norton, 1960), 38.

27. Ibid., 16n. The note was added to the English translation with Freud's express authorization. We can therefore suppose that it authentically expresses his thought.

28. This provides the occasion to give homage to Didier Anzieu, one of the rare contemporary psychoanalysts to have taken this text of Freud seriously, in his book *Le Moi-peau* (Paris: Bordas, 1985).

29. Freud, *The Ego and the Id*, 15.

30. Notably in letter 52 to Fliess where Freud describes these "signs of perception" as a first surface of inscription, anterior to any psychical system, the unconscious as well as the conscious.

31. Freud, "General Considerations on Hysteria" (1909), in *SE* 9:229.

32. Among others, see Freud, "The Economic Problem of Masochism" (1924), in *SE* 19:164–65.

33. Freud, *The Interpretation of Dreams*, tr. A. A. Brill (New York: Modern Library, 1994), 231–32.

34. Freud, "Introduction to Narcissism" (1915), in *SE* 14:75–76. See also Mikkel Borch-Jacobsen, *The Freudian Subject*, tr. C. Porter (Stanford, CA: Stanford University Press, 1988), 113–25.

35. Merleau-Ponty, *The Visible and the Invisible*, 270 [translation slightly modified].

36. Breuer and Freud, *Studies on Hysteria*, 38. Recall that Anna had glimpsed in a mirror "a pale image, not her own but her father's, with death's head."

3. RETURN TO DESCARTES

1. See the analysis I make of it in *"Ego fatum* ou le miroir de Zarathoustra," *Lignes* 7 (February, 2002).

2. I tried to show this in *Faire part.*

3. See A. Damasio, *Descartes' Error: Emotion, Reason, and the Human Brain* (New York: Harper Perennial, 1995).

4. "When I analyze the event expressed in the sentence 'I think,' I acquire a series of rash assertions which are difficult, perhaps impossible, to prove—for example, that it has to be something at all which thinks, that thinking is an activity and operation on the part of an entity thought of as a cause, that an 'I' exists, finally that what is designated by 'thinking' has already been determined—that I *know* what thinking is." See Friedrich Nietzsche, *Beyond Good and Evil*, section 16, in *The Basic Writings of Nietzsche*, tr. W. Kaufmann (New York: Modern Library, 2000), 213.

5. The first to offer an opinion on this was probably Ferdinand Alquié, *La découverte métaphysique de l'homme chez Descartes* (Paris: Presses Universitaires de France, 1950).

6. Descartes, *Meditations on First Philosophy*, Second Meditation, paragraph 4, in *The Philosophical Writings of Descartes*, ed. and tr. J. Cottingham, R. Stroothoff, D. Murdoch (Cambridge: Cambridge University Press, 1985), II:16–17. Hereafter, the citations for the *Meditations* will be given parenthetically in the text. For example, M II, 4:16–17 refers to the Second Meditation, paragraph 4, and the number after the colon corresponds to the page in volume II of *The Philosophical Writings*.

7. This is the thesis Derrida put forward in his study, "The Cogito and the History of Madness," in *Writing and Difference*, tr. A. Bass (Chicago: University of Chicago Press, 1980), 31–64.

8. A misinterpretation like this is what commits a mind as subtle as Jean-Claude Milner's to defend the Lacanian interpretation of Descartes in his *L'Oeuvre Claire* (Paris: Seuil, 1995), 39–42. For a logical approach to this problem, one may consult Jean-Claude Pariente, "La première personne et sa fonction dans le Cogito," in the collection *Descartes et la question du sujet* (Paris: Presses Universitaires de France, 1999).

9. Such an ethics also possesses a political meaning. We may regret that from Spinoza to Foucault, the most rigorous thinkers of a politics of resistance have always seen it in a non-Cartesian perspective, while refusing to root it in an originary affirmation of the ego. This is still the case with the excellent book by Françoise Proust, *De la résistance* (Paris: Cerf, 1997), which makes use of the entire weight of this concept. How does one not see that this is always an ego that stands with an other to resist the intolerable—and that it draws on the power to surge forth in its free self-affirmation?

10. Foucault's position in *The History of Madness* was one that Jean-Luc Marion supports today in "The Originary Otherness of the Ego: A Re-Reading of Descartes' Second Meditation," in his *On the Ego and God: Further Cartesian Questions*, tr. C. Gschwandter (New York: Fordham University Press, 2008), 3–29.

11. Letter to Arnauld, 29 July 1648 in Descartes, *Philosophical Writings*, III:357.

12. See the letter to Clerselier from 12 January 1646, or the *Responses to the Second Objections*, in *Philosophical Writings*, II:100: if the ego "does not deduce existence from thought by means of a syllogism, but recognizes it as something self-evident by a simple intuition of the mind. This is clear from the fact that if he were deducing it by means of some syllogism, he would have to have had previous knowledge of the major premise 'Everything which thinks is, or exists'; yet in fact he learns it from experiencing in his own case that it is impossible that he should think without existing. It is the nature of our mind to construct general propositions on the basis of our knowledge of particular ones."

13. At least on this point I subscribe to the critique of contemporary humanism made by Alain Badiou, *Ethics: An Essay on the Understanding of Evil*, tr. P. Hallward (London: Verso Books, 2002).

14. Descartes, *Principles of Philosophy*, I, section 51; *Philosophical Writings*, I:210.

15. On the distinction between the truth of the world or of Being, foreign to what it reveals, and this other truth or immanent self-revelation that "reveals nothing other than itself," I am guided by Michel Henry's analysis in *C'est moi la verité* (Paris: Seuil, 1996)—but only to a certain point: for him, this self-revelation belongs not to my life but to an absolute and divine Life that no longer coincides with the life of my ego. This scission is what I cannot accept, with the belittling of the ego that follows from it: I am probably too Cartesian for that.

16. "I, Antonin Artaud, I am my son, my father, my mother / and me; / leveler of the imbecile periple / where engendering goes to hell."

17. Jaako Hintikka has done so in his now classic study "Cogito ergo sum: Inference or performance?" *Philosophical Review* 71 (1962), 3–32.

18. "Thus I shall be uncertain not only about whether you are in the world and whether there is an earth or sun; but also about whether I have eyes, ears, a body, and even whether I am speaking to you and you are speaking to me. In short, I shall doubt everything." Descartes, *The Search for Truth*, in *Philosophical Writings*, II:409.

19. As Levinas strongly emphasizes, "the denomination here is only pronomination . . . the pronoun already dissimulates the unique one that is speaking, subsumes it under a concept. But it designates only the mask or the person of the unique one, the mask that leaves the I evading concepts." See Levinas, *Otherwise Than Being or Beyond Essence*, tr. A. Lingis (Dordrecht: Kluwer Academic Publishers, 1991), 56.

20. I am guided here by Michel Henry, *Genealogy of Psychoanalysis*, tr. D. Brick (Stanford, CA: Stanford University Press, 1998), which gave us new access to Descartes' thought.

21. Descartes, *Principles of Philosophy* I, section 6, in *Philosophical Writings*, I:194; on this primordial experience of freedom, see also section 39.

22. Letter to Father Mesland, 9 February 1645, in *Philosophical Writings*, III:245. On this question, we can also consult J.-M. Beyssade, *La philosophie première de Descartes* (Paris: Flammarion, 1979), 190–99.

23. M III, 33:33. We often find this thesis in his work—for example, in his "Responses to the First and Third Objections" or in the *Principles of Philosophy*, I, section 21—and I am amazed that eminent historians still refuse to admit the discontinuity of Cartesian time.

24. Descartes, "Responses to the Fifth Objections," in *Philosophical Writings*, II:255.

25. Though it is today contested, I feel in close agreement with the interpretation proposed by Martial Guéroult in his *Descartes selon l'ordre des raisons* (Paris: Aubier, 1953), esp. vol. 1:153–58, on the "precariousness" of the ego cogito, and 272–85, on the discontinuity of time.

26. Descartes, *Principles of Philosophy* I, section 21, in *Philosophical Writings*, I:200; my emphasis.

27. The only one of all of our contemporaries to take the theory of continuous creation seriously is Levinas. For him, the discontinuity of time and its "continuation through the rupture" makes resurrection "the principal event of time": "in continuation the instant meets its death, and resuscitates . . . Recommencement in discontinuous time brings youth, and thus the infinition of time." See Levinas, *Totality and Infinity*, tr. A. Lingis (Pittsburgh: Duquesne University Press, 1969), 284.

28. See notably his letter to the Cambridge Platonist Henry More (aka Morus) from February to April of 1649 in *Philosophical Writings*, III:371–75.

29. The closest to him is probably Kant, for he too is a thinker of the Moment, and his whole reflection on time is condensed in this fragment from the *Opus Postumum*: "Time has no duration. Its being (now, future, at the same time, before, after) is a Moment." I tried to reconstitute the Kantian theory of the Moment in the last part of *Le Don de la Loi* (Paris: Presses Universitaires de France, 1999).

30. Descartes, "Synopsis" to the *Meditations*, in *Philosophical Writings*, II:10.

31. [The epigraph is one of Descartes' first maxims, dating from his earliest writings, which Jacques Maritain characterizes as his "Juvenilia"; this motto is reproduced in *Philosophical Writings*, I:2.]

32. In Jean-Luc Marion's *On Descartes' Metaphysical Prism*, tr. J. Kosky (Chicago: University of Chicago Press, 1999), the author characterizes Cartesian philosophy as an "unfolded ontology," divided between an ontology of the cogitatio (which ends up at the primacy of the ego) and an ontology of causality

(which leads to the primacy of God). There is nothing to say back to this analysis. I would only add that the second ontology seems to me to renege on the promises of the first, effacing anything in the thought of the ego that was able to transgress the closure of onto-theology.

33. Meister Eckhart, Sermon 52, "The Poor Are Happy in Spirit," in *The Essential Sermons, Commentaries, Treatises, and Defense*, ed. and tr. E. Colledge, B. McGinn, and H. Smith (Mahwah, NJ: Paulist Press, 1981), 203.

34. For example, see the already-cited passage from the *Principles of Philosophy*, section 6, where he puts forward the hypothesis that God may "take pleasure in deceiving us."

35. Plato, *Republic* X, 617e, tr. A. Bloom (New York: Basic Books, 1991), 300.

36. Descartes, *Responses to the Sixth Objections*, section 8, in *Philosophical Writings*, II:289.

37. Georges Bataille, preface to "Madame Edwarda," in *My Mother; Madame Edwarda; The Deadman*, tr. Austryn Wainhouse (New York: Marion Boyars, 1988), 137–38.

38. Once is not enough, so I adopt here Levinas's point of view. See *Of God Who Comes to Mind*, tr. B. Bergo (Stanford, CA: Stanford University Press, 1998), 63–64; and the preface to *Totality and Infinity*, 27–30.

39. M II, 5:17. I am inspired here by the remarkable analysis given by Etienne Balibar, "*Ego sum, Ego existo*, Descartes au point d'hérésie," *Bulletin de la Société française de philosophie* 86 (1992).

40. Descartes, *Discourse on Method*, IV, section 2, in *Philosophical Writings*, I:127; my emphasis. On these rapprochements, see J.-P. Marcos, "Le Sujet suppose vouloir," *Le Moment cartésien de la psychanalyse* (Paris: Arcanes, 1996), 82–83.

41. This is the pious interpretation that Marion proposes in *On Descartes' Metaphysical Prism*, 275–76.

42. Meister Eckhart, "Commentary on Exodus," in *Meister Eckhart: Teacher and Preacher*, tr. and ed. B. McGinn, F. Tobin, et. al. (Mahwah, NJ: Paulist Press, 1986), 45; also cited by Stanislas Breton in *Deux Mystiques de l'excès* (Paris: Cerf, 1985), 98. This thesis is not Eckhart's last word on this question: in his other works, he was trying instead to establish the radical privilege of the ego by situating it in some way beyond "God." Here is the full passage:

Four things are to be remarked upon here. The first is that these three words "I," "am," and "who" belong to God in the most proper sense. The term "I" is the pronoun of the first person. A distinguishing pronoun signifies the pure substance—pure, I say, without any accident, without anything foreign, the substance without quality, without this or that form, without this or that. These things belong to God alone, who is above accident, species, and genus. I say they are his alone, so that he says in the Psalm: "I alone am" (Ps. 140:10).

43. Even if he always very strongly insisted on the sovereign freedom of the ego, to the point of claiming that it "in some way makes us the same as God and seems to exempt us from being subject to him." See the Letter to Queen Christina from 20 November 1647, or section 152 of the *Passions of the Soul.*

44. Nietzsche, *The Gay Science*, no. 125, tr. J. Nauckhoff and A. Del Caro (Cambridge: Cambridge University Press, 2001), 120.

45. Fichte, *The Destination of Man (1800)*, tr. P. Sinnett (London: Chapman Brothers, 1846), 67 [translation modified—compare *The Vocation of Man*, tr. P. Preuss (Indianapolis: Hackett Press, 1987), 63–64: "I know nothing and do not exist. There are images: they are all that exists, and they know about themselves in the manner of images—images which drift by without meaning or purpose. I am myself one of these images. No, I am not even that, but only a distorted image of these images." The older version is closer to the French syntax cited by Rogozinski.]

46. Kant, "Paralogisms of Pure Reason," in *The Critique of Pure Reason*, tr. W. Pluhar with P. Kitcher (Indianapolis: Hackett Press, 1996), 384. See my analysis of them in *Kanten—esquisses kantiennes* (Paris: Kimé, 1996), 75–91.

4. THE EQUIVOCATIONS OF PHENOMENOLOGY

1. Artaud, *The Theatre and Its Double*, tr. M. Richard (New York: Grove Press, 1958), preface.

2. Husserl, *Cartesian Meditations*, tr. D. Cairns (Dordrecht: Martinus Nijhoff, 1964), 25; see also Husserl, *The Crisis of European Sciences*, tr. D. Carr (Evanston, IL: Northwestern University Press, 1970), 78–80.

3. [The author has already intimated the well-known distinction in German between *Körper* and *Leib*, two words used for "body." The former can mean any body whatsoever, including material bodies, astronomical bodies, and dead bodies, or corpses. The latter is the word typically used to describe a living body, including a human body. In most English translations of Husserl, it is usually rendered as "Body." In his *Phenomenology of Perception*, Merleau-Ponty renders it as *le corps propre*, which then becomes the infelicitous "proper body" in English. It is worth noting that the German word belongs to the family of words deriving from the verb *leben*, to live, and it is precisely to place the emphasis on *life* that Merleau-Ponty later on renders it as *la chair*, the flesh (which is then, perversely, returned to German as *die Fleisch*). Didier Franck's book *Le corps et la chair* examines this difference in Husserl and takes issue with Merleau-Ponty's interpretation of it. Rogozinski is following Franck (see note 19 below) by rendering *Leib* as *la chair* and by distinguishing the *corporal* and the *carnal*, which has required us to modify translations of Husserl accordingly.]

4. This concept of the *Ichleib* appears rather early in Husserl, as early as in *Thing and Space: Lectures of 1907*, tr. R. Rojcewicz (Boston: Kluwer Academic Publishers, 1997), where it plays a decisive role in the constitution of spatiality.

5. Husserl, *Ideas: General Introduction to Pure Phenomenology*, tr. W. R. B. Gibson (New York: Collier Books, 1962), book I, section 49, 137.

6. Husserl, *Fifth Logical Investigations*, tr. J. N. Findlay (New York: Routledge and Kegan Paul, 1976), 2:541.

7. Husserl, *Thing and Space*, 34.

8. Husserl, *The Basic Problems of Phenomenology: From the Lectures, Winter Semester, 1910–1911*, tr. I. Farin and J. G. Hart (Dordrecht: Kluwer Academic Publishers, 2006), 79–82.

9. I rely here on the analysis proposed by Rudolf Bernet in *La vie du sujet* (Paris: Presses Universitaires de France, 1994), 303–4.

10. Husserl, *Basic Problems of Phenomenology*, 78.

11. Husserl, *The Crisis of European Sciences*, 184.

12. On the dangers of an "excessive" reduction and its consequences for the destiny of phenomenology, see the fine book by François-David Sebbah, *L'Epreuve de la limite* (Paris: Presses Universitaires de France, 2001).

13. Husserl, *The Idea of Phenomenology*, tr. L. Hardy (Dordrecht: Kluwer Academic Publishers, 1999), Second Lecture, 25. See also the critical analysis given by Michel Henry in *Material Phenomenology*, tr. S. Davidson (New York: Fordham University Press, 2008).

14. See Husserl, "Zur Phänomenologie der Intersubjektivität. Texte aus dem Nachlass" in *Zweiter Teil: 1921–1928 (Husserliana XIV)*, ed. Iso Kern (Leuven: Springer, 1973), section 58.

15. Husserl, *Erste Philosophie (1923–1924), Zweiter Teil: Theorie der Phänomenologischen Reduktion (Husserliana XIII)*, ed. R. Boehm (Dordrecht: Martinus Nijhoff, 1959), section 35.

16. Husserl, *Ideas* II:223: "the [flesh] is *my* [flesh], and it is mine in the first place as my 'over and against,' my *ob-ject*, just as the house is my object, something I can see, something I touch or can touch, etc." See also section 22 (page 103): "What we find then is ourselves as the spiritual Ego related to the stream of lived experiences—'spiritual' here is used in a mere general sense, referring to the Ego that has its place precisely not in Corporeality; e.g., I 'think,' i.e., I perceive, I represent in whatever mode, I judge, I feel, I will, etc., and I find myself thereby as that which is one and the same in the changing of these lived experiences, as 'subject' of acts and states."

17. We will find this self-criticism in an unpublished text from 1933 called "Universal Teleology," in *Husserliana XV: Zur Phänomenologie der Intersubjektivität. Texte aus dem Nachlass. Dritter Teil: 1929–1935*, ed. I. Kern (Dordrecht: Springer-Verlag, 1973), 594.

18. Husserl, *Lectures on the Phenomenology of the Consciousness of Internal Time*, ed. M. Heidegger, tr. J. Brough (Dordrecht: Kluwer Academic Press, 2008), 69: "What 'individual' means here is the original temporal form of sensa-

tion, or, as I can also put it, the temporal form of original sensation, here of the sensation belonging to the current now-point and only to this."

19. On this question, see Husserl's unpublished texts cited by D. Franck in *Chair et corps* (Paris: Minuit, 1982), 189–90. Let me take a moment to underscore just how much my research has benefited from this important book.

20. See, for example, *Husserliana XV*, 587 and 598.

21. Derrida, *Speech and Phenomenon*, tr. D. Allison (Evanston, IL: Northwestern University Press, 1973), 82.

22. Husserl, *Erste Philosophie*, section 40.

5. THE FIELD OF IMMANENCE

1. Gilles Deleuze and Felix Guattari, *What Is Philosophy?* tr. H. Tomlinson and G. Birchill (London: Verso, 1994), 42.

2. Aristotle, *On the Soul* III, 426b16, in *The Basic Writings of Aristotle*, ed. R. McKeon (New York: Modern Library, 1941), 585. See also *On the Senses*, 7: 447–49.

3. At first glance, self-*givenness* of the ego could come from a phenomenology of givenness, such as the one elaborated by Jean-Luc Marion in *Being Given*, tr. J. Kosky (Stanford, CA: Stanford University Press, 2002). But immanent *self*-givenness is not just one "case" among others of givenness in general; it radically differentiates itself from other modes of givenness that open to or could be subordinate to a transcendence. I am not sure that the phenomenology of givenness and of the "saturated phenomenon" takes account of this difference.

4. On this essential distinction, see Husserl, *Ideas* II, 152–54. [Note that *Empfindnisse* is translated here as "sensings," which is closer to Levinas's translation into French as *sentance*, which is adopted by Rogozinski, instead of "impressions sensibles," used by Eliane Escoubas in her French translation of *Ideas* II; *Empfindung*, conversely, is translated as "sensation" in both English and French.]

5. Michel Henry commits this error: it leads him to restrain the extremity of the field of immanent life by totally dissociating life from the horizon of the world. This then prohibits him from seeing the possibility of a *transcendence* in *immanence*.

6. See the unpublished manuscripts from the 1930s cited by Nathalie Depraz, "Temporalité et affection dans les manuscrits tadifs de Husserl," *Alter* 2 (1994): 72–73.

7. Husserl, *Thing and Space: Lectures of 1907*, tr. R. Rojcewicz (Boston: Kluwer Academic Publishers, 1997), appendix IX, 330.

6. THE CARNAL SYNTHESIS: THE CHIASM

1. Husserl, *Ideas* II, 156. As one recalls, this scission between the eye and the look, this impossibility of seeing oneself seeing, ruins the Lacanian theory of the mirror stage.

2. Artaud, *Oeuvres complètes* XI (Paris: Gallimard, 1974), 74 [Translation mine].

3. In a different context where it is not a question of the chiasm, Husserl described the formation of these "communities of resonance" in which the affective excitations of the ego "are sustained by resonating together (by 'appealing' to one another)" and ultimately converge in a unique affection. See, for example, Husserl, *Analyses Concerning Passive and Active Synthesis: Lectures on Transcendental Logic*, tr. A. Steinbock (Boston: Kluwer Academic Publishers, 2001), 520–23.

4. [*Ecart* is a fairly ordinary word in French, with a broad scope of synonymous meanings in English, including a gap, a spread, a hiatus, an interval, a divergence, a separation, a difference, or even a set-aside (much like the change one saves for a rainy day); the verbal form *écarter* can mean to spread (one's legs), to brush aside, to step or get away from (from the car, for you are under arrest), to keep away (from danger), to separate, and even to eliminate. In this, and the subsequent chapters, the author begins to assign it a conceptual function, though he too uses synonyms for it, including *intervalle* and *hiatus*. I have rendered it most frequently as either "divergence" or "gap" depending on the context. And I have rendered *fonction d'écart* as the "function to open up a divergence" precisely because it is a function that *inserts* a gap, *opens* a divergence, or *marks* a difference.]

5. Husserl, *Ideas* II, 153.

6. Ibid., 158. He often insists on the "disincarnating" character of sight: "I must apprehend my [flesh] . . . then I can make for myself an 'image' of my [flesh] in outer appearance, whereby my [flesh] of course necessarily loses the property of [flesh]." See Husserl, *Thing and Space*, 330.

7. Husserl, *Ideas* II, 167.

7. HOW TOUCHING TOUCHES ITSELF TOUCHING: THE (IM)POSSIBILITY
OF THE CHIASM

1. "Nor is it fusion; it is contact with the other. To be in contact is neither to invest the other and annul his alterity, nor to suppress myself in the other. In contact itself the touching and the touched separate, as though the touched moved off, was always already other, did not have anything in common with me." See Levinas, *Otherwise Than Being*, 86.

2. Sartre affirms this at least three times in the chapter on the body in *Being and Nothingness*, no doubt to oppose himself to Husserl. I have analyzed the Sartrian critique of the chiasm in "Scotomes: Point de vue sur Sartre," *Les Temps Modernes* 531–533 (1990).

3. Merleau-Ponty, *The Visible and the Invisible*, tr. A. Lingis (Evanston, IL: Northwestern University Press, 1968), 141 and 215.

4. Ibid., 248.

5. Merleau-Ponty, *Phenomenology of Perception*, tr. C. Smith (New York: Routledge & Kegan Paul, 1962), 92. [Translation modified.]

6. Ibid., 93 [emphasis by Rogozinski; translation modified]; see also *The Visible and the Invisible*, 147. We see that from one book to the next, Merleau-Ponty always encounters this aporia.

7. Merleau-Ponty, *The Visible and the Invisible*, 141–42 and 149. For him, the chiasm does not perform a true *synthesis* of heterogeneous elements; rather, it connects only "ensembles unified in advance by means of differentiation" (262). [Translations slightly modified.]

8. Ibid., 254.

9. Husserl had indeed seen that objective simultaneity is formed on the basis of nonsimultaneous originary impressions: see, for example, section 38 or appendix VII of the 1905 *Lectures on the Phenomenology of Consciousness of Internal Time*, 80–84 and 119–20.

10. Derrida, *On Touching: Jean-Luc Nancy*, tr. C. Irizarry (Stanford, CA: Stanford University Press, 2005), 34.

11. Ibid., 174–75. We find a similar critique of the chiasm in Michel Henry, *Incarnation, une philosophie de la chair* (Paris: Seuil, 2000). I tried to confront these two approaches in "Le chiasme et le restant," *Rue Descartes* 35 (2002).

12. On this aporia of the arrival, whose impossibility of the tactile chiasm is only a particular case, I would like to refer to the last part of my book *Faire part—cryptes de Derrida*.

13. Derrida, *On Touching*, 175. This is a surprising affirmation, repeated several times in the text.

8. IN CONTACT WITH THE UNTOUCHABLE: THE REMAINDER

1. Aristotle, *On the Soul* II:423ab, in *The Basic Works of Aristotle*, ed. R. McKeon (New York: Modern Library, 2001), 577ff. See the commentary on this by Jean-Luc Chrétien, *L'Appel et la Réponse* (Paris: Minuit, 1992).

2. Husserl, *Husserliana XV*:296–98. Husserl thus does not always cede to this "metaphysics of the touch" (of perfect coincidence, of plenitude, of the immediateness of contact) that Derrida attributes to him a little too quickly.

3. Plato, *Timaeus* 52bc, tr. B. Jowett, in *Complete Dialogues of Plato*, ed. E. Hamilton and H. Cairns (Princeton, NJ: Princeton University Press, 1961), 1179.

4. It is from this perspective that I interpret the remarkable works by F. Tustin, especially her *Autisme et psychose chez l'enfant*.

5. Merleau-Ponty, *The Visible and the Invisible*, 243.

6. [An earlier occurrence of this word, *immonde*, was translated by its ordinary usage as "filthy," but here, the addition of the hyphen, *im-monde*, suggests that the accent should be placed on both the *monde*, the world, and the privative *im-*, hence, "nonworldly," which certainly fits in this context.]

7. [The phrase here, *sa part maudite*, can refer to the "dirty or shameful part," where the "part" in question could be an organ, an activity, or simply a thought; the phrase also refers to the title of one of George Bataille's major works, translated into English as *The Accursed Share*.]

8. Husserl, *Ideas* I, 184 [translation modified].

9. THIS IS (NOT) MY BODY: THE REMAINDER OF INCORPORATION

1. "The body is the being-exposed of being," writes Jean-Luc Nancy in *Corpus* (tr. R. Rand [NewYork: Alephoe, 2008]), and this exposition is manifest according to him by the explosion or separation of bodies, their opening, their escape-from-self. But the surprising concept of the body he elaborates in this beautiful little book supposes a deliberate rejection of every thought of the flesh, of carnal immanence, and an equally deliberate confusion of certain traits of the *Leib* and *Körper*.

2. Mishima, *Sun and Steel*, tr. J. Bester (New York: Kodansha International, 1970), 41–42. I am very close here to the analysis made by Francois Noudelmann in "Le corps tragique. Lecture de Mishima," *Césure* 9 (1995). We might glimpse an analogous phantom in Celine, when he opposes the "fairy" body of the dancer to the filthy and mortifying flesh of the Jew.

3. Freud, *The Wolfman*, ed. M. Gardiner (New York: Basic Books, 1972), 226.

4. See Bettelheim, *Symbolic Wounds: Puberty Rites and the Envious Male* (Glencoe, IL: Free Press, 1954), 115.

5. On the ambivalent value of the sacrificial remainder in ancient India, see the very rich analyses of Charles Malamoud, *Cuire le monde* (Paris: Decouverte, 1989), 13–33; see also Detienne and Vernant, *La cuisine du sacrifice en pays grec* (Paris: Gallimard, 1979). I tried to analyze the social and political function of these rites in "Le restant de l'universel," *Universel, singulier, sujet* (Paris: Kime, 2000).

6. Bataille, "The Use Value of D. A. F. de Sade," in *Visions of Excess: Selected Writings, 1927–1939*, tr. A. Stoekl (Minneapolis: University of Minnesota Press, 1985), 94.

7. Aristotle, *Metaphysics Zeta 10* (1035b), in *Basic Writings*, 798. On this determination of the whole, its relation to the parts, and the "mutilation" that can affect it without destroying it, see *Metaphysics Delta 26* and *27*.

8. Aristotle, *Politics* I-2 (1253a), in *Basic Writings*, 1129. We encounter these "examples" in other essential texts: in the introduction to *On the Parts of Animals* (640b–641a: a hand of bronze or of wood, the eye, or the hand of the cadaver) or again in *On the Soul* (412b: an eye of stone), at the moment when it is a matter of clarifying the relation between soul and body.

9. Plato, *Timaeus* 69c–70a, in *Complete Dialogues*, 1193.

10. For example, see the *Politics* 1293b (in *Basic Writings*, 1215) and 1298a (in *Basic Writings*, 1225). Platonic politics are grounded on the metaphysical principle articulated by Diotima in *Symposium* 205e: "but my speech denies that eros is of a half or of a whole—unless, comrade, that half or whole can be presumed to be really good; for human beings are willing to have their own feet and hands cut off, if their opinion is that their own are no good. For I suspect that each does not cleave to his own (unless one calls the good one's own and belonging to oneself, and the bad alien to oneself) since there is nothing that human beings love other than the good," in *Symposium*, tr. S. Benardete (Chicago: University of Chicago Press, 2001), 36.

11. See Husserl, *Ideas* II, 211.

12. Sartre, "Venice from my window," in *Modern Times: Selected Non-Fiction*, tr. R. Buss (London: Penguin Group, 2000), 25. Freud makes us aware of an analogous experience in "The Uncanny."

13. Guy de Maupassant, "Horla," in *Short Stories of the Tragedy and Comedy of Life*, vol. 2 (BiblioBazaar, 2008 [collection originally published in 1903]), 32. [The short story "The Horla" was originally written in 1887, in the style of a journal whose author is disturbed by thoughts and feelings of anguish. He senses the presence of a being that he calls the "Horla" (taken from the French *hors* [outside] and *là* [there]). The journal records how its author's sanity and his sense of alienation are put into question as the Horla progressively dominates his thoughts, which becomes increasingly intolerable.]

14. Althusser, "Idéologie et appareils idéologiques d'Etat," *Positions* (Paris: Editions sociales, 1976), 79–137. As we have seen, it is an interpellation of this type that according to Lacan ensures the "subjection" of the subject to the signifier.

15. Husserl, *Ideas* II, 101 and 156 (on the problem of localization of sounds and the differences between hearing, sight, and touch).

16. See Tomatis, *The Ear and Language*, tr. B. Thompson (New York: Stoddart, 1997), 108–26 and 156–66. [Alfred Tomatis was an ear, nose, and throat specialist and the son of an opera singer. His most famous client was Maria Callas, who came to him in the 1950s when she lost her ability to sing a certain set of notes. A series of tests revealed that Callas could no longer hear the frequencies of the notes she wanted sing, leading Tomatis to postulate his law: the voice can reproduce only what the ear can hear. On the basis of this discovery, he was able to cure Callas by working on her ear, specifically, the tiny bone and muscle structures of the inner ear. Once those muscles were properly exercised and restored to health, Callas could once again hit the high notes. This experimental discovery has led to several audio-vocal applications and treatments.]

17. See Freud, *New Introductory Lectures on Psychoanalysis* (31st lecture), ed. James Strachey (New York: W.W. Norton, 1990), 57–80, as well as the fundamental text *The Ego and the Id*.

18. See Gisela Pankow's excellent book *L'homme et sa psychose* (Paris: Aubier-Montaigne, 1969), 92–103. On the question of verbal hallucination, one must read the book by J. Naudin, *Phénoménologie et psychiatrie. Les voix et la chose* (Marseille: Presses Universitaires de Marseilles, 1997).

10. BEYOND THE OTHER

1. "Fleisch ähnlich Körperlichkeit" is how Husserl sometimes describes it. See *Husserliana XV*:249.

2. Husserl, *Cartesian Meditations*, tr. D. Cairns (Dordrecht: Kluwer Academic Press, 1999), 109. Hereafter citations from this text will be designated as *CM*, followed by the page number, in the main body of the text.

3. Husserl, *Husserliana XIII: Zur Phänomenologie der Intersubjektivität. Texte aus dem Nachlass. Erster Teil: 1905–1920*, ed. Iso Kern (Dordrecht: Kluwer Academic Publishers, 1973), 6.

4. Plato, *Sophist* 231a, in *Complete Dialogues*, 973.

5. *Husserliana XV*:206.

6. de la Boétie, *The Politics of Obedience: Discourse on Voluntary Servitude* (1548) (New York: Kessinger Publishers, 2004), 6.

7. Merleau-Ponty, *The Visible and the Invisible*, 134.

8. Freud, *Sketch for a Scientific Psychology* (1895), in *SE* 1:330ff. We may regret that he took no account of it in another elaboration of his theories.

9. See Jean-Luc Marion, *God without Being* tr. T. A. Carlson (Chicago: University of Chicago Press, 1991), 11–15. Marion justly concludes (38–39) that "the idol always culminates in a self-idolatry," and we can say as much for the idolatry of the other.

10. After having celebrated in *Totality and Infinity* the "frankness" of the face of the other, his "rightness" that "could not lie," Levinas ended by recognizing in his last book the "ambiguity" of the face, "trace lost in the trace," "possibly mask." Levinas, *Otherwise Than Being*, 93–94. I am not sure that he draws all the consequences of it on the ethical plane.

11. S. Thibierge, *Pathologies de l'image du corps* (Paris: Presses Universitaires de France, 1999), 197–98; other examples of this syndrome are described on pages 35–39 and 64–65.

12. "It is in the function where the sexual object files towards the descent of reality and is present as a packet of meat that this form of desexualization, so manifest that it is called a reaction of disgust in the hysteric, emerges." See S, XI:157.

13. Odon de Cluny, cited in M. Surya, *Bataille: An Intellectual Biography*, tr. K. Kijalkowski and M. Richardson (London: Verso, 2002), 28. [The text in question is from one of the many severe and forceful moral sermons by Saint Odo of Cluny (878–942 A.D.), second Abbot of Cluny, collected together with letters and essays in three volumes called *Collationes* II.]

14. Freud, *The Ego and the Id*, 33. We find an interesting analysis of this problem in M. Borch-Jakobsen, *The Freudian Subject* (Stanford, CA: Stanford University Press, 1988), 203–235.

15. Kant, *Critique of Judgment*, tr. W. Pluhar (Indianapolis: Hackett Press, 1987), section 48, 180.

16. Kant, "The Doctrine of Virtue," section 24, in *The Metaphysics of Morals*, tr. M. J. Gregor (Cambridge: Cambridge University Press, 1996), 171; see also section 48 in the appendix of part 1 ("The Doctrine of Right") on the possibility of a synthesis of respect and love. In *Le Don de la Loi*, I tried to elucidate the Kantian theory of respect—but I was unable to do so due to having discovered the function of the remainder.

17. Freud, *The Ego and the Id*, 24.

18. Husserl, *Husserliana XV*:105.

11. THE CRISIS OF THE CHIASM

1. Kierkegaard (Johannes Climacus), *Philosophical Fragments*, tr. H. Hong and E. Hong (Princeton, NJ: Princeton University Press, 1985).

2. F. W. J. Schelling, *Philosophical Inquiries into the Nature of Human Freedom*, tr. J. Gutmann (Lasalle, IL: Open Court Publishing, 2001), 46–47.

12. FROM HATRED TO LOVE

1. Husserl, *Ideas* II, 160.

2. "I don't know if in French the word *'remanence'* exists, but it translates extremely well what I mean . . . which always arises from and *se soulever* from what had once wanted to subsist, I meant remaner, remain in order to re-emanate, emanate by keeping its remainder, to be the leftover that will arise again." Artaud, Letter to Le Breton (1946), in *Oeuvres Complètes* XI:194.

3. Plato, *Phaedo* 105de, in *Collected Dialogues*, 87.

4. A. Kolnai, *Le Dégout* (Paris: Agalma, 1997; originally published in 1929), 39–43 and 70–71. In the *Critique of Judgment*, Kant had already claimed that disgust imposes itself on jouissance.

5. Freud, *Dora: An Analysis of a Case of Hysteria*, ed. P. Rieff (New York: Touchstone, 1997), 83.

6. See Schilder, *The Image and Appearance of the Human Body* (New York: Routledge, 1999, originally published in 1935), 24–29 and 70–74.

7. Cited by S. Thibierge, *Pathologies de l'image du corps* (Paris: Presses Universitaires de France), 72. See also 179–180.

8. See "The Man Who Fell out of Bed," in Oliver Sacks, *The Man Who Mistook His Wife for a Hat* (New York: Touchstone Press, 1998), 55–58.

9. Descartes, *Passions of the Soul*, sections 79–80, in *Philosophical Writings*, I:356. He tries in a genial manner to define these passions in an immanent fashion without any consideration for the relation to others, by leading them back to the internal movements of the soul and the "animal spirits." Hatred would in this way be provoked by the penetration of a foreign element into the body, harmful to the "principle of life."

10. Proust, *Sodom and Gomorrah*, vol. 4, *In Search of Lost Time*, tr. C. Prendergast and J. Sturrock, (New York: Penguin Classics, 2003), 11–15. [The scene in question is early in part 1, when the narrator realizes, after having observed his flirtation with Jypien, that Monsieur de Charlus is homosexual, and he describes the very different perspective in which he now sees Charlus.]

11. This distinction perhaps recuperates the one Rousseau established between "amour-propre" and "amour de soi" as originary auto-affection; see the careful analyses of this question in P. Audi, *Créer* (Paris: Encre Marine, 2005), 362–66. On narcissism and its sociopolitical significance, see the works of Bernard Steigler.

12. Kant, *Critique of Judgment*, 115.

13. Freud, "Instincts and Their Vicissitudes," in *General Psychological Theory*, 91.

14. Spinoza, *Ethics*, book V, proposition 4, tr. G. H. R. Parkinson (Oxford: Oxford University Press, 2000), 292. Hereafter references to this text will be made with standard shorthand, followed by the page number to this text, as in E5p4:292.

15. Spinoza, E3p44:198.

16. Lacan, *Séminaire VIII: Le Transfert*, 173.

17. Lucretius, *Of the Nature of Things*, IV:1153–70, tr. M. F. Smith (Indianapolis: Hackett Press, 2001), 131. See also Plato *Republic* 474d.

18. Freud, *Group Psychology*, 43–44.

19. "It is precisely the facility with which (the good breast) dispenses milk—and thus gratifies the child—which excites desire, as *if this gift were inaccessible*" (emphasis mine). See Melanie Klein, *Envy and Gratitude: A Study of Unconscious Forces* (London: Hogarth Press, 1957), 20–21.

20. Spinoza, EVp23s:303. "This idea which expresses the essence of the body under a species of eternity is, as we have said, a certain mode of thinking which belongs to the essence of the mind, and which is necessarily eternal."

21. See Empedocles, "On Nature," in *The Presocratic Philosophers*, ed. G. S. Kirk, J. E. Raven, and M. Schofield (Cambridge: Cambridge University Press, 1957), 326–28 and 423–24. [The version in *Empedocles: The Extant Fragments*, ed. and tr. M. R. Wright (New Haven, CT: Yale University Press, 1981), 166, is somewhat different and reads as follows:

And these things never cease their continual exchange of position, at one time all coming together into one through love, at another again being borne away from each other by strife's repulsion. (So, insofar as one is accustomed to arise from many) and many are produced from one as it is again being divided, to this extent they are born and have no abiding life; but insofar as they never cease their continual exchange, so far they are forever unaltered in the cycle.

The French translation used by author is more different still, and if one renders that into English from the French, it results in the following: "Sometimes by love, together they constitute / a unique ordering, sometimes each of them / can be separated by the enemy hatred / until the time when they are grounded in the One and are engulfed in shadow / And thus it is that the One has learned to be born from the many."]

22. Ibid., B10–20, in *Presocratic Philosophers*, 326–27.

13. FROM ARCHI-AGONY TO RESURRECTION

1. F. Lhermitte, *L'image de notre corps* (Paris: Editions de la Nouvelle Revue Critique, 1939), 148.

2. On the enigma of this knotting of life and death—and the question of knowing which of the two "resists" the other—one must read the lovely pages written by Françoise Proust in *De la résistance* (Paris: Cerf, 1997), 117–51.

3. "If the body shows scratches, especially on the shoulder, similar to *kimali*, the erotic scratches impressed during sexual dalliance, this means that the deceased has been guilty of adultery or has been too successful with women, to the annoyance of a chief, man of power, or a sorcerer." See Malinowski, *Crime and Custom in Savage Society* (Totowa, NJ: Littlefield, Adams, 1966), 88. The rite of the "interrogation of the cadaver" had been described in L. Thomas, *Anthropologie de la mort* (Paris: Payot, 1975), 409–10.

4. See S. Follin, *Vivre en délirant* (Paris: Les Empecheurs de penser en rond, 1992), 301.

5. Kierkegaard, *This Sickness unto Death*, tr. H. Hong and E. Hong (Princeton, NJ: Princeton University Press, 1983), 18.

6. See Winnicott, "Fear of Breakdown (1963)," in *Psychoanalytic Explorations*, ed. C. Winnicott, R. Shepard, and M. Davis (Cambridge, MA: Harvard University Press, 1989), 87–95.

7. For all of this, Artaud's thought (and his madness) still has much to teach us. For a first approach, see my study "J'ai toujours su que j'étais Artaud le mort," in *Europe* (2002).

8. Derrida had clearly seen that the work of mourning presupposes an originary "mourning of the self" in which I survive myself. In *Faire part*, I sought to explain his conception of mourning and of "survivance," his aim of a "mourning of

mourning," and the impossible statement "I am dead," which subtends his entire oeuvre.

9. See Freud, "Mourning and Melancholia," in *General Psychological Theory*, 164–79; as well as the developments of N. Abraham and M. Torok in *L'Ecorce et le Noyau* (Paris: Aubier-Flammarion, 1978).

10. Freud, "Thoughts on War and Death," in *Character and Culture*, ed. J. Strachey (New York: Macmillan, 1963), 132–33.

11. Spinoza, *Ethics* V, P238, S303.

12. [Rogozinski here refers to a text of Husserl's, which in French translation (by P. Beck, N. Depraz et. al., in *Alter* 1 [1993]: 271–90, is called "Le monde anthropologique." A translation of this text does not exist in English, but it corresponds to text number 28, dating from the end of August 1936, in *Husserliana XXIX—Die Krisis des europäischen Wissenschaften und die transzendantale Phänomenologie Ergänzundsband. Texte aus dem Nachlass 1934–1937*, ed. R. N. Smid (Dordrecht: Kluwer Academic Publishers, 1993), 321–38.]

13. The same argument is also valid against the hypothesis of a time that would have preceded my birth: against the absurd notion of a consciousness of not-yet-being-there. Just as it cannot die, the immanent ego is never born. See Husserl, *Ideas* II, 107–10, and appendix VIII of the *Analyses Concerning Passive and Active Synthesis*, 451–73.

14. Nietzsche, *Twilight of the Idols*, "What I Owe to the Ancients," in *The Portable Nietzsche*, ed. Walter Kaufmann (New York: Penguin, 1954), 561. I here rejoin by other means the interpretation of the eternal return given by Didier Frank, *Nietzsche et l'ombre de dieu* (Paris: Presses Universitaires de France, 1996).

15. I have exposited on this "affective" interpretation of the Eternal Return in "*Ego fatum* ou le miroir de Zarathoustra," *Lignes* 7 (2002).

16. Schreber, "Bodily Integrity Damaged by Miracles," in *Memoirs of My Nervous Illness*, tr. I. Macalpine and R. Hunter (New York: New York Review of Books, 2000; originally published by Harvard University Press, 1955), 141–51.

17. See R. Jaulin, *La Mort sara* (Paris: Plon, 1967). In Mircea Eliade, *Mystical Births*, the author shows that such rites are found in nearly identical forms among the Amerindians, the Australian Aborigines, and the Siberian shamans. It is indeed a question of a symbolic invariant that transcends the cultural or ethnic differences to the extent that it is rooted in an originary carnal experience common to all humans.

18. Plato *Phaedo* 88ab, in *Collected Dialogues*, 70.

19. Plato *Phaedo* 77e, in *Collected Dialogues*, 61.

20. See the *Apocalypse of Saint John* (20:6–14). In this text, the "second death" comes after a "first resurrection," but it uniquely strikes down the bad powers,

just as the Just are resuscitated for eternity. I am obviously using this term in a very different sense.

21. Artaud, "Je n'admets pas" (1947), in *Oeuvres*, 1589.

14. TOWARD DELIVERANCE (*INSTASY*)

1. Freud, "Instincts and Their Vicissitudes," 89. This "part" of the ego rejected outside of itself corresponds exactly to what I call the "remainder."

2. On the paradoxical temporality of the messianic event, its relation to historical time, and the risk of imposture and of the disaster to which it is exposed, I refer to the works of two friends: F. Proust, *L'Histoire à contre-temps* (Paris: Cerf, 1994); and G. Bensussan, *Le Temps messianique* (Paris: Vrin, 2001).

3. Levinas, "Messianic Texts," in *Difficult Freedom: Essays on Judaism*, tr. S. Hand (Baltimore: Johns Hopkins University Press, 1997), 88. In the same text (pp. 81–87), he evokes the amazing passage of the Talmud that sees that the Messiah has already come in a distant past without having been recognized.

4. Descartes, letter to Father Mesland, 9 February 1645, in *Philosophical Writings*, III:245. On this question, we can also consult J.-M. Beyssade, *La philosophie première de Descartes* (Paris: Flammarion, 1979), 190–99.

5. *Exodus* 3:11–14 (King James Version).

6. This is how Meister Eckhart understands it: "when at night one asks someone who wishes to remain hidden and not be named, 'who are you?' he responds *ego sum qui sum*, I am who I am." See his "Commentaries on Genesis," in *The Essential Sermons*, 82–122.

7. "I am with them [the children of Israel] in this distress and I will be with them in other distresses." It is in this sense of being-with that Rachi interpreted the Word.

8. It is this priority of the gift of the I over the givenness of the law that I had not seen when I was writing *Le Don de la Loi*, which led me to determine the *Gesetzgebung* as the most originary givenness and to erect the Law as "subject of the subject." By coming back from Kant to Descartes—and by better understanding the Word of Sinai—I have managed to overcome this idolatry of the Law.

9. *Exodus* 4:5–7 (King James Version). [Rogozinski is using the edition prepared by Chouraqui, unavailable in English, necessitating some minor changes to suit Rogozinski's argument.]

10. Paul, *Letter to the Philippians* 2:6–9 (King James Version). We know that Gregory of Nyssa interpreted the story of Exodus on the leprous hand of Moses as an allegorical anticipation of this "kenosis" of the Christ.

11. Saint John of the Cross, *The Dark Night of the Soul*, tr. E. Allison Peters (Garden City, NY: Image Books/Doubleday, 1959), book II, chap. 6.

12. Saint John of the Cross, *The Living Flame of Love*, tr. D. Lewis (New York: Cosimo Classics, 2007), stanza II, paragraph 2, 34–35.

13. Husayn Mansur Hallaj, *Diwan* (920), poems 57 and 41.

14. See the sermon 52, "The Poor Are Happy in Spirit," in Eckhart, *The Essential Sermons,* 203.

15. Hölderlin, "Remarks on Oedipus," in *Essays and Letters on Theory*, tr. and ed. Thomas Pfau (Albany: State University of New York Press, 1988), 103–8; see also in the same work the "Remarks on Antigone," 109–16. To approach these texts, the density of which defies every reading, I have relied notably on the clarifying commentaries of F. Dastur and P. Lacoue-Labarthe. One can find another approach to the *Ungeheure* in my book *Kanten*.

16. I have tried to describe certain modes of exclusion of a remainder by a political community: in the case of the revolutionary Terror and in the case of the Indian caste of the untouchables; see, respectively, "Etranger parmi nous: La Terreur et son ennemi," *Césure* 9 (1995); and "Le Restant de l'universel," in *L'Universel, le Singulier* (Paris: Kimé, 2000). These are just some markers along the path of research in progress.

Bibliography

Abraham, Nicholas, and Torok, Maria. *L'Ecorce et le Noyau* (Paris: Aubier-Flammarion, 1978).

Alquié, Ferdinand. *La découverte métaphysique de l'homme chez Descartes* (Paris: Presses Universitaires de France, 1950).

Althusser, Louis. "Idéologie et appareils idéologiques d'Etat," in *Positions* (Paris: Editions sociales, 1976).

Anzieu, Didier. *Le Moi-peau* (Paris: Bordas, 1985).

Aristotle. *The Basic Works of Aristotle*, ed. R. McKeon (New York: Modern Library, 2001).

Artaud, Antonin. *Oeuvres complètes* XI: 74 (Paris: Gallimard, 1974).

———. *The Theatre and Its Double*, tr. M. Richard (New York: Grove Press, 1958).

Audi, Paul. *Créer* (Paris: Encre Marine, 2005).

Badiou, Alain. *Ethics: An Essay on the Understanding of Evil*, tr. P. Hallward (London: Verso Books, 2002).

Balibar, Etienne. *"Ego sum, Ego existo*, Descartes au point d'hérésie." *Bulletin de la Société française de philosophie* (1992).

Balmès, Francois. *Ce que Lacan dit de l'etre* (Paris: Presses Universitaires de France, 1999).

Baltrustratis, Jurgis. *Le Miroir* (Paris: Seuil, 1978).

Bataille, Georges. *My Mother; Madame Edwarda; The Deadman,* tr. Austryn Wainhouse (New York: Marion Boyars, 1988).

———. "The Use Value of D. A. F. de Sade," in *Visions of Excess: Selected Writings, 1927–1939,* tr. A. Stoekl (Minneapolis: University of Minnesota Press, 1985).

Bensussan, Gerard. *Le temps messianique* (Paris: Vrin, 2001).

Bernet, Rudolf. *La vie du sujet* (Paris: Presses Universitaires de France, 1994).

Bettelheim, Bruno. *Symbolic Wounds: Puberty Rites and the Envious Male* (Glencoe, IL: Free Press, 1954).

Beyssade, Jean-Marie. *La philosophie première de Descartes* (Paris: Flammarion, 1979).

Bloomfield, Maurice. *The Mystiques de l'excès Hymns of the Atharva-Veda*, ed. and tr. R. T. H. Griffith (Cambridge, MA: Harvard University Press, 1895).

Boétie, Etienne de la. *The Politics of Obedience: Discourse Voluntary Servitude* (1548) (New York: Kessinger Publishers, 2004).

Borch-Jacobsen, Mikkel. *The Freudian Subject* (Stanford, CA: Stanford University Press, 1988).

Breton, Stanislas. *Deux* (Paris: Cerf, 1985).

Breuer, Josef, and Sigmund Freud. *Studies on Hysteria* (1895), tr. and ed. J. Strachey with the collaboration of A. Freud (New York: Basic Books, 2000).

Chrétien, Jean-Luc. *L'Appel et la Réponse* (Paris: Minuit, 1992).

Cordié, Anny. *Un enfant psychotique* (Paris: Seuil, 1993).

Damasio, Antonio. *Descartes' Error* (New York: Putnam, 1994).

Deleuze, Gilles. *Immanence—A Life*, tr. A. Boyman (New York: Zone Books, 2005).

———. *The Logic of Sense*, tr. M. Lester and C. Stivale, ed. C. Boundas (New York: Columbia University Press, 1990).

Deleuze, Gilles, and Felix Guattari. *What Is Philosophy?* tr. H. Tomlinson and G. Birchill (London: Verso, 1994).

Depraz, Nathalie. "Temporalité et affection dans les manuscrits tadifs de Husserl." *Alter* 2 (1994).

Derrida, Jacques. *Aporias*, tr. T. Dutoit (Stanford, CA: Stanford University Press, 1993).

———. *Margins: Of Philosophy*, tr. A. Bass (Chicago: University of Chicago Press, 1982).

———. *On Touching-Jean-Luc Nancy*, tr. C. Irizarry (Stanford, CA: Stanford University Press, 2005).

———. *Speech and Phenomenon*, tr. D. Allison (Evanston, IL: Northwestern University Press, 1973).

———. *Writing and Difference*, tr. A. Bass (Chicago: University of Chicago Press, 1980).

Descartes, Rene. *The Philosophical Writings of Descartes*, Vols. 1–3, ed. and tr. J. Cottingham, R. Stroothoff, and D. Murdoch (Cambridge: Cambridge University Press, 1985).

Detienne, Marcel. *Les Maîtres de vérité dans la Grèce archaique* (Paris: Maspero, 1967).

Detienne, Marcel, and Jean-Pierre Vernant. *La cuisine du sacrifice en pays grec* (Paris: Gallimard, 1979).

Eckhart, Meister. *The Essential Sermons, Commentaries, Treatises, and Defense*, ed. and tr. E. Colledge, B. McGinn, and H. Smith (Mahwah, NJ: Paulist Press, 1981).

———. *Meister Eckhart: Teacher and Preacher*, tr. and ed. B. McGinn, F. Tobin et al. (Mahwah, NJ: Paulist Press, 1986).

Empedocles. *Empedocles: The Extant Fragments*, ed. and tr. M. R. Wright (New Haven, CT: Yale University Press, 1981).

Fichte, J. G. *The Destination of Man* (1800), tr. P. Sinnett (London: Chapman Brothers, 1846).

———. *The Vocation of Man*, tr. P. Preuss (Indianapolis: Hackett Press, 1987).

Follin, Sven. *Vivre en délirant* (Paris: Les Empecheurs de penser en rond, 1992).

Franck, Didier. *Chair et corps* (Paris: Minuit, 1982).

———. *Dramatique des phénomènes* (Paris: Presses Universitaires de France, 2001).

———. *Nietzsche et l'ombre de dieu* (Paris: Presses Universitaires de France, 1996).

Freud, Sigmund. *Dora: An Analysis of a Case of Hysteria*, tr. Philip Rieff (New York: Touchstone, 1997).

———. *The Ego and the Id*, tr. Joan Rivière, ed. James Strachey (New York: W. W. Norton, 1960).

———. *General Psychological Theory*, ed. Philip Rieff (New York: Touchstone, 1991).

———. *Group Psychology and the Analysis of the Ego* (New York: W. W. Norton, 1922).

———. *The Interpretation of Dreams*, tr. A. A. Brill (New York: Modern Library, 1994).

———. *New Introductory Lectures on Psychoanalysis* (1933), ed. James Strachey (New York: W. W. Norton, 1990).

———. *The Standard Edition of the Complete Psychological Works of Sigmund Freud*, ed. J. Strachey et al. (London: Hogarth Press, 1957).

———. *The Wolfman*, ed. M. Gardiner (New York: Basic Books, 1972).

Guéroult, Martial. *Descartes selon l'ordre des raisons* (Paris: Aubier, 1953).

Haar, Michel. *Heidegger and the Essence of Man,* tr. W. McNeill (Albany: State University of New York Press, 1994).

———. *The Song of the Earth*, tr. R. Lilly (Bloomington: Indiana University Press, 1992).

Hallaj, Huseyn Mansour. *Diwan* (Paris: Seuil, 1981).

Heidegger, Martin. *Being and Time*, tr. J. Macquarrie and E. Robinson (New York: Harper and Row, 1962).

———. *The Concept of Time*, tr. W. McNeill (Oxford: Blackwell Publishers, 1992).

———. *Four Seminars*, tr. A. Mitchell and F. Raffoul (Bloomington: Indiana University Press, 2003).

———. *Fundamental Problems of Phenomenology*, tr. A. Hofstadter (Bloomington: Indiana University Press, 1988).

———. *Gesamtausgabe*. Vol. 39, *Hölderlins Hymnen "Germanien" und "Der-Rhein," 1934* (Frankfurt am Main: Vittorio Klostermann, 1993).

———. *The Heidegger Controversy: A Critical Reader*, ed. R. Wolin (Cambridge, MA: MIT Press, 1993).

———. *The History of the Concept of Time: Prolegomena*, tr. T. Kisiel (Bloomington: Indiana University Press, 1992).

———. *Introduction to Metaphysics*, tr. G. Fried and R. Polt (New Haven, CT: Yale University Press, 2000).

———. *Kant and the Problem of Metaphysics*, tr. R. Taft (Bloomington: Indiana University Press, 1990).

———. *The Metaphysical Foundations of Logic*, tr. M. Heim (Bloomington: Indiana University Press, 1984).

———. *Nietzsche*. Vol. 2, *The Will to Power as Knowledge*, tr. D. F. Krell (New York: Harper and Row, 1984).

———. *Nietzsche*. Vol. 3, *The Eternal Recurrence of the Same*, tr. D. F. Krell (New York: HarperOne, 1991).

———. *Nietzsche*. Vol.4, *Nihilism*, tr. D. F. Krell (New York: HarperOne, 1991).

———. *Off the Beaten Track*, tr. J. Young and K. Haynes (Cambridge: Cambridge University Press, 2002).

———. *Pathmarks*, ed. W. McNeill (Cambridge: Cambridge University Press, 1998).

Henry, Michel. *C'est moi la verité* (Paris: Seuil, 1996).

———. *Genealogy of Psychoanalysis*, tr. D. Brick (Stanford, CA: Stanford University Press, 1998).

———. *Incarnation, une philosophie de la chair* (Paris: Seuil, 2000).

———. *Material Phenomenology*, tr. S. Davidson (New York: Fordham University Press, 2008).

Hintikka, Jaakko. "Cogito ergo sum: Inference or performance?" *Philosophical Review* (1962), 71 (1): 3–32.

Hölderlin, Friedrich. *Essays and Letters on Theory*, tr. and ed. Thomas Pfau (Albany: State University of New York Press, 1988).

Husserl, Edmund. *Analyses Concerning Passive and Active Synthesis: Lectures on Transcendental Logic*, tr. A. Steinbrock (Boston: Kluwer Academic Publishers, 2001).

———. *The Basic Problems of Phenomenology: From the Lectures, Winter Semester, 1910–1911*, tr. I. Farin and J. G. Hart (Dordrecht: Kluwer Academic Publishers, 2006).

———. *Cartesian Meditations*, tr. D. Cairns (Dordrecht: Martinus Nijhoff, 1964).

———. *The Crisis of European Sciences*, tr. D. Carr (Evanston, IL: Northwestern University Press, 1970).

———. *Husserliana XIII: Erste Philosophie (1923–1924), Zweiter Teil: Theorie der Phänomenologischen Reduktion)* , ed. R. Boehm (Dordrecht: Martinus Nijhoff, 1959).

————. *Fifth Logical Investigations*, tr. J. N. Findlay (New York: Routledge and Kegan Paul, 1976).

————. *Husserliana XIV: Zur Phänomenologie der Intersubjektivität. Texte aus dem Nachlass. Erster Teil: 1905–1920*, ed. Iso Kern (Dordrecht: Kluwer Academic Publishers, 1973).

————. *Husserliana XV: Zur Phänomenologie der Intersubjektivität. Texte aus dem Nachlass. Dritter Teil: 1929–1935*, ed. I. Kern (Dordrecht: Springer-Verlag, 1973).

————. *The Idea of Phenomenology*, tr. L. Hardy (Dordrecht: Kluwer Academic Publishers, 1999).

————. *Ideas: General Introduction to Pure Phenomenology*, book 1, tr. W. R. B. Gibson (New York: Collier Books, 1962).

————. *Ideas Pertaining to a Pure Phenomenology and to a Phenomenological Philosophy*, book 2, tr. R. Rojcewicz and A Schuwer (Dordrecht: Kluwer Academic Publishers, 1989).

————. *Lectures on the Phenomenology of the Consciousness of Internal Time*, ed. M. Heidegger, tr. J. Brough (Dordrecht: Kluwer Academic Press, 2008).

————. *Thing and Space: Lectures of 1907*, tr. R. Rojcewicz (Boston: Kluwer Academic Publishers, 1997).

Janicaud, Dominique. *The Shadow of That Thought*, tr. M. Gendre (Evanston, IL: Northwestern University Press, 1996).

Jaulin, Robert. *La Mort sara* (Paris: Plon, 1967).

Kant, Immanuel. *Critique of Judgment*, tr. W. Pluhar (Indianapolis: Hackett Press, 1987).

————. *The Critique of Pure Reason*, tr. W. Pluhar with P. Kitcher (Indianapolis: Hackett Press, 1996).

————. *The Metaphysics of Morals*, tr. M. J. Gregor (Cambridge: Cambridge University Press, 1996).

Kierkegaard, Sören (Johannes Climacus). *Philosophical Fragments*, tr. H. Hong and E. Hong (Princeton, NJ: Princeton University Press, 1985).

————. *This Sickness unto Death*, tr. H. Hong and E. Hong (Princeton, NJ: Princeton University Press, 1983).

Kirk, G. S., and J. E. Raven. *The Presocratic Philosophers; a Critical History with a Selection of Texts* (Cambridge: Cambridge University Press, 1957).

Klein, Melanie. *Envy and Gratitude: A Study of Unconscious Forces* (London: Hogarth Press, 1957).

Kolnai, Aurel. *Le Dégout* (Paris: Agalma, 1997; originally published in 1929).

Lacan, Jacques. *Ecrits*, tr. B. Fink (New York: W. W. Norton, 2007).

————. *Seminar I: Freud's Papers on Technique, 1954–55*, ed. J.-A. Miller, tr. J. Forrester (New York: W. W. Norton, 1992).

————. *Seminar II: The Ego in Freud's Theory and in the Techniques of Psychoanalysis, 1954–55*, ed. J.-A. Miller, tr. S. Tomaselli (New York: W. W. Norton, 1991).

————. *Seminar III: The Psychoses, 1955–56*, ed. J.-A. Miller, tr. R. Grigg (New York: W. W. Norton, 1997).

————. *Seminaire VII: Le Transfert (1960–61)*, ed. J.-A. Miller (Paris: Seuil, 2001).

————. *Séminaire IX: L'Identification*, ed. J.-A. Miller (Paris: Piranha, 1990).

————. *Séminaire X: L'angoisse (1962–1963)*, ed. J.-A. Miller (Paris: Seuil, 2004).

————. *Seminar XI: The Four Fundamental Concepts of Psychoanalysis*, ed. J.-A. Miller, tr. A. Sheridan (New York: W. W. Norton, 1998).

————. *Séminaire XIV: La logique du fantasme* (Paris: Schamans, 1981).

————. *Séminaire XV: D'un Autre à l'autre*, ed. J.-A. Miller (Paris: Seuil, 2006).

Levinas, Emmanuel. *Difficult Freedom: Essays on Judaism*, tr. S. Hand (Baltimore: Johns Hopkins University Press, 1997).

————. "Dying for . . . ," in *Entre Nous*, tr. M. B. Smith and B. Harshav (New York: Columbia University Press, 2000).

————. *Of God Who Comes to Mind*, tr. B. Bergo (Stanford, CA: Stanford University Press, 1998).

————. *Otherwise Than Being or Beyond Essence*, tr. A. Lingis (Dordrecht: Kluwer Academic Publishers, 1991).

————. *Totality and Infinity*, tr. A. Lingis (Pittsburgh: Duquesne University Press, 1969).

Lhermitte, François. *L'image de notre corps* (Paris: Editions de la Nouvelle Revue Critique, 1939), 148.

Lucretius. *Of the Nature of Things*, IV: 1153–1170, tr. M. F. Smith (Indianapolis: Hackett Press, 2001).

Malamoud, Cathérine. *Cuire le monde* (Paris: Decouverte, 1989).

Malinowski, Bronislaw. *Crime and Custom in Savage Society* (Totowa, NJ: Littlefield, Adams, 1966).

Marcos, Jean-Pierre. "Le Sujet suppose vouloir," in *Le Moment cartésien de la psychanalyse* (Paris: Arcanes, 1996).

Marion, Jean-Luc. *Being Given*, tr. J. Koskey (Stanford, CA: Stanford University Press, 2001).

————. *God without Being*, tr. T. A. Carlson (Chicago: University of Chicago Press, 1991).

————. *On Descartes' Metaphysical Prism*, tr. J. Kosky (Chicago: University of Chicago Press, 1999).

————. *On the Ego and God: Further Cartesian Questions*, tr. C. Gschwandter (New York: Fordham University Press, 2008).

————. *Reduction and Givenness: Investigations of Husserl, Heidegger, and Phenomenology*, tr. T. Carlson (Evanston, IL: Northwestern University Press, 1998).

Maupassant, Guy de. *Short Stories of the Tragedy and Comedy of Life*, Vol. 2 (BiblioBazaar, 2008) [collection originally published in 1903].

Merleau-Ponty, Maurice. *Phenomenology of Perception*, tr. C. Smith (New York: Routledge & Kegan Paul, 1962).

———. *The Visible and the Invisible*, tr. A. Lingis (Evanston, IL: Northwestern University Press, 1968).

Milner, Jean-Claude. *L'Oeuvre Claire* (Paris: Seuil, 1995).

Mishima, Yukio. *Sun and Steel*, tr. J. Bester (New York: Kodansha International, 1970).

Nancy, Jean-Luc. *Corpus*, tr. R. Rand (New York: Alephoe, 2008).

Naudin, Jean. *Phénoménologie et psychiatrie. Les voix et la chose* (Marseilles: Presses Universitaires de Marseilles, 1997).

Nietzsche, Friedrich. *The Basic Writings of Nietzsche*, tr. W. Kaufmann (New York: Modern Library, 2000).

———. *Ecce Homo: How One Becomes What One Is*, tr. R. J. Hollingdale (New York: Penguin Classics, 1992).

———. *The Gay Science*, tr. J. Nauckhoff and A. Del Caro (Cambridge: Cambridge University Press, 2001).

———. *The Portable Nietzsche*, ed. Walter Kaufmann (New York: Penguin, 1954).

Noudelmann, François. "Le corps tragique. Lecture de Mishima." *Césure* 9 (1995).

Ott, Hugo. *Heidegger: A Political Life*, tr. A. Blunden (New York: Basic Books, 1993).

Pankow, Gisela. *L'homme et sa psychose* (Paris: Aubier-Montaigne, 1969).

Pariente, Jean-Claude. "La première personne et sa fonction dans le Cogito," in *Descartes et la question du sujet* (Paris: Presses Universitaires de France, 1999).

Plato. *Complete Dialogues of Plato*, ed. E. Hamilton and H. Cairns (Princeton, NJ: Princeton University Press, 1961).

———. *Symposium*, tr. S. Benardete (Chicago: University of Chicago Press, 2001).

———. *Republic*, tr. A. Bloom (New York: Basic Books, 1991).

Poe, Edgar Allan. "The Facts in the Case of M. Valdemar," in *The Portable Edgar Allan Poe*, ed. J. G. Kennedy (New York: Penguin Books, 2006).

———. "William Wilson," in *The Portable Edgar Allan Poe*, ed. J. G. Kennedy (New York: Penguin Books, 2006).

Proust, Françoise. *De la résistance* (Paris: Cerf, 1997).

———. *L'Histoire à contretemps* (Paris: Cerf, 1994).

Proust, Marcel. *Sodom and Gomorrah*, Vol. 4, *In Search of Lost Time*, tr. C. Prendergast and J. Sturrock (New York: Penguin Classics, 2003).

Raffoul, François. *Heidegger and the Subject*, tr. D. Pettigrew and G. Recco (New York: Humanity Books, 1998).

Rogozinski, Jacob. "Chasser les héros de notre âme," in *Penser après Heidegger* (Paris: L'Harmattan, 1992).

———. "*Ego fatum* ou le miroir de Zarathoustra." *Lignes* 7 (February 2002).

———. "Etranger parmi nous: La Terreur et son ennemi." *Césure* 9 (1995).

———. *Faire-part—cryptes de Derrida* (Paris: Lignes-Léo Scheer, 2005).

———. "J'ai toujours su que j'étais Artaud le mort." *Europe* (2002).

———. *Kanten—esquisses kantiennes* (Paris: Kimé, 1996).

———. "Le chiasme et le restant." *Rue Descartes* 35 (2002).

———. *Le Don de la Loi* (Paris: Presses Universitaires de France, 1999).

———. "Le Restant de l'universel," in *L'Universel, le Singulier* (Paris: Kimé, 2000).

———. "Sans je ni lieu: la vie sans être d'Antonin Artaud," in *Michel Henry, l'epreuve de la vie* (Paris: Editions du Cerf, 2000).

———. "Scotomes: Point de vue sur Sartre." *Les Temps Modernes* Issues 531–533 (1990).

Sacks, Oliver. *The Man Who Mistook His Wife for a Hat* (New York: Touchstone Press, 1998).

Saint John of the Cross. *The Dark Night of the Soul*, tr. E. Allison Peters (Garden City, NY: Image Books/Doubleday, 1959).

———. *The Living Flame of Love*, tr. D. Lewis (New York: Cosimo Classics, 2007).

Sami, Ali. *Corps reel, corps imaginaire* (Paris: Dunod, 1977, 1994).

Sartre, Jean-Paul, *Being and Nothingness*, tr. Hazel E. Barnes, (New York: Citadel Press, 1956).

———. "Venice from My Window," in *Modern Times: Selected Nonfiction*, tr. R. Buss. (London: Penguin, 2000).

Schelling, F. W. J. *Philosophical Inquiries into the Nature of Human Freedom*, tr. J. Gutmann (Lasalle, IL: Open Court Publishing, 1936, 2001).

Schilder, Paul M. *The Image and Appearance of the Human Body* (New York: Routledge, 1999; originally published in 1935).

Schreber, Daniel Paul. *Memoirs of My Nervous Illness*, tr. I. Macalpine and R. Hunter (New York: New York Review of Books, 2000; originally published by Harvard University Press, 1955).

Sebbah, François-David. *L'Epreuve de la limite* (Paris: Presses Universitaires de France, 2001).

Spinoza, Benedict. *Ethics*, tr. G. H. R. Parkinson (Oxford: Oxford University Press, 2000).

Surya, Michel. *Bataille: An Intellectual Biography*, tr. K. Kijalkowski and M. Richardson (London: Verso, 2002).

Thibierge, Stéphane. *Pathologies de l'image du corps* (Paris: Presses Universitaires de France, 1999).

Thomas, Louis-Vincent. *Anthropologie de la mort* (Paris: Payot, 1975).

Tomatis, Alfred. *The Ear and Language*, tr. B. Thompson (New York: Stoddart, 1997).

Tustin, Frances. *Autisme et psychose chez l'enfant* (Paris: Seuil, 1982).

Wallon, Henri. *Les origins du caracterè chez l'enfant* (1932) (Paris: Presses Univer-sitaires de France, 1983).

Winnicott, Donald W. *Psychoanalytic Explorations*, ed. C. Winnicott, R. Shepard, and M. Davis (Cambridge, MA: Harvard University Press, 1989).

Index

Tactile chiasm, 170, 300; and the crisis
of the chiasm, 181, 184, 196, 208,
243, 270; in Derrida, 170; and
incorporation, 159, 160, 171, 243,
270; in Merleau-Ponty, 55, 171; and
the remainder, 172, 183, 201, 206,
270, 300; and subjectification, 160,
171; and temporality, 153–154, 164,
170–172; and truth, 55, 183, 206;
visual chiasm, 160, 182, 201. *See also*
Quasi-chiasm, as visual
Tomatis, Alfred, 206
Transcendence, 39, 40, 41, 43, 44, 45,
46, 54–56, 59, 125, 126, 128, 132, 135,
139, 141–143, 157, 177, 189, 212, 220,
221, 223, 224, 226, 238, 239, 241, 286,
289–290, 292, 294, 306; of Dasein,
16, 39, 42–43; of the ego, 53, 135, 140,
142; of the Other, 108, 114, 126, 212,
223, 230, 233; transcendence-in-
immanence, 44, 132, 177, 189, 223,
224, 241; of vision, 68, 70; of the
world, 59, 126, 128, 139, 146, 157, 180,
187, 190, 218, 236, 239. *See also*
Immanence
Transfiguration, 184, 214, 263, 287, 293;
and instasis, 295, 297, 298, 304, 306;
and love, 184, 259, 260, 262–268; and
the "mourning of mourning," 273, 274,
277, 278; movement of disfiguration
and transfiguration, 259, 260, 267, 279,
291, 295–298, 300–301, 304, 306; of
others, 230, 262, 263, 265; and
resurrection, 282, 285, 287, 295, 300;
and truth, 262, 282, 292

Wallon, Henri, 50, 57, 58, 61, 159
Winnicott, Donald, 275

Michael G. Levine, *The Belated Witness: Literature, Testimony, and the Question of Holocaust Survival*

Jennifer A. Jordan, *Structures of Memory: Understanding German Change in Berlin and Beyond*

Christoph Menke, *Reflections of Equality*

Marlène Zarader, *The Unthought Debt: Heidegger and the Hebraic Heritage*

Jan Assmann, *Religion and Cultural Memory: Ten Studies*

David Scott and Charles Hirschkind, *Powers of the Secular Modern: Talal Asad and His Interlocutors*

Gyanendra Pandey, *Routine Violence: Nations, Fragments, Histories*

James Siegel, *Naming the Witch*

J. M. Bernstein, *Against Voluptuous Bodies: Late Modernism and the Meaning of Painting*

Theodore W. Jennings, Jr., *Reading Derrida / Thinking Paul: On Justice*

Richard Rorty and Eduardo Mendieta, *Take Care of Freedom and Truth Will Take Care of Itself: Interviews with Richard Rorty*

Jacques Derrida, *Paper Machine*

Renaud Barbaras, *Desire and Distance: Introduction to a Phenomenology of Perception*

Jill Bennett, *Empathic Vision: Affect, Trauma, and Contemporary Art*

Ban Wang, *Illuminations from the Past: Trauma, Memory, and History in Modern China*

James Phillips, *Heidegger's* Volk*: Between National Socialism and Poetry*

Frank Ankersmit, *Sublime Historical Experience*

István Rév, *Retroactive Justice: Prehistory of Post-Communism*

Paola Marrati, *Genesis and Trace: Derrida Reading Husserl and Heidegger*

Krzysztof Ziarek, *The Force of Art*

Marie-José Mondzain, *Image, Icon, Economy: The Byzantine Origins of the Contemporary Imaginary*

Cecilia Sjöholm, *The Antigone Complex: Ethics and the Invention of Feminine Desire*

Jacques Derrida and Elisabeth Roudinesco, *For What Tomorrow . . . : A Dialogue*

Elisabeth Weber, *Questioning Judaism: Interviews by Elisabeth Weber*

Jacques Derrida and Catherine Malabou, *Counterpath: Traveling with Jacques Derrida*

Martin Seel, *Aesthetics of Appearing*

Nanette Salomon, *Shifting Priorities: Gender and Genre in Seventeenth-Century Dutch Painting*

Jacob Taubes, *The Political Theology of Paul*

Jean-Luc Marion, *The Crossing of the Visible*

Eric Michaud, *The Cult of Art in Nazi Germany*

Anne Freadman, *The Machinery of Talk: Charles Peirce and the Sign Hypothesis*

Stanley Cavell, *Emerson's Transcendental Etudes*

Stuart McLean, *The Event and Its Terrors: Ireland, Famine, Modernity*

Beate Rössler, ed., *Privacies: Philosophical Evaluations*

Bernard Faure, *Double Exposure: Cutting Across Buddhist and Western Discourses*

Alessia Ricciardi, *The Ends of Mourning: Psychoanalysis, Literature, Film*

Alain Badiou, *Saint Paul: The Foundation of Universalism*

Gil Anidjar, *The Jew, the Arab: A History of the Enemy*

Jonathan Culler and Kevin Lamb, eds., *Just Being Difficult? Academic Writing in the Public Arena*

Jean-Luc Nancy, *A Finite Thinking*, edited by Simon Sparks

Theodor W. Adorno, *Can One Live after Auschwitz? A Philosophical Reader*, edited by Rolf Tiedemann

Patricia Pisters, *The Matrix of Visual Culture: Working with Deleuze in Film Theory*

Andreas Huyssen, *Present Pasts: Urban Palimpsests and the Politics of Memory*

Talal Asad, *Formations of the Secular: Christianity, Islam, Modernity*

Dorothea von Mücke, *The Rise of the Fantastic Tale*

Marc Redfield, *The Politics of Aesthetics: Nationalism, Gender, Romanticism*

Emmanuel Levinas, *On Escape*

Dan Zahavi, *Husserl's Phenomenology*

Rodolphe Gasché, *The Idea of Form: Rethinking Kant's Aesthetics*

Michael Naas, *Taking on the Tradition: Jacques Derrida and the Legacies of Deconstruction*

Herlinde Pauer-Studer, ed., *Constructions of Practical Reason: Interviews on Moral and Political Philosophy*

Jean-Luc Marion, *Being Given That: Toward a Phenomenology of Givenness*

Theodor W. Adorno and Max Horkheimer, *Dialectic of Enlightenment*

Ian Balfour, *The Rhetoric of Romantic Prophecy*

Martin Stokhof, *World and Life as One: Ethics and Ontology in Wittgenstein's Early Thought*

Gianni Vattimo, *Nietzsche: An Introduction*

Jacques Derrida, *Negotiations: Interventions and Interviews, 1971-1998*, ed. Elizabeth Rottenberg

Brett Levinson, *The Ends of Literature: The Latin American "Boom" in the Neoliberal Marketplace*

Timothy J. Reiss, *Against Autonomy: Cultural Instruments, Mutualities, and the Fictive Imagination*

Hent de Vries and Samuel Weber, eds., *Religion and Media*

Niklas Luhmann, *Theories of Distinction: Re-Describing the Descriptions of Modernity*, ed. and introd. William Rasch

Johannes Fabian, *Anthropology with an Attitude: Critical Essays*

Michel Henry, *I Am the Truth: Toward a Philosophy of Christianity*

Gil Anidjar, *"Our Place in Al-Andalus": Kabbalah, Philosophy, Literature in Arab-Jewish Letters*

Hélène Cixous and Jacques Derrida, *Veils*

F. R. Ankersmit, *Historical Representation*

F. R. Ankersmit, *Political Representation*

Elissa Marder, *Dead Time: Temporal Disorders in the Wake of Modernity (Baudelaire and Flaubert)*

Reinhart Koselleck, *The Practice of Conceptual History: Timing History, Spacing Concepts*

Niklas Luhmann, *The Reality of the Mass Media*

Hubert Damisch, *A Theory of /Cloud/: Toward a History of Painting*

Jean-Luc Nancy, *The Speculative Remark: (One of Hegel's bon mots)*

Jean-François Lyotard, *Soundproof Room: Malraux's Anti-Aesthetics*

Jan Patočka, *Plato and Europe*

Hubert Damisch, *Skyline: The Narcissistic City*

Isabel Hoving, *In Praise of New Travelers: Reading Caribbean Migrant Women Writers*

Richard Rand, ed., *Futures: Of Jacques Derrida*

William Rasch, *Niklas Luhmann's Modernity: The Paradoxes of Differentiation*

Jacques Derrida and Anne Dufourmantelle, *Of Hospitality*

The authorized representative in the EU for product safety and compliance is:
Mare Nostrum Group
B.V Doelen 72
4831 GR Breda
The Netherlands

www.ingramcontent.com/pod-product-compliance
Lightning Source LLC
Chambersburg PA
CBHW030636270326
41929CB00007B/99